SICKLES
THE
INCREDIBLE

SICKLES
THE
INCREDIBLE

BY
W. A. Swanberg

 Stan Clark Military Books
Gettysburg, Pennsylvania

Reprinted 1991 by special arrangements with Charles Scribner's Sons by:

Stan Clark Military Books
915 Fairview Avenue
Gettysburg, Pennsylvania 17325
717-337-1728

Picture credit abbreviations:
  MOLLUS / Mass. Comm. / USAMHI
    Military Order of the Loyal Legion of The United States,
    Massachusetts Commandery. United States Army Military
    History Institute.
  GNMP
    Gettysburg National Military Park

FOR
Dorothy, Jack and Sally

Two Views of Mr. Sickles

"Here is a man still in his prime . . . whose career has been as diversified and romantic as if he had filled out a full century of endless action . . . His recent coup d'etat against the Erie Ring would alone make any man famous. Few characters in our country, or in our history, have passed through so many ordeals."

—*John W. Forney* in 1872

"One might as well try to spoil a rotten egg as to damage Dan's character."

—*George Templeton Strong* in 1872

I have said to you before that I do not deem it a wise course, nor recommend it to any friend; but I have adopted it; it is mine, and I will follow it come what may.

—*D. E. Sickles*

Author's Note

The writer has tried to be scrupulous in his effort to portray a complex and enigmatic man. The great majority of conversations in this book are direct or indirect quotations from many different sources which are identified in the footnotes. In less than a half-dozen instances, speeches are given which are not a matter of actual record but which logic would seem to dictate must have been made under those historical circumstances.

Contents

SICKLES
THE
INCREDIBLE

CHAPTER I

The People's Choice

As cannon boomed along the Potomac and the parade got under way, Mr. Sickles leaned back in his carriage and proceeded to enjoy the fun. Flags and bunting decorated almost every building along Pennsylvania Avenue, excited people lined the walks, and the weather was well-nigh as balmy as May. Clad in top hat and frock coat with a white carnation in his lapel, Mr. Sickles looked excessively young and handsome to be the member-elect from the Third District of New York. He was in the pleasant process of stepping upward from local to national politics, with the happy perquisite of prefixing "Honorable" to his name, and perhaps he could not be blamed for an expression of self-satisfaction.

He had been elected, hadn't he? He had been elected despite some of the most sulphurous vilification ever heard outside of a Bowery barroom. *Infamous scoundrel,* they had called him; *moral bankrupt, man of shocking personal habits, disciple of debauchery,* and others as choice. That proper lawyer, George Templeton Strong, had informed his diary that Sickles was "one of the bigger bubbles in the scum of the [legal] profession, swollen and windy, and puffed out with fetid gas." [1]

Unfortunately there was some truth in all this, but only half-truth. His detractors did not mention that Sickles also had a streak of genius, intelligence that fairly crackled, the combativeness of a fighting cock, and powerful friends who regarded him a little nervously as *the* heir apparent if he could

1

only keep out of the gutter. He looked sedate enough there in his carriage, but Washington would soon learn that sedateness was not the natural air of Daniel Edgar Sickles.

Up ahead, the Marine Band was playing, an eight-company military escort marched in splendid array, and some 200 United States Marshals from all parts of the country were astride their horses, led by Jonah D. Hoover, the Marshal for the District of Columbia and a good friend of Sickles. Ladies in new spring bonnets waved lacy handkerchiefs from the upper windows of Willard's Hotel as the procession passed by, and Sickles cocked an appreciative eye in their direction. Women had been hard on his reputation but he loved them nevertheless. As the parade reached the sprawling National Hotel at Sixth Street, there was a slight delay. Then a rousing cheer went up from the spectators as an elegant open barouche, drawn by four horses and bearing President Pierce and President-elect Buchanan (both friends of Sickles) pulled out and entered the honored position in line.

Sickles nudged his companion, crusty Representative-elect John B. Haskin of Westchester County, New York.

"I hope Old Buck can stick it out," he remarked dryly.

He was referring to a most untimely indisposition which had stricken Mr. Buchanan at this climactic point in his long career. Less than a week earlier, the President-elect had visited Washington to arrange final details for occupancy of the White House, and had stayed at the National Hotel. On his return to his Pennsylvania country estate he had been seized with violent cramps and diarrhoea—a miserable ailment for an elderly man expected to display himself as leading actor in a slow and elaborate public ceremony.[2] But the inauguration of a President is an event that takes no account of human frailties short of mortal illness. Fortified with soothing syrups, Buchanan was in the parade, albeit looking somewhat wan and apprehensive as he nodded and tipped his hat to the celebrants crowding the avenue.

Sickles had to admire Old Buck's grit. He also could not repress a warm glow of gratification at the fact that his own per-

sonal planning and manipulation had set the dignified Pennsylvanian on the highroad to the executive mansion. He had bet
his shirt on the right horse and had won a good deal more than
a mere seat in Congress. The stakes were incalculable—high
enough to make a man a bit light-headed.

The procession moved on with the music. Forward from the
Presidential barouche was a gilded float drawn by six horses,
on which a curvaceous young woman clad in white satin por-
trayed the Goddess of Liberty. Ahead of that was the crack
company of Montgomery Guards, a Washington military unit
uniformed in blue and gold. They were led by Captain Philip
Barton Key, another friend of Sickles—a tall and dashing figure
with gold-plumed cap who rode his iron-gray horse with nonchalance.

Captain Key was not quite as nonchalant as he looked. Under
President Pierce he held the office of United States Attorney
for the District of Columbia, a post he did not wish to lose.
Would the incoming chief magistrate retain him? Like thousands of other office-holders, he was nervously pondering the
future and wondering what wires he could pull to avoid the unpleasant necessity of seeking other employment.

It was nearing one o'clock when the head of the procession
reached the north gate of the Capitol, which even then was being
enlarged to give the Representatives a spacious new hall. The
military formed a double line presenting arms, the Messrs.
Pierce and Buchanan entered between the muskets, and within
fifteen minutes the assembled notables were in their places to
witness the solemn investiture of the nation's new leader.

The gallery was reserved for the ladies, with a special seat of
honor for Miss Harriet Lane, the poised niece of the bachelor
President-elect, who was destined to be mistress of the White
House for the next four years. Among this murmuring bevy—
the wives of men who were to make tragic history—was a dark-
haired, lustrous-eyed beauty who seemed not long out of her
teens. She was an appealing creature in ruffled crinoline, a dé-
colleté bodice that revealed softly proportioned shoulders and

arms, and an absurd hat topped with jonquils. She was Mrs. Sickles, wife of the new member from New York. It is doubtful that Mrs. Sickles paid close heed to the inaugural address of Mr. Buchanan, a cautious speech in which he expressed hope that there might be an end to the animosity between North and South which had caused "no good and much evil." [3] More likely her thoughts were on her husband, looking so personable and assured down below.

With his election and his intimacy with Buchanan, Sickles was riding a flood tide of political fortune that might carry him far. Teresa Sickles was delighted at his meteoric rise and his even more exciting prospects. Still, being the wife of the magnetic New Yorker involved hardships a lady did not discuss in public. Mrs. Sickles must have wondered whether in his new eminence, with the Capitol as his stage and the whole nation as his audience, he would mend his ways and become respectable.

Down at the rostrum, Mr. Buchanan finished his speech and received spirited applause. That emaciated ancient, Chief Justice Roger Brooke Taney, advanced and swore him in. James Buchanan, triumphing over bodily distress, was President, and few of the glowing witnesses were prescient enough to know that the ship of state was weighing anchor for a slow but inexorable voyage into disaster.

The following evening, March 5, 1857, the inaugural ceremonies were officially ended with the biggest ball ever given in Washington. Six thousand tickets had been sold at the extravagant price of ten dollars each, all of them bearing the engraved likeness of President Buchanan. Since no hall in the city would accommodate anywhere near such a throng, a rough wooden building had been erected for the purpose in Judiciary Square next to the city hall. Though from the outside it resembled a huge railroad conductors' shanty, inside it was splendidly decked with a white ceiling flecked with golden stars, and walls decorated with the national colors. [4]

Representative Sickles was there with his lady, surrounded by a group of friends. The new Congressman was a small man of thirty-seven with the alert, energetic compactness of a bull terrier. He wore his hair at collar length, as was the custom among legislators, and his face was clean-shaven except for a full, drooping mustache that trailed from an aggressive nose. There was a penetrating quality about his eyes, and under them were faintly visible sacs hinting of many a reckless outing. Faultlessly attired in a dark suit with colorful silk vest and cravat, Mr. Sickles was an arresting figure because he combined good looks with an air of subdued violence.

When Marshal Hoover came up and swept Mrs. Sickles away in a waltz, the Representative turned to his friends. One of them was Samuel Butterworth, a staunch Tammany politician who was Superintendent of the Assay Office in New York and was frankly worried as to whether he would be retained in that post. Butterworth was in no condition for dancing that night. En route by train to the inaugural with New York's postmaster, Isaac V. Fowler, the two men had drunk a few toasts to the incoming administration and had got a little careless. Fowler's revolver—pistols were a common masculine accessory at the time—had dropped from his pocket, discharged, and inflicted a flesh wound in Butterworth's thigh.[5] His leg was now bandaged and he was limping, but he was hanged if he was going to waste a ten-dollar ticket.

With him was Emanuel B. Hart, another Tammany stalwart and one of Sickles' most intimate friends. Hart at present held no office, but he felt it was his due after all he had done for the party to be rewarded with a post of some importance. Sickles had already reassured Butterworth and Hart. Both had worked whole-heartedly for his election, and it was unthinkable that their labors should go unrecognized.

Considering that he was a mere Representative in a throng that bristled with Senators, generals, justices and bemedalled ministers, Sickles drew a surprising amount of respectful attention as he stood apart from the crowd with a glass of wine in his hand. Judge Jeremiah Black, soon to be announced as Bu-

chanan's Attorney General, stopped to congratulate him, as did
Senator Slidell of Louisiana and the new Vice President, John
Breckinridge. Others who paused to pass a friendly word were
Senator Douglas of Illinois, Colonel John Forney of Pennsylvania, and the Chevalier Henry Wikoff, who held no title at all
except that of the most sophisticated busybody in Washington
society.

There was a momentary interruption around eleven P.M. as
the President entered, followed by Miss Lane on the arm of
Senator Jones. Amid a ripple of applause, the orchestra struck
up "Hail to the Chief," and the wooden hall fairly groaned
under its burden of enthusiastic humanity. Though still pale,
the President had recovered sufficiently from his illness to lead
a cotillion, which he now proceeded to do.

Others had not been so lucky. The sensation of the hour was
what had already become known as the "National Hotel disease." Several dozen other guests who had put up at the hostelry
at the same time as Mr. Buchanan were still violently ill. The
story was current that before the President-elect had arrived,
the hotel management had distributed arsenic liberally around
the house to get rid of the rats that infested it. It was said that
the poisoned rats, frantically seeking water, had plunged into
the hotel's reservoir from which cooking and drinking water
was drawn, and thus the unfortunate guests had unwittingly
been downing rat poison.[6] The National's proprietor, a man
named Calvert, indignantly denied this and was threatening to
sue the city for $75,000, claiming that the illness was caused by
an "unwholesome miasma" emanating from a nearby city sewer.[7]

In any case, there had been a mass exodus from the National,
the biggest hotel in town. Among its patrons had been Mr. and
Mrs. Sickles, and although both of them still felt very well they
had quickly moved into the house of the hospitable Marshal
Hoover.

But at the ball, all was gayety. Three thousand dollars worth
of wines had been stocked for the occasion, along with four hundred gallons of oysters, twelve hundred quarts of ice cream and

other delicacies. Sickles asked and was given a dance with Miss Lane, and was also seen with the gorgeous Creole, Mrs. Senator Slidell, as his partner. It was later in the evening when Philip Barton Key disentangled himself from the throng and sought out Sickles.

The two men were already well acquainted, having a mutual friend in Marshal Hoover. Key, standing almost a head taller than the Congressman, passed a few amiable remarks and then got down to the subject uppermost in his mind—his position as United States Attorney.

Though he did not mention it, Key had been under some slight criticism because of his failure to convict Representative Philemon T. Herbert of California in the previous year. Herbert had created the scandal of 1856 by drinking deeply at Willard's Hotel, then engaging in a furious argument with a waiter named Keating—a quarrel the legislator ended by jerking out a pistol and shooting Keating dead.[8] While there were some who wryly said that Washington waiters were notoriously so dilatory and insolent that a man could hardly be blamed for shooting one, it was felt in other quarters that Key had not been properly active in the prosecution.

Sickles, whose eye level was somewhere in the region of the tall District Attorney's silk cravat, listened with a good deal more than ordinary attentiveness.

"There is no one I would rather oblige than you," he said to Key with a warm smile, "and I think I can do it. I will speak to the President about it."

This was a promise he could make with perfect assurance. Though Buchanan was so proper and reserved that he habitually addressed his niece and social coadjutor as "Miss Harriet," [9] the Representative from New York knew from experience exactly how to penetrate this monumental formality. Key murmured his thanks as Teresa Sickles came up on the arm of Henry Wikoff. Mrs. Sickles was duly introduced to Mr. Key, and the District Attorney snatched her away for the next dance.

Mr. Wikoff, a knowing fellow who had spent years flitting

between European capitals, and who noticed everything, saw that Teresa and Key made a most attractive couple. It is doubtful that Sickles even noticed his wife's departure, for he was busy talking politics with Samuel Butterworth and Emanuel Hart.

CHAPTER II

Politicking on the Potomac

Gossip—a commodity that seemed to trail around Daniel Sickles like a nimbus wherever he went—had arrived in Washington with him. It was said that he had been involved in a shocking affair with a woman in New York, which was true enough, though not the half of it. There was talk that as an attorney he had become enmeshed in certain affairs that brought him dangerously close to criminal prosecution, which was also true.

Yet there were those who swore by him, and not entirely because he had the President's ear and was regarded as a "comer." As one contemporary commentator put it, "To serve his friends he will do anything tolerated by the license of modern politics; when he resolves upon the overthrow of a political enemy, the strongest man finds him formidable." [1]

To Sickles, politics was the highly practical art of rewarding loyalty and friendship, and he worked at it with unflagging zeal. Less than a fortnight after the inauguration, he attended a stag whist party at the home of his host, Jonah Hoover. Among those present were Sickles' Congressional colleague, Haskin, a reporter for the Congressional *Globe* named John J. McElhone, and Philip Barton Key. Though Key's worries about his post might have been considered a confidential matter, Sickles mentioned it in the hearing of others while the cards were being dealt.

"I've urged your reappointment to the President," he said to Key. "I think it will be done as you wish." [2]

Key thanked him for his intercession and said he hoped Sickles would continue his good offices. In taking the part of Key, who was neither a friend of long standing nor an ally who had labored faithfully for his election, Sickles was not going by the book, and yet he may have seen some mutual advantage in the transaction. In the ensuing weeks, he was busy in the interests of a host of far more deserving friends, among them Butterworth, Hart, and Charles K. Graham, a young New York civil engineer who had long backed Sickles in the Tammany Wigwam.

It was on behalf of Graham that Sickles encountered a bit of the sort of unpleasantness not unknown to him in previous Tammany maneuvers. Early in May, by which time he had moved into a suite at Willard's, he received an angry note from one J. McLeod Murphy, who held the position of Civil Engineer at the Brooklyn Navy Yard. In it, Murphy said he was informed that Sickles had assailed his character in an effort to remove Murphy from his well-paid post, and demanded to know if this was true. In reply, Sickles wrote Murphy tartly, saying that the engineer had neither specified what had allegedly been said about him nor who his informants were.

"Your note seems only a vague menace," he finished, "apparently intended to deter me from my duty as a Representative. As such I have already taken too much notice of it."

Two days later, a friend of Murphy named Major L. D. Watkins called on Sickles at Willard's and began questioning him about his reported remarks about Murphy. Sickles, never known for patience, soon became testy.

"I do not admit the right of any person to interrogate me in this vague manner," he snapped.

"Well, sir," Major Watkins replied, "Mr. Murphy considers your note to him insulting."

Thereupon he handed Sickles a letter, which the legislator opened. Dated May 4, it read in part:

> Sir: . . . The evasive and insulting language which you have seen fit to employ leaves me no alternative. My friend, Major L. D. Watkins, who bears this note, will receive any answer you

have to make. He has but a single question to ask— Will you
meet me? And if so, when and where? Very respectfully,

                           your obt. servant, J. McLeod Murphy

This, in short, was a challenge to settle the matter on the field
of honor with weapons to be chosen by mutual agreement.
Sickles told Watkins that the note would receive his attention,
and the major left.

Though not lacking in physical courage, Sickles could see no
advantage in fighting a bloody duel over a trifling difference
with an office-holder he scarcely knew. He had no real quarrel
with Mr. Murphy. It was merely that he wanted his friend
Graham to have Murphy's job. After a moment's thought, he
dashed off the following message to Murphy:

Sir: . . . There is certainly not a word in my note to which
you refer that can possibly be deemed an imputation upon your
honor. Therefore it presents no ground upon which you have a
right to demand either an explanation or a meeting.

                           Very resp., etc., D. E. S.

As far as he was concerned, that was the end of it, but J. Mc-
Leod Murphy had other ideas. At eight o'clock on the morning
of May 6, Sickles was sound asleep in his Willard's Hotel bedroom when he was aroused by a knock at the door. He got up
sleepily in his nightshirt and opened the door a crack. With that,
Murphy threw his weight against the door and catapulted himself into the room. He was a bearded man, slightly bigger than
the Congressman, and he carried a cowhide horsewhip.

"I have come to settle with you!" he shouted, his face purple
with rage.

He raised the whip and was about to strike with it. Sickles,
though somewhat at a disadvantage, being barefooted and in his
nightshirt, dove at the man. He managed to seize the whip and
wrest it away from Murphy, in so doing taking a solid blow in
the face. The whip fell to the floor and the two men closed in
combat, lurching around the room and upsetting a chair in their

struggle. At length Sickles secured a firm hold on Murphy's throat and forced him into a corner. Choking for breath, Murphy gasped that he had had enough and was satisfied. Sickles then released him and allowed him to leave, keeping the cowhide whip as a souvenir of the encounter.

This, at any rate, was the story Sickles gave out to the newspapers. J. McLeod Murphy related quite a different version to the newsmen. He had speedily got the better of the Congressman, Murphy declared, and after a few minutes of battle Sickles was so badly beaten that he begged Murphy to desist. Murphy then let him go and departed, leaving the whip with him purposely as a reminder to keep a more civil tongue in his head thereafter.[3]

Perhaps both combatants fought better in print than they did in the hotel bedroom. In point of trophies, the battle seemed a standoff, since Sickles was left with the whip and also with a swollen eye that soon turned black. He was in a bitter mood about the bruised eye when Forney, Hoover, Wikoff, and other friends called on him at the hotel, which he did not leave for several days because of the disfigurement. Immediately after the battle he dispatched a hot note by messenger to Secretary of the Navy Isaac Toucey. The note got quick results.

On the following day, Secretary Toucey announced that he had refused to accept Murphy's resignation and had dismissed him instead because of his "unwarranted assault" on Representative Sickles.[4]

Two days later came the official appointment of Sickles' friend, Charles K. Graham, as Civil Engineer of the Brooklyn Navy Yard in Murphy's place.[5]

But Murphy had the last word. Returning to New York, he published a "card" in the *Evening Post* of that city, a newspaper that for long had regarded Sickles as the very essence of evil. It read:

> Had I known Mr. Sickles' previous history as I do now, I should have treated his innuendos with contempt. His whole career has been a series of unparalleled debaucheries. Gradu-

ating from the worst sinks of iniquity in this city, he has led the life of a professional vagabond. In debt to everybody, a fashionable roué with a degree of acquired smartness that belongs to men who are only "bold and bad" enough to challenge the laws of morality, and to fight the easy virtue of frail women, he stands before the public . . . a disgraced and vanquished man, and as such I take my leave of him.

—Jno. McLeod Murphy [6]

Sickles had been assailed before, often by experts. Yet no one had done a more punishing job than Murphy in this newspaper blast that enlivened dinner-table conversation in thousands of New York homes and also found its way to Washington. Being a lawyer and a good one, the Congressman could have sued on the ground that Murphy's assault tended to damage his reputation.

Sickles did not sue. Possibly he felt a little uneasy about defending his reputation in the courtroom, for he had never been overly careful about keeping it above reproach. Besides, he was too busy a man to be dragged into pointless quarrels. His labors involved him more in cloakroom sessions and private parleys than in any unusual activity on the House floor, but they bore fruit in a number of official announcements that warmed the hearts of Sickles' friends.

Samuel Butterworth was retained in his position as Superintendent of the New York Assay Office.

Emanuel B. Hart was appointed Surveyor of the Port of New York.

Captain Isaiah Rynders, an old Sickles crony, was given the post of United States Marshal for the Southern District of New York.

And Philip Barton Key was reappointed as United States Attorney for the District of Columbia. [7]

There were a number of lesser appointments naming friends of Representative Sickles, even down to a sandy-haired young man named S. B. Beekman, who had solicited votes for Sickles in New York's Third District and was rewarded with a clerkship in the Department of the Interior. All in all, if any further evidence were needed that Daniel E. Sickles stood in well with the President, it was in.

Clearly Key was grateful for his retention, for it was soon noticed that he was on the most companionable terms with Sickles, and more particularly with Sickles' dark-eyed wife, Teresa. There was a hop at Willard's every Thursday night, and although Sickles loved to dance he was usually too busy to attend. Teresa was often seen with Key as her partner, gaily tripping through a quadrille or a german. Every Saturday the Marine Band played on the south terrace of the White House, a romantic spot perfumed with eglantine and roses, and Mrs. Sickles occasionally appeared there on the arm of Captain Key as the stirring notes of brasses pealed off toward the unfinished and tomb-like Washington Monument.

There was little gossip about this at first, for there was nothing unusual about it. The social mores of the capital had become adapted to the exigencies of lawmaking. Legislators were invariably so busy with night sessions, committee meetings, and plain nocturnal politicking over whiskey punch, that their wives either accepted other escorts or spent lonely evenings at home with fancywork or a book. Several Washington clergymen had protested solemnly against this custom, characterizing it as a pernicious practice certain to weaken family ties if not leading to downright immorality, but these warnings were in vain.

Furthermore, Teresa Sickles was regarded as little more than a child by the more seasoned of the legislators' wives, and it was hardly surprising that she should seek the gayety of the capital in her first year there. Almost every night in the week there was an entertainment somewhere. The National Hotel, after a month of total eclipse, caused by the "endemic" which had proved fatal to several persons, had closed its doors for a stern housecleaning and complete renovation of the kitchen.[8] It was now reopened, and after some hesitation Washingtonians began attending dances there without any noticeable ill effects. At Brown's Hotel, just up the Avenue from the National, a large deputation of blueblood Southern legislators and their wives made their home, and they were traditionally lavish in giving receptions and dinners.

So Mrs. Sickles, always gowned in the latest importation, found plenty to do even though her husband was seldom with her. Occasionally she appeared in society with Henry Wikoff, whom the Sickleses had known in New York and who was called the "Chevalier" because of certain romantic escapades which had occupied him in Europe. But more often her escort was Philip Barton Key.

After the summer recess, Mr. and Mrs. Sickles returned to Washington in the late fall of 1857 contemplating a significant change in their way of life. Daniel Sickles loved to entertain and to live graciously, in spite of his preoccupation with politics. In his opinion, one could hardly give parties of distinction in a public hotel. He solved this problem by leasing the Stockton Mansion, a spacious, three-story white brick house on Lafayette Square which in the previous year had been occupied by the huge, amiable Representative James Orr of South Carolina and his family.[9]

In addition to furnishing a patrician setting for sociability, the Stockton place offered other advantages. It was located in the very nesting place of Washington aristocracy. And it was only a stone's throw across the Avenue from the White House, where James Buchanan was working sixteen hours a day in a conscientious effort to satisfy office seekers and keep the Union from splitting asunder. Sickles, who never hesitated to call on the busy President, found this propinquity convenient.

Before the Sickleses moved in with their three-year-old daughter, Laura, the Stockton Mansion was redecorated from kitchen to attic in the latest baroque fashion. Sickles purchased a glittering new carriage and pair, as well as two fine saddle horses. He staffed his house with a cook, a butler, a chambermaid, a coachman, and a footman. He stocked his cellar with a connoisseur's selection of Madeira, port, and sherry as well as more potent liquors. All this was living on a scale almost equal to that of the rich Senator William Gwin, or the equally rich Postmaster Aaron Brown, and there were some who wondered where the money came from. It was obvious that the Representative could not afford such grandeur on his Congressional salary of $3000 a year, but it was said that he came from a wealthy family.

That winter, the Sickles household became the scene of a gradually increasing number of dinners and entertainments. They began modestly enough, with the guests coming mostly from the ranks of old friends such as Hoover, Haskin, Wikoff, and Sickles' Congressional colleague from New York's Sixth District, the unprepossessing but persuasive John Cochrane. Another visitor whom Sickles soon came to admire was blunt, bearded Edwin McMasters Stanton, a good friend of Buchanan who had electioneered for Old Buck and was now doing a thriving legal business in Washington.

These intimates were of a uniformly Northern origin. The exception was Philip Barton Key, whose iron-gray horse was often seen tied at the Sickles hitching-rail.

It was impossible that Key's doings could go unnoticed, for he was "the handsomest man in all Washington society." [10] His paternal grandfather had been master of a manor house on Pipe Creek in northern Maryland, a magnificent place operated by a regiment of slaves. A grand-uncle had served with distinction in Congress under Jefferson. Chief Justice Taney, who had sworn in no less than eight Presidents during his long tenure, was Key's uncle. His father was the late Francis Scott Key, lawyer, churchman, and poet who, by the dawn's early light, had been inspired to pen hasty verses to the flag, which had surprised him by catching the public fancy and becoming the words to the national anthem. Scott Key, indeed, had been United States Attorney for the District of Columbia under Jackson, so that his son now seemed to hold the post by princely succession.

Sickles, of course, knew better than that. Key owed his job to the potent intercession of Representative Sickles.

By blood and background Key was in perfect rapport with

the state's-rights, slave-owning Southern aristocrats who completely dominated capital society, were traditionally powerful in government councils, and had grave doubts that anything good could come from north of the Mason-Dixon line. He was an intimate of the Gwins, Senator and Mrs. Clement Clay of Alabama, and many others of the elect. Added to all this, he was probably the most eligible catch in the city, being a widower whose wife had died five years earlier. Even had he not been extraordinarily handsome, he would have been fair game for ambitious mothers of marriageable belles.

Thus there was no lack of surprised observers when Key began to appear quite regularly at the new Sickles domicile. Not that anyone—even allowing for those rumors—had anything against Daniel and Teresa Sickles. Not at all. It was simply that Key was a charter member of Southern society. To find him bestowing his amiable attentions upon the household of the new and still unaccepted Congressman from the North was almost as startling as if President Buchanan had suddenly begun holding conferences with a House page boy.

In this watchful city where gossip flew like rockets, it was widely known that Sickles had used his influence with the President to secure Key's reappointment. Was Key repaying a political debt in social currency?

Whether or not this was true, Key's friendship with the Sickleses added luster to the New York couple's entertainments. As the season wore on, others of the purple paid their respects at the Stockton Mansion in the wake of the District Attorney. The socially prominent Representative George H. Pendleton of Ohio and his beautiful wife Alicia—who was Key's younger sister—began to favor the Sickles home with their presence. Mayor James Berret, a good friend of Key, was among the callers. Asthmatic Senator Clay and his witty, vivacious wife Virginia—herself an arbitress of fashion—were guests. Even the Gwins came, as did Postmaster General Brown and his wife. On the Thursday nights of the Sickles fortnightly dinners, Jackson Place in front of the Stockton Mansion was jammed with pol-

ished calashes and broughams bearing the crests of some of the
capital's proudest families.

These visitors found the Sickleses to be gracious hosts whose
cuisine, wines, and cigars were irreproachable. They had to
admit that Sickles was unfailingly genial and attentive, with a
genuine talent for witty talk and repartee. In a knot of males,
he had a genius for telling an off-color story, building it up
gradually to a crackling climax. As for his wife—well, she was
as delightful as she was decorative, no more than twenty-one and
always dressed as if she had just stepped out of a bandbox. No
one could help liking her.

Yet there were some who had the impression that the Congressman was just a shade too eager, too ambitious. Restless,
kinetic, he had the air of a mountain climber who has won hand-
holds on a succession of subsidiary heights but never for a moment removes his eye from the summit.

But at least one frequent guest of the Sickleses was untroubled by such an impression. He was young Samuel Beekman
of New York, who owed his job as clerk in the Interior Department to the good offices of Daniel Sickles. Beekman was invited
to the Stockton Mansion as a loyal supporter, a friend from back
home, and a young bachelor who was new in Washington and
was therefore somewhat lost.

To Beekman's uncomplicated way of thinking, no one could
possibly ascend the social scale any higher than Congressman
Sickles and his wife. He always addressed Mr. Sickles defer-
entially as "Sir," and he treated Teresa Sickles with something
approaching devotion. In fact, it was noticed with some amusement that Beekman hovered around Mrs. Sickles like a bee
around a blossom. Undoubtedly he was a mite smitten with
the lady,[11] and if so it was no wonder, for she combined the
Latin dash of her Italian father and the admirable figure of her
still beautiful American-born mother. What was more, according to one observer "she was as kind to a raw boy just let loose
on society as to a Secretary of State." [12]

Another young man to whom she was kind was Henry Watterson, then eighteen, by no means a "raw boy" but a precocious youth with weak eyes and rather delicate health. Watterson, who lived at Willard's with his parents, occasionally took Teresa to dinner when her husband was absent or busy, and when he fell ill that winter, Teresa was one of several volunteer nurses who sat with him and kept him posted on the news. He developed an entirely proper fondness for her, as well as sympathizing with her for what he termed "a husband's neglect." [13]

As for Mr. Sickles, he was far too busy to notice. That winter, the quarrel as to whether Kansas was to enter the Union as a slave or a free state was assuming furious proportions in the House, and Sickles was solidly behind the Administration's peculiar proposal to settle the dispute by handing Kansas bodily over to slavery. Yet he was clearly on his good behavior, avoiding wrangles which in his Tammany days he would have welcomed. At a night session on February 5, 1858, the Kansas issue reached new turbulence when Lawrence Keitt, the fire-eating Representative from South Carolina, shouted at slavery-hating Galusha Grow of Pennsylvania, "Sir, I will let you know that you are a Black Republican puppy."

"Never mind," Grow snarled. "No negro-driver shall crack his whip over me."

Keitt sprang at Grow. The Northerner knocked him down with a solid blow to the jaw. With that Barksdale of Mississippi leaped into the fray, as did Washburne of Illinois, Lamar of Mississippi, Covode of Pennsylvania, and a half-dozen others. Instantly the aisle was thronged with struggling, cursing legislators. Barksdale's wig was sent skimming from his bald pate in the melee, and in his haste to retrieve it he put it on again backward. Covode picked up a heavy brass cuspidor, a formidable weapon, but fortunately order was restored before he could bring it down on a Southern skull.[14]

Sickles, though entirely in accord with the Southern bloc on the Kansas question, held aloof from such unseemly strife. Those who had known him as a Tammany brawler—notably Haskin and Cochrane—noticed how his deportment had im-

proved. It was evident that ambition for high office was having a
restraining and dignifying effect on the one-time bottle-swinging
valiant of Wigwam free-for-alls.

In any case, he was so busy that virtually his only social appearance with his wife was at the regularly scheduled Sickles
entertainments. He kept a sharp eye on his political fences and
gave close attention to letters from constituents. Two or three
evenings a week he had George Wooldridge, a crippled clerk
of the House, over at the Stockton Mansion to attend to his
correspondence. Wooldridge, who hoisted his partially paralyzed
frame around on crutches, came from a Catskill village in New
York and had been a clerk at the state capitol in Albany when
Sickles was in the legislature there. The two men were close
friends, and it was Sickles who had secured Wooldridge his post
in Washington, where he acted as the Congressman's confidential
secretary in addition to his duties at the House.

On top of these chores, Sickles was forced to give thought to
pecuniary matters, for his expenses were enormous. To meet
them he took legal work on the side, making frequent trips to
New York and elsewhere in the interest of his clients. Then too,
he regarded himself as a connoisseur of women. Handsome and
masterful enough to outweigh his somewhat unimpressive stature, he was an expert at flattery and subtle persuasion, and
some women found him irresistible. This pursuit took time,
for it had to be done *sub rosa*. What with women, politics and
the law, Sickles was a man eternally in a hurry, always going
somewhere, doing something, seeing someone. The fact that
he was able to keep abreast of the turgid political current despite
all these side interests is proof that he possessed an explosive
quickness of intellect.

Teresa had long since become resigned to her husband's
philandering. A spirited young woman left alone with a fine
household staffed with servants, she had to seek her own entertainment. She sought it more and more with Barton Key. The
couple were together at the theater, at teas, at hops. But most
of all they went riding together, for Key was a splendid horse-

man and Teresa an accomplished equestrienne. Congressman Haskin, riding one day through the lonely cemetery near the Corcoran country residence, was a bit surprised to see Teresa and Key cantering toward him. They greeted him pleasantly and rode on.[15]

Although by now their frequent companionship was causing gossip, Sickles was unaware of the talk and had no suspicions. Indeed, in the opinion of no less a man than Senator Clay, Sickles "forced his wife into Barton's company." [16] Some observers thought him a "pusher" who would use any tool at hand to aid his upward climb, and that he regarded Key's intimate friendship as a sure *carte d'entrée* into social circles which as yet had given only tentative acceptance.[17] In this view, if his attractive wife could help his career, why not make use of her?

The unhappiest witness of this arrangement was young Beekman. He had foolishly become infatuated with Mrs. Sickles. She was unfailingly kind to him, but she seemed something more than kind to the tall District Attorney. Beekman watched the growing friendship of Key and Mrs. Sickles with bitter jealousy in his heart. He did not trust to gossip. He rented a horse and spied on the couple on some of their outings.

One night in March, Beekman had a few drinks at Willard's bar with a fellow Interior Department clerk from New York, Marshall J. Bacon. Beekman's loosened tongue soon got to wagging on the subject that tormented him—Teresa Sickles. He made remarks impugning Mrs. Sickles' virtue, and said flatly that her friendship with Key was anything but an innocent one. Becoming more specific, he said he knew of at least one instance in which Mrs. Sickles and Key had taken a room at an inn together, remaining there more than an hour.

All this was entirely too spicy for Bacon to keep under his hat. When Bacon met Wooldridge the next day, he repeated to the clerk what Beekman had told him, undoubtedly with the warning, "Don't breathe a word of this."

This placed Wooldridge, a youngish man who appears to have been motivated by worthy impulses, in a difficult position. He had already heard some of the gossip about Mrs. Sickles, and it worried him. Now this shocking tale of Beekman's, via Bacon, listed chapter and verse to what had previously been no more than innuendo. Wooldridge was loyal to Sickles, to whom he owed his job, and he knew that the Representative's domestic happiness and political future could easily be shattered by the scandal that seemed to be brewing. Wooldridge pondered the problem. At last he decided that it was his duty to inform Sickles of the Beekman story and let him handle it in his own way.

This he did, as diplomatically as possible, taking Sickles aside in the House chamber the following day. Sickles immediately dispatched a note by messenger to Beekman, requesting him to call at the Stockton Mansion at seven that night.

Beekman obeyed. At seven he was admitted by a servant into the Stockton place and escorted into the study, where Sickles was waiting with Wooldridge. Sickles was smoking his inevitable slim cigar and pacing the floor angrily, while Wooldridge sat quietly to one side, his crutches between his knees.

"Now, young fellow," Sickles snapped, "what's all this you have been saying about my wife and Mr. Key?"

Beekman was stunned that his supposed confidence had reached the ears of the last person in the world he wanted to hear it. Cowed by the menacing attitude of his political sponsor, he quickly backtracked. He admitted that he had "uttered several trifling jokes about the female sex in general" to a friend in casual conversation, but that was all. He swore that he had said nothing derogatory about Mrs. Sickles.

"I have been informed," Sickles insisted, "that you have been publicly circulating calumnies against my wife and Mr. Key."

Beekman again denied it. The talk grew stormy, with Sickles demanding that Beekman admit making the offensive remarks, something he doggedly refused to do, and at length he left the house angry and upset.[18]

Still dubious, Sickles then arranged an interview with Key

and told him of the gossip attributed to Beekman. Key was incensed.

"This is the highest affront that can be offered to me," he said in cold rage, "and whoever asserts it must meet me at the point of a pistol." [19]

He demanded to know the author of the rumors, and Sickles told him. The irate District Attorney then left with the promise that he would communicate immediately with the three men involved in the tale-bearing and prove its falsehood.

Using his old friend Marshal Hoover as personal messenger, Key on March 26 sent a volley of notes aimed at this end. The first was to Wooldridge, asking him his authority for the rumors he had mentioned. Wooldridge replied at once with the following explanation:

P. B. Key, Esq.

Dear Sir: Marshall J. Bacon informed me on Tuesday afternoon, March 23, that Mr. Beekman said that Mrs. Sickles had been out riding on horseback three different times with Barton Key during Mr. Sickles' last absence to the city of New York, and that they stopped at a house on the road toward Bladensburg, and that Mrs. Sickles had a room there and remained one hour and a half; also that she took off her habit, and that he had no doubt there was an intimacy between Mr. Key and Mrs. Sickles.

There was much more of the same kind of conversation; and Mr. Bacon told me also in a manner that assured me it was so, that Mr. Key boasted that he only asked 36 hours with any woman to make her do what he pleased. Yours, &c,

G. B. Wooldridge

Key's next note, to Bacon, elicited the reply that Beekman was his informant. Hoover then journeyed with a note from Key to Beekman, asking if he was "responsible for the vile calumnies" attributed to him by Bacon and Wooldridge.

By now, Samuel Beekman must have realized that in uttering

those careless remarks at Willard's he had unwittingly projected himself into a most touchy affair of honor. If he admitted
that he had made the remarks in question, he stood an excellent
chance of being challenged to a duel by either Key or Sickles,
both of whom were known as seasoned men with a pistol. Beekman wanted no duel. In a sweat, he swore he had made no such
statements, writing Key that "I disavow that I was ever their
author, and pronounce everything therein as a lie, and also the
statement of Mr. Bacon that I was their author."

Beekman was so shaken by the whole affair that a few days
later he resigned his clerkship—undoubtedly feeling that he
would be ousted anyway—and returned to New York to seek
other employment and ponder the perils of a loose tongue.

As for Key, he wrapped the sum total of the day's correspondence in an envelope and dispatched it via Hoover to Sickles,
with a little note which as much as said, "Here's an end to this
nonsense":

> Hon. D. E. Sickles—
> My Dear Sir: I send by Jonah Hoover a copy of the corre-
> spondence had today, and you will perceive any effort to fix the
> ridiculous and disgusting slander on me of the parties con-
> cerned, was unsuccessful. Respectfully and truly yours,
>   Philip Barton Key [20]

Sickles seemed satisfied. He sent a reply to Key telling of his
pleasure at the settlement of the matter and expressing the hope
that their friendship would continue as before.

"I like Key," he said to Hoover. "This thing shocked me when
I first heard about it, and I am glad to have the scurrilous business cleared up." [21]

Key must have been relieved to receive this token of trust,
but apparently the District Attorney was still a trifle uncertain
about Sickles' feelings, for he did not go in person to discuss
the matter with him. Instead he went to Haskin, who was privy
to most of it, and declared to Haskin the utter purity of his
attitude toward Teresa Sickles.

"I regard her almost as a child," he said. "It is ridiculous to suppose that I could have anything but honorable intentions toward her." [22]

He asked Haskin to pass this reassurance along to Sickles, which Haskin did at the next opportunity.

Despite his own well-publicized moral lapses, Daniel Sickles was a man of intense personal pride who would not countenance the breath of scandal attaching to his wife. He had a hair-trigger temper which could explode whenever he was humiliated or balked in any design. Yet now he maintained a remarkable equanimity. He loved his young wife with a negligent affection which he did not realize was mortifying to her. He had no doubts about her virtue, for he had known her since childhood, but he well knew that her impulsiveness and naiveté might lead her into innocent indiscretions. He warned her, as subsequent events showed, and let it go at that.

The Congressman was busy, even for a Congressman. Politics, ambition—and certain more confidential affairs—had to be served. And Teresa and the District Attorney continued to meet each other, with somewhat more circumspection but ever nearer the brink of danger.

CHAPTER III

After the Ball

For most of the winter, Mrs. Senator Gwin had been planning a ball to make all previous balls pale by comparison—a fancy dress affair to which no one would be admitted unless properly disguised by costume and mask. The bluff, hearty Senator put her right on that score. A native of Tennessee who had made his fortune in the California boom, William Gwin said he would vote Black Republican before he would burlesque his Senatorial dignity by draping his plump figure in some play-acting nonsense. Let the women and the younger blades disguise and prettify themselves to their hearts' content. Not he—and certainly not such as Senator Davis, or Senator Seward.

The invitations were sent out weeks in advance, and Seward and others of the enemy were among those invited. Perhaps that was why Senator and Mrs. Gwin planned so grandly for this ball, which was to be remembered long after the glories of ante-bellum Washington society were forever gone. For already the quarrel between North and South was becoming so acrimonious as to strain old friendships and even break them. In Congress, several duels had narrowly been averted. Already Miss Harriet Lane and Mrs. Senator Douglas were not on speaking terms, because the Senator had vigorously fought Mr. Buchanan's effort to incorporate Kansas into the Union under the pro-slavery Lecompton constitution. Who could tell how soon capital society would be truly split in twain?

So, although the Gwins were as Southern as though they still lived in Nashville, they invited the Sewards, the Douglases, and many others from the benighted North. Whether anyone realized it, this was to be the last occasion on which a number of distinguished gentlemen and their ladies were to meet on terms approaching social cordiality.

Philip Barton Key was invited as a matter of course, even though there had been considerable worried talk about him since he dropped several young women to whom he had been attentive and began spending his leisure with Teresa Sickles.

Mr. and Mrs. Sickles received an engraved invitation early in March, requesting their presence at the Gwin mansion, masked, on April 8. Sickles, to be sure, had endeared himself to Southern legislators by his sturdy championing of the Administration's pro-Southern policies. In so doing, he had been representing the feelings of the majority of his constituents as well as his own, for most New Yorkers disliked Abolitionists, regarded slavery as none of their affair, and knew that their city did a spanking business with the South which might be catapulted into ruin by any sectional rupture.

Like a hundred other women, Teresa devoted careful thought to her costume, considered a dozen possibilities, then made her choice and ordered it from New York. Even Sickles gave the matter some study, for the Gwin ball was one function he meant to attend. But he was a man with many irons in the fire, and first he had to make a business trip to New York. The day before he left—hardly a week after the Beekman incident—he stopped at Haskin's seat in the House.

"I'll be gone a few days, John," he said. "I wonder if you'd look in on Teresa while I'm away, to see if she wants anything." [1]

Haskin agreed. Sickles left next morning, and around four o'clock that very afternoon Haskin happened to be driving along Pennsylvania Avenue with his wife and children, on their way to Georgetown to buy some shoes. As they passed the White House, Haskin recalled his promise. Though they were late, he turned his carriage into Jackson Place and stopped at the Stockton Mansion. He helped his wife to alight and, as he later described it, "rushed upstairs, opened the front door and the door to the little library without knocking." [2]

Mr. and Mrs. Haskin immediately became aware that they had intruded on a private tête-à-tête. Teresa and Key were seated together at a small round table. Teresa, a wooden spoon in her hand, was in the act of mixing a bowl of salad. On the table stood a bottle of champagne, about half gone, and two glasses.

Teresa dropped the spoon and flushed as she arose, but she was still the thoughtful hostess.

"How nice of you to stop!" she exclaimed. "Perhaps—would you have some wine with us?"

The Haskins explained that they had to hurry along. Teresa introduced Mrs. Haskin to Key, for they had never met. There was a brief and rather strained conversation, and then the visitors took their leave.

As the Haskins returned to their carriage, Mrs. Haskin said with some asperity, "We won't go there again, John. She's a bad woman." [3]

Haskin must have shaken his head over this incident, coming so soon after the Beekman exchange which one would have thought would have counseled discretion. But he was no tale-bearer, and Sickles was not to learn of the champagne scene until much later, when it made no further difference.

When Sickles returned from New York, he brought with him a buccaneer's costume for the ball and also an illness. It is not written what ailment he had, but it may well have been a common cold. At any rate, by the night of the ball he was ill enough to be in bed, and Teresa was driven off alone by John Thompson, the Scot coachman. She was clad in red cape, pointed bonnet, and on her arm she carried "a basket of goodies for her grandmother"—surely a fetching Little Red Ridinghood.

The Gwin mansion, at 19th and I Streets, just off the Avenue, was already besieged by a snarl of carriages which liveried coachmen were trying to untangle. Inside, the huge ballroom, said to be not far from the White House's East Room in size, was festooned with streamers and alive with music, movement, and excited talk. One of the guests was Major John De Havilland, the capital's poet laureate, who wore a clanking suit of armor and whose muse was so inspired by the affair that he penned a long metrical description of the ball after the manner of Pope. Wrote the major, doing honor to the rule excluding all political partisanship from the gathering:

> No carking cares of state can enter here,
> To damp the spirits or repress the cheer.
> Frowns and annoyance are denied the door,
> And Pleasure rules upon the waxen floor.
> No Slavery, but to Beauty, here is seen,
> Nor Abolition, save of Discord's mien.
> Chivalric sway all hearts and minds maintain,
> From sunny Texas up to snowy Maine . . .[4]

Perhaps the feelings between representatives of the two sections were not quite so amicable as the major's poesy had it, but there certainly was no unpleasantness. The room was a riot of color, the costumes splendid. At one end, the gracious Mrs. Gwin, attired as a Lady of the Court of Louis Quatorze, greeted an unending line of guests. In such a large gathering, some duplication of costume was inevitable. Teresa Sickles soon discovered that the brunette Mrs. Hughes of Virginia, daughter of Secretary of War Floyd, had also arrived in the guise of Red Ridinghood, but this should not have desolated her. There were three French Marchionesses (Mrs. Jefferson Davis, Miss Hale of New Hampshire, and the Baroness de Stoeckl), three English Huntsmen, and no less than six Spanish Cavaliers.

Barton Key, in fact, was one of the Huntsmen—an appropriate costume for such a devoted horseman. He made a striking figure in white satin breeches, lemon-colored high-top boots, a cherry velvet jacket and jaunty cap, with a silver bugle slung over his shoulder.[5] He soon found Teresa and took her away in a galop, a lively dance then coming into vogue.

Jonah Hoover, swathed in lace and ruffles as Claude Melnotte, must have raised an eyebrow at this, so short a time after he had carried those notes for Key. So too must the classic Mrs. Pendleton, Key's sister, as well as others. Mrs. Pendleton, personifying the *Star-Spangled Banner,* did honor to her poet father and his anthem in a costume that was one of the sensations of the evening. Decorating the corsage of her white satin gown was a golden spread-eagle, while in silver letters the motto "E Pluribus Unum" trailed on a tricolor sash, and a crown of thirteen stars flashed on her proud head.

There was a ripple of excitement when President Buchanan arrived, torn away from "carking cares of state" to pay his respects to the Gwins and undoubtedly wishing that his whole quarreling nation could settle its differences as easily. The six-foot President was now sixty-seven, and yet he still presented an impressive figure in the inevitable black suit and white silk cravat, his florid face topped by snow-white hair. His "infirmity" —a muscular weakness of the neck which made him cock his head far to port like a puzzled barnyard fowl—was no longer noticed by his intimates.

The mettlesome Mrs. Senator Clay could not forgo the opportunity to twit the President. She had cast aside her glamor and come garbed as Mrs. Partington, a fictional Yankee lady from Beanville who uttered salty remarks in atrocious grammar—a rustic Mrs. Malaprop. She was acting the part to perfection.

"Lor! Air you ralely Old Buck?" she shrilled at Mr. Buchanan. "I've often heern tell o' Old Buck up in Beanville, but I don't see no horns."

"No, Madam," the President replied, a little cynical for once. "I'm not a married man."

Mrs. Clay even condescended to pass a few words with that double-dyed Northerner, Senator Seward of New York, despite an earlier threat to her husband that "Not even to save the nation could I be induced to . . . speak to him." [6]

Daniel Sickles was indeed missing something special, but New York City was far from unrepresented. There was Scottish-born James Gordon Bennett, the unscrupulous and remarkably cross-eyed publisher of the New York *Herald,* clad in kilts. There was Representative Cochrane, a sinister-looking matador. Decked out as the painter Van Dyck was Mr. Mathew Brady, the fashionable New York photographer whose ambition was to snap every important personage of the day and who was thinking of opening a gallery in Washington. To be photographed by Brady was almost *de rigueur* in smart society, and both Daniel and Teresa Sickles had recently sat for him.

The Southern stalwarts, of course, were there in a body. Mr. Keitt of South Carolina, who had recently been toppled to the House floor by Mr. Grow's Abolitionist fist, made a brave-looking Buckingham, while Mr. Clingman of North Carolina was a Gentleman of the Twentieth Century, clad in a blue coat with metal buttons and white satin breeches. Mr. Jefferson Davis, remembering his Senatorial dignity, appeared in ordinary dress, but the foreign legations were attired in all manner of colorful panoply.

> How rich the medley, and how gay the throng!
> Greek meets with Greek—Turk pushes Turk along;
> Knights pair with Gipsies—Monks with stately Dames;
> The peasant girl the gallant courtier claims.

So wrote Major De Havilland, with an enthusiasm justified by the glittering scene before him. The major even remarked on the beauty of Teresa Sickles with appreciative verses:

> Lo! little "Riding Hood," with artless grace,
> Reveals the sweetness of her youthful face.

Mrs. Sickles was one of the belles among a host of pretty women. She danced on the arms of a dozen partners, but in the end it was Key to whom she returned. Later, when the Gwins' fine wines had had their effect, they were together almost exclusively, and Key was careless enough to call further attention to this by gaily blowing a few blasts on his hunting horn.

At two A.M., when Teresa left with Key, many eyes followed them—some scornful, some cynical, some mirroring concern.

Red Ridinghood and the English Hunter climbed into the Sickles carriage. Coachman Thompson later recalled in court that Mrs. Sickles directed him to drive along "back streets," and that they lingered for quite a while in front of the National Hotel before Key got out and bade her goodnight.[7]

The coachman, being ordinarily observant, could not help noticing numerous remarkable incidents thereafter. It was Mrs. Sickles' habit to ride out almost every weekday around one P.M. to pay social calls on her friends, with Thompson handling the reins. She would hand him a list of the addresses at which she intended to call, and he would follow the most direct course in complying. But on several occasions she gave him no list at all. Instead, she directed him to the old Congressional burying grounds near the East Branch of the Potomac. There, inside the cemetery, Key would be waiting on his iron-gray mount. Teresa and Key would saunter off out of the coachman's sight, leaving him to mind the horses, and would return an hour or more later.

Then there was that night in May when Mr. Sickles was away on one of his frequent trips. Key arrived early that evening and stayed far beyond midnight, sitting with the lady of the house in the small library at the front of the drawing room. Thompson knew this, because around one A.M. he thought he heard the front bell pulled. So did Bridget Duffy, the house-maid, and the two went to the top of the staircase. From that vantage point they saw Key and Mrs. Sickles come out of the library. Mrs. Sickles went to the front door and opened it, but no one was there. Key and the mistress thereupon returned to the library.

Click went the lock on the door from library to hall.

Click went the lock on the door from library to drawing room.

Thompson turned to Bridget Duffy with a knowing grin. "They ain't up to no good work," he said.

Bridget blushed and ran to her room.[8]

Sickles, who had an ear so sharp that it never missed the softest vibrations of political gossip, heard not a word about any delinquencies at his own fireside. The Congressman was busy supporting Buchanan's policies, busy with legal work, busy with women. More cautious than in the past, he now carried on his illicit affairs in secrecy. His political confreres, who had been worried about that, had to admit that he maintained a studiously respectable front.[9] He seemed to have drawn a lesson from past errors—as well as the sound advice of associates —so that the violence and contempt for public opinion that had once marked him were no longer in evidence. The *enfant terrible* of New York politics, it seemed, was growing sensible.

In the legislative arena likewise he had won first-term laurels. He was often closeted with Buchanan, and in June he made an effective speech in the House praising the Administration's stand against "English aggression" in stopping and searching American vessels suspected as slave traders.[10] By the time the session ended, the new Congressman from Manhattan seemed more than ever a man destined for the heights.

On July 1st, the Sickleses closed their Washington house and moved to New York. Sickles was up for re-election in the fall, and he had a little politicking to do.

That summer, a veritable miracle came to pass. An enterprising Yankee named Cyrus Field had organized a group of American and British financiers in a combine aimed at spanning the Atlantic with an underwater cable. Many laughed at "Field's Folly," but in August, after several disheartening failures, the cable was completed and the nation went mildly crazy. President Buchanan and Queen Victoria exchanged congratulatory messages over almost 2000 miles of sunken wire. It was generally believed that this new marvel, which would bring news from Europe instantly instead of in the fortnight or so required by vessels, would cement the world in new amity.

Somehow it was overlooked that for years the North and

South had been in closest communication by telegraph and by personal discussion in Congress—a communion that had resulted not in accord but in steadily increasing friction.

But the city of New York, ever eager for a jubilee, planned a mammoth Cable Celebration for September 1st.

The Sickleses had been summering at their impressive home on the Hudson River at Ninety-first Street in Bloomingdale, then a rural section well north of the teeming city. Sickles, always happiest in a crowd of intimates, was often seen at Delmonico's and at the Tammany Wigwam, his two favorite resorts, where he renewed his friendship with Emanuel Hart, Samuel Butterworth, Charles K. Graham and others. Though he loved the theater and was a good friend of the actors John Brougham and Edwin Forrest, most of his cronies were more noted in the legal and political fraternities. They included such Tammany disciples as Captain William Wiley, John Graham, August Belmont, Thomas Francis Meagher, and James Topham Brady.

John Graham, Charles' elder brother, was a hard-drinking lawyer of considerable ability who in 1850 had won applause by horsewhipping the unpopular James Gordon Bennett on Broadway while Mrs. Bennett looked on screaming.[11] Belmont, a former member of the fabulous Rothschild banking house in Germany, had come to America, struck it rich as a financier, and developed a passion for politics and the racetrack—in both of which pursuits Sickles was right at his elbow. Meagher, a fiery Irish revolutionist from Waterford, had been sentenced by the British to the penal colony in Tasmania, had escaped and come to New York to be idolized by his Anglophobe countrymen and to essay a new career at the bar. Brady was then at the summit of his powers as one of the most eloquent pleaders of the day.

Sickles was fond of surrounding himself with men who were able, brilliant, or unusual in some way. All of these regarded Sickles as a valued friend long before he became the outstanding young leader of the Democratic Party with a great future before him.

The day of the great celebration dawned. Broadway presented

a magnificent sight, with every business establishment decorated with flags, streamers, and mottoes proclaiming the "wedding of Europe and America." Mr. Barnum's Museum bore huge portraits of Buchanan and Queen Victoria. Sedate Trinity Church had unbent to allow its steeple to be draped with the flags of all nations. Mathew Brady's photographic gallery (on the second floor above Thompson's Saloon) flaunted an enormous transparency showing a bridge across the ocean, and Neptune in chains.

New York was choked with a half million visitors. Hotels were so inadequate that many unfortunates had to sleep in Central Park. But not Philip Barton Key. He had visited with the Sickleses on his way up to Saratoga, where he had vacationed for several weeks, and now he was with them again on the return trip. Another guest at Bloomingdale was Daniel Dougherty, a Philadelphia politician and good friend of Buchanan and Sickles. Key and Dougherty found Sickles a pleasant host as well as a man who could arrange little conveniences. When the parade got under way, they were not forced to cope with the sweaty multitude that packed Broadway. They were comfortably installed, along with the Sickleses and the Haskins, in a big second-floor parlor of the ornate Metropolitan Hotel from which they could peer out through a welter of Chinese lanterns and see the whole display.[12]

In the great parade, headed by six thousand soldiers, rode Mr. Buchanan and Lord Napier, the British Minister, sandwiched among a myriad of dignitaries, floats, and marching groups including such diverse elements as the coroners, the governors of the almshouses, the hoop-skirt makers, the Cadets of Temperance, and, paradoxically, the distillers.[13]

That evening, fireworks were exploded with such abandon that the City Hall cupola caught fire. There was a vast municipal banquet at the Metropolitan Hotel, where a score of toasts were proposed. To one of them—"The Arts of Peace"—Daniel Sickles responded with his usual fluent charm even though he had never been known as an especially peaceful man.[14]

Everybody felt a little silly three days later when the cable went dead and never worked again.

It turned out that Sickles had a fight on his hands for his Congressional post that fall. Some of his Tammany enemies denounced him, and the quarrelsome brethren ended by splitting into factions and nominating two candidates. Sickles had to defeat not only his Republican opponent, Amos Williamson, but also another Democrat. He took to the hustings with relish, for he loved a fight and could win over a crowd and demolish a heckler with finesse. Aided by Butterworth, Hart, and other Tammany friends, he beat Williamson by a slim 148 votes.[15]

The defeated candidate shouted fraud—not surprisingly, for fraud seemed part and parcel of New York elections of that era. Williamson secured affidavits that Sickles had imported illegal voters wholesale from Brooklyn, and contested the election, but in the end the result was allowed to stand. Late in November the Sickleses returned to Washington with their formidable train of servants and baggage and reopened the Stockton Mansion.

Shortly before their return, Barton Key, at Sickles' request, had represented him in a minor legal question about the lease of the house.[16]

He liked Key. If there had been a moment of suspicion at the time of the Beekman incident, that was all forgotten.

CHAPTER IV

Sir, I Do Assure You

Washington in 1858 was a Southern city entirely surrounded by slave territory, a capital where Southerners had called the tune politically and socially for decades and had not the slightest intention of allowing any change. Lafayette Square bristled with this lordly attitude. It was inhabited by some of the most powerful of the Southern Democrats dedicated to the proposition that the rising Republicans were sordid money-grubbers bent on humiliating the South, and, gad sir, unless they mended their ways there was always the remedy of secession.

The square was a center of elegance and wealth, hallowed by the shades of such immortals as Henry Clay, Dolly Madison, Daniel Webster, John Randolph, and Stephen Decatur, all of whom had lived there. Its leafy little park, surrounded by an iron fence with massive gates surmounted by gilt eagles, was a place where the children of statesmen and legislators played under the watchful eyes of nursemaids. A little back from the center, circled by beds of roses and easily visible from the White House's north portico, stood Clark Mills' equestrian statue of Andrew Jackson, erected in 1853, representing the general doffing his cocked hat, just as he does today. Iron benches were scattered along the walks, and just to the west of the statue was a dwarf Spanish chestnut known as the "wishing tree," which was believed to have miraculous powers. Young lovers and married couples often came to stand under it in the hope that its spreading branches would confer happiness.[1]

The Sickles home, formerly the residence of Senators and Cabinet members, overlooked this scene from the west side of the square. To the north, at the corner of H Street, was the fine old Decatur House from which Stephen Decatur sallied forth in 1820 to fight his duel with Commodore Barron and was carried home to his wife with only a few hours to live. Now the place was owned by John Gadsby, a rich landowner and slave dealer. Sixty paces east on H Street was fashionable St. John's Church, shepherded by the Reverend Smith Pyne and attended by notables including President Buchanan, who often snorted that Pyne's sermons were "too long, too long." [2]

Dr. Pyne, when later asked if the Sickleses were members of his congregation, said cautiously that he "believed" they were, which suggests that they were occasional but not regular communicants. [3]

Also around the square were the homes of Treasury Secretary Howell Cobb of Georgia, Senator John Slidell of Louisiana, and others of the elect including the Southern-loving banker W. W. Corcoran and the Benjamin Ogle Tayloes, transplanted Virginia aristocrats. The Tayloes—to whom Barton Key was related— lived in a handsome residence on the east side of the square adjoining the old Dolly Madison place. Next to the Tayloe house and only a stone's throw from Pennsylvania Avenue was a spacious three-story brick building once occupied by Chief Justice Taney, Key's uncle, and now the home of the National Club, better known simply as the Club House. This establishment was frequented by government officials and Washington business men. It was a place where a friendly drink could be enjoyed with all-male gossip, and although it was sedate enough it was rather frowned on by residents who wanted to preserve the square's original character.

Key, who lived at the C Street residence of his sister and brother-in-law, the Pendletons, was a member of the club and often stopped there, particularly after the Sickleses moved in across the park. From the entrance of the Club House, the chaste white front of the Sickles place could easily be seen.

When the Sickleses returned to this patrician milieu late in 1858, they had more of a feeling of "belonging" than during the previous winter. True, there were still a few doors that had not been opened to them, but at any rate they had a year behind them and had made astonishing progress.

Now they resumed their progress. Sickles was appointed to membership in the House Committee on Foreign Relations, a post of importance reflecting his steady rise. His social star likewise rose. Among the guests at the Stockton Mansion that winter were such notables as Secretary and Mrs. Cobb, Attorney General and Mrs. Black, Representative Lawrence O'Bryan Branch of North Carolina, the Slidells, the Orrs, and the President himself. And always there was the ubiquitous Henry Wikoff, a man who could enliven any party.

To many a lady, the "Chevalier" Wikoff seemed a fictional romantic hero brought to life. Heir to a Philadelphia fortune, he had been a globe-trotting idler for most of his forty-five years. He had been everywhere. In France he had been friendly with Louis Napoleon before he became king, and was also said to have been employed by the British to spy on the French. His most publicized achievement was an infatuation with an Englishwoman named Miss Gamble, whom he pursued from London to Genoa, where he kidnaped her. For this the Chevalier had served fifteen months in an Italian prison and had written a book about his exploits titled, "My Courtship and Its Consequences," which became a best seller.[4] To the Sickleses he was friend, confidant and dinner-party ornament.

The up-and-coming New York couple were also busy with plans for little Laura, who had thus far escaped baptism. They had discussed the matter with Dr. Pyne and with Mrs. Slidell, who was to be godmother. President Buchanan gladly agreed to be godfather. Sickles was nominally an Episcopalian, while Teresa was a Roman Catholic, and the fact that the christening was to take place at Protestant St. John's showed that the father's wishes were inflexible in all important matters. But when the appointed day arrived, Laura was ill with whooping cough and the ceremony had to be postponed.

The brilliance of the Sickles entertainments that winter did not go unnoticed. "His [Sickles'] coaches, dinners and parties were irreproachable," wrote the sociable newsman Ben Perley Poore, "and Mrs. Sickles was noted for her magnificent jewelry and beautiful toilettes. Mr. Buchanan was a frequent guest at their house." [5] Representative Branch, too, was impressed. "Yesterday I dined with Sickles of New York," he wrote his wife on one occasion. "He lives in great style keeping one of the finest carriages &c &c in the city . . . [Mrs. Sickles] is young pretty and very stylish." [6]

Senator Gwin was said to spend $75,000 a year in Washington.[7] The Sickleses' manner of living, while it did not equal the lavishness of the Gwins', was grand enough to cause speculation. Poore later wrote that the Sickles establishment was rumored to be "kept up by a New York steamship company [and] frequented by the lobby." [8]

*   *   *

In October of 1858, Mrs. Nancy Brown, wife of one of the White House gardeners, had a conversation she was later to remember. Mrs. Brown lived on Fifteenth Street near the angle-wise intersection of Vermont Avenue, which was only two short blocks north of Lafayette Square and yet was in a poor neighborhood inhabited by a conglomeration of whites and negroes. One morning, a tall, distinguished-looking man rode up, dismounted from his iron-gray horse, and addressed Mrs. Brown pleasantly.

"Is that house for rent, Madam?" he asked, pointing with his riding crop to the vacant place cater-corner across the way at No. 383 Fifteenth.

"I don't know," the woman replied. "You'll have to ask the colored man."

The "colored man" was John Gray, owner of the house, who

some time previously had moved to new quarters near Capitol Hill. Mrs. Brown gave the gentleman Gray's address and he thanked her and rode off. About three weeks later he returned and, seeing Mrs. Brown, told her he had rented the house for a Senator friend. Not long afterward a tradesman brought a wagonload of wood and piled it near the back door of the brick house.[9]

But it was not until December or January that Mrs. Brown noticed any sign of life at No. 383. One chill day she saw the tall gentleman come up the street, this time on foot, and enter the house. He came out again, got an armload of wood and re-entered. Soon there was smoke curling from the chimney, indicating that he had lighted a fire.

Mrs. Brown was curious, for she had never seen the Senator the man had mentioned. In fact, this seemed an unlikely neighborhood for a person of such importance to seek lodging. She kept a sharp eye at the window. A few minutes later, a woman came into view, walking rather uncertainly up Fifteenth Street. She was young and attractive, and Mrs. Brown noticed that she wore a plaid silk dress under a black raglan cloak, and a black velvet shawl fringed with bugles.

The woman turned in and entered No. 383 in a manner that appeared nervous and furtive, keeping her shawl drawn so as to conceal most of her face. She remained inside for perhaps an hour or more, and then she left the place hurriedly alone. Shortly after her departure, the tall gentleman came out, locked the door, and walked away.

Now thoroughly alert to a mystery she could only guess at, Nancy Brown kept the brick house under vigilant surveillance. There was still no sign of any regular occupant there, but occasionally, at intervals of a week or a few days, the same man and woman returned to pay further brief visits. Once or twice they arrived together, but more often the man arrived first, to be followed shortly thereafter by the woman. When he did so, he always carried wood in with him, and he did something else that did not long remain a puzzle to the interested observer.

He hung a bit of red ribbon out on one of the upstairs shutters. This, Mrs. Brown reasoned, must be a signal to the approaching woman to reassure her that the man was inside and waiting for her.

Nancy Brown had no further doubt as to what the brick house was being used for, and she was highly curious as to the identity of the couple. One day, while shopping on the Avenue, she saw the woman being driven by in a fine carriage, and she asked a friend who the woman was.

"Why, that's Mrs. Sickles," the friend replied.

In a similar manner, Mrs. Brown learned that the tall gentleman was Mr. Key, the District Attorney.

Nancy Brown was not the only observer of the comings and goings of Key and Mrs. Sickles at the brick house on Fifteenth Street. A housepainter named John M. Seeley, whose back yard adjoined that of the brick house, was well aware of it, as was his wife Sarah Ann and his sixteen-year-old blonde daughter, Matilda. Mrs. Seeley and her daughter were in the habit of going upstairs so they could get a better view of the arrival and departure of the couple. Mrs. Seeley's interest was all the further whetted since she recognized Key, having lived in Georgetown some years earlier when Key also lived there.

Directly across Fifteenth Street from the brick house was the home of a colored woman, Mrs. Baylis, who had a young son named Crittenden. Mrs. Baylis noticed the visits across the way, as did the boy. Indeed, it got so that whenever Key and Mrs. Sickles approached their rendezvous, dozens of people both white and colored were on the *qui vive,* with corner loafers murmuring coarse jokes and housewives spying from behind bedraggled curtains. On one occasion when Key and Mrs. Sickles came up the street together, a pair of policemen happened to be passing the time of day nearby. The couple apparently were impressed by this symbol of authority, for they walked on hurriedly without entering the brick house—an incident that afforded the Fifteenth Street gossips malicious amusement for days.[10]

Key, a strapping man of thirty-nine and the father of four

children, was known as a gallant but not as a libertine. Despite his robust appearance he worried a good deal about his health,[11] but always seemed to find enough reserves of strength to carry him to parties and hops. Occasionally he felt too ill to go to his office in the city hall and the work was left to his assistant, Robert Ould.[12] Some came right out and said the District Attorney was lazy. For a man of uncertain health, he carried on his back-street affair with the Congressman's wife with remarkable diligence and also managed to be with her at countless parlor gatherings. Later, when circumstances warned them to be on guard, they worked out a scheme whereby they could meet in society without—as they naively supposed—arousing suspicion.

Even John Cooney, who succeeded Thompson as the Sickles coachman, was aware of this. On one occasion that winter when Mrs. Sickles was making afternoon calls, Cooney drove her to Mrs. Secretary Thompson's. Shortly after she entered, Key arrived and joined her inside. A half-hour later she emerged alone and rode to the next stop, Mrs. Postmaster General Brown's. No more than ten minutes later, Key joined her there as if by pure chance. The process was then repeated at the home of the lively Mrs. Rose Greenhow.[13]

This deception became so transparent that even the two lovers must have been aware of it. They resorted to other tricks, devising a code with which they could communicate by note with less danger. Key formed a habit of signaling to Teresa from Lafayette Square by waving a white handkerchief, a signal she could easily see from her window.[14] Others could see it as easily, for a half-dozen witnesses later testified that they had seen the District Attorney facing the Sickles place and waving his handkerchief in a "rotary motion." He also carried a pair of opera glasses which he would train on Teresa's window and detect her answering signals.

By midwinter the "secret" affair was known, though perhaps not to its full extent, by almost everybody in Washington except for one person—Daniel Sickles.

Among those who knew were the Sickles servants. One day

when a domestic saw Key standing out in the square twirling his handkerchief, she remarked scornfully to a belowstairs companion, "There is Disgrace, waiting to meet Disgust." [15]

Another who knew was Albert A. Megaffey, a prosperous contractor and fellow member of the club who was friendly with Key and enough older to feel free about offering sound advice. In the previous June he had taken Key aside and warned him in fatherly fashion that his attentions to Mrs. Sickles were causing gossip. In February of 1859, Megaffey repeated the warning, this time making it stronger. Key once more fell back on his threadbare insistence that he had only "paternal" feelings toward Teresa. And when Megaffey, who knew better, suggested that Key might get into actual danger over the matter, the District Attorney bridled and patted the breast of his coat.

"I am prepared for any emergency," he snapped.[16]

The reply has a flavor of desperation. Key was a crack shot, and like many gentlemen of the day he sometimes carried a pistol. Very possibly he had reached the point where he was expecting at any moment to receive a challenge from Daniel Sickles so that the issue could be settled one way or the other by bullets at twenty paces.

While the fuse sputtered slowly over this powder-keg, Edwin Stanton returned after a year in California as special United States counsel to settle conflicting land claims in that state. Perhaps affection was not the terrible-tempered attorney's long suit, and yet his attitude toward the youthful Representative Sickles warmed rapidly into real fondness. Both were intimates of Buchanan. Both were politicians driven by ambition and skilled at devious manipulation. Both had wives considerably younger than themselves, for Stanton was then forty-six and his wife Ellen only twenty-nine. Between the bleak Ohioan and the sleek New Yorker was cemented a friendship that was to persist so steadfastly through years of personal and political strife that— for better or for worse—Stanton had a large hand in shaping the career of Daniel Sickles.

But if Sickles numbered his friends in the hundreds, Teresa was lonely and afraid. She desperately needed a friend and confidante in whom she could trust, something she could not find in the circle of capital *grandes dames*. A few months earlier she had made the acquaintance of Octavia Ridgeley, a young Washington lady, and the two became firm friends, often making afternoon calls together. It was a friendship that was to involve Octavia in the most harrowing scene of her life.

On Thursday, February 24th, was held the last dinner party ever to be given by Daniel and Teresa Sickles. Key was not invited, for earlier there had been a minor difference between the host and hostess about him, Sickles suggesting that perhaps she was overdoing it with Key.[17] Daniel Dougherty, in town on a political mission from Philadelphia, was a guest, as were Henry Wikoff, Octavia Ridgeley, and many others. The regal Mrs. Clay arrived with Mrs. Senator Pugh, and later penned this impression of her hostess and the party:

> She [Mrs. Sickles] was so young and fair, at most not more than twenty-two years of age, and so naive, that none of the party of which I was one was willing to harbor a belief in the rumors which were then in circulation. On that, Mrs. Sickles last "at home," her parlors were thronged, one-half of the hundred or more guests present being men. The girl hostess was even more lovely than usual. Of an Italian type of feature and coloring (she was the daughter of a famous musician, Bagioli of New York) Mrs. Sickles was dressed in a painted muslin gown, filmy and graceful, on which the outlines of the crocus might be traced. A broad sash of brocaded ribbon girdled her slender waist, and in her dark hair were yellow crocus blooms. I never saw her again, but the picture of which she formed the center was so fair and innocent, it fixed itself permanently upon my mind.[18]

"*I never saw her again,*" wrote Mrs. Clay, summing up in those five words a world of tragedy. To the Alabama matron, a shrewd observer who could be sharply censorious when the occasion demanded, Mrs. Sickles was anything but an adventuress.

The party broke up around ten P.M. and most of the guests moved on to Willard's, where a hop was in progress. Teresa left in a carriage with Wikoff and Miss Ridgeley, while Sickles tarried a while to see everyone off before proceeding to the hotel.

It was past two when the Sickleses returned home. The day had been such a busy one that the Congressman had not had time to read his mail, so he now sat down in his study and went through a handful of letters.

One of them was in a cheap yellow envelope. Its oddly punctuated message, with one word missing as if in haste, must have staggered Daniel Sickles:

> Washington, Feb. 24, 1859
>
> Hon. Daniel Sickles—
> Dear Sir: with deep regret I inclose to your address the few lines but an indispensable duty compels me so to do seeing that you are greatly imposed upon.
> There is a fellow I may say, for he is not a gentleman, by any means by the [name] of Phillip Barton Key & I believe the district attorney who rents a house of a negro man by the name of Jno. A Gray situated on 15th Street b'twn K & L streets, for no other purpose than to meet your wife Mrs. Sickles. He hangs a string out of the window as a signal to her that he is in and leaves the door unfastened and she walks in and sir I do assure you
>   with these few hints I leave the rest for you to imagine.
>   Most Respfly
>   Your friend R. P. G.[19]

But One Course Left

Sickles arose Friday morning somewhat earlier than usual, strode across proud Lafayette Square and into grubby Fifteenth Street. He must have eyed the stark brick front of No. 383 with distaste before he knocked at a few neighboring doors and asked questions.

Then he went on to the Capitol, where he sought out McElhone, the *Globe* reporter, and asked him to insert the following personal advertisement in the next day's *States* and *Star*:

> R. P. G., who recently addressed a letter to a gentleman in this city, will confer a great favor upon the gentleman to whom the letter was addressed by granting him an early, immediate and confidential interview.[1]

A little later, Sickles found the clerk, George Wooldridge, behind the Speaker's chair in the House.

"George," he said, "I want to speak to you about a painful matter. Late last night I received this letter."

Although the House was in session and a speaker was droning somewhere in the background, he began reading the note aloud. But emotion overcame him, his voice broke, and he handed the missive to Wooldridge. The clerk read it and the two retired to an anteroom, where Sickles flung himself into a sofa. He had inquired in the neighborhood of No. 383, he went on, and had learned it was true that Key had rented the place and was meeting a woman there.

"My hope," he said, "is that this is not my wife, but some other woman. As my friend, you will go there and see whether it is or not." He collapsed in convulsive sobs for a moment. "Get a carriage—I'll show you the house." [2]

The two men were driven to Fifteenth Street, where Sickles pointed out Gray's house. After taking Sickles back to Lafayette Square, Wooldridge returned to Fifteenth Street and began a quiet investigation. Every person he queried in the neighborhood knew about the meetings which had taken place at the brick house. He spoke with the colored woman, Mrs. Baylis, who lived almost directly opposite, and arranged to rent an upper room from her for a few days with the idea of spying from this vantage point and thus making positive identification of the woman.

"Them white folks was at the house jest yesterday afternoon," Mrs. Baylis told him as he left.

That afternoon, despite the doubts that racked him, Sickles addressed the House briefly on a Navy yard appropriation bill. When Wooldridge reported to him what Mrs. Baylis had said, he seized the crippled clerk's shoulder excitedly.

"Then it can't be Teresa!" he cried. "She was at home all yesterday afternoon preparing for the dinner party! Key's got some other woman on the string." [3]

Yet he was not sure, for the description seemed to tally. He instructed Wooldridge to continue his inquiries with the greatest of caution, not mentioning Mrs. Sickles' name. Wooldridge did so on Saturday, spending several hours snooping in the vicinity of the brick house. He soon discovered that Mrs. Baylis was mistaken about the day and that the latest assignation had taken place on Wednesday. He further learned that the woman in question frequently wore a black raglan cloak and a black velvet shawl fringed with bugles. It was Teresa beyond a doubt. But Wooldridge, a thorough man, even went to the Sickles home and questioned the servants. They admitted they had often seen

Mr. Key across the way in the square, making signals with his handkerchief which seemed to be directed at the Sickles house.

When Wooldridge returned to the Capitol around 4:30 and reported this to Sickles, the Congressman went white. Perhaps a quarter-hour later, the Rev. Smith Pyne, in his carriage, saw Sickles striding across Lafayette Square and was startled by the New Yorker's stricken expression. He later described it as "wild," "defiant," and "desolate." [4]

That evening at the Stockton Mansion was a tormented one. Sickles entered tight-lipped, and instead of dining downstairs he ordered Bridget Duffy to bring him a tray of food in his bedroom. So far he had mentioned nothing of his suspicions, but the increasing grimness of his manner during the past two days could scarcely have been unobserved by the apprehensive Teresa. Octavia Ridgeley was with her, staying for the weekend on what proved to be the unhappiest visit of her life.

Sickles summoned Teresa to the bedroom.

Then the servants and Miss Ridgeley—all of them privy to a secret which Sickles had just learned—heard the broken, confused, passionate sounds from a husband confronting his wife with proof of her shame and infidelity. They heard agitated talk and sobbing from both of them. Bridget, with marvelous restraint, later declared, "There was some unhappy feeling between Mr. and Mrs. Sickles." [5] Octavia, with more descriptive facility, said that Sickles' groans were "fearful . . . They seemed to come from his very feet." [6]

So, for Teresa Bagioli Sickles, ended the dinners with famous men and accomplished women, the gay hops at Willard's, the thrilling swell of the Marine Band on the President's lawn, the signals, the trysts, the guilt. She was not yet twenty-three years old, but in its essence her life ended that evening.

Around 9 o'clock, Sickles called Bridget and Octavia to the bedroom. With tears streaming from his eyes, he handed them a paper which he asked them to sign as witnesses. Teresa sat there wordless, her head bowed, her face buried in a lacy handkerchief. The paper, written jerkily in her girlish hand, read:

I have been in a house in Fifteenth Street, with Mr. Key.
How many times I don't know. I believe the house belongs to a
colored man. The house is unoccupied. Commenced going there
the latter part of January. Have been in alone and with Mr.
Key. Usually stayed an hour or more. There was a bed in the
second story. I did what is usual for a wicked woman to do. The
intimacy commenced this winter, when I came from New York,
in that house—an intimacy of an improper kind. Have met
half a dozen times or more, at different hours of the day. On
Monday of this week, and Wednesday also. Would arrange
meetings when we met in the street and at parties. Never would
speak to him when Mr. Sickles was at home, because I knew he
did not like me to speak to him; did not see Mr. Key for some
days after I got here. He then told me he had hired the house
as a place where he and I could meet. I agreed to it. Had nothing to eat or drink there. The room is warmed by a wood fire.
Mr. Key generally goes first. Have walked there together say
four times—I do not think more; was there on Wednesday last,
between two and three. I went there alone. Laura was at Mrs.
Hoover's. Mr. Key took and left her there at my request. From
there I went to Fifteenth Street to meet Mr. Key; from there to
the milk woman's. Immediately after Mr. Key left Laura at Mrs.
Hoover's, I met him in Fifteenth Street. Went in by the back
gate. Went in the same bedroom, and there an improper interview was had. I undressed myself. Mr. Key undressed also. This
occurred on Wednesday, 23rd of February, 1859. Mr. Key has
kissed me in this house a number of times. I do not deny that
we have had connection in this house, last spring, a year ago,
in the parlor, on the sofa. Mr. Sickles was sometimes out of
town, and sometimes in the Capitol. I think the intimacy commenced in April or May, 1858. I did not think it safe to meet
him in this house, because there are servants who might suspect
something. As a general thing, have worn a black and white
woollen plaid dress, and beaver hat trimmed with black velvet.
Have worn a black silk dress there also, also a plaid silk dress,
black velvet cloak trimmed with lace, and black velvet shawl
trimmed with fringe. On Wednesday I either had on my brown
dress or black and white woollen dress, beaver hat and velvet

shawl. I arranged with Mr. Key to go in the back way, after leaving Laura at Mrs. Hoover's. He met me at Mr. Douglas'. The arrangement to go in the back way was either made in the street or at Mr. Douglas', as we would be less likely to be seen. The house is in Fifteenth Street between K and L Strets, on the left hand side of the way; arranged the interview for Wednesday in the street, I think, on Monday. I went in the front door, it was open, occupied the same room, undressed myself, and he also; went to bed together. Mr. Key has ridden in Mr. Sickles' carriage, and has called at his house without Mr. Sickles' knowledge, and after my being told not to invite him to do so, and against Mr. Sickles' repeated request.

—Teresa Bagioli

This is a true statement, written by myself, without any inducement held out by Mr. Sickles of forgiveness or reward, and without any menace from him. This I have written with my bed-room door open, and my maid and child in the adjoining room, at half past eight o'clock in the evening. Miss Ridgeley is in the house, within call.

—Teresa Bagioli

Lafayette Square, Washington, D.C., Feb. 26, 1859

Mr. and Mrs. Pendleton dined here two weeks ago last Thursday, with a large party. Mr. Key was also here, her brother, and at my suggestion he was invited, because he lived in the same house, and Mr. Sickles wished to invite all those from whom he had received invitations; and Mr. Sickles said, "do as you choose."

—Teresa Bagioli

Written and signed in the presence of O. M. Ridgeley and Bridget Duffy. Feb. 26th.

—Octavia M. Ridgeley
—Bridget Duffy [7]

Sickles, even in his desolation, was still the lawyer. He wanted written proof and he had it, in his wife's own hand, down to the last grimy little detail. Would Teresa, even in her terror and shame, have given it to him without some promise that what poor shreds of self-respect she had left would be protected?

Would she have given it had she known it would be published in the newspapers from New York to San Francisco, not to mention London and Paris? It seems unlikely. One can only speculate on the use Daniel Sickles—a man who always had a plan—planned to make of this pathetic document. It would hardly be necessary in a divorce suit. Undoubtedly the confession was part of Teresa's punishment, but there must have been more to it than that. Possibly—as was later suggested in some quarters—Sickles wanted the paper as evidence in his favor should his rage lead him to violence. In any case, Teresa Sickles' confession of guilt was to serve no purpose other than to proclaim her shame before all the world.

That night Teresa slept on the floor in an adjacent room, symbolizing her exclusion from her husband's bed. He had already taken her wedding ring. On Sunday morning he arose and shaved—a rite this meticulous man performed every day of his life come weal or woe. He was seized with paroxysms of sobbing, and occasionally he called on God to witness his troubles. Teresa, utterly crushed, remained upstairs. Little Laura, awed by the trouble between her parents, played spiritlessly with the Sickles Italian greyhound, Dandy.

Always, in a crisis, Daniel Sickles sought his friends. He had dispatched a telegram to Emanuel Hart in New York begging him to come. He now sent notes to George Wooldridge and to Samuel Butterworth, who happened to be in Washington on a Tammany errand. The Congressman had a delicate problem to solve. Some practical policy had to be adopted toward the affair. Sickles, who unquestionably had his eye on the Presidency at some future date, was faced by a scandal that might mean sheer political ruin. He had lost his wife. Could he, by some last-ditch prestidigitation, save his career?

He was still gripped by grief, his eyes bloodshot from weeping, when Wooldridge clumped in on his crutches. It was not until later—sometime after noon—that Butterworth arrived. To spare Sickles' feelings, Wooldridge related the details of the discovery to the newcomer.

"I am a dishonored and ruined man," Sickles told Butter-worth. "I cannot look you in the face!" [8]

His old Tammany ally, who also was acquainted with Key, discussed the matter with Sickles at some length. He saw his political associate, of whom great things were expected, facing a dire emergency where a misstep would assuredly mean disaster, and he counseled moderation. It was an interview frequently interrupted by fresh outbursts of sobbing on the part of Sickles, and on one occasion he bolted from the study and fled to his bedroom, with Butterworth following and trying to soothe him. Wooldridge, badly shaken, remained in the study and began looking through the stereoscope in an effort to quiet his nerves.

"You may be mistaken in your belief that this is generally known," Butterworth told Sickles. "You must do everything you can to keep it from the public."

"It's the town talk," Sickles replied bitterly. "The whole world knows it."

Butterworth was silent for a moment. "If that is so," he said at last, "there is but one course left for you as a man of honor. You need no advice." [9]

Sickles was pacing the floor, gnawing at an unlighted cigar. He paused as he reached the window, then started.

Across Jackson Place, no more than fifty feet away, Philip Barton Key's tall figure moved alongside the iron fence surrounding the park. Key was clad smartly in broadcloth coat and top hat. He slowed his pace as he came opposite the house. Dandy, the little greyhound, ran over and fawned on him, but he paid scant attention to the dog. Eyeing the upper windows of the house, he drew a white handkerchief from his pocket, raised it and waved it several times before he passed on.

Sickles uttered a strangled imprecation. "That villain," he screamed, "is out there now, making signals!" [10]

He pounded down the stairs, with Butterworth following. There was a hurried conversation in the hall. Then Butterworth donned his coat and left the house alone—a point to be remembered. As for Sickles, he rushed upstairs again to the cabinet where he kept his guns.

Butterworth must have hurried, for he overtook Key on the Avenue just opposite the White House. The two men said good-day and stopped to pass a few commonplace words. Perhaps they chatted only a minute or two, but it was long enough for Sickles to arm himself and come catapulting out of the house. As the two men separated, Sickles was rounding the square at a fast clip on the north side. He turned into Madison Place, passed the Club House, and came within hailing distance of Key, who was walking toward the Club House from the other direction.

"Key, you scoundrel," Sickles shouted, "you have dishonored my bed—you must die!" [11]

A dozen-odd witnesses saw and heard what followed. The square was busy that Sunday, and the two combatants seemed almost surrounded by pop-eyed strollers, yet no one raised a hand to avert violence.

Sickles took deliberate aim and fired. Key dodged behind a tree, crying "Don't shoot!" as he retreated. As Sickles aimed again, Key reached into his pocket, drew out an object, and hurled it at his assailant. Ironically, it was the opera glass he had used in his observation of Teresa's window. It struck Sickles harmlessly and fell to the ground.

Sickles had a steady hand and many hours of target practice behind him. The next shot took effect. Key screamed and pitched into the gutter, still begging for mercy. Sickles fired again—some witnesses said twice again. Then he walked up to the prostrate figure, aimed the weapon point-blank at Key's head, and pulled the trigger. But the gun misfired, and suddenly several passersby came to their senses and stayed his hand. Samuel Butterworth, who had witnessed the whole proceeding, came up and took Sickles' arm.

"Is the damned scoundrel dead yet?" Sickles asked as Butterworth led him away. [12]

Key was still breathing faintly when he was carried the short distance into the Club House. But a few minutes later, when he was examined by one Dr. Coolidge, an Army surgeon who happened by, he was dead. One bullet had pierced a thigh near the groin, and another had punctured the liver.

One of the witnesses was young J. H. W. Bonitz of Wilmington, North Carolina, a White House page boy. His eyes popping, Bonitz legged it back to the executive mansion, found the President and told him the news.

Mr. Buchanan all but collapsed. "I was afraid it would happen!" he groaned. "I must see Sickles—I must see him at once!"

How many times had he cautioned Sickles against his own worst enemy, sudden impulse? Now he had surrendered to the most violent impulse of all. While Old Buck was opposed to murder on principle, he was even more aghast at the implications of this particular homicide—namely, the abrupt ruin of a career which until now had held such bright promise. After some thought, he did a queer thing.

He told young Bonitz that as an eyewitness he would be held in jail without bond unless he left Washington immediately. He presented Bonitz with a razor as a personal memento, and a sum of money for more practical purposes, and advised him to clear out of town. The young man departed for North Carolina, warmly grateful for the Presidential solicitude that enabled him to avert a sojourn behind bars. Unacquainted with the law, he did not know that he would not have been jailed, nor did it occur to him that Buchanan's motive might have been to remove a witness whose story could be damaging to Sickles.[13]

Meanwhile, Sickles and Butterworth hailed a carriage and were driven to the home nearby of Attorney General Black, where the Congressman formally surrendered himself to the silver-haired Cabinet member who had regarded him as a protégé. These formalities over, he was driven in company with a number of friends and officials back to his own home, where he picked up some personal belongings preparatory to entering the District jail. He had declined to seek his freedom on bail, declaring that he sought nothing more than a speedy trial and complete vindication.

Wooldridge was still viewing the stereoscope in the study when the retinue arrived, and he learned to his horror that the Congressman had done the worst possible thing for a man with ambitions for the Presidency. Sickles was allowed a moment with Teresa on his promise that he would not harm her. Mayor Berret was among those present, and after Sickles had poured brandy for himself and his tense-faced guests, he was taken away to the jail. Even in his gloom and despair, he did not forget the public.

"He made gestures as of salutation as he left the house," Mayor Berret later recalled. "I suggested to him that he had better not allow his attention to be called to the crowd." [14]

Late that afternoon, Sickles entered the jail, at Fourth and G Streets, a decrepit and noisome dungeon described by one contemporary commentator as "the worst in the land." [15] He recoiled as the stench of the place struck his nostrils, and possibly regretted his brave decision to waive any request for freedom on bail.

"Don't you have a better room?" he wryly asked the jailer who led him to his cell.

"No," the jailer replied, shrugging. "This is the best place you members of Congress have afforded us." [16]

CHAPTER VI

The Dignity of a Homicide

The New York *Times* correspondent hastened to telegraph a dispatch beginning: "The vulgar monotony of partisan passions and political squabbles has been terribly broken in upon today by an outburst of personal revenge which has filled the city with horror and consternation—I cannot unfortunately add, with absolute surprise." [1]

Perhaps it was not absolute surprise, but Washington had never known such numbing shock as seized it that day. On hearing the news, Senator Clement Clay rushed into his wife's room at Brown's Hotel.

"A horrible, horrible thing has happened, Virginia!" he exclaimed. "Sickles . . . has killed Key—killed him most brutally while he was unarmed!" [2]

Representative Lawrence O'Bryan Branch sat down to write his wife in North Carolina a description of the killing, ending it, "What is the world coming to?" [3]

While attendants were washing blood from the floor in the Club House parlor, the bars at Willard's and the National were abuzz. Mr. Buchanan, in the White House, must have reflected that bachelorhood had its advantages. The reverberations spread quickly. In New York, George Templeton Strong confided some tart opinions to his diary:

> The news of the day is that the Honorable Dan Sickles has attained the dignity of a homicide . . . Were he not an un-

mitigated blackguard and profligate, one could pardon any act of violence committed on such provocation. But Sickles is not the man to take the law into his own hands and constitute himself the avenger of sin.

Butterworth of this city is in a yet worse position. He had no wrong to avenge and no passion to cloud his sense of right and wrong, but he seems to have gone forth at Sickles' request and engaged Key in conversation until Sickles could get his pistols and come up and use them. He clearly deserves hanging.[4]

Indeed, the law began to eye Butterworth with dark suspicion when it became known that he had conferred with Sickles only minutes before the shooting. The suspicion deepened when Butterworth was asked at the coroner's inquest whether he expected Sickles' attack on Key, and he refused to answer.[5] This did not seem like a proper attitude for an innocent man. Newspapers came out flatly with the statement that Butterworth had willingly served as Sickles' decoy in chatting with Key and delaying him so that Sickles could blaze away at him before he reached the safety of the Club House.[6] They also published "artist's sketches" of the murder showing Butterworth leaning negligently against a fence nearby, viewing the assault much like a spectator at a sporting event.[7] Things were getting a little warm for Butterworth and he suddenly felt the need of a lawyer to protect his interests. He retained the eminent Reverdy Johnson, one of the ablest attorneys of the day.

The exact nature of Butterworth's role was of prime importance on two counts. If it could be shown that he had acted deliberately in concert with Sickles, then he was an accessory before and during the fact and was liable to grave punishment. Such action would also indicate that Sickles' mind was sufficiently cool to lay a trap for Key and make intelligent arrangements for a successful homicide—a fact which would weaken any claim that he was a victim of temporary aberration induced by passion.

Two days later, Butterworth came out with a careful statement that he was entirely unaware that Sickles planned to kill Key.

He was the most astonished man in the world, he said, when he heard the shooting and saw Key fall. His explanation of his movements ranks high on the list of fancy tales. He stated that Sickles asked that he go with him to the Club House to make inquiries as to whether Key had made signals to Teresa from there. Butterworth assented and left, "supposing Mr. Sickles was with him or following." [8]

Somehow, Butterworth got halfway across the square without realizing that Sickles was not with him. Somehow he managed to don his overcoat and overtake Key, who by this time must have been well on his way to the club.

He spoke with Key. Then, although both he and Key were going to the Club House, Butterworth left the District Attorney and took another route through the park, possibly not wishing to be too close when bullets started to fly. Flimsy as it was, Butterworth's story could not be disproved and he was not even indicted.

Meanwhile, Teresa's confession—the paper she would surely never have surrendered without assurance that it would be kept inviolate—was published on the front pages of the newspapers. It was an act of such utter ruthlessness that one hesitates to lay blame. Yet who could have released the paper for publication but Daniel Sickles? Ordinary men in his predicament would have said goodbye to public life as a matter of course and sought merely to avoid punishment for murder. But Sickles was a fighter whose abnormally combative instincts were aroused by any effort to put him in the wrong or to stay him in his career. With his whole future in the balance it is possible that he could have found justification in putting aside the unfaithful Teresa as one to whom he owed nothing—not even honorable treatment—and publishing the confession as proof to the public of the great wrong he had suffered at the hands of Key.

As for Teresa, her misery was only beginning. Emanuel Hart had now arrived from New York, and he took charge of the Sickles household and labored manfully to help his old colleague. As future witnesses, Nancy Brown, John M. Seeley and his wife, and others were brought to the house to gaze at Teresa as they would at some sideshow monstrosity and affirm that she was the woman they had seen enter the brick house with Key.[9] She had no other callers. Mrs. Clay, Mrs. Greenhow, and other former friends may have felt compassion for her, but the rigid code of the day had to be observed. It simply would not do to visit her.

"Those who have known her," sighed the New York *Times*, "will grieve sorely at the necessity of giving her up as lost." [10] *Harper's Weekly* added a resounding understatement: "it would appear . . . that neither Mr. Key nor Mrs. Sickles acted with ordinary prudence," and sang a mournful four-stanza threnody for the fallen woman whose exile was so inexorable. It began:

> Bridle your virtue,
>   Tether the tongue;
> Pity the fair vine
>   Blighted so young!
> Why not the tomb?
>   Sad, shattered life;
> Think of her doom—
>   Widow, yet wife! [11]

While Key was buried at the Presbyterian Cemetery in Baltimore, and souvenir seekers were cutting chunks out of the tree behind which he had vainly sought shelter,[12] Sickles was learning first-hand about the capital's accommodations for felons. The filthy District jail was alive with vermin, and the fastidious Congressman would awake of mornings to find himself acrawl. The sanitary facilities of his cell were indifferent, consisting of one iron bucket. This was surely no fit treatment of a friend of the President, and pressure was brought to bear resulting in his removal a few days later to the less odorous apartment of the warden himself. He was allowed the companionship of his dog. He received an endless stream of calls from friends including Wikoff, Speaker Orr, Vice President Breckinridge, Secretary Cobb, Attorney General Black, and most of the rest

of the Cabinet.[13] His father, who had known incessant worry
about his tempestuous son but had never expected him to become involved in murder, came down from New York and had
a sorrowful interview with him. President Buchanan did not
visit him but sent a note of condolence, and was later to make
his sympathy felt in a more concrete way.

To a reporter, Sickles said, "Satisfied as I was of his [Key's]
guilt, we could not live together on the same planet." [14]

The newspapers, so long surfeited with political bickering,
made the most of the new sensation with a freedom almost equal-
ing latter-day journalism. Column after column was written
about the affair day after day, and when fact was exhausted the
writers fell back on speculation. Among the items published
were:

"It is reported that Mrs. Sickles is *enceinte,* and has made an
affidavit that she became so in consequence of her intercourse
with Key." [15]

"The published statement that Mrs. Sickles is *enceinte* is untrue." [16]

"It is insinuated that Mr. Sickles knew of the too great intimacy between his wife and Mr. Key some months ago, and that
only when he found it must become generally known did he
determine to take Key's life." [17]

"It is freely rumored that a brother of the deceased announces
his purpose to kill Sickles on sight." [18]

The city throbbed with speculation as to the identity of the
mysterious R. P. G. whose note had precipitated the killing.
There were many wild stabs, among them that the first and last
initials of Rose O'Neal Greenhow fitted. In New York, the
diarist Strong, ordinarily no rumor-monger, inscribed these
startling words in his journal:

> People say the confession extorted from his wife and put on
> paper before witnesses was the dodge of a Tombs lawyer, and
> shows the homicide to have been premeditated from the
> first . . . That Sickles seduced his mother-in-law and silenced

her husband by telling him there was another Mrs. Bagioli in
Italy, and also seduced the daughter before their tardy marriage, appeared granted. The story has long been generally received . . . Some people talk of relations between the lady
and Old Buck [the President], of which Dan had full notice
and in which he acquiesced, and which put that venerable
sinner in Dan's power. Some say other things as bad. There is
hardly a kind or degree of baseness that somebody is not quite
ready to vouch for.[19]

The prisoner expressed a wish for spiritual solace, and the
Rev. E. H. Haley, a Presbyterian pastor who lived near the jail,
visited him daily in his cell and also sought to bring comfort
to Teresa. The latter he found an impossible task. Teresa was
passing her days in weeping, obsessed by her guilt and the
shame she had visited on her daughter. Rev. Haley found her in
such mental agony that he feared for her sanity and even felt
she might try to take her own life. He begged Sickles to relent
enough to give back the token she wanted most of all—her
wedding ring. Sickles said he bore her no resentment but was
"unalterably determined" never to see her again. He consented
to return the ring, but broken, as a symbol of their sundered
marriage.[20]

Not until March 10th was Teresa well enough to return to
New York with her mother and child. Before she left, Laura
visited her father and expressed curiosity at the bars on the
windows, the bare stone walls, and the general gloominess of the
place she had been told was his "new office."

"Why aren't you going to New York with us, Papa?" she asked
innocently.

"Because I have too much work to do, my child," he replied.
"I am terribly busy, but will see you a little later."

After she left, he flung himself on his cot and wept.[21]

But in his extremity, the Congressman was certainly not without friends. He received sympathetic letters by the score, some
from total strangers. James Topham Brady, John Graham, and
Thomas Francis Meagher, able lawyers all, arrived post-haste

from New York to defend their rash ally. His old crony, Captain William Wiley, came to lend moral support. He needed friends, for there were also critics. For one, his political arch-enemy, the New York *Evening Post*, was gunning for him. Said the *Post*:

> The wretched man, Daniel E. Sickles, has in his career reached the stage of assassination, and dipped his hands in human blood . . . He is a person of notorious profligacy of life . . . a certain disgrace has for years past attended the reputation of being one of his companions . . . Sickles was excluded from decent society in this city long ago; and it would be almost a miracle if, in the school to which he took his young wife, she should have preserved her innocence . . . It is certain that the man who makes no scruple to invade and destroy the domestic peace of others—he who, in his own practice, regards adultery as a joke and the matrimonial bond as no barrier against the utmost caprice of licentiousness—has little right to complain when the mischief which he carries without scruple into other families enters his own.[22]

And there were many who agreed with the Brooklyn *Times* when it said: "A man of gentlemanly feeling, of ordinary courage, would have challenged the offender and met him face to face, risking his own life for the sake of his honor." [23]

So Brady, Graham, and Meagher had certain prejudices to overcome in the interest of their client. But when Daniel Sickles went to trial on April 4th, these three had Edwin Stanton allied with them in the defense, as well as Philip Phillips, a shrewd Washington attorney, not to mention three other lawyers of the capital, the Messrs. Chilton, Magruder, and Ratcliffe. Sickles had no less than eight high-ranking lawyers representing him, four of them close personal friends.

Against this formidable crew stood one man—plump, mild-looking Robert Ould, who had been Key's assistant and was now elevated to the office of District Attorney by Buchanan to prosecute the killer of his predecessor. This contest was obviously so one-sided that friends of Key pleaded with the President to appoint some outstanding lawyer to assist Ould, but he refused.[24] Buchanan was not forgetting the prisoner's labors in his behalf in the election year of 1856 and thereafter. At the last moment, Key's friends retained John Carlisle, an able Washington attorney, to aid in the prosecution, paying him out of their own pocket, so that the prosecution was outnumbered only eight to two.[25]

The newspapers had made the private affairs of Daniel and Teresa Sickles the exciting property of every literate chambermaid and bootblack in the land. Millions of Americans were hanging on every word when Prosecutor Ould, in his opening argument to the jury, brought out the astonishing fact that Sickles had carried three different pistols on his person on the murder day, and characterized him as "a walking magazine . . . a moving battery which could place itself in any position like a piece of flying artillery on a field of battle." [26] But once he came to grips with Stanton and his colleagues, Ould was outclassed in a variety of infighting at which he proved marvelously unskilled. He was placed by inference in the unhappy position of defending adultery—something he indignantly denied, insisting that he was merely prosecuting a killer—but he did not shout as loud or as dramatically as his opponents, and his point tended to become lost in the shuffle.

It was the aim of the defense to show that Sickles was rendered temporarily insane by rage and grief at the time of the slaying— the first such defense in American jurisprudence—and also that he was justified on the score of the "unwritten law" in killing "the defiler of his marriage bed." James Brady pictured with Hibernian emotion the agony of a man who discovers that his wife has been seduced by his friend. John Graham callously referred to Teresa as a "prostitute." Mr. Ratcliffe made the point that the penalty for adultery in Maryland was one hundred pounds of tobacco, and allowed that if Sickles had taken recourse to the law instead of the pistol, he would have been granted "a chew of tobacco" as recompense for the ruin of his wife.[27]

Seated in the wooden prisoner's cage, Sickles was pale and tense as he heard every grubby little detail of his shame told and retold by ten lawyers for the benefit of newspapermen and spectators. Often he broke into audible sobs. Several times during the trial he was so overborne with emotion that recesses had to be called to allow him to recover some pretense of composure. Angry Edwin Stanton treated him with the greatest solicitude even as he heaped ridicule on the prosecution, browbeat the judge, and spoke with feeling of the sanctity of the home.

"It would have been well," Stanton said, referring to Key's signals with the handkerchief, "if Mr. Key had attached as much importance to the dignity of a banner as did his distinguished sire"—author of "The Star-Spangled Banner." [28]

So much was said about the handkerchief signals that Brady received a letter from an anonymous young lady in Vermont who strongly defended Sickles and inconsistently signed herself, "one of the order of frailty—one of the simple waiters for the wave of some masculine pocket handkerchief." [29]

Though Carlisle did his best for the prosecution, he was not in charge. Ould, who was, gave such a futile performance that it seemed that Key was on trial for seduction, not that Sickles was on trial for murder. Butterworth was not even called as a witness. An obvious counter for the prosecution would have been a searching inquiry into Sickles' own behavior. As one editorialist put it, "Unless his conduct as a husband has been scrupulously correct, he cannot properly plead the justification of a wounded marital honor." [30] Such a scrutiny would have been embarrassing to Sickles for it would have disclosed that his conduct had been anything but scrupulously correct and that Teresa had far more to forgive than he.

In truth, the prosecution did some snooping and came up with affidavits that Sickles had recently met a certain woman in Philadelphia and had joined her in trysts at Barnum's Hotel in Baltimore. There was also evidence of his infidelity elsewhere.[31] Astonishingly, this evidence was not used, and the prisoner re-

mained in the eyes of the jury a man of unblemished personal
life.

No one was really surprised when Sickles, who had not testified, was acquitted on April 26th.

Stanton was so excited that he did a jig in the courtroom,
then called hoarsely for three cheers.[32] Enthusiastic spectators
responded with a will. Captain Wiley rushed up, embraced
Sickles and kissed him on the cheek.[33] Escorted by Wikoff, Rev.
Haley, and members of his counsel, the somewhat pallid Sickles
left the court. Outside the crush was so dense they had trouble
getting through, and cheering citizens called on the vindicated
Congressman for a speech.

In his suite at the National, James Brady gave a reception
for the members of the jury, a pleasant entertainment that was
interrupted when a crowd appeared outside to serenade the
defense counsel. As for Sickles, he was congratulated on his
victory that evening by some 1500 well-wishers.[34]

President Buchanan, it was said, was delighted. One wonders
how Prosecutor Ould, who held his office at the pleasure of
the President and may have suspected that any really energetic
conduct of the prosecution might turn the President's pleasure
to anger, must have felt.

Said the Baltimore *Patriot:* "We may somewhat account for
the seeming tenderness and extreme delicacy of the prosecution on remembering the fact that the accused was a fast friend
of the highest officer of the nation." [35]

Another editorialist sounded an ominous note which should
have warned Sickles that his victory might become Pyrrhic: "It
is due to truth to say that the facts which have been brought out
during the trial—the cold-blooded manner in which Key was
killed, the overwhelming disgrace heaped upon the poor, silent,
friendless wife, and the transparent efforts which have been
made to manufacture public sentiment for the benefit of the
prisoner—have gone far toward depriving Mr. Sickles of sympathies which he enjoyed on the first intelligence of the catastrophe." [36]

Old Buck had stood by his protégé. But in New York, Sickles' home city, the farcical aspects of the trial did not sit well with the press. It was even suggested that Sickles might do well to leave New York and choose some new field for his exertions.

On the evening of his acquittal, Sickles was congratulated by the brunette Mrs. Phillips, the Alabama-born wife of one of the defense counsel, who patted him on the back and said archly, "Well, we have got you off this time. Now you be a good boy." [37]

This was asking a lot of the impulsive Congressman. On the following day, he took a walk with Wiley and Wikoff and visited the spot near the Club House where Key was killed.

"Of course I intended to kill him," he told them. "He deserved it." [38]

CHAPTER VII

End of a Career

When Teresa arrived in New York with her daughter from the capital, she took refuge in the home of her parents near Central Park. She had a refuge and little else. Old friends cut her on the street. Small boys hurled obscenities at her. Even butchers and grocers snubbed her. According to the mores of the day, it was sinful to have any traffic with this woman on whom the scarlet letter had been branded by every newspaper in the land. Only Emanuel Hart stood by her with a warmth of sympathy and understanding which won her everlasting gratitude.

As for Sickles, he must have been relieved that by the time he was acquitted Congress was finished. He closed the Stockton Mansion and informed the owner he would not need it again, ever. He returned to New York and his Bloomingdale place, badly in need of a rest after an ordeal that had sapped even his almost limitless stamina. He well realized that he was under a cloud. This was no novelty to him, and doubtless he felt that a little time and some judicious fence-mending would dissipate the overcast and place him in the warm sunlight of political favor once more. He had already been elected for the next term of Congress, so he had no stumping worries for more than a year. Despite published rumors that he would sail to Europe for a holiday, he remained at Bloomingdale in comparative quiet.

There was another published report, however, which no one in his right mind would have questioned, namely: "There is no shadow of possibility that Mr. Sickles will ever be reunited with his wife." [1]

To his friends, this was so obvious that it hardly needed expression. Naturally he would never return to the wife who had shamed him. If he ever were so foolish, that way lay ruin.

But as July came on, there were odd portents. Sickles, it was said, had been seen in the company of Teresa. On one occasion he had even taken her on a brief excursion on his boat on the Hudson. His friends, who thought they knew him so well, could not look into the heart of this extraordinary man and realize that he was not quite all iron and ambition—that in him were wells of tenderness and affection quite as deep as his capacities for egotism and wilfulness. They could not know that Daniel Sickles, while in his prison cell, had had time to reflect on his troubles and come to the conclusion that he was not blameless.

However negligent he had been as a husband, Teresa seemed to hold a special place in his heart which no mistress could touch. Sickles had been torn by a gamut of emotion ranging from homicidal frenzy to deepest shame and remorse—a shock that frequently reduced him to helpless weeping and made him seek comfort in religion. His bitterness may not have melted, but it softened. From his cell he had started a correspondence with his wife. A month after the killing, while he still awaited trial, she wrote him:

> Good morning, dear, dear Dan—Mr. Fields has just left. He brought me a kind, good letter from you. Thank you many times for all your kind expressions and God bless you for the mercy and prayers you offer up for me. Do not ask if I never think over the events of the past month. Yesterday, at each hour by the clock, I thought, "One month ago this day, at this hour, such and such things were going on in our once happy home." That fearful Saturday night! . . . If I could have foreseen the scenes of the following day I would have braved all dangers, all things, to have prevented them. Oh that Manny Hart could have been with us! . . .

I have been out of the house but three times since I came home; and you know how much exercise I have been in the habit of taking . . . Last night I walked with Manny Hart; but my body trembled, my legs seemed to give way under me and my heart beat violently.

The verses you send me are very beautiful. I will keep them always, and I thank you sincerely for them . . . Perhaps I spoke hastily of George Wooldridge. I promise you not to mention his name, Wiley's or Butterworth's again in any of my letters unless necessary. One thing I will assure you of, and that is that I did *not* tell Mr. Butterworth to mind his own business or something to that effect . . . Mr. Butterworth, I think, only needed encouragement from me to flirt. I may be mistaken but I doubt it. But let all suppositions be forgotten and unthought of—the reality is bad enough without suspecting or supposing things . . .

No, dear Dan, I cannot say you ever denied me what was necessary, and you gave me many things I did not deserve— everyone knows this . . . I shall commence a pair of slippers for you in a few days, my dear Dan. I will not stop working on them until they are finished. Will you wear them for me? Or would you dislike to wear again anything that I have made? . . .

Can I say or do anything for you that you have not spoken of—if so, write me. Do not be angry at anything I have written you. I swear that I have not written a word to cause you pain . . . Write when you can, and think and feel as leniently as possible of me and my unhappy position. God bless you for the two kisses you send me—and with God's help and my own determination to be good, true and faithful to you and myself hereafter, those kisses shall never leave my lips while I am called *wife* and you *husband.* I swear it by Laura . . . God bless you, pray for me, and believe in the sincerity and gratitude of—

—Teresa [2]

A man who sends prayers, kisses, and a poem is not unyielding. The casual attitude of Sickles toward his wife concealed a powerful inner attachment of whose strength perhaps even he was unaware until disaster came. And Teresa was an essentially religious woman: she had sinned, and she must atone. Key she must blot out of her memory. With an intensity born of desperation she sought to rebuild her crumbled world. During the first days of the trial she sent her husband flowers and followed them with this letter:

> I cannot tell you, dear, dear Dan, how *much* pleasure your letter written yesterday gave me. I am so glad the flowers were acceptable. You are not wrong in supposing that I was pained at your silence, and equally pained at receiving the letter you sent me. You know, Dan, I *never* affect to love or dislike a person—and I am, in a certain way, as frank as any breathing creature. You say if I can hate those whom you love and who love you then it is vain for you to appeal to me again on such a subject. Dear Dan, it would be as impossible for me to love those who hate me and have injured me, have called me every vile name, as I believe it would be to have you love me again or ever wipe out the past. I enclose a letter written last night. I send it to show you how I felt about all you said. *It tells the fearful story of my heart . . .*
>
> You say that any object you have loved remains dear to you. Do I now stand upon a footing with the other women I know you have loved? I have long felt like asking you what your love affairs have been—love of the heart, or love of their superior qualities such as you have often informed me I did not possess, or attraction of face and form, or an infatuation? If during the first years we were married my good conduct did not keep you true to me, can I suppose for a moment the last year has? *Ask your own heart who sinned first, and then tell me, if you will.*[3]

Teresa had always been aware of the incongruous and often humiliating position imposed on her by the fact of being Daniel Sickles' wife. Now she had suffered greatly because of her own wickedness, and for once she was willing to point out that she had not been the first to err. She grasped and clung to a wild hope that atonement could work a miracle and that a rebuilding of their marriage was not impossible. What else could she hope for, for her and her daughter? And Sickles, who had once had a hungry eye on the White House—who had broken Teresa's wedding ring to signify the end of their marriage— felt remorse and pity.

In mid-July, three months after the trial, his friends were staggered when he told them that he and Teresa had been reunited. Men like Brady and John Graham remonstrated with him, pointing out that a reunion would be sheer political sui- cide, particularly after the defense's pitiless portrayal of Teresa as a wanton had won his acquittal. Renounce her and he had some chance of picking up the remnants of his career. Rejoin her and he was finished. But Sickles' mind was set.

The news soon leaked out to the press, which had already seized on the affairs of Teresa, as it had long before of Sickles, as provocative items which could be speculated about with pleasant freedom from the danger of libel. A storm of protest and denunciation broke out in large print.

Said the New York *Dispatch:* "His warmest personal and political friends bitterly denounce his course." [4]

The *Sunday Courier:* "His political aspirations, his career in life, once so full of encouraging brightness, and his business prospects, have all been blasted by this act." [5]

The New York *Sun* gave new credence to one of the wildest of the rumors—that Teresa had actually conspired with Sickles in the murder of Key: "It will interest, though it will scarcely surprise our readers to learn, that Daniel E. Sickles and his wife have harmonized their little difficulty—if a difficulty ever existed between them—and are again enjoying each other's refined and elevating society." [6]

But it remained for the *Sunday Mercury* to give full rein to malice with the publication of "An Epithalamium in Honor of the Reunion of a Distinguished Couple, Who had been Parted for a Brief Period by Circumstances over which Neither of Them had any Control." This bit of poesy began:

Hail, matchless pair! United once again
In newborn bliss forget your bygone pain.
Hail! Turtle doves, returning to a nest
Defiled yet dear—determined to be blest!
What though the world may say, "With hands all red,
Yon bridegroom steals to a dishonored bed!"
And friends, estranged, exclaim on every side:
"Behold! Adultery couched with homicide!" [7]

There was more in the same vein. Only Horace Greeley, the queer but kindly philosopher of the *Tribune,* flew in the face of convention by commending Sickles for his forgiveness. James Gordon Bennett of the *Herald* surprisingly came out with a measured and not unfriendly editorial appraisal in which he suggested that the Congressman had rejoined his wife "on the advice of his attorneys." [8]

This was an absurdity Sickles could not allow to stand uncorrected, priding himself as he did on making his own decisions. He immediately wrote a letter to the *Herald* which was published next day. In it he paid his respects to that newspaper and dealt with his more venomous critics with restraint and dignity:

Through the course of sad events, which during the last few months have brought so much affliction upon my family, I have been silent. No amount of misrepresentation affecting myself only could induce me now to open my lips; nor could I deem it worth while under any circumstances to notice what has been said or can be said in journals never regarded as the sources or the exponents of public opinion, for in these it is too often obvious that only unworthy motives prompt the most vindictive assaults upon the private life of citizens holding public stations . . .

Referring to the forgiveness which my sense of duty and my feelings impelled me to extend to an erring and repentant wife, you observe, in the course of your temperate and dignified article, that, "It is said, however, that the last phase of the

affair was brought about through the advice of his lawyers."
This is entirely erroneous . . . My reconciliation with my wife
was my own act, done without consultation with any relative,
connection, friend or adviser. Whatever blame, if any belongs
to the step, should fall alone upon me. I am prepared to defend
what I have done before the only tribunal I recognize as having
the slightest claim to jurisdiction over the subject—my own
conscience and the bar of Heaven. I am not aware of any statute
or code of morals which makes it infamous to forgive a woman;
nor is it usual to make our domestic life a subject of consultation with friends, no matter how near and dear to us. And I
cannot allow even all the world combined to dictate to me the
repudiation of my wife, when I think it right to forgive her and
restore her to my confidence and protection.

If I ever failed to comprehend the utterly desolate position of
an offending though penitent woman—the hopeless future, with
its dark possibilities of danger, to which she is doomed when
proscribed as an outcast—I can now see plainly enough in the
almost universal howl of denunciation with which she is followed to my threshold, the misery and perils from which I have
rescued the mother of my child . . .

There are many who think that an act of duty, proceeding
solely from affections which can only be comprehended in the
heart of a husband and father, is to be fatal to my professional,
political and social standing. If this be so, then so be it . . . so
long as I do nothing worse than to reunite my family under the
roof where they may find shelter from contumely and persecu-
tion, I do not fear the noisy but fleeting voice of popular
clamor . . . if I know the human heart—and sometimes I think
that in a career of mingled sunshine and storm I have sounded
nearly all its depths—then I may reassure those who look with
reluctant forebodings upon my fortune to be of good cheer,
for I will not cease to vindicate a just claim to the respect of my
fellows; while to those motley groups, here and there, who look
upon my misfortune only as weapons to be employed for my
destruction, to those I say, once for all, if a man make a good
use of his enemies, they will be as serviceable to him as his
friends.

In conclusion, let me ask only one favor of those who, from whatever motive, may deem it necessary or agreeable to comment in public or private on this sad history; and that is, to aim all their arrows at my breast, and for the sake of my innocent child, to spare her yet youthful mother, while she seeks in sorrow and contrition the mercy and the pardon of Him to whom, sooner or later, we must all appeal.

Very respectfully, your most obedient servant,

—Daniel E. Sickles [9]

It was a remarkable letter, courageous, persuasive, and moving. But the code of the day was inflexible. The confession forced from Teresa and published abroad, the ruthless courtroom mutilation of her name, the utterly false rumors that she was a trull who welcomed all comers, the known transgressions of Sickles—all these outraged the sensibilities of 1859. Custom demanded that the woman taken in adultery be exiled from society, and for Sickles to forgive her after saving his own neck by proclaiming her shame was considered the last step in degradation. Many friends who had stoutly stood by him during the trial now abandoned him in disgust.

In New York the prevailing question was, "Why did he do it?" Few could credit him with sincerity and generosity in his motives. It was bruited about that Sickles had rejoined his wife only after she had blackmailed him with the threat of publicizing certain damaging letters of his which she held. It was also rumored that he had forged notes in the name of his father-in-law, Antonio Bagioli, and had been reconciled with Teresa rather than to face prosecution. [10] Even the staid Strong wrote in his diary, "Probably the lovely Teresa had a hold on him and knew of matters he did not desire to be revealed . . . He must have been in her power somehow, or he would not have taken this step and sacrificed all his hopes of political advancement and all his political friends and allies . . . He can scarcely shew himself at Washington again . . ." [11]

The wiseacres were wrong. But Sickles' reputation was now

so badly smeared that his critics saw villainy in an act of unself-
ishness.

Driven by ambition, devoted to his friends, sensitive to criticism, Sickles, in his reunion with Teresa, achieved nobility.
The cost was incalculable. For him to stroll into Delmonico's,
where once everyone had greeted him with welcoming halloos,
and find familiar backs turned to him, must have been bitter.
To contemplate political oblivion was even worse.[12]

Unhappily, the sacrifice could not accomplish the impossible.
The reconciliation was blighted from the start by the tall, handsome ghost of Barton Key. The past could not be recaptured,
but even so Teresa at least had the continued "confidence and
protection" of her husband.

When Sickles returned to Washington that fall—astonishing
the prophets who said he would not dare go—he necessarily
went alone. And when he got there he was a pariah. He was
walking through the motions of the last scene before the curtain
dropped.

His career, everybody agreed, was finished.

CHAPTER VIII

Father to the Man

When Daniel Edgar Sickles was born in New York City on October 20, 1819, Monroe was in the White House and New York was a city of less than 150,000 people who did not yet know the blessing of gas lights.

His father, George Garrett Sickles, was a shrewd patent lawyer, politician, and opportunist who traced his lineage back six generations to the time when the first Sickles—then named Van Sicklen—left Holland for New Amsterdam.[1] He was a gambler who plunged in various enterprises, sometimes with success and sometimes failure, so that the family fortunes had a way of fluctuating from near-opulence to something approaching poverty. He was a brilliant, erratic man with a strong streak of poetry in him. The mother, Susan Marsh Sickles, was a devout Episcopalian and a woman whose letters reveal unusual gentleness and warmth of spirit.

Their son was a handsome, blue-eyed, chestnut-haired boy with a headstrong impulse for self-expression, "remarkable for a determined resistance to corporal punishment."[2] He was a problem from the start.

Since there is little recorded of him during these early years but examples of his self-will and determination, these qualities must have been paramount. He ran away from home several times. His parents were alternately overjoyed by his quick wit and appalled by his wilfulness. Undoubtedly they were baffled by this only child whose hot-headed insubordination was tem-

pered by moments of winning amiability and what seemed the
promise of genius, and felt that if they could control his obsti-
nacy he might make a great mark in the world. But how to control it? When he was about fifteen they tried putting the control-
ling in other hands. They sent him to an academy at Glens Falls,
New York, a place devoted to turning callow boys into finished
young gentlemen. This experience misfired after a few months
when a master reprimanded Daniel and the boy flared back at
him and quit school in a rage.

One of his favorite haunts in Glens Falls had been the work-
room of the *Messenger,* the local weekly newspaper, for journalism had begun to fascinate him. From Stephen Adams, the proprietor, he got a job as printer's devil and general helper, and
here he learned typesetting with astonishing ease and was also
allowed to compose minor news items. It was his first intimate
contact with an institution which was to absorb him, praise him,
and damn him for much of his life, and the experience sharp-
ened his native facility with words.

His abandonment of school was a further problem to his per-
plexed parents, who logically feared that without any authority
over him he might become involved in all manner of devilment.
They entreated him to return, but it was some eighteen months
before he quit the composing stick in Glens Falls and went
back home. This was during one of the low periods of George
Sickles' endeavors, when investments had gone mouldy, and he
was unable to offer his son much financial help. Daniel went to
work as typesetter for a printer named Turney in Fulton Street.
He was a dextrous and accurate fellow with type, but he was
also a young man with spring-steel energy and a hunger to sam-
ple life in all its forms. He began traveling with a group of
rowdies and experimenting with the fleshpots of the big city, so
that it was not long before his father, who had so earnestly desired his return to New York, was instead pondering how to get
him safely away.

It happened that around this time some of George Sickles' un-
promising investments, many of them in real estate, took a sharp

upturn so that in a remarkably short time he was lifted from a mere competence to comparative wealth. He rode the tide, opened a fine office at 74 Nassau Street, and was shrewd enough or lucky enough in his enterprises to see his fortunes soar. He bought a handsome country place near Livingston, New Jersey, and after much coaxing he persuaded Daniel to quit his printer's job and join his parents there. The sins of New York were comfortingly distant, and the plan was for the young man to make a grass-roots study of scientific agriculture and eventually become a country gentleman.

Daniel, surprisingly, stuck it out for a year; then, after a bitter quarrel with his father, left home with a few shillings and walked to Princeton, where he got work in a newspaper office. His plan now was to continue his education, and he sought to enter the college there—an impossibility because of his lack of funds. Discouraged, he moved on to Philadelphia, where he worked for a time on *Burton's Magazine*. Here he was recognized by a family acquaintance, and thus George Sickles caught up with his son.

The father now realized that he was confronted by a will fully as strong as his own. He sensibly wrote his son that all would be forgiven and his wishes for an education would be granted if he would return home. Daniel, a born Knickerbocker, cheerfully agreed. In 1838 he was installed in the fantastic household of some family friends, the Da Pontes on Spring Street in New York, to be prepared for college.

Patriarch of this learned and Bohemian clan was old Lorenzo Da Ponte, then eighty-nine, a Venetian-born Jew of brilliant intellect who had managed to encompass in his long career the diverse occupations of teacher, poet, Catholic priest, librettist for Mozart, rake, bookseller, grocer, and professor of Italian at Columbia College. In Europe his affairs with women had been almost as notorious as those of his good friend Giovanni Casanova.[3] Da Ponte had three sons, the youngest being Lorenzo L. Da Ponte, who followed in his father's intellectual footsteps and was professor of belles-lettres at New York University. Although

scholarly pursuits were poorly paid, and the old man often had
to stave off creditors, he was never one to take the practical view.
He had added to his expenses by adopting a girl whose background is obscure but who was born Maria Cooke and came
from Croton Falls in Westchester. A lovely young woman, Maria
had married Antonio Bagioli, a musician of some distinction
who had come from Italy as maestro of the visiting Montressor
Opera Company and had decided to stay.

The Bagiolis, at that time a part of this bookish and breezy
household, had a black-haired, year-old baby girl named Teresa.

Young Professor Lorenzo Da Ponte was charged with the duty
of filling in the gaps in Daniel's secondary education, and the
pair developed a close affection. In effect, young Sickles became
a member of the household for about two years, which in itself
must have been a liberal education. Bourgeois concepts got
short shrift there. Old Da Ponte could discourse about art, literature, and music—and women—in a dozen languages. The
place, flowing as it did with wine, *gemütlichkeit* and learning,
was a noisy, orderless island of intellectual freedom where Des-
cartes or Goethe might be discussed with profundity while the
infant was suckled in a corner and spaghetti boiled over in the
kitchen.

Thus Sickles met his future wife about the time that she was
learning to talk. The younger Da Ponte found him a student of
remarkably quick perception, and within a year he entered New
York University, still under the Da Ponte wing and still frequenting the Da Ponte domicile, which must have fascinated
him. In this multilingual household where it was necessary for
the family to decide what language they would use at any given
time, Sickles picked up an acquaintance with French, Spanish,
and Italian which was to be useful later on. It is doubtful that
he studied hard, but Professor Da Ponte regarded him as a
promising student and boon companion, and the two were inseparable.

At the age of ninety, old Lorenzo Da Ponte felt death creeping
on him, and characteristically he composed an ode to his own

demise, *Parti de la Vita* (Farewell to Life), on the very day before he died. When young Lorenzo Da Ponte was stricken with pneumonia six months later and died within a few days, Sickles was crazed with sorrow. At the funeral he "raved and tore up and down the graveyard shrieking"; the mourners were forced to carry him away bodily.[4] Daniel Sickles, a young man who always wanted his own way, had encountered in death a power he could not control.

He had no further interest in college. He left school, taking the step with the impulsive haste that had already become characteristic. In 1840 he entered the law office of the noted Benjamin F. Butler, Attorney General under Van Buren, and mastered the law with the ease with which he acomplished anything he undertook. In 1843 he was admitted to the bar. In one of his early cases—a patent suit heard in Washington by a board of commissioners headed by the venerated Daniel Webster—he won Webster's praise for his astute presentation.

During this time he had already made his entry into Democratic politics, which in New York City meant Tammany. This came as second nature to him, for George Sickles had been a stalwart of the Wigwam and the boy had been brought up in an atmosphere of political flim-flam and the extravagant rituals affected by the tribe. Already the most dapper young blade in the legal fraternity, he was known as a spendthrift and night-prowler after women. And along the way he was rushing headlong into scandalous adventures perhaps a trifle too ominous to be dismissed as youthful scrapes.

In 1837, Sickles was indicted along with one Melvin S. Whitney for obtaining money under false pretenses. A few years later the Court of General Sessions ordered him to show cause why he should not be prosecuted for appropriating funds belonging to a man named Moore.[5] It was also said that on another occasion he projected the publication of a political paper, sold some $1000 or more in subscriptions, then put the money in his pocket and "went off to spend it at a fashionable watering place." [6] No prosecution is recorded in any of these cases. One

must draw the conclusion that Sickles was either unjustly accused, that he or his father made good the shortages, or that
political pressure was brought to bear in his favor.

He was still a welcome guest at the household of the Da
Pontes, and also at the Bagiolis, where he watched Teresa grow
to schoolgirl age. Signor Bagioli had now made his mark as a
musician and teacher and was in comfortable circumstances. It
was rumored, of course, that Sickles seduced the still lovely Mrs.
Bagioli and silenced her husband with threats to expose his
earlier indiscretions. So many rumors hovered about the young
lawyer—some of them inspired by hatred or political enmity
and demonstrably untrue—that it is impossible to pin them all
down. There is no doubt, as one observer put it, that "he had
drunk to the dregs the cup of dissipation." [7] Whether his wild-
ness reached outright criminality may be questioned, but it is
clear that the smallish, dashingly handsome young man was at
times dangerously close to its edges.

He plunged enthusiastically into politics, which in Tammany
of that era was itself a form of dissipation, and seldom missed a
meeting at the Wigwam at Frankfort and Nassau Streets. At this
edifice of connivance and thuggery, with its downstairs bar dispensing heady spirits, any meeting might dissolve in a free-for-
all featuring brass knuckles and knives. A man who could rise
before this assemblage of toughs and deliver forthright opinions
might be somewhat wanting in principles but he was certainly
no weakling.

Here Sickles, with his talent for making friendships, allied
himself with Brady, Wiley, John Graham, and others. Tammany
at this time was torn by one of the most violent of its internal
dissensions, the struggle between the Hunker faction, which
largely opposed anti-slavery agitation, and the abolitionist Barn-
burners. Sickles and his friends were prominent Hunkers, and
at one of the less comradely meetings he was picked up bodily
and flung down a stairwell. He managed to seize a railing in his
descent and fell stunned and bleeding but not seriously injured. [8]
After that, he made it a point to become adept with the pistol. [9]

He was armed both with a pistol and bowie knife at a later meeting when infuriated enemies advanced on him, and with these weapons he managed to cover his retreat to a window, from which he jumped to safety on Frankfort Street.[10]

His audacious partisanship brought him enemies aplenty, but it also brought him powerful Tammany friends, among them the unscrupulous Fernando Wood and the plug-ugly Captain Isaiah Rynders. He became the youngest member of the party's General Committee. In 1847 he made his first venture into public life when he was elected to the state assembly—this despite the fact that he had just been prosecuted for the alleged theft of a mortgage from one William Kemble. Kemble claimed that Sickles had borrowed $800 from him and had given a mortgage as security. He had returned the mortgage to Sickles for recording, Kemble complained, and after that Sickles refused to give him either the $800 or the mortgage. There was a directed verdict of acquittal, since the mortgage was not made out directly to Kemble.[11]

Money, indeed, was a constant need to Sickles, for it poured through his fingers. His father had long since refused to finance his tastes for tailored clothing, boned turkey on ice, gambling at the races, vintage champagne, and agreeable women, and as a result he was often hard pressed. One of his expenses was a vivacious brunette prostitute named Fanny White whom he had met in a Mercer Street bordello.[12] Fanny's charms were for sale, but Sickles wanted exclusive enjoyment of them. This came high, particularly since she had a liking for gems, furs, and other luxuries which he could not bring himself to deny her. There were also unverified rumors that his relationship with Fanny was a two-way affair and that he accepted money from her earnings to help him in his election campaign[13]—a report that caused him to be branded by an enemy newspaper with an ugly word: pimp.

Ugly words or no, Assemblyman Sickles took Fanny up to Albany with him and scandalized even those who had come to expect the unusual from him by introducing her at the table of the hotel where he boarded and even escorting her into the Assembly with him. This was too much for that august body. They passed a vote of censure on him.[14] Typically, that same winter he wrote his father from Albany requesting the loan of fifty dollars so that he could buy an overcoat.[15]

Though his outrageous conduct shocked old-timers in the state capital, they had to admit that politically the cheeky New Yorker was razor-sharp. Governor William Marcy grudgingly said that as a debater Sickles excelled any man of his years, and the astute Henry Raymond declared that as a parliamentary leader he was unsurpassed.[16]

But the Assembly and Fanny took only a portion of his time, for Sickles had already seen in Tammany how a judicious mixture of initiative, personality, and political acumen could push a man speedily to high station. He now had his eye on the national scene. In 1848 he was a delegate to the Democratic Convention in Baltimore, where he helped nominate his friend, Franklin Pierce, for the Presidency.

Away or at home he was one of the most gregarious of men. He loved nothing better than to drink and talk with friends. He was a "regular" at Delmonico's famous establishment and also a member of a coterie which met at the magnificent Astor House and included Greeley, Brady, Hart, Edwin Forrest, John Van Buren, and Henry G. Stebbins.[17] It was a group in which poetry was argued as well as politics or business, and Sickles, a confirmed theatergoer, felt quite competent to discuss Lear or Othello with the great tragedian Forrest. These men liked him for his personal magnetism, his quick intelligence and ready wit, his flashes of generosity, and his remarkable ability as a raconteur.

Money to him was something to spend and enjoy, something that could easily be replaced somehow. When he was caught short he borrowed from friends sums little and big, and sometimes had difficulty in repaying them. Among his letters are dunning notes, generally friendly: "If you can let me have that $15," [18] or "I will renew your note that falls due 5 August but on one condition, that it is drawn to my order . . ." [19]

Yet when he happened to be in pocket he was equally amiable in making loans to hard-pressed cronies. There was a warm depth of sentiment and loyalty in his character that helps to explain his popularity.

He was rising speedily in the legal world, being retained in at least one case by the foxy James Gordon Bennett. He was regarded by one shrewd observer as "a lawyer by intuition—careful in reaching his conclusions, but quick and bold in pushing them." [20] Between Sickles and his parents there was genuine filial devotion, and they were often torn between their love for their son and their worries over his excesses. His letters show that he treated them with respect and tenderness, often going out of his way to make some little representation of affection.

But it was not in Daniel Sickles to keep out of trouble. In 1852, his Tammany friend Robert J. Dillon was running for office against one Nelson Waterbury. Waterbury's adherents prepared a circular addressed to the voters urging his election, and took them to the Broadway post office for delivery. Sickles, always eager to help a friend, determined to spike this appeal to the populace. He led several carriage-loads of rowdy cronies to the post office, charged into the place, tore open mail bags, and carried away the Waterbury literature. For this he narrowly missed prosecution for robbing the mails, but this case, like most of the others, never came to trial. [21]

To this same Robert Dillon, Sickles later addressed a letter which reveals the very essence of his reckless, proud nature. Dillon had obviously protested to him about some unwise "idiosyncrasy," and Sickles replied:

> I cannot play the courtier to the multitude much less to individuals. I have never done it and never will. You waste your own time and pain me by requesting it.
>
> I know all the consequences of yielding to this idiosyncrasy and have many a long year since resolved to enjoy it even at the price which must inevitably be paid.
>
> I have said to you before that I do not deem it a wise course,

nor recommend it to any friend; but I have adopted it; it is
mine, and I will follow it come what may.

Video meliora prologue, deleriora sequa.

—D. E. Sickles [22]

Meanwhile, George Sickles and Signor Bagioli were growing
concerned about Daniel and Teresa. Sickles somehow found
time to return to the Bagiolis and to watch Teresa grow into
something lovely even though it could not quite yet be called
young womanhood. They often went riding together, with
Teresa gaily setting the conversation in Italian or French as the
whim dictated, and Sickles following the lead with considerable
facility. Now they were showing all the signs of infatuation.

Both fathers opposed the match, giving as their reason
Teresa's tender age. But it seems more likely that Bagioli, at
least, had reservations about the acceptability of a son-in-law
who brazenly sported in town with a harlot and even took her to
Albany with him.

Both fathers urged the couple to delay, but Sickles was never
one to wait for something he wanted. Teresa quitted her school-
ing at the Manhattanville Convent of the Sacred Heart, and the
pair were married by Mayor Kingsland on September 27th,
1852. Teresa was just sixteen. Sickles was a month short of
thirty-three. Six months later, at the urging of the devoutly
Catholic Teresa, the marriage was given religious sanction by
Archbishop John Hughes.[23]

Possibly the gossips were right in saying that Sickles seduced
the girl. In any case he married her, and it unquestionably was
a love match even though his interpretation of marriage did not
bind him to sexual fidelity.

He liked to set his own rules. He was born with violent, un-
disciplined impulses no one had been able to curb. He was
trained in the saloon-cutthroat arena of hoodlum Tammany
politics where many a criminal gained high office. With this
equipment and background, it was hardly to be expected that
he would be a model of rectitude.

But if Daniel Sickles had a bit of the scoundrel in him, he combined it with magnificent gifts. This paradox was to keep him in perpetual violence and turmoil, shuttling between fame and disgrace, but always in the center of the stage because that was at all costs exactly where he wanted to be.

CHAPTER IX

The Colonel at Court

In January of 1853 Sickles' loyal labors in the Tammany fold were rewarded with a highly prized political plum. He was made corporation counsel of New York City, a post that paid a flattering salary with extra emoluments and also left room for profitable legal work on the side. He was well pleased with the job, which was a fitting acknowledgement of his status as "the prominent young leader of the Democracy in the Empire State," [1] and he doubtless would have held it for a year or more had not fate taken a hand.

In May, President Pierce cast about for a suitable minister to England and hit on James Buchanan for the post. Buchanan, himself a former Secretary of State and a veteran of decades of political wars, was agreeable provided that the Senate would confirm him in advance. He sought out his good friend, the newspaperman-politician John Forney, and asked him if he knew of someone who might serve as a competent secretary of legation—a question Forney answered in the negative at the moment but filed away in his mind.

Shortly thereafter, Forney made a trip to New York and met Sickles at a political gathering. He had previously encountered the New Yorker casually at the Baltimore convention, and he was now impressed anew with his ability and personal charm. Half in jest, Forney mentioned Buchanan's search for a secretary in London and asked Sickles if he would be interested in the job.

"How much does it pay?" Sickles inquired.

"Twenty-five hundred a year," the Pennsylvanian replied.

Sickles smiled. "Why, bless you, my dear fellow, that would hardly pay for my wine and cigars. My annual income is fifteen times more than that. I could not think of such a sacrifice." [2]

But later that day he gave the matter more serious thought. A shrewd political analyst, he must have reviewed the possible consequences of accepting such a position. It would remove him temporarily from the Tammany councils. On the other hand, it would broaden his perspective, instruct him in the intricacies of statecraft, and might be a pleasant lark. Most important, it would place him at the side of James Buchanan, one of the most powerful Democrats who had narrowly missed the Presidential nomination in 1852 and might very possibly make it in 1856. Sickles was far too aware of the value of political alliances to shrug off this opportunity to gain the friendship of a potential President. Next day he boarded a train for Lancaster and called on Buchanan at his country estate.

Buchanan, as Forney put it, had previously known Sickles only as a "brilliant lawyer, politician, and man of the world, who had a host of friends and not a few enemies, like all men of force and originality." [3] He was delighted by the electric personality of the young New Yorker. He sent Sickles' name to President Pierce as his choice for secretary.

Pierce applauded the selection, but it happened that his Secretary of State was William Learned Marcy, the New York Democrat who had been governor when Sickles was in the Assembly. Marcy had had intra-party differences with Sickles, and furthermore he was aghast at the idea of confiding an important post in the delicate mission to a man who had flaunted his liaison with a prostitute in the very halls of the statehouse.

Marcy said no. He flatly refused to sign Sickles' commission.

But President Pierce liked Sickles, and there was heavy pressure from Tammany in favor the appointment. Marcy was overruled; he still balked at signing the commission, so Assistant Secretary of State Dudley Mann signed it. [4] Sickles hastened to

Washington, where Marcy pointedly ignored him but the President shook his hand, gave him an encouraging talk, and told him of the necessity of America being represented by discerning men in the important London post.[5]

Sickles did a great deal of traveling between New York and Washington that spring, for he was not only pushing his own interests but was also using his influence to obtain a diplomatic post for his friend, the New York financier August Belmont. This effort was likewise crowned with success when Belmont was appointed chargé at The Hague.[6] Sickles had an astonishing way of getting what he wanted, and working at it to the exclusion of other matters. His father wrote to him in Washington at this time expressing affection but also pointing out that two of his notes were due, one for $475 and the other for $250. "Now it is hardly fair," George Sickles complained a little peevishly, "that you should entirely neglect your personal affairs to help others, and to ask me to fill the breach . . ."[7]

Undoubtedly Teresa was delighted over her husband's new post, but she was pregnant and was saddened because Sickles thought it best for her to join him later. Her childlike devotion is evident in a note she addressed to "My own dear darling Dan" in which she mentioned suffering some of the upsets incidental to pregnancy and went on:

> I hate the idea of your going away without me, and know that I could not leave [sic] you were it in my power. You know what is best, and I shall act as you wish me to, however much I may dislike it. God only knows how I can get along without you . . . Come home to dinner, come home as early as you can. God bless you my own dear darling *pet*—may God bless you forever and ever is my prayer.
>
> Your truly devoted and most dearly attached wife and baby.
>   —Teresa [8]

So when Sickles sailed in September, Teresa was not with him. However, according to an opposition newspaper which went into some detail about the matter, he did not go alone. He took with him Fanny White, whose liaison with him had now persisted intermittently for more than five years.[9]

In London, Buchanan was highly pleased with his secretary. Sickles had served a brief term in the New York State Militia, attaining the rank of major, and he now seems to have promoted himself one grade to a colonelcy, a title calculated to impress the British. To Harriet Lane, who had remained temporarily at the Buchanan Pennsylvania estate, the minister wrote:

"Col. Sickles is a very agreeable as well as an able man. He possesses much energy of character, & will make a favorable impression here. I think it will not be long before his lady follows him . . . I understand she is only a child, and so is Col. Sickles. Their respective parents are quite rich, but I do not think the Col. has a large income." [10]

In another letter dated October 14th, Buchanan informed his niece, "Mrs. Sickles is, I believe, very anxious to come to England; & it is probable she may do so in the spring." [11]

Naturally Teresa was anxious to join her husband and show him their new daughter, but one gets the impression that Sickles was in no hurry for the reunion. His geniality and zest had completely won over the staid and distant Pennsylvanian, and Buchanan was already being quietly approached by forward-looking Democrats for the 1856 Presidential campaign. Sickles himself was one of these forward-looking Democrats. The ease and speed with which he had penetrated the defensive armor of Buchanan is proof of his magnetism. The two were such boon companions that they lodged together. Buchanan kept heaping praise on his secretary. "I am warmly and strongly attached to him," he wrote Forney. "He is a man of fine talents, of excellent manners & of a brave and loyal temper. My personal relations with him have been everything I could desire." [12] The only complaint the minister had to make about his young aide was that "he writes a very bad hand, and spends a great deal of money." [13]

To be the intimate of the man who might well be the next President must have repaid Sickles for his financial sacrifice and also for the absence of his wife.

According to an article published years later in the antagonistic New York *World,* Sickles kept Fanny White in London
with him long enough to make use of her in a daringly impudent fashion to pay off an old score. He was angry at James
Gordon Bennett because the crabbed Scot in his *Herald* had
denounced his appointment to the London post and called him
unfit. At one of Queen Victoria's drawing-room receptions, said
the *World,* Colonel Sickles appeared with Fanny White on his
arm, and she was presented to Her unsuspecting Majesty as one
"Miss Bennett of New York." [14] Certainly never before had a
royal personage been made the instrument of conveying such an
oblique transatlantic insult. The affront to the queen did not
become known in court circles, but news of it leaked out across
the waters and reached New York, as undoubtedly was the intention.

This was sheer wormwood to the grim publisher because it
struck his one vulnerable spot. Bennett had become the most
hated man in New York as a result of the venom and unscrupu-
lousness with which he had lifted his *Herald* from a starveling
sheet to the most powerful paper in town. When Sickles' friend
Graham horsewhipped him in 1850 with the aid of a band of
Tammany bully boys, Graham was actually applauded for the
act. It was said that Bennett had not a single real friend, and indeed he appeared to want none. His imperviousness to insult
had caused enemies to switch their attack to his unfortunate
wife, and it was broadly—and falsely—hinted around the city
that her virtue was anything but unsullied. So virulent was this
campaign that the luckless woman had fled New York and spent
most of her time in Europe.

Now, to have Sickles present a notorious Jezebel to the Queen
under the name of Bennett made the editor writhe. It set off a
series of vitriolic attacks on Sickles in the *Herald* which persisted for four years.

Meanwhile, Buchanan was troubled by matters large and
small. One of the small ones was the question of court dress.
Previously, American ministers abroad had worn a sober but

distinctive uniform prescribed by the State Department for official functions. Secretary Marcy, a democratic sort, changed all this. He decreed that the nation's representatives should wear only the "simple dress of an American citizen." [15]

Though Buchanan regarded his own experience and ability as superior to Marcy's,[16] he followed this annoying regulation until at one function, to his horor, he was mistaken for a footman. Thereafter he solved the problem by wearing a plain dress sword "to distinguish me from the upper Court servants," [17] while Sickles on at least one occasion decked himself out in his militia officer's uniform, a splendid thing encrusted with ribbon and braid.[18]

One of Buchanan's primary concerns in statecraft was something that scarcely seemed any of his affair—the hoped-for acquisition of Cuba from Spain. This was an idea dear to the hearts of Southern legislators such as Senator Slidell, whose aim was to convert the island into two slave states, and the minister, though personally opposed to slavery, was solidly behind the project on the grounds of strategy and profit.[19]

The American minister at Madrid at the time was the fiery Pierre Soulé, a Louisianan who wanted Cuba. The minister at Paris was George Mason, a Virginian who wanted Cuba. The chargé in the Netherlands was August Belmont, who also wanted Cuba. All of these men were well aware that Spain was in one of her chronic states of political turmoil and financial exhaustion, and the machinations among them to push the Cuban scheme amounted to intrigue. It was Sickles' first full-dress introduction to the idea, which was later to loom large in his affairs, and he fell in enthusiastically with it.

When Teresa arrived in London in the spring of 1854 with her infant daughter, her natural charm and the cosmopolitan ease and knowledge of languages she had acquired in the Da Ponte household made her an instant success in the legation circle. One must assume, or hope, that by this time Fanny White had been sent back to New York to resume her Mercer Street profession. In any case, Teresa became friendly with Harriet

Lane, who had arrived that winter, and during a period when Miss Lane returned to America to attend to some property matters, Teresa became Buchanan's official legation hostess.

It was a duty that required close contact between the snowy-haired old Pennsylvanian and the bride not yet eighteen. By this time Buchanan must have been aware of Sickles's philandering, which was common London gossip, and it is possible that he felt compassion for Teresa—a sentiment that could easily develop into something warmer. Rumor began to murmur that the elderly bachelor was smitten with the wife of his secretary of legation.[20]

It was during this interval that General John A. Thomas, an Assistant Secretary of State, arrived in London on official business with his lady. Mrs. Thomas could not forgo this opportunity to be presented at court, and she spoke to Buchanan about it. The minister assented and told her to place herself in charge of Mrs. Sickles, who would accompany her to St. James' Palace.

Mrs. Thomas, whose home was in New York, could scarcely have been unaware of the various scandals involving Sickles. It it also conceivable that she had heard something about Buchanan's rumored attentions to Teresa.

Whatever the reason, she "decidedly declined" to go to court under the wing of a young lady she regarded as a schoolgirl, and demanded a more suitable sponsor.[21] Buchanan was outraged. There were warm words, and the upshot was that Mrs. Thomas, to her chagrin, was not presented at court at all. Undoubtedly she read more than was implied in the minister's championing of Teresa. It is certain that Buchanan did not forget the slight, for one of his first acts when he became President was to arrange the removal of General Thomas from the State Department.[22]

Despite rumor, despite Sickles' back-street amours, Teresa's straightforwardness and simplicity made her a favorite with such formidable British dames as Lady Palmerston and Lady Clarendon. She, Miss Lane, and Mrs. Lawrence—wife of the military attaché—were universally known as the "three American Graces." [23] But her social success must have been tinged with disillusion. In her naiveté she had married Sickles in the belief that she could reform him, win him over, remould him into a faithful husband. True, he was kind and indulgent as ever, but he was also as wayward as ever, and she began to realize that he was an incorrigible philanderer.

Another of Sickles' peculiarities was a touchy sense of patriotism—an aspect of his character that exploded like fireworks on July 4th, 1854.

For some years the expatriate Bostonian, George Peabody, had grown steadily richer as a London banker and broker, and had never passed by an opportunity to improve relations between his native and adopted countries. A gourmet and a speaker of some ability, he liked to give little dinners to which he would invite prominent Britons and Americans. It was his special pleasure to celebrate British-American friendship on Independence Day by sponsoring a large banquet at London's Crystal Palace. At this gathering, toasts would be drunk to the Queen and President, and speeches given on the theme of international amity.

This mutual well-wishing grated on Sickles' nationalism. To him Independence Day was strictly an American holiday and no property of the British at all. He protested the idea to Peabody and suggested what he considered a better one—a special subscription dinner attended exclusively by Americans. There was a good deal of parleying about this. Peabody gave ground on some points, for Sickles was a hard man to overcome in an argument, but the banker got his back up somewhat at what he considered unwarranted interference with an old custom and did not concede everything the New Yorker urged, although Sickles seemed to believe he had.[24]

The dinner—provided by Peabody—was given July Fourth at the sedate Star and Garter Hotel at Richmond on the Thames. There were a hundred and fifty guests present, and when Sickles arrived he was annoyed to find that many of them were Englishmen. He was further incensed to see life-size oil portraits of Queen Victoria and the Prince Consort on the wall near the head of the table, with a comparatively small portrait of George Washington sandwiched in between. There was no likeness at all of Sickles' good friend, President Pierce.

His choler rose when he noted in the printed program that the toast to Washington had been assigned to a Briton, Sir James Tennent, and that the toast to the Queen preceded that to the President. To complete his disgust, the lines of the "Star-Spangled Banner" and "Hail, Columbia" had been printed with all uncomplimentary jabs at the British—"the foe's haughty host," "the hireling and slave," "their foul footsteps' pollution," etc.—politely removed.[25]

Sickles fumed over his roast beef and joined only perfunctorily in the preliminary toasts. Then came the climactic moment. George Peabody arose and delivered a warm encomium of the virtuous sovereign—who had loaned the famous Winterhalter portraits from the palace itself—and ended with the shouted toast:

"Gentlemen . . . the Queen!"

The party rose to a man, right foot on chair, glass held aloft toward Victoria's portrait in the traditional salute. To a man, except for Sickles. He remained rooted in his chair, a flush spreading over his face.

Some of the celebrants—one of them was Buchanan—noticed this shocking affront. The banqueters sought to ignore it, but they could scarcely be indifferent when Sickles, a few moments later, got up and marched stiffly from the room.

The incident provoked heated drawing-room talk for months. Coming from a diplomatic representative charged with the duty of promoting international comity, it caused Buchanan great embarrassment. Colonel Sickles, the minister explained to his British friends, had meant no reflection on the Queen but had merely been upset over what he felt was Peabody's failure to keep his agreement.[26]

Colonel Sickles, still simmering, wrote an anonymous letter

to the Boston *Post* in which he arraigned Peabody in his old home city as a cheap trickster and renegade American who had so far forgotten his native land as to pervert the Independence Day holiday into a pro-British celebration and to curry favor with the Queen. He also exchanged tart notes with Peabody. The banker wrote to ask if Buchanan was interested in the matter. Sickles replied that he was not, that he (Sickles) was fighting in his own behalf.

George Peabody thereupon gave him the back of his hand. "If Mr. Buchanan has nothing to do with the matter," he wrote, "I wish no controversy with you." [27]

So infuriated was Sickles at this that he challenged Peabody to a duel—an invitation the banker declined.

There was some difference of opinion as to whether Sickles' choler was caused by outraged chauvinism or whether he might have had a canny eye cocked across the Atlantic in the direction of voters who admired anyone who tweaked the British lion's tail. "The occasion was a first-rate one for a sly display of democratic jealousy of royalty," one observer commented. "Mr. Sickles . . . was bent on making political capital out of this rare chance . . . and he anticipated with relish the enthusiastic admiration his conduct would excite [at home]. In the frenzy of the moment he hoped the Queen would henceforth refuse to receive him, and that he would be compelled to return home an object of patriotic ovation, leading him straight to the door of the next Presidency." [28]

Indeed, the secretary was extraordinarily busy at this time defending his country's honor and his own. Almost simultaneously, his old Tammany friend John Van Buren, who had drifted into another bloc of the party and was allied with Secretary Marcy, arrived in England on a visit. Sickles was furious at Van Buren because of an incident in the previous November, when Van Buren had made a speech at Tammany Hall. In it he made a passing and innocuous reference to Sickles, when he was suddenly interrupted by a wag in the audience who shouted, "Where is Fanny White?"

Van Buren laughed, replied, "I did not inquire," and went on with his speech.[29]

The incident probably was magnified in transmission. On July 20th, the plump Van Buren was in his room at Queen's Hotel in London when one Major A. H. Sibley appeared as Sickles' emissary and presented Van Buren with a challenge.

Van Buren, who had a greater liking for pressed duck than the sword, calmly explained the matter and stressed his own innocence of any intent to insult, and a duel was averted.[30]

But these episodes were merely surface bubbles on a swell of ominous events. The Cuban intrigue had been brewing and foaming with greater vehemence as a result of Spain's seizure of the American merchant vessel *Black Warrior* in Cuban waters in May. Americans were indignant, and the time seemed ripe to take concrete steps about acquiring the Pearl of the Antilles. In mid-August Sickles was back in Washington to confer with President Pierce and Marcy.

He told these gentlemen of the revolutionary mutterings in Spain and suggested that a secret American subsidy to the revolutionists might throw the country into such chaos that Cuba would gladly be sold. Or, if the sale was repugnant to Hispanic pride, possibly a five-million-dollar grant to the powerful Queen Mother, Maria Christina, or a generous payment to the Spanish treasury, might persuade the Spaniards to give the troubled island its freedom. The assumption was that once Cuba was free, it would soon become part and parcel of the United States.[31]

Sickles stayed at the White House a week, communing with the President and working night and day on a memoir which he titled, "On the State of Europe; its Bearing upon the Policy of the United States" [32]—a subject on which he was not too diffident to feel qualified to speak. Pierce was impressed, and Sickles returned to London with instructions for the ministers in Europe to meet and compose a statement on the American démarche in Cuban policy.

He lingered in London only long enough to confer with Buchanan, then was on his way to Paris to see Mason and finally to Madrid to see Soulé. He was laying the groundwork for one of the world's prize diplomatic fumbles. While in the Spanish capital he was presented to the twenty-four-year-old Queen Isabella II, a plump young woman already notorious for her affairs with men. It was only a brief audience, and probably the queen scarcely noticed the spruce young American who bowed before her. Not being gifted with omniscience, neither of them knew that they would meet again when they were older and had passed through separate and peculiar ordeals.

In October, the blunderbuss which Sickles had so carefully oiled and primed was unlimbered for action. Buchanan, Mason, and Soulé—with Sickles and Belmont—gathered at the pleasant Belgian resort town of Ostend. Here they put their heads together for several days and came forth with the so-called Ostend Manifesto, a pugnacious statement redolent of the old "manifest destiny" doctrine.

The United States, they used many words to say, should make every effort to buy Cuba from Spain, but if this failed, the United States would be justified in taking the island by force.

In Europe, foreign chancelleries were in a froth over this swipe at international convention. In Washington, Pierce and Marcy were swamped with protest. Their ministers, they saw, had gone too far. They promptly disowned and repudiated the manifesto—an act that must have been humiliating to its framers, placing them as it did in the position of naughty boys who had been spanked.

Disgruntled though they were, Sickles and Buchanan had other fish to fry. The next Presidential campaign was looming closer, and Buchanan was receiving more letters from across the water urging him to throw his hat in the ring. To Forney he had written denying any Presidential aspirations in terms remarkable in implying the opposite of what they said.[33] Actually, Old Buck was eyeing the White House with the fervor of a knight-errant viewing the Holy Grail, and Sickles was at his elbow enthusiastically promoting the crusade.

When he quit the London post and sailed for New York with

Teresa and the baby in November, his plans were well formed. His $2500 salary as secretary had pinched him—as almost any salary would have—and he had been forced to borrow money freely. In return he gave drafts on the United States Treasury, and when he reached Washington Secretary of the Treasury Guthrie refused to honor these drafts.[34]

This left the unhappy London creditors high and dry, but Sickles still had Buchanan in his vest pocket. A month later he received a letter from the minister which said in part:

"Your refusal to rise when the Queen's health was proposed is still mentioned in society, but I have always explained & defended you." [35]

CHAPTER X

Target, Washington

In New York, Sickles resumed his law practice and began inflating the Buchanan-in-1856 balloon by conferences with and letters to influential Democrats in the Empire State and elsewhere. In backing Buchanan he was by no means betting on a sure thing. There were other strong Democratic aspirants—Pierce, Douglas, and Marcy were among them—and the political situation was further confused by the deepening North-South schism, the increasing strength of the Republicans, and the unpredictable potency of the Whigs and Know-Nothings.

Being Sickles, he immediately became enrolled in controversy. One of his quarrels in 1855 was with D. Wemyss Jobson, a British-born dental surgeon and patent counsellor who had aided Dr. John Allen of New York in a lawsuit for infringement of Allen's patent for making artificial teeth. Jobson complained that Allen had refused to pay for his services, and he retained Sickles and his father to represent him in an action against Allen.

Jobson became suspicious when no move was made against Allen. His suspicions grew when he did a little snooping and found, as he claimed, that Dr. Allen was frequenting the Sickles offices. He heard rumors that the Sickleses had gone over to the opposition and that "Allen had made it all right with old Sickles." Jobson talked with James Gordon Bennett about it, and the publisher said he was not surprised since Sickles had betrayed Bennett "and every person that ever trusted him."

Stalemated in his suit against Allen, Jobson vented his spleen

in an angry pamphlet in which he accused the Sickleses of un-
ethical practices and downright treachery.[1]

Little alarums like this were routine to Daniel Sickles. In the
autumn of 1855 he was nominated for the state senate, making
his campaign a test of the indorsement of Buchanan by New
York State Democrats, and was elected. In the senate at Albany,
where he was a member of a minority of only four Democrats,
he endeared himself to many righteous New Yorkers who had
formerly despised him, by his able leadership of a fight against a
bill which would have struck a blow against wealthy old Trinity
Church—his mother's church.

Trinity, founded well before the Revolution as a parish of the
Church of England, had been granted a substantial glebe at the
time of its chartering. These lands, which had then been pasture
or meadow, were transformed by New York's quick growth into
fabulously valuable real estate in the heart of the city. Trinity's
shrewd board of directors had kept much of this land, and on it
were business buildings paying huge rentals. The church, many
of whose members were among the wealthiest and most prominent men in the city, was anything but poverty-stricken. It was
drawing a vast income from its holdings, which its critics declared was being used mainly to increase its wealth, with only
a small proportion going for missionary and charitable causes.
The Trinity Church Bill, sponsored largely by other less opu-
lent Episcopal churches, would have wrested control from Trinity's own vestry and spread the real-estate income among other
churches in the diocese.

Sickles heeded his mother's plea and fought the bill with all
his power. Nor was he unaware that the fight would make him
important friends. In Albany he rallied the opposition and delivered a well-organized and effective speech defending the
"vested constitutional rights" of Trinity and not forgetting
that—

> I was born and reared within the bosom of this church and
> in this parish. The graves of my humble ancestors lie within

its sacred enclosures. The marriage vow, the baptismal blessing, were pronounced upon those from whom I sprang, by the side of its altars. It is the only church that now remains within my district to take care of the poor . . .[2]

The bill was defeated. Sickles' legal opinion was so well-grounded that it still stands a hundred years later. Perhaps Trinity's vestrymen would have been happier had they been rescued by someone more known for godliness, but at any rate, they were thankful for their rescue.[3]

Unlike most political specialists, Sickles seemed able to keep several pots boiling at the same time and to give all of them the needed stirring. He announced his intention to run for Congress in 1856. When Buchanan returned from England in April of that year, Sickles saw to it that he was given a welcome worthy of a coming President. The retiring minister rode triumphantly up Fifth Avenue to the Everett House on Union Square, where he was greeted by Sickles, Senator Slidell, Mayor Fernando Wood, and a host of other notables who tendered him a magnificent and well-publicized reception.[4] Ever since his typesetting days Sickles had respected the power of the printed word, and one of his many accomplishments was an uncommon ability to treat genially with newspapermen and get a "good press."

The Buchanan boom was now gathering thunder. Forney was working at it in Pennsylvania, and in New York Sickles and Slidell invaded Wall Street and raised huge campaign funds from business men and capitalists who feared that the election of the Republican Frémont would mean war with the South and the ruin of commerce.[5]

In the midst of all this, Sickles carried on a feud with Bennett and the *Herald*. When Bennett somewhat later penned a bitter attack in which he referred to "this double-dealing Dan E. Sickles" and accused him of betraying a legal client, Sickles was not too busy to sue him both for civil and criminal libel. He retained his old friend John Graham in the criminal suit—a chore relished by the little lawyer who had personally cowhided

Bennett seven years earlier. At a court hearing, Graham let loose
a memorable diatribe:

> Who is James Gordon Bennett? No prosecution you can in-
> stitute against him involves the freedom of the press. The press
> disowns him as a member. No press will defend the licentious-
> ness of his journal . . . My client is determined to give the
> author of this libel an opportunity to confront—I was going to
> say, his peers—but where the peers of this man Bennett would
> come from, I know not. That twelve such men lived at this
> time on the face of the earth, or that twelve such men ever dis-
> graced it by their existence, is a fact which to the credit of the
> human species I distinctly deny. If you were to congregate and
> concatenate all the monsters that have ever disgraced the hu-
> man form, I doubt whether you would be able to find among
> them twelve bad enough to make the peers of this infamous
> wretch.[6]

The suit never came to trial, but this was a small matter. Buchanan was elected President in the fall of 1856 by a narrow
margin. Sickles was elected to Congress by a comfortable plural-
ity. The target, which was Washington, had been hit in the
bullseye and the future was a delightful thing to contemplate.
As a man entering into national politics, Sickles felt a need for
a properly impressive setting. It was at this time that he bought
the riverside mansion on Ninety-first Street in suburban Bloomingdale, performing his customary miracle of being pinched for
funds and yet living like a king. It is not known whether his
London creditors were still unsatisfied or whether his proud
father had "filled the breach."

So Teresa, installed as mistress of the household, continued
her efforts at adjustment to a marriage that did not conform to
the pattern outlined in the popular romances of the day. She had
a husband who petted her, bought her jewels, insisted that she
dress in the latest fashion, and quite frankly preferred to sleep
with other women. At nineteen she had reached the stunned
realization that a man could be perfectly enchanting and yet
shrug off a spouse's obligation of at least nominal fidelity.

In truth, the time Sickles allotted for domesticity approached the vanishing point as politics virtually took over his waking hours. In 1857 he became embroiled in one of Tammany's eternal inner eruptions when he supported his friend, the notorious Fernando Wood, for mayor. Daniel Tiemann was nominated instead, but Wood incontinently ran for the office anyway. Wood lost by a close margin, and the anti-Wood members of the Tammany General Committee decided to expel Sickles and C. Godfrey Gunther, another Wood supporter.

They met for this purpose at the Wigwam on December 9th. Both factions came armed with brass knuckles, blackjacks, and more lethal weapons. The bar was lined three deep, and soon the political discussion degenerated into a free-for-all fight with fists flying, bottles swinging, and the niceties of debate lost in a welter of howls and sulphuric curses. The Tammany policemen had always been gentle with the men of the Wigwam who controlled their jobs, but the riot became so bloody, with several men injured and one shot, that forty officers had to swing their clubs to restore order. The meeting broke up with no action taken, and Sickles was still a member of the General Committee.[7]

With reason, he felt exultant. All of his long-laid plans, despite the whims and pitfalls of unpredictable politics, had worked out precisely as he wished. His dear friend Buchanan would soon be in the White House, and he would be posted at Old Buck's elbow. Could anything be more promising?

"It was indeed a triumph," Sickles wrote a friend, commenting on his election to Congress. "All the old fogies were against me . . . It is a glorious triumph for the Young Democracy & I mean they shall profit by it."[8]

*　　*　　*

Hardly more than two years later, gunfire roared in Lafayette Square. Sickles was acquitted of murder. He took back his repentant wife, and after that no one had any doubt on one point: Daniel E. Sickles was finished.

CHAPTER XI

Man with Smallpox

When Sickles reached Washington late in 1859, his arrival was entirely lacking in the fanfare of inauguration time two years earlier. Many had said he would not have the nerve to appear in the capital again after what had happened. Those observers had an improper conception of the Sickles nerve. He was there, but alone and quietly. Teresa had remained in New York with Laura. If her Dan had the courage to face ostracism in Washington, she—the branded adulteress—had not, nor did he want her to. He took a suite at Willard's and soon discovered how few friends he had.

Buchanan was still in the White House, of course, and he was still friendly. Yet the President could not blink the fact that Sickles had alienated himself from society and jettisoned his own political future. The relations between them, though cordial, had sharply changed. Old Buck no longer viewed the younger man as a brilliant protégé with unlimited prospects, but rather as a luckless has-been, a lame duck who held office only because he had been elected before he shot Key and forgave his wife and who would quit Washington forever when his term was ended in 1861—if he could stick it out that long.

Still numbered among his friends were Edwin Stanton, Henry Wikoff, and a few others, and as long as he lived Sickles would never forget their loyalty. But to this gregarious extrovert who needed popularity as much as he needed food and drink, the whittling down of his circle of intimates from hundreds to a handful was a thrust to the heart. His humiliation at Delmonico's was now repeated at Willard's bar and at the National. Men he had known well—men who had courted his favor—now stopped talking at his approach and moved away uneasily.

In Congress, if anything, it was worse.

"I am desirous of adding a line in reference to Mr. Sickles of New York," one corespondent wrote, "and particularly in regard to the universally accepted opinion that he is not spoken to by his fellow members. It is quite true that there is very little disposition manifested by any of the representatives to establish intimate relations with Mr. Sickles; but justice to the man himself requires that I should state that he seems to desire no such relations. Every day . . . when debate has begun, he walks in quietly from the side door and takes his seat . . . Resting his head on his gloved hand, he remains seated, taking no part in the discussions—voting, when called upon, in a low voice. He dresses in exquisite taste, and has cultivated a large pair of brown whiskers. He seems conscious that public opinion is greatly against him . . ." [1]

Mrs. Chesnut, the patrician lady from South Carolina, was conscious of it too when she walked into the House gallery.

"I have seen only two men in all my life who were sent to Coventry thoroughly and deliberately," she wrote. "One was a fine young officer in all his bravery of naval uniform, traveling with a rich old harridan at her expense . . . That was at Saratoga. In Washington, I saw Mr. Sickles sitting alone on the benches of the House of Representatives. He was as left to himself as if he had smallpox." [2]

Mrs. Chesnut made it clear that this universal quarantine was invoked not because Sickles killed Key—it was felt he was justified in that—but because "he condoned his wife's profligacy and took her back." This fact throws into relief the merciless moral code of the time, which would have banished the fallen Teresa from all friendly human contact. Sickles ironically was being made to suffer for an act of warmth and forgiveness, qualities he was seldom accused of having.

This session of Congress must have been the bitterest of ordeals, with the pain of obloquy and the contempt of former friends rendered all the more lacerating by the certain knowledge that he was appearing for the last time on the stage of national events. There was no handrail now to stay his plunge. He was ruined and he knew it. He stayed on with a fortitude such as few men have. His realization of hopelessness was evidenced by his failure to run for re-election in 1860.

For years he had cheerfully broken all the rules laid down for the personal conduct of a successful politician, and had not only got away with it but appeared to profit by it. Now he had kicked the most sacred cow of all, and was confronted by a massive unanimity of disapproval with which even his charm and ability could not cope. For the first time in his life he sank into something much like humility. When he addressed the House on December 13th, 1859, he almost apologized for his temerity, saying:

> It would have been more agreeable to me if some other gentle-
> man . . . had risen to discharge the duty which, in my humble
> judgment, remains to be performed . . . Seldom asking the in-
> dulgence of the House heretofore, I would not now trespass on
> its patience if I did not feel myself compelled to protest . . .
> against much that has been said on this floor . . . in the name
> of the North.[3]

And yet time slowly began to exert a beneficent influence. When he returned to Washington after the sumer recess in 1860 there were some legislators who, either because they admired his courage or felt that he had suffered enough, thawed somewhat toward him. His temper was beginning to rebel against taking a permanently silent role even if this was to be his swan song. More than this, events of such enormity were taking place that one man's disgrace tended to become lost in the shuffle.

The long prologue to the nation's bloody tragedy was drawing to its climax with such a spate of virulence and insult as Congress had never seen. To many Southerners, the election of

Linc   1 had ended any hope for peaceable settlement. The fate
of st   e-torn Kansas was argued with increased vehemence, and
in o   debate Congressman Haskin gestured so excitedly that a
loac   pistol dropped from his pocket, causing a furore.[4] There
wei   ew and stronger threats of secession. Disaster loomed, and
in   ember the House appointed a Committee of Thirty-three
on   Perilous State of the Union, to explore the empty barrel
of   npromise.

       les had always been a Democrat, a Buchanan man, a New
Y   r defending New York interests—which is to say he had
v   solidly with the Southern bloc. He was still that way on
I   mber 10th when he delivered a ringing speech attacking
"   illusion . . . that this Union can be preserved by force"
       lefending the last-resort right of a state to "seek safety in a
       ate existence"—i.e., to secede from the Union. He went on
       ake the astonishing threat that New York City might one
       secede from the state:

> No man will ever pass the boundaries of the City of New
> ork for the purpose of waging war against any state of this
> nion . . . The City of New York is now a subjugated depend-
> cy of a fanatical and puritanical state government . . . Noth-
> g has prevented the City of New York from asserting her right
> govern herself except that provision of the federal constitu-
> on which prohibits a state from being divided without its
> wn consent . . . When that restraint shall no longer exist
> . . she will repel the hateful cabal at Albany and . . . as a
> ree city, open wide her gates to the civilization and commerce
> of the world.[5]

Clearly, the man sent to Coventry was feeling his oats again.
This was the sort of talk Southern legislators loved to hear. It
encouraged them in their belief that the North was so hopelessly
divided that it could make no effective resistance to secession.

And secession, so long a threat, became reality. South Carolina began the parade ten days later, soon to be followed by
others. Buchanan, who sought to mediate and as a result had

won the contempt of both factions, crumbled under the strain. He teetered, placated, and sought inspiration in prayer. In a crisis where firmness and strength were needed, weakness overbore him. Frantically he sought to delay and dump the whole accursed problem into the bony lap of the Republican Mr. Lincoln two months hence. He tied his own hands impossibly with his opinion that the administration had no constitutional right to coerce any state, and when the secessionist South Carolinians seized Fort Moultrie and threatened Fort Sumter, the President did not know what to do.

Sickles knew what to do. The New Yorker who had so recently upheld the right of a state to peaceful secession was outraged by the rebellious violence in Charleston Harbor. With Major Anderson holding Sumter with a small force and being menaced by warlike Palmetto men, Buchanan even considered withdrawing the force—a move Sickles heatedly opposed. "Support him!" he urged the President. And while Buchanan temporized, Sickles and Edwin Stanton—now Attorney General—cooked up a sly trick to force the President's hand.

Unknown to Buchanan, they broadcast telegrams to Northern politicians asking them to fire salutes, stage parades, and send congratulations to the President for upholding Anderson at Sumter.[6] Sickles boarded a train for Philadelphia, where he persuaded Daniel Dougherty to round up some artillery and have a hundred guns fired to applaud the President for his firmness. Hurrying on to New York, he got Captain Isaiah Rynders to do the same.[7]

This oblique pressure had the effect of stiffening Buchanan's spine. He achieved a measure of determination. Major Anderson stayed where he was. For years thereafter Sickles and Stanton enjoyed a private joke about how they had kept Anderson at Sumter and thus sponsored the first shot fired against the rebellion.

The crisis, so paralyzing to the President, worked like a heady stimulant on Sickles. He was always in some sort of crisis, be it financial, legislative, sexual, or homicidal, and these situations

invariably galvanized him into action, not always wise. His actions now were wise. The Congressman from New York was
gaining in stature. His sudden rupture with the firebrand Southerners whom he had wined and dined and defended for years
was perfectly consistent and logical because in their rage they
had gone beyond the law.

Sickles, the lawyer, viewed secession as a matter of constitutional law and would reluctantly say goodbye to the dissident
states so long as they departed peacefully and legally. But it was
crystal clear to him that the Carolinian cannonballs were illegal.
By resorting to violence his former friends from Dixie had forfeited his sympathies.

His dander was rising. In a speech before the House on January 16th, 1861, he branded the Southern attack on the United
States vessel *Star of the West* as "naked, unmitigated war," and
declared:

> It will never do, sir, for them [the South] to protest against
> coercion and, at the same moment, seize all the arms and
> arsenals and forts and navy-yards and ships . . . When sover-
> eign states by their own deliberate acts, make war, they must
> not cry peace . . . when the flag of the Union is insulted, when
> the fortified places provided for the common defense are as-
> saulted and seized, when the South abandons its Northern
> friends for English and French alliances, then the loyal and
> patriotic population of that imperial city [New York] are unani-
> mous for the Union.[8]

For a man personally so headstrong and violent, Sickles had
a remarkable respect for law in government. His former Southern colleagues must have been surprised at his attitude, but
there was no staying them now. As a breather in the crisis,
Sickles offered a resolution in the House calling for the celebration of Washington's birthday as a national holiday. The measure was passed, and Secretary of War Joseph Holt and General
Winfield Scott thought this a fine opportunity to make a military display with the small forces then in the capital. They
scheduled a parade of the soldiery for February 22nd.

Ex-President Tyler, the venerable Virginian, was in Washington attending the ill-fated Peace Convention, and when he got wind of this plan he rushed to Buchanan to protest. The parade, he said, would be resented by the touchy Southerners as a display of force. He did not explain just how a peaceable group of marching men compared with cannon fired on United States ships and soldiers as a "display of force." The President, seeking to placate everybody, gave in. He ordered Holt to call off the parade.

Sickles heard of this next morning, February 22nd. He pounded into the White House, where Buchanan was conferring with Holt.

"Mr. President," Sickles snapped, "there are ten thousand people out on the streets of Washington today to see the parade which was announced. I have just heard that it has been countermanded, and the report is exciting great indignation. I come to ask if it is true, and if so whether the parade may yet be carried out."

Buchanan wavered. Sickles pressed. The President finally said wearily to Holt, "Go ahead with the parade." [9]

Holt did his best, but at this late hour most of the soldiers had been ordered away. Only a handful remained, and the brave "show of force" fizzled into a pipsqueak affair which hardly would have done credit to a chowder and marching club. Southern sympathizers who witnessed the spectacle had good cause to jeer.

Already, on February 5th, Sickles had given the House the latest reflections of his agile mind and had shown how dramatically Southern violence had transformed him. The secession movement, he said—

originated . . . as a peaceful remedy for grievances. As such it had thousands, and tens of thousands of friends in the North who were disposed to meet it on middle ground and say, "If you cannot abide with us, bitter as the lesson may be, we will yield to the necessity for a separation." That was the December phase of the secession movement. In January it assumed a new attitude. No longer peaceable; no longer disposed to await the consent of the government or the deliberations of Congress . . . and we are menaced, as the penalty of resistance, with all the terrors of civil war . . . In February, secession assumes another and yet more questionable shape. I can only character-ize it as the Mexican method of revolution . . . In February, secession is spoliation and war. What next? Let us not lift the veil. But I will say, in the presence of this new and latest phase of the revolution, that it can have no friends in the North.[10]

No friends in the North . . . It was an ominous warning of what was to come. The Peace Democrat saw peace glimmering. In two short months the somewhat tarnished member from New York had abandoned his old friends in Secessia because he saw them clearly in the wrong. But matters had long since passed the point where reason prevailed. On March 4th, James Bu-chanan left Washington with a sigh of relief, and the Republi-can Mr. Lincoln took over the problem of how to parley with cannonballs.

CHAPTER XII

The Making of a General

In April, 1861, Daniel Edgar Sickles, private citizen, was back at the law with his father at their Nassau Street offices, and keenly unhappy about it. For years he had held public posts of steadily increasing importance, and now—just when events were reaching a crisis—he was excluded. The Union was only a memory. There was even talk that the rebels were moving large forces toward Washington and that the capital was in imminent danger. For Sickles, with his craving to be in the center of any turmoil, the role of bystander was galling.

As if this were not enough, other circumstances combined to make his existence dreary. His reunion with Teresa had been a failure despite all good intentions. At bottom he could not forgive her affair with Key, nor could he abstain from humoring his "idiosyncrasy"—his ceaseless quest for women. On her side, Teresa bitterly reproached herself for the eclipse of her husband's career which the reunion had caused. It was said that she was desperately unhappy, that she could not sleep and had resorted to opiates.[1]

Furthermore, some of Sickles' Tammany friends still eyed him askance—the more so because of his Congressional attacks on the Southern resort to force, for Tammany was still largely a Copperhead tribe that paid only lip service to the Union. One of the paradoxes of his career was that he often seemed to profit most through guile, and to suffer from acts of honesty and sincerity.

The depth of his malaise is indicated by the fact that he was seriously considering joining the colors as an aide to his old friend, Colonel Abram Vosburg of the state militia, when a better idea came along. One day he and Captain William Wiley— the man who had so enthusiastically embraced him on his acquittal in Washington—went into Lorenzo Delmonico's famous establishment at Broadway and Chambers Street. At the bar they met several acquaintances, and the talk naturally turned to the war with the South. It was suggested to Wiley that he should get up a company or regiment to aid in the defense of Washington.

"If he will," Sickles said jocularly, "I'll go as a private."

Wiley considered the idea over his drink. It struck him that Sickles, with his qualities of leadership and his brief experience with the state militia, ought to make an excellent officer.

"If you will command a regiment," he proposed to Sickles, "I will raise, arm, and equip it." [2]

Neither of them knew, of course, that this light barroom talk was to produce the commander who would win—or almost lose, depending on the authority—the battle of Gettysburg. Sickles and Wiley got busy. From Governor Edwin Morgan they got authorization to raise a regiment. From a local Union Defense Committee they obtained five hundred dollars to make a start, and the two friends had handbills printed and posted urging men to volunteer. Sickles also made recruiting speeches and saw to it that his efforts were publicized in the papers. Indignation against the South was running high with the surrender of Fort Sumter, and within a fortnight he and Wiley had raised a regiment of eight companies.

There were plenty of critics who sneered that since Sickles was in such bad odor that he was barred from almost everything else, he was only too willing to climb aboard the bandwagon of patriotism and seek to recoup some standing by active participation in the war. These detractors made the common mistake of ascribing all his actions to selfish motives. Naturally he was seeking some escape from the wreckage of all his hopes, but he was also fired with anger at the Southerners who he felt had betrayed him as well as the nation. Regis de Trobriand, a French-born New York newspaperman who knew him well and had no axe to grind, had no doubt about his sincerity, saying:

> During the time of discussion he had been among those most conciliatory in regard to the pretensions and aggressions of the South. But when the sword was drawn, he was one of those most ready to throw away the scabbard . . . Disgusted with the bad faith of his old allies, and irritated at the false position in which they had put the Democrats of the North, he considered his party as in duty bound, more than any other, to carry on the war *à outrance,* unto the complete triumph of the national government.[3]

No sooner was his regiment on hand than Sickles received an order from Governor Morgan to raise a full brigade of five regiments.[4] The project he had started in a fairly modest way was mushrooming, and he went to work with a will, pleased at the prospect of becoming a brigadier general. His friend, Charles K. Graham, still in the Brooklyn Navy Yard post Sickles had got for him, joined in the recruiting and quit his position, bringing with him four hundred Navy Yard workers who were eager for a slap at the South. A former Assembly colleague, Dennis Meehan, came in with a hundred men. Sickles even made recruiting trips to upstate New York and found more hundreds of men who were itching to shoulder a musket.

One of those who joined out of a sense of duty was a muscular, handsome young man named Joseph Hopkins Twichell, a clergyman from Plantsville, Connecticut, who was recently out of Yale, where he had pulled an oar on the crew. Twichell was opposed to war, but was even more strongly opposed to slavery and disunion, and he regarded the conflict as a sad necessity. He became one of the brigade's regimental chaplains, and although at first he had some reservations about the character of the commander—he wrote his father, "The intimate friendship of Gen. Sickles, I did not regard as a promise of extraordinary piety" [5]—he soon came to admire Sickles' energy and efficiency.

When someone asked the commander where the brigade was going, "The General said that he now thought our first destination would be Richmond, Va." Twichell liked that.[6]

By the middle of May, Sickles and Wiley had succeeded in organizing a full brigade of more than 3000 men. Sickles proudly christened it the Excelsior Brigade, after the inscription on the New York State seal, and got ready for training. Then came a crusher. A telegram from Governor Morgan ordered Sickles to disband all but eight of his forty companies. The raising of so many troops in New York City, the governor said by way of explanation, was causing dissatisfaction in the interior counties.[7]

Sickles was outraged. He had expended great time and effort in recruiting, and the more than 2000 men he would have to discharge would be furious at the humiliation of slinking home as civilians after they had been sent to the wars with brass bands and patriotic speeches. He sniffed a strong scent of politics behind the move, for Governor Morgan was a staunch Republican and Sickles had few friends among that party in Albany or anywhere else.

Furthermore, under the peculiar custom of the day the rank of a volunteer officer was dictated by the number of men he brought into the army. If he recruited a regiment he became a colonel, while if he brought in a brigade he was rewarded with the shining star of a brigadier general. Sickles was not the sort of man who could regard rank as unimportant. The governor, he was convinced, was pole-axing him for personal and partisan reasons, a treatment he was not inclined to accept supinely.

Bristling, Sickles caught the next train to Washington, where he saw President Lincoln and explained his problem. It was the first meeting between these two men, so utterly unlike in every way, who were destined to be linked socially and politically in an unusual intimacy. Always a fertile plan-maker, Sickles broached one which he felt would neatly circumvent the governor. He suggested that if the state would not take his men, the federal government accept them direct as United States Volunteers.

Much as he wanted men, Lincoln saw that this was a ticklish procedure. Until then the raising of troops had been the prerogative solely of the states, and mixed up in it were delicate considerations of local pride, patronage, and influence.

"I like that idea of United States Volunteers," Lincoln admitted, "but you see where it leads to. What will the governors say if I raise regiments without their having a hand in it?"

Sickles urged that the "power to raise armies" granted to Congress by the constitution was ample authority. Furthermore, he pointed out that patriotic ardor was now running high, that men were willing and eager to enlist and that this feeling should be exploited before it faded. The President was impressed by this faultlessly dressed, highly persuasive New Yorker whose reputation was so beclouded. Lincoln was anxious to make the suppression of the rebellion a united movement of the North embracing all shades of political opinion, and Sickles and many of his men were Democrats who had opposed his election. In the end, Lincoln called in Secretary of War Cameron, who approved the idea, and Sickles was instructed to hold his men and promised that they would be accepted.

"We will see how this beginning ends," was the way Lincoln put it.[8]

Sickles left with a provisional appointment as brigadier general and a pleasant feeling that he had outmaneuvered the governor. But his satisfaction melted when he reached New York. Trouble was brewing. Wiley, who served as his quartermaster—and who, astonishingly, had his headquarters at Delmonico's—had hired two of that restaurant's chefs to cook for the brigade. These cooks were accustomed to preparing such delicacies as stuffed pheasant and crepes suzettes. Even with volunteer help, they found it impossible to prepare enough food for 3000 men in improvised kitchens, and some were going hungry and were loud in their complaints. To complicate matters, the expense of feeding and housing the men was enormous, and Wiley was doing it on credit. The cost for the first two weeks alone had been $12,000, and now that the number of men was quintupled, so was the cost. Some of the creditors were beginning to weaken in their patriotism.

Wiley had thoughtfully hired a brass band for the troops, but many of them resentfully said they couldn't eat music. A new menace arose in the question of sanitation. Most of the men were quartered in the state barracks near the post office, with the excess being herded into rented lofts and garrets which were barren and unheated. At none of these places were there adequate facilities for cleanliness. Sickles' men, many of whom had no change of clothing or even soap or razors, were roaming the streets so dirty, tattered, and unshaven as to frighten women and children. For want of anything better to do some of them were getting drunk and disorderly.[9]

To add to the bedlam, a steady stream of recruits was still trickling in, and accommodations had to be found for them. Chaplain Twichell was sent to find quarters for them—a thankless task, for he wrote, "I learn that the quarters I rented yesterday proved unsatisfactory to our men . . . and this morning there were some signs of mutiny. We must get into new barracks at once or there will be loss through desertion." [10]

The police complained, and now the Board of Health became alarmed. Sickles' men, this body said, were filthy, lice-ridden, and a menace to public health. Unless something was done, there was danger of pestilence, and something had better be done quickly or the whole bag and baggage would be ejected from the city.

In desperation, Sickles made a deal with the proprietor of a bath house and barber shop on Crosby Street, who agreed to bathe, shave, and cut the hair of all the recruits at ten cents a head.[11]

This mass purification staved off ruin for a time, but now a new threat arose. The state authorities, incensed at Sickles' temerity in keeping his whole brigade when he was commanded to discharge all but a regiment—and further angered by his direct dealing with Lincoln—summarily ordered him to vacate the state barracks. The President, indeed, had found the problem of circumventing state control over recruiting a tougher one than he had anticipated. Officials in Albany were up in arms over this transgression on their traditional privilege, and weeks were consumed in stalemated controversy over the question.[12]

With his men turned into the streets, Sickles had to act quickly. He managed to secure permission for them to be quartered temporarily at the Fashion race track on Long Island, a place with which he was thoroughly familiar as a spectator and bettor at the races. He sent anguished telegrams to the War Department in Washington protesting at the delay and pleading that his troops be accepted before they melted away in desertion. He was informed that the men could not yet be mustered in as the problem of jurisdiction was not settled, but he was offered the use of land adjacent to Fort Wadsworth on Staten Island as a camp until the question could be ironed out. Thankful for this small favor, he moved his brigade out to what proved to be a barren wasteland near the island's shore.[13]

He called the place Camp Scott in honor of the venerable general of the Union army. He now had space and air for his men, but space and air were only two of the requirements for a moderately comfortable existence. Sickles had ordered tents, but only a few had arrived and most of the men perforce slept in the open—a fitful slumber haunted by the buzzing and stabbing of a million mosquitoes. The food problem was still anything but well in hand, with meat inclined to spoil from lack of refrigeration. Sickles had been able to borrow only three hundred rifles from the armory, and his men had to trade off using them in drill.[14]

These men, most of them, wanted to fight. They were honest citizens who had enlisted in a laudable flush of patriotism, had left steady jobs and kissed mothers and sweethearts goodbye, and were under the innocent delusion that they would march directly to some vague place south of Washington where they would meet the rebels and trounce them for good and all. In their enlistment enthusiasm they had pictured the war as a stirring affair carried on to the tune of martial music and culminating in swift victory. Instead, they were the unoffending victims of a snarl of inefficiency and red tape which they could not understand. They thought they had joined the army, but as yet they were not even accepted. No one seemed to want them. They were still in New York after weeks had passed, and what was worse, were living in a condition approaching misery, with poor food and very little shelter. The glamor of warfare had glimmered. They were sick of promises. Inevitably they began to desert.

Sickles was doing his best for them, and they knew it. They admired the little general with his fancy uniform and cocky strut. They were thankful when he bought—on credit—a circus tent from his old friend P. T. Barnum. The big canvas gave shelter to many men pending the arrival of the regular army tents.[15] But still . . .

Sickles hurried off to Washington to see Lincoln again. The President greeted him kindly.

"Your camp has gone all to pieces, I hear," he said.

"Not yet, your Excellency," the New Yorker replied, but he admitted that things were in a fairly parlous state and again urged that his brigade be accepted by the government.

Lincoln was sympathetic, and said that if Sickles could hold his men three days longer, a mustering officer would come "and take you all in out of the cold." [16]

Encouraged, Sickles went back to New York and gave the good news to his officers—news which, it developed, was a little premature. Two days later, he spent a few hours in the city and returned to Camp Scott to find that a whole company of ninety men had deserted en masse. Making inquiries, he learned that the company had just left for the ferry, having been enticed by bounties and the promise of early action to join another regiment being organized in the city. The general took a detachment of men and headed post-haste for the ferry. Arriving there, he found the vessel loosening its hawsers and about to steam off with his absconding company.

"Stop!" he roared to the captain. "You are aiding men to desert from the army!"

The captain obeyed when Sickles' men leveled their muskets at him. The discomfited deserters disembarked and were promptly arrested with their officers. A few hours later, a captain and two lieutenants from the New York regiment which had attempted to lure the company away, appeared at Camp Scott to inquire about the men. They were likewise arrested.

Sickles decided that the time had come to discourage this sort of thing with a show of swift military justice. At ten o'clock that night the officers involved in the desertion were given a summary court-martial and were condemned to be shot at midnight. The sentence, duly confirmed by Sickles, was read to the terrified men and at 11:45 they were given fifteen minutes for prayers and preparation for death while a firing party was detailed for the execution.

The condemned men begged for mercy, but the grim arrangements proceeded. At midnight, just as the firing squad was lining up, the officers in charge of the detail opened sealed orders from General Sickles. To the vast relief of the culprits, it was a reprieve until the findings of the court should be submitted to the President for approval.[17]

But by morning the misdoers, instead of feeling gratitude at their deliverance, were experiencing a slow burn of indignation. Somehow, although they were still under arrest, they managed to get word to a Brooklyn attorney named Reynolds who immediately took up the cudgels for them. Calling Sickles a "pseudo brigadier general," he drew up a habeas corpus action and declared that since the men had never been officially sworn into the army they were at liberty to do as they pleased and Sickles had no authority whatever over them. This was a delicate legal point indeed, and if it could be carried the burgeoning brigadier would very likely be left with nothing but his shoulder straps, if that.[18]

Probably no man was ever so harried, balked, and assailed as Daniel Sickles in his efforts to raise a brigade for a good cause. The wonder is that he did not give up in disgust. But Sickles was ever at his best when the going was rocky. The staid *Tribune* had to admit that Camp Scott "deserved creditable mention" for its orderliness,[19] and Chaplain Twichell was impressed with Sickles' insistence on temperance and discipline on the part of his men.[20] But the food was still bad, the mosquitoes were still biting, and what was worse, no salaries were being paid to this brigade which still had not been accepted into the army despite its pleas that it be allowed to go out and win the war. Men were forced to write home for extra clothing and a few dollars for tobacco and supplies.

"I have seen enough already in this camp to show me that I shall get used to things which before have been night-mares," wrote Twichell, and the general must have seconded the motion.[21]

At long, long last, Washington moved. The federal-state quarrel was solved. Two regular army officers arrived at Camp Scott, and they were cheered to the echo. They promptly swore in the weary men of the brigade as United States Volunteers. The recruits were wild with relief and joy that day, and uproarious shouts of "On to Richmond!" were heard everywhere. Now, surely, they would get out of this hateful place and head south for action against the rebels.

Unfortunately, this was not so. Another stalemate loomed.

In maintaining many hundreds of men for something more than two months, Sickles and Wiley had been forced to beg for credit to the bursting point. They owed for food, rent, supplies, horses, forage, fuel, tents, and a thousand other items. The sum total of their debts, in Wiley's estimate, had reached the staggering sum of $283,000,[22] while Sickles' own later estimate was closer to $400,000.[23] Wholesale suppliers who had been influenced by patriotism or profit to extend this credit now looked with suspicion on the idea of allowing the brigade to leave before the bills were paid. They said in effect, "You can go, but not until you settle these debts." When the money was not forthcoming, they secured judgments against Sickles.[24]

The unhappy Excelsior Brigade had to mark time while this quarrel was settled.

To expect either Sickles or Wiley to pay anything like this amount was absurd. To expect the government to pay promptly was equally fantastic, for Washington was in a chaos of confusion and the federal bookkeepers were months behind in their accounts. Very likely Sickles and Wiley had been a little glib in their promises to pay, what with their early enthusiasm and their ignorance that the bills would mount so high. It was a dilemma for which blame should not have been laid on any person, but rather on the anarchy concomitant with war. Sickles was filled with a passionate determination to lead his troops into battle come what may, and to him any other consideration was of small consequence. Employing all his genius for persuasion, he sought to coax the creditors to be patient in the assurance that the government would pay the bills when it got around to it.

The answer was no. The creditors wanted cash on the barrelhead.

At this critical moment, a disastrous event came obliquely to his aid. On July 21st was fought the battle of Bull Run, and when routed Federal soldiers came streaming into the capital with fearful stories that the powerful rebels would surely advance on Washington, Secretary Cameron in panic looked around for more men. Any men. Even men encumbered by debt. He bethought himself of Sickles' brigade up there in Staten Island, and sent an order: Come.

Finally, on July 22nd, 1861—three full months after recruiting had begun—a chastened Excelsior Brigade broke camp and entrained for Washington. Brigadier General Sickles had won his first battle of the War Between the States.[25]

In so doing he had lost an old friend. Captain William Wiley was left in New York with angry merchants waving bills in his face. Wiley gave out a statement describing just how he felt about it:

> So he [Sickles] marched off with three regiments, and paraded them before Lincoln, and said he had done all this out of his own pocket. There were piles of judgments against him in the offices. He had no more to do with the brigade than the receiving of the recruits.
>
> It was fifteen months before I could get a settlement. He left me in the lurch. I called a meeting of the creditors at the Astor House . . . and they passed some resolutions to ask the Secretary of War to pay the bills . . . I left him [Sickles] on account of it; denounced him then, and have done so since.[26]

All this may have been true, or partly true. But the real wonder is that by July 22nd Sickles had any regiments left to march off with.

CHAPTER XIII

The Unmaking of a General

In Washington, the Excelsior Brigade was assigned space in a meadow just outside the city, and work began toward transforming what was still a motley force of willing but untrained men into something resembling soldiers. It soon became clear that the immediate Confederate threat had subsided and that the enemy was posting his forces somewhere a few miles south of the Potomac.

Sickles was proud of his men; he had a hunch that if he had had the opportunity to lead them at Bull Run, things might have been different. He later wrote, "It is not for me to say how the fortunes of that day might have been influenced by the presence of five thousand well-drilled troops, officers and men, all well known to each other, and animated by a strong *esprit de corps.*" [1]

This was written in a moment of exaggeration. He had something less than 5000 men. [2] They were not well-drilled and there is some doubt about their *esprit de corps* after what they had been through.

But in the late summer of 1861, Sickles had reason to feel that he was bouncing back from oblivion. He was a brigadier general with a star on his shoulders, a salary of $300 a month and forage for four horses, and almost unlimited authority over five regiments. His provisional nomination as brigadier would have to be confirmed by the Senate before it was a solid reality, but he had no doubt that could be managed. For him—a man often touched by the humors of chance—the war had come at a moment most opportune.

His sojourn near Washington enabled him to continue an easy-going familiarity with the White House which had persisted through two previous administrations. This doubtless would have come about in any case, since he had a strong affinity for the Executive Mansion as a place he had hoped—perhaps still hoped—to occupy some day, but it was aided by his close friendship with that astonishing man, Henry Wikoff.

Wikoff, then forty-eight, had inherited a considerable fortune and spent most of his adult life in an uninterrupted international quest for pleasure, which to him meant intimacy with the high and mighty mixed with a generous dash of intrigue. Personally attractive, urbane and courtly, he was the arch-dilettante of his age. Of him, John Forney took a deep breath and said:

> Ranging through all society, he can talk of love, law, literature and war; can describe the rulers and thinkers of his time, can gossip of courts and cabinets, of the boudoir and the salon, of commerce and the church . . . of Dickens and Thackeray . . . of Lincoln and Stanton, of Buchanan and Pierce, of the North and the South, of the opera and the theater, of General Sickles and Tammany Hall, and of the inner life of almost every capital of the world.[3]

A strange man, Wikoff, touched with genius but also touched with scalawaggery. He had been on excellent terms with Buchanan, and even though the Democrats had been swept out of office he saw no reason why his pleasant visits at the White House should cease. He had been introduced to Mrs. Lincoln, and that lady had immediately succumbed to his charm. The President's wife, keenly sensitive to malicious newspaper gibes about her Western background, was uneasy and insecure in her post as First Lady, and felt need of a social counsellor. This was Wikoff's forte, and he moved into a position at Mary Lincoln's right hand.[4]

In this position he was anything but hampered by being one
of the few friends of the almost friendless James Gordon Bennett, whose New York *Herald* was almost as influential as its
proprietor was hated. Bennett, of whom it was said that he
would sell his soul for a news scoop, had long since inaugurated
his policy of installing news spies or tipsters at key spots—persons who mingled socially in the political centers, were not
known as newspaper representatives, and could therefore pick
up unguarded gossip and news beats which known reporters
would never learn. In Washington, one of Bennett's most valuable spies was Wikoff. Bennett, never above prostituting his
journal for what he considered a desirable end, had earlier been
scornful of Lincoln, but now he took a new tack and backed the
President. More particularly, the *Herald* began covering the
activities of the First Lady with the fondest solicitude, dwelling
on her intelligence and beauty, warmth of heart, and taste in
clothing. Wikoff was behind most of this flattery. When she confided in the Chevalier, Mrs. Lincoln was moving into danger, a
fact that soon was to be made shockingly clear.[5]

But Wikoff's propensities for mischief were then unsuspected
and he was constantly in the White House. With the Chevalier
installed there, Sickles was not far behind. The new brigadier
general was a frequent caller at the Executive Mansion, where
his wit and sparkling personality quickly won the friendship of
the First Lady.

Sickles also took the opportunity to thank President Lincoln
for his support when things looked blackest, and to give his
views on the prosecution of the war. Cordial relations already
existed between the President and the Democrat who had so
stoutly opposed his election. Lincoln liked any man who could
gets things done and wanted to fight. The busy chief executive
took the time to review the Excelsior Brigade, standing in front
of the White House with Sickles as the regiments passed by. "I
have seldom seen a finer military show," commented N. P.
Willis in a piece about it in the *Home Journal*. "Sickles is a soldier, and a brave one . . . He has plenty of talent, everybody

knows, and is not likely (with so much at stake) to outrun discretion in his zeal." [6] This was a fairly canny observation, and Willis, a friend of Sickles, was thoughtful enough to send him a clipping of the article.

The War Department, whose unpretentious structure was just west of the White House—and within shouting distance of the old Stockton Mansion—was another frequent port of call for Sickles. Here his friend Stanton was now serving as legal counsel to Secretary of War Cameron. Stanton likewise was a Democrat, but his staunch service to the Union in the waning months of the feeble Buchanan administration was not forgotten, and he was soon to enter the highest councils of the new regime.

After almost three months near Washington, Sickles' brigade moved its camp in October to a spot on the Potomac in Maryland just opposite Acquia Creek, where it became part of the division commanded by Brigadier General Joseph Hooker. The meeting between the small, handsome Sickles and the tall, handsome Hooker was a significant one, the beginning of an acquaintance that would follow a rough road to friendship.

Hooker, a man of violent impulses, had come within an inch of dismissal from West Point for insubordination. In the Mexican War he had got into hot water because of his ill-natured criticism of General Scott. If old Scott had had the last word, he would not have got so much as a lieutenancy in the Union army, but Lincoln needed men who knew something about running a war, and he took on the big man with the schoolgirl complexion. Personally brave, often genial, Hooker was the prey of vanity, hot temper, and unrestrained ambition. He had the traditional West Pointer's contempt for political generals, and when two such forceful individuals as he and Sickles collided, the chips were certain to fly until they had established some method of peaceful coexistence, if such a thing were possible.

Their first quarrel came when Hooker reprimanded Sickles for allowing his brigade to take too many ambulance wagons on what was supposed to be strictly a foot-soldier training march in Charles County. Stung, Sickles protested over Hooker's head to General George B. McClellan, the young Galahad who had recently been elevated to command the newly-organized Army of the Potomac. Hooker's wry rejoinder to McClellan was, "In my official intercourse with veteran politicians suddenly raised to high military rank, I have found it necessary to observe their correspondence with especial circumspection." [7]

Sickles was doing a good deal of anxious shuttling between camp and Washington. His nomination as brigadier general would come up before the Senate for confirmation in the not distant future, and he had learned that although the President was on his side, a number of influential Senators were opposed to him. Some of this opposition arose from personal or political spite against a prominent Democrat whose reputation was not unblemished, but there was also some suspicion of his loyalty. There were Republican Senators who feared that a man such as Sickles, who had long hobnobbed in Congress with the Southern fire-eaters, might march his brigade over on the side of Jefferson Davis at the first opportunity. [8]

Alarmed, Sickles took every step he could to win over the opposition. He went to General McClellan—himself a Democrat —and got the Young Napoleon's recommendation. Via Wikoff, he managed to get approving notice in the one-time enemy sheet, Bennett's *Herald*. [9] He made frequent trips to Washington, where he visited the Senators who held the dreaded power of shearing him of his stars, and gave them earnest assurances of his loyalty and worthiness. He buttered Hooker by writing him that the public applauded his efforts to break the Confederate blockade of the lower Potomac, and adding, "The President spoke warmly and enthusiastically of you." [10] He was not above flaunting his acquaintance with Lincoln in the face of his commander under the guise of relaying a compliment. In fact, as was usual in his crisis, he sought the help of any person who could aid him, and Hooker was one of these. Hooker happened to be a close friend of Senator Nesmith of Oregon, and Sickles asked him to intercede with the Senator—something Hooker was not inclined to do. In a letter to Nesmith explaining his failure to come to Washington, Hooker wrote that he would have made the journey "if I had anyone to leave my command with except Sickles, with whom I would expect to have it dishonored less than twelve hours after leaving." [11]

This was hardly a just appraisal, for Sickles, with all his gadding about and string-pulling, had real affection for his Excelsiors and was determined that they should distinguish themselves in the coming conflict. His own military training and experience were sorely lacking, but he was a quick learner and he possessed the qualities of a born leader. His men admired and respected him. With Hooker and the Senate he was in for trouble, but he was not too busy to send fond letters home to his parents and to Laura, now a pretty little girl of seven. A delightful note he received from Laura, dated October 27th, shows that the general and politician did not forget he was also a father:

> Many thanks my darling Papa, for your affectionate letters. I hope dear Papa that you will write just as often as you can, we are all so happy when your letters are received . . . We have not seen poor old Nero for five days, and we are afraid that he has been killed. Poor dear old Nero!
>
> Mamma, Grandmamma and I, spent the day with Grandma Sickles, on Wednesday, and had a very pleasant time.
>
> How very fine your soldiers and horses must appear, and how glad I should be to see them. Will you let us all come to see you one of these days? Grandma Sickles says she intends to make you a visit.
>
> Oh how happy we shall be if you can come to us at Christmas! Accept an affectionate embrace and 10,000 kisses dear good Papa, from your Laura.[12]

Was the unhappy Teresa sitting at her daughter's shoulder as she wrote? There are no letters between Sickles and Teresa to be found in this period, and it may be that they seldom corresponded. But to his father and mother he wrote frequently. Elderly Susan Sickles replied to one letter with motherly solicitude and knowledge of her son's failings: "I must close my letter by saying may God bless you and trusting you will not be too venturesome in your projects," and adding:

> Teresa tells me you have not the Shirts I mean the night Shirts I made for you. I think you had better send for them . . . I present you with a locket with my miniature and my hair. I request you to wear it in your pocket as a protection and a Sheald.[13]

Difficulties of several kinds were now looming so ominously that the surprising thing is that Sickles had time to write at all.

One of them was in his own beloved Excelsior Brigade. These men, when they had been rescued from their misery at Staten Island, had felt that the time for action was near. Now the sad truth was brought home to them that war could be a slow, uneventful, wearisome business of watching, waiting, and training. The dashing young General McClellan was a great one for riding about hell-for-leather as though great doings were in the offing, but nothing ever seemed to come of it. His vast Army of the Potomac was living far too literally up to its name and sitting squarely on the Potomac. The rebels were right over there across the river. They even had the nerve to plant batteries commanding the stream so that Union vessels had to run a gauntlet of solid shot and it was becoming harder to supply the capital. This outraged the aggressive Hooker, and he proposed to McClellan an ambitious plan to smash the offending batteries and relieve the humiliating Potomac blockade, but the plan died somewhere in a headquarters pigeonhole.[14]

Nothing happened. It slowly dawned on the disillusioned soldiers that trouncing the rebels was going to be no three-months outing. The way things were going it would take all winter—maybe even more.

On picket duty of quiet moonlit nights, Sickles' men heard rebel pickets just across the river. The Johnnies would bellow tauntingly, "How did you like Bull Run?" and the Union men would shout back, "How about Laurel Hill?" with the parley usually ending in a salvo of furious curses. To have the enemy so near and yet to be able to do nothing about it was frustrating and made them feel that something was fishy up there somewhere in the brass.[15]

So boredom grew, and with it grew dissension, bickering, and downright ugliness and insubordination. Frequently the men managed to smuggle in liquor. Young Joseph Twichell, chaplain of the Second Regiment, watched these portents uneasily.

"The use of rum is undoubtedly our worst evil among both officers and men," he wrote his father. "I have witnessed some disgraceful scenes of debauchery . . ."[16]

The situation became so serious that Sickles felt obliged to order two Massachusetts soldiers shot for disobedience. Morale was not improved when a bitter feud broke out between the Second Regiment's commander, hard-drinking Colonel George Hall, and the lieutenant colonel, H. J. Potter. The two men quarreled incessantly, and junior officers took sides in the argument so that the regiment was split in spiteful animosity.[17]

"I pray God," Twichell wrote, "that we may have fighting enough outside, to leave no room for it within."[18]

Early in November, Hooker's division had moved some eighteen miles downriver to Budd's Ferry, where the waiting began all over again. Here Sickles' friend Charles Graham, colonel in command of the Fourth Regiment, decided that as long as action would not come, he would create it. Without a by-your-leave from any superior, Graham took four hundred picked men across the Potomac one night, moved into rebel territory, shot two pickets, burned some forage, made a reconnaissance of enemy positions, and returned with two secessionists as prisoners.

Sickles, who was panting for action himself, was pleased at Graham's unauthorized sortie. Hooker, when he received the report on it, was less so. He wrote McClellan that since the foray had involved no losses, he would not censure Graham. But McClellan, outraged at the cheek of the young colonel from Brooklyn, ordered him placed under immediate arrest[19]—an action serving as proof to Graham's adherents that that McClellan fellow didn't want to fight.

On November 10th occurred an event that temporarily relieved the camp's disgruntlement. Thaddeus Sobieski Constantine Lowe, the Yankee aeronaut who was known as "the Professor" although he had only a grammar-school education, came down the Potomac to Hooker's camp with his balloon. Since all attempts to get official permission to move across the Potomac had failed, Hooker had decided that it might at least be instructive to soar aloft and view the Confederate batteries and positions from on high, and he had requested Lowe's services.

The naval tug containing the balloon, its equipment and staff was brought safely into the mouth of Mattawoman Creek, and Hooker strolled down there with Sickles to watch the proceedings. Helpers started the gas generators and the big silk bag slowly began to fill, disclosing a huge portrait of George Washington on its side.[20]

To Sickles, always fascinated with the new and adventurous, it was unthinkable to remain landbound while this mighty sphere explored the skies. When Professor Lowe took off early that evening, Sickles was with him in the swaying basket. The atmosphere was clear, and masses of enemy campfires could be seen at Dumfries and Occoquan as well as farther beyond the river, showing that the Confederates were there in considerable force. Sickles was so intrigued with this new method of reconnaissance that he went up repeatedly in ensuing weeks, recording the locations of the enemy batteries across the river. The rebels, refusing to allow this observation to go unprotested, frequently blazed away fruitlessly at the balloon with their cannon. General Sickles was so magnificently attired in a well-tailored uniform glittering with the insignia of his rank that the balloon men commented about it among themselves.[21]

In December, James Gordon Bennett exploded a bombshell when his *Herald* published long and verbatim excerpts from Lincoln's forthcoming message to Congress—a document supposedly secret until its delivery. There was a howl of rage from competing newspapers, and before long the House Judiciary

Committee began to inquire into the question of just how such sacred stuff could leak out. Bennett blandly suggested that he had made shrewd surmises, but the feeling was general that there was a snooper in the White House. Soon things began to grow a little warm for Henry Wikoff.

While this pot was coming to a boil, the inefficient Simon Cameron was removed from his post as Secretary of War, where he had succeeded mainly in creating chaos, and was replaced by Edwin Stanton. For Sickles this was an immensely cheering event. He signalized it by rechristening his uneasy village of tents Camp Stanton. The elevation of his good friend to head the War Department could hardly fail to advance his military fortunes—always providing the Senate would confirm his nomination as brigadier. This was a growing worry. In Wikoff he had a loyal ally and Washington informant, and on January 30th, 1862, he addressed him a chatty letter touching on this and other matters:

My Dear Wikoff:

What is the news? Of course I am exceedingly anxious to know what the Senate is doing . . . Did Mrs. L. think of the Senators? Remember me to her very cordially.

. . . Perhaps the Maryland Senators—Kennedy and Pearce —oppose me because I do not hunt for runaway negroes in this part of Maryland, while Wilson opposes me because he thinks I do occupy myself in negro catching. The Maryland Senators rather incline towards the South & perhaps sympathize with the feelings in this part of the State which is not only against the Government but irritated by the presence and annoyances of a large body of troops.

Everywhere in the Brigade—except a fraction of the 3rd Regt —there is *the sharpest possible solicitude* for my confirmation, a feeling which is shared by the Squadron in the river near me. When the news comes their bunting will be all out for a holiday & my camps will ring with huzzas.

. . . Did you have an opportunity to sound Stanton about

giving me "a Chance"? Nothing is so ruinous to an army as
doing nothing—it is as demoralizing as a defeat. My men have
been looking at the enemy and living in the mud for three
months. I cannot endure it much longer.

Faithfully Yrs. Sickles [22]

The letter hints that Sickles had sought the aid of Mrs. Lincoln, possibly in interceding with certain doubtful Senators.
And it makes it clear that in his eagerness for action and his
knowledge that his command was disintegrating through disuse,
Sickles was going over the head of General Hooker, over the
head of General McClellan, and appealing directly to Secretary
Stanton for "a chance" at the enemy.

His chance for action came soon, but against a different sort
of enemy. In Washington, Congressional suspicion in the mon-
strous *Herald* scoop was directed squarely at Wikoff, and the
Chevalier was subpoenaed to appear before the Judiciary Committee on February 10th. Before the Committee, Wikoff admitted he had telegraphed portions of Lincoln's message to the
Herald, but when it came to telling just how he had got his
hands on the document, he balked. He was, he said, "under obligation of strictest secrecy." [23] Thereupon the Sergeant-at-Arms
arrested him for contempt and he was clapped in the Old Capitol Prison—not an entirely new experience to Wikoff, but not
a pleasant one either.

It was widely believed that Wikoff, in his peculiar position
as White House majordomo and confidant, had wheedled the
document out of Mrs. Lincoln, and according to the newsman
Ben Perley Poore, "this opinion was confirmed when General
Sickles appeared as his counsel." [24]

The general, Poore said, "vibrated between Wikoff's place
of imprisonment, the White House and the residence of Mrs.
Lincoln's gardener, named Watt." This John Watt was a sly
scoundrel who had been head gardener for several years and
had somehow managed to hold his job even though he had been
accused of peculating White House funds before the Lincolns

arrived. Mary Lincoln's unsteadiness of judgment led her so far astray as to repose implicit faith in the man; she allowed him far more freedom around the executive mansion than one would expect for a gardener, and had once even taken him along as a companion on a trip to New York.[25]

Sickles worked energetically to save Wikoff and also Mrs. Lincoln from the consequences of this folly—so energetically that when the general was summoned before the Committee there was a lively clash and Sickles came close to following his crony to jail for contempt. But he managed to smooth the matter over with one of the most implausible explanations ever made outside of fiction. Watt was brought in as a witness and he solemnly clarified the whole business. He had happened to stroll through the White House library one day, he said, and he read portions of Lincoln's message, which lay open on the desk. The next day he repeated it to Wikoff. That was all there was to it.[26]

The Committee pronounced itself satisfied. Lincoln, it was said, had himself appeared before its members and asked them to "spare him disgrace." The only result of all these alarums was that Wikoff lost his pleasant position as Mrs. Lincoln's social counsellor and was ejected from the White House for good, and that John Watt was fired. The whole affair was conducted under heavy wraps, and no one ever explained how Watt could have such a marvelously retentive brain as to commit thousands of words to memory at a glance. It seems obvious that Watt lied and that Wikoff somehow got a copy of Lincoln's message and held it before him while he telegraphed it to New York. Whether he secured it with the knowledge or connivance of Mrs. Lincoln may be doubted if one is charitable.

The fishy aroma of this transaction lingers even after almost a century. While Sickles was "vibrating" between Wikoff, Watt, and the White House, he accomplished something that has never been officially explained. Since Watt emerged as the whipping boy in the affair, losing a position he prized dearly, Sickles must have exerted some unusual pressure on him to persuade him to testify as he did. Had Sickles managed to dredge up proof of some previous misdoing against the gardener, or had Watt been rewarded in some way for consenting to be the scapegoat? Sickles must have known all the answers, but he never disclosed them.

As for Wikoff, his status as the *Herald*'s Washington Paul Pry was finished, but in any case he had his freedom and no important person was compromised.

So Sickles, after paying a few more calls on various Senators, returned with some satisfaction to Camp Stanton, where he doffed his attorney's mantle and became a general again. But conditions at the camp had gone from bad to worse. Incessant rains had made the place "a floating sea of mud." [27] Sullen soldiers who for some reason had not been paid for two months were building corduroy roads so that subsistence could be brought in and they would not starve. Hooker was disgruntled because he had submitted to McClellan a plan for destroying the enemy batteries disclosed by the balloon observations, and nothing had come of it. The camp was surrounded by secessionist planters who cordially hated the men in blue and did their best to make life miserable for them, even refusing to sell them needed produce. When a group of these planters entered camp on a pass from Hooker to look for runaway slaves, and took a shot at a cowering negro without even asking his identity, Sickles angrily ordered the men to leave, and later got into a controversy with Hooker about it.[28]

Worse yet, the Hall-Potter feud had waxed into a campaign of bitterness and recrimination that infected the whole Second Regiment.

"The Col., Lt. Col. and numerous captains and lieutenants are under arrest," wrote Chaplain Twichell, "pending their trial on charges preferred the one against the other. Hate and envy rage implacably." Sadly the chaplain reflected, "I feel painfully at times the utter inadequacy of my own ministry to meet the needs of the occasion." [29]

Thousands of discouraged men, afflicted by a veritable disease of boredom, were turning their energies against each other.

No one could meet the needs of the occasion but General Mc-Clellan, by ordering some movement—any movement—against the enemy across the river. And McClellan, with his nervous apprehension that he was faced by insuperable forces, always found new reasons for delay even though Washington was complaining.

For Sickles, the cruelest blow of all fell when he received a letter from the Adjutant General in Washington dated March 20, 1862:

> Sir:
>
> The Senate having on the 17th instant negatived your appointment as Brigadier General of Volunteers, I am instructed by the Secretary of War to inform you that the President does hereby revoke it.[30]

Sickles had fallen in love with the stars on his shoulder straps. With some justification he felt he had earned them. But Hooker was not unhappy at losing the peppery brigadier whose pipeline to Washington had somehow failed him. Hooker promptly appointed Colonel Nelson Taylor of the Third Regiment to assume command of the Excelsior Brigade—a move that further infuriated Sickles and caused him to dispatch a bristling note to Hooker which read in part:

> I respectfully bring to the attention of the Brigadier General Commanding the Division the fact, of which I cannot believe him to be ignorant, that I am the Senior Colonel of the Brigade, having been mustered into service as Colonel of the 1st Regiment on the 29th of June, 1861, which muster was afterwards duly confirmed by the letter of appointment of the President of the United States.
>
> . . . Until superseded in command by a Brig. Genl. regularly assigned on duty with the Brigade, I respectfully claim that I am entitled to the command as the senior officer present.
>
> For these reasons I respectfully protest against Special Orders No. 132 as illegal, unauthorized and unjust. I shall obey him

—since obedience to superior authority is the first duty of a
soldier—and shall avail myself of the right to appeal for redress
to the General Commanding the Army.[31]

In fact, he went a good deal higher than the General Commanding. Although he was fuming, he addressed a temperate
letter to Lincoln himself, requesting that he be continued in
command. "I ask," he wrote, "to be permitted to vindicate at
the head of this column of brave and loyal men, the justice and
fitness of your generous confidence in conferring upon me the
distinction and responsibility of a high command." [32]

But Lincoln, however sympathetic he was, was too busy with
larger affairs to meddle in the quarrel. And from Hooker,
through his adjutant, Sickles got no sympathy at all:

General:

   I am directed by the Brigadier General Commanding the
Division to acknowledge your communication of this date, and
to inform you that Special Order No. 132 relieving you from
duty with the 2nd Brigade was issued advisedly.

   If in its operation, the Commanding General, to whom you
propose to address your protest, should find the order to be
"illegal," "unauthorized" and "unjust" he entertains no doubt
that it will be revoked.[33]

Unless some miracle could be arranged, Sickles was knocked
down to a colonel, and what was more discouraging, a colonel
without a command. His loyal colleague from the Navy Yard,
Colonel Graham, promptly resigned his command in protest.
The men in the ranks were likewise indignant. One of them,
Felix Brannigan, an Irish-born private in Graham's regiment,
wrote his sister heatedly: "I suppose that before this you have
heard that we have lost both Sickles and our Colonel, they have
been most shamefully treated by the War Department. Political
influence I doubt not was bro't to bear against the former, and
the latter resigned in consequence. We all deplore the loss, and
hope for their restoration." [34]

To heap further weight on Sickles' burden of misfortune, the immovable Army of the Potomac was finally on the move. Confronted at last by a flat order for action from Lincoln, McClellan was shifting his forces by water in a bold flanking operation designed to get at Richmond from the Peninsula of Virginia. There would be action galore, and Sickles would miss out on it.

But he could never accept defeat. He issued a stirring order of farewell to his soldiers, then packed off for Washington, intending to work the miracle. The *National Republican* of April 9th carried a brief item concealing a world of determination and purpose:

"Gen. Sickles is at Willard's."

CHAPTER XIV

On to Richmond!

In Washington, Sickles plunged into feverish activity, angrily feeling himself a victim of personal animosity and political intrigue. His friend Thomas Francis Meagher's nomination as brigadier general had been approved by a unanimous vote of the Senate in February, and was not Meagher likewise a strong Democrat? He was, but one difference was that Meagher had never consorted publicly with prostitutes, had never shot anyone or taken to his bosom a wife who was cast out of society. Sickles regarded all these matters as irrelevant and having no bearing on the question of his fitness for important command.

Furthermore, as he well knew, one potent segment of the opposition came from Governor Morgan and other influential Republicans in Albany who were infuriated at his success in stealing the brigade from New York State sponsorship and smuggling it into the army via the back door as United States Volunteers. The wires had been burning between Albany and Washington with appeals to Republican Senators to slap this Democratic upstart down once and for all, and they had been effective.

Sickles deftly began pulling every string in sight to salvage his future in the army. He felt reasonably sure he could persuade Lincoln to renominate him if there was fair assurance that the Senate would confirm him. On the Senate he now trained all his batteries of logic and cajolery. He worked energetically on Senator Henry Wilson, the Abolitionist head of the Military Affairs Committee. He also importuned Senators Wade, Fessenden, Grimes, and others of the Republican group who had opposed him.[1] From his father in New York he received a letter full of sympathy and indignation in which George Sickles said:

> I know that the Republican Party could not act towards you as you have acted towards the Nation . . . To me it seems cruel that you should be willing to sacrifice everything—even life itself, and be refused the poor privilege by a set of drivelling apes . . .[2]

George Sickles also passed along encouraging news. Horace Greeley, the eccentric of the *Tribune,* was circulating a petition asking that Sickles be renominated and was getting many signers, one of them being William Cullen Bryant, the editor of the *Evening Post* which had for so long assailed him. Greeley, who had strongly supported Lincoln ever since the Chicago convention and whose rallying cry, "Onward to Richmond!" had become a byword, wielded considerable influence with the administration and should be a useful ally.

Surprisingly, even Bennett's *Herald* threw a few posies in Sickles' direction. It mentioned a minor reconnaissance he had made into Virginia with part of his men early in April and said that on this assignment "he had won the admiration of the portion of the brigade that accompanied him." [3] When one recalls the hatred that had persisted between Bennett and Sickles for several years, culminating in a libel suit against the publisher, this kindliness is astonishing.

There had already been signs that the Sickles-Bennett war was ended. The publisher had been gentle with Sickles during the Key trial, and even when the Congressman was reunited with his wife. Possibly the fact that Bennett and Sickles had in Wikoff a mutual friend had helped to smooth the waters. Now that Wikoff was cast out of the White House, perhaps Bennett, who viewed almost everybody from a standpoint of their importance as a news source, felt that Sickles, with his familiarity with the Lincolns, might be useful.[4]

As for Sickles, his reverses since the Key affair had sobered
him. He needed every friend he could get. If he took a mistress
now—as he doubtless did, being Daniel Sickles—it was quietly,
with discretion. Previously he had been satisfied to have Democratic newspapers on his side. Now he wanted them all, and
from this point on he took the most delicate care to foster
friendly relations with reporters and editors. The press, which
had ruined him, could also save him, and that included James
Gordon Bennett.

In his fight to win back his brigadier's appointment, he was
far from friendless. Lincoln admired a fighter, and was well
aware of the New Yorker's abilities. Furthermore, the President
could not blink the fact that in accepting the Excelsior Brigade
as United States Volunteers he was partly responsible for bringing the wrath of New York Republicans on Sickles' head. Lincoln would do what he could.

Stanton was a solid ally. The new Secretary of War was an
expert in duplicity, and was even then sneering at Lincoln behind his back, but toward Sickles he was unfailingly loyal.
Sickles also succeeded in winning the support of Reverdy Johnson, who had been Butterworth's attorney in the Key killing,
and the influential Marylander was exerting pressure on the
Senators from his own state as well as others.[5] These were hopeful signs, but the issue yet hung on a razor's edge and there was
nothing for Sickles to do but make friends and wait for the decision. Pride entered into the question of whether he was to be
a brigadier general, but there was more than that. To him it
was a question of simple justice, and the answer would decide
whether he was to be forever beaten down and exiled from opportunity because of past sins.

The Capitol was still abuilding, with its unfinished dome
open to bats and starlings, but in almost every other way Washington had changed sharply in the few years since the Sickleses
had dispensed hospitality at the Stockton Mansion. The Dolly
Madison house just across the square had been taken over by
McClellan as his headquarters, but now the Young Napoleon

was off to the wars and the place was quiet. The former Club House, where Key had died, was now the residence of Secretary Seward. At Willard's bar, formerly a sanctuary for legislators, solons could hardly find room what with all the contractors, promoters, and officers in blue lined up in excited and not too optimistic discussion of the new move against Richmond. The Southern chivalry had flown in a body, and although there was still a feeble attempt at social life, it had dwindled sadly. Mrs. Rose O'Neal Greenhow, who had so often entertained the Sickleses in the palmy days, was now an inmate of the Old Capitol Prison, having spied so successfully for the rebels that it was said she was largely responsible for the Union disaster at Bull Run. Mrs. Philip Phillips, who had warned Sickles to be "a good boy," was also in custody as a Confederate spy. Senator Gwin himself had been arrested for disloyalty. The capital, so naively confident before Bull Run, was now pervaded by uneasiness and gloom in the face of a war that loomed as a far more serious matter than anyone had foreseen.

But Sickles, ever the optimist, could not conceive that the Union might be defeated. He had his own problems to solve, and meanwhile his friend Edwin Forrest was in town presenting Hamlet, Lear, Richard III, and Macbeth. Sickles must have enjoyed these entertainments and also dined with the tragedian while waiting to see what would happen.

On April 25th, the first hurdle was gained. On Stanton's official recommendation, the President renominated Sickles for a brigadiership, and one of the newspapers, which persisted in calling him a general although he was actually only a colonel, remarked that "Gen. Sickles was at the Capitol yesterday in very good spirits." [6] There still remained the question of whether he could swing the Senate. He did not fail to dispatch a letter of thanks to Greeley for his help, saying, "The expression of your confidence in me has impressed favorably those in authority— especially I may mention Senator Wade . . . It is right you should know that the confidence of the President and Sec. of War has not been impaired . . ." [7]

Greeley deserved thanks. On May 13, the Senate confirmed
the nomination by the painfully close vote of 19–18. The colonel
was a brigadier again by the grace of one Senator. When the
news trickled down to the Virginia Peninsula, where the war had
suddenly become a very bloody affair indeed, Hooker may not
have applauded it but Sickles' own Excelsior Brigade cheered.

"Immense enthusiasm was aroused yesterday by the news of
Gen. Sickles' confirmation," wrote Chaplain Twichell. "We will
give him a rousing welcome when he comes." [8]

Twichell, a young man of extraordinary intelligence and
analytical ability, had felt some doubt early in 1861 when he
first realized he was to serve under the beclouded ex-Congress-
man. A year had passed—a year during which he had been in close
contact with his commander and had seen him beset by all manner of woes—and he was completely won over. He had not
merely resigned himself to the general's peculiarities but had
become a loyal and devoted partisan. So had at least two others
of the regimental chaplains, Father Joseph O'Hagan and the
Rev. C. H. A. Bulkley. So had the overwhelming majority of
the brigade's soldiers. Whatever his other failings, Sickles possessed a power to captivate men, to inspire them with real affection, to kindle in them that spark of camaraderie mingled with
respect and obedience that can only be kindled by the born
leader.

While Sickles had been winning his brigadier's battle, the
Army of the Potomac had engaged in more sanguinary conflicts
that had the newspapers agog. General McClellan had landed
his men at Fortress Monroe, on the tip of the Peninsula, and
had begun an advance toward Richmond. He had lost precious
weeks in besieging the Confederate stronghold at Yorktown
until the enemy abandoned it. In a somewhat confused pursuit,
Hooker's division was in the van, and when the rebels turned
to give battle on May 5th near Williamsburg, Fighting Joe assaulted them without immediate support. His men fought val-
iantly, but so did the enemy, and help arrived not a moment too

soon, for his division was exhausted and bleeding. Reinforcements saved the day. That night the rebels relinquished Williamsburg and continued their retreat toward Richmond.

In this costly engagement the Excelsior Brigade, led by Colonel Taylor, had bravely taken its first fierce baptism of fire and had suffered fearsome losses. In its five regiments, 772 men were killed or wounded.[9] "The slain unburied . . . lay in heaps," Twichell wrote. "I shall remember it long." [10]

When Sickles rejoined his brigade at Bottom's Bridge, he found it to be officially the Second Brigade of Hooker's Division of the Third Army Corps, led by grizzled old General Samuel Heintzelman. He received a warm welcome from his officers and men, including his admiring young aide-de-camp, Lieutenant J. L. Palmer. The restored commander issued a prideful order to his soldiers announcing his return and praising their valor in the ringing phrases at which he was so facile:

> . . . At Williamsburg you won imperishable renown. As long as this war has a place in history, the courage, constancy and steadiness which you displayed in that unequal combat will make the 5th of May memorable in our annals. The enemy has felt your power, and the nation appreciates your worth.
>
> Yet greater achievements are within our grasp. We are near Richmond . . . Richmond, the capital of the enemy, must fall before the invincible Army of the Potomac . . .[11]

Sickles, the commander whose only battles had been against secessionist planters and Senators, was now leading men who had had a strong taste of war. During the previous year, the Excelsiors had cursed their stay at Camp Scott, hated their sojourn near Washington, and abominated their mud-hole at Camp Stanton, and now finally they were engaged in the business they had enlisted for. The reality was far different from what they had pictured it, and some of them were not sure they liked it even as well as Camp Stanton. Nevertheless they had toughened and matured. It was sad to bury old friends in hostile soil, but at any rate the enemy was giving precious ground and the cocky rebs were laughing on the other side of their faces now. McClellan, two months earlier an object of doubt and suspicion in Washington because of his "slows," had become the toast of the North. Richmond was now menaced instead of Washington. Newspapers speculated as to whether McClellan would take the Confederate capital or whether he might be beaten to the honor by General McDowell, advancing from the direction of Fredericksburg.[12] Almost daily there were wild rumors that Richmond *had* been taken, and joy was unrestrained north of the Mason-Dixon Line.

After Williamsburg, the Army of the Potomac pursued the retreating rebels for some forty miles without serious opposition. By the end of May some of the Yanks got within a few miles of Richmond—close enough to hear the ringing of the city's church bells. In these movements, Sickles became acquainted with commanders who were later to loom large in his destiny. There was George Gordon Meade, the nervous and irascible Pennsylvanian. There was Daniel Butterfield, a dapper little non-West Pointer from New York State who waxed his mustache to needle-sharp points. There was Oliver Otis Howard, a handsome young New Englander who had studied for the clergy but had been diverted from this calling by a West Point appointment; and many others. On the other side, doing their best to smash the Union advance, were former friends with whom Sickles had often dined and politicked in Washington— Howell Cobb, Roger Pryor, Lawrence Branch, all of them Confederate brigadiers.

With their backs to the wall, the rebels came back on May 31st with a furious offensive near Fair Oaks Station, some six miles east of Richmond. For two days the Union forces more than held their own in a battle with frightful casualties. When it was over, many Federal officers felt they had won a victory and wondered why they were not allowed to follow it up.

It was here that Sickles had his first encounter with the front-line realities of warfare, and he acquitted himself admirably with his brigade. A brigadier general's job in this man's war was anything but a post of safety involving only the thoughtful scrutiny of maps in some hut well behind the lines. He was expected to be out there with his men among the whining minie balls, to inspire them with his presence and with his own contempt for danger. In the heat of the second day's action he sent Colonel Hall with the Second Regiment in a savage and successful bayonet charge, and handled his forces with enough skill to win a commendation from the exacting Hooker.[13] One correspondent was so impressed as to write:

> Gen. Sickles had several narrow escapes; he was always to be found in the thickest of the fight. Had those gifted Senators who refused to confirm his nomination, but witnessed the enthusiasm of his troops when serving under him, and his military qualifications for the office, they would do penance until re-elected.[14]

During the assault, the Excelsiors captured a horse-drawn omnibus bearing the legend "Columbus Hotel, Richmond, Va.," which the rebels had used as an ambulance. Delighted, a lieutenant drove it to brigade headquarters and presented it to Sickles for his personal use. Sickles had a better idea. He sent it on to his corps commander, profane old General Heintzelman, with a suggestion that when he reached Richmond, he patronize the Columbus Hotel.

"It seems that those damned fellows of Sickles have got into Richmond already," Heintzelman guffawed, "and are keeping hotel." [15]

There was no doubt at all in anybody's mind that Richmond was the next stop. Young General Howard had his horse shot under him and his left arm badly wounded, but stayed with his brigade through the crisis and had the arm amputated later. General Philip Kearny had lost his right arm in the Mexican War, and the two afterward had a mutual joke, saying that they needed only one pair of gloves between them.[16] But the aftermath of the battle was anything but a joking matter. One officer recalled that the stench of the dead in the summer heat

"was so strong that it caused vomiting among our sturdy em-
ployes, accustomed to care for the sick." [17] Medical care was
shockingly inadequate. Hundreds of wounded, some of them
with wounds crawling with maggots, were loaded like cordwood
in stifling boxcars headed for the hospitals at the rear, and many
died en route. Men who had come through battle unscathed
fell prey to heat, bad water, dysentery, and fever. Chaplain
Twichell was appalled at the suffering and horror all around
him, and only his sense of duty and the rightness of his cause
sustained him. He wrote his father:

> I think of you at home a great deal now . . . Never was it so
> inviting or so dear, or sweet to remember. Yet, I know not what
> could induce me to leave here now. I wish to witness the "great
> day" which will blow the trumpet of freedom for the oppressed,
> and proclaim to the world that the Republic is not a failure.[18]

With death a commonplace and burial a constant chore, a
covey of civilian embalmers had descended on the army, plying
their trade in shacks and tents behind the lines. Some of them
were not above promoting their wares to the living, suggesting
to soldiers the advantages of making advance arrangements for
the embalming and shipment home of their bodies rather than
to lie in a nameless battlefield grave. Prices varied from twenty
dollars for the embalming of a private up to a hundred dollars
for officers, depending on rank.[19]

As always in war, the ridiculous accompanied the tragic. A
young Excelsior man named Rednor was brought in with a
painful leg wound, and to forget his misery he could think of
nothing better than to bring out his fiddle and squeak out a gay
jig, not noticing that three New Hampshire men were being
buried a few yards away. And there was the affair of the stray
cow. Soldiers with fever needed milk, and the surgeons speedily
appropriated the animal when it wandered into camp. But
McClellan's order was to respect rebel property, and when the
owner came with a provost guard, the cow had to be returned.
Nor would the rebel sell the cow. Nor would he sell any milk.

The commanding general's chivalry might be admirable, but it seemed extreme when it caused men to die.[20]

After Fair Oaks there was a three-week lull while McClellan temporized and pondered the injustice of Washington in expecting him to attack an enemy which he now believed greatly outnumbered him. This was not so, the direct opposite being true, but the belief was fixed in the young general's mind. With operations at a standstill there was opportunity for social life among the officers, in which the gregarious Sickles was in his element. He was so thoroughly at home in any gathering that he was already one of the best-known of the brigadiers. A trio who caught his fancy were Frenchmen of royal blood, the deaf Prince de Joinville and his two nephews, the Comte de Paris and the Duc de Chartres, the latter two known by their non-Gallic comrades as Captain Parry and Captain Chatters.[21] Exiled by Napoleon III, they had offered their services to the Union cause and had become members of McClellan's staff. With his passable French, Sickles knew better than to call them Parry and Chatters. He got along famously with all of them and particularly with the tall young Comte de Paris, pretender to the throne of France.[22] It would have taken even more than Sickles' vivid imagination to conceive that one day in another world he would be pushing the young count to seat himself on the throne Napoleon had vacated.

Meanwhile, there were the inevitable reconnaissances, and on one of them amiable young Lieutenant Palmer, Sickles' aide-de-camp, ran squarely into a rebel outpost before he knew it. He was riddled with bullets, but his mates managed to carry his body back to camp. Sickles came out of his tent, moved almost to tears at the loss of his faithful subaltern, and, in Twichell's words, "mourned as for a son." [23]

McClellan, who had received some reinforcements and was pleading for more, finally moved on June 24th in an effort to push the enemy into the defensive works of Richmond itself. As part of an ambitious offensive, Hooker sent Generals Sickles and Grover into the attack along the Williamsburg Road. Press-

ing forward through mud in a soaking rain, the men in blue
met peppery resistance but were making sizeable gains when a
baffling order arrived from McClellan directing them to withdraw to their defenses. Hooker, despite his rage at this incomprehensible sacrifice of hard-won ground, relayed the order to
his subordinates.

Sickles, filled with the ardor of a successful attack, was furious. He sent back an aide to report that he was driving the
enemy and protesting the order to retire. But Hooker curtly
repeated the command and the men were withdrawn.

Two hours later McClellan arived. When he learned of the
earlier successes he ordered the attack repeated. Once more
Sickles sent his brigade forward, this time with artillery support, but now the rebels had stiffened and although the advance was continued it was at the cost of heavy losses. A tragic
error had occurred somewhere along the chain of command,
and the engagement ended indecisively. It was McClellan's last
offensive move against Richmond, so tantalizing near and yet so
far away.[24]

For the Confederates had made good use of the time given
them. Stonewall Jackson, after soundly defeating the Union
General Banks in the Shenandoah, had made a quick march to
the beleaguered Richmond area. The rebels, now led by
Robert E. Lee, performed a military miracle; they left Richmond thinly protected and fell hard on the Union right at
Mechanicsville, sending it rolling back. Hooker and Kearny,
fighters both, were almost mutinous in their rage at McClellan.
They begged to be allowed to drive for Richmond, but Little
Mac said no. Confederate records later revealed that their capital was so sparsely defended that a determined assault could
hardly have failed to take it.

Instead, the Army of the Potomac, cleanly outgeneraled, was
driven into retreat by a foe considerably inferior in numbers.
In the bitter Seven Days fighting, the Federals held their own
at Gaines Mill, Glendale, and White Oak Swamp, and yet the
order was to fall back, fall back. The Northern newspapers, so

prone to regard the war as a sort of fairy-tale pursuit of fleeing rebels, refused to give credence to the thought that the knightly McClellan was beaten. It was even hinted for the hundredth time that Richmond had actually fallen and that the War Department "for reasons no doubt satisfactory" was withholding news of the triumph.[25]

The men of the Army of the Potomac knew better. The easy promise of "Richmond in one more push" had gone glimmering, and what had seemed sure victory was now very close to utter disaster.

During all this fighting the Excelsior Brigade, though steadily reduced by deaths, wounds and illness, had been forged into a body of hard-bitten, battle-wise soldiers educated in the necessities of war and in the tricks of self-preservation. Colonels Hall and Potter, while still far from friendly, had no time for their old bickerings and both had emerged as intrepid leaders. Sickles himself had gained in stature. Newspaper reports might be fanciful, but Chaplain Twichell had watched his commander with an eye grown mature and discerning.

"Gen. Sickles is among us all the time—at home among his men and his men feel confidence in him," he wrote his father, later adding that the general "is brave as a lion and is much admired for his judgment. He has the making of a first class soldier in him which circumstances will not fail to develop." [26]

But McClellan was retreating—a skilful retreat, it was called, but a retreat nevertheless. Enormous quantities of stores were burned to prevent their falling into rebel hands, and large numbers of wounded were left behind with their surgeons to be captured by the advancing gray hosts. The Army of the Potomac hurled back the last determined Confederate assault at Malvern Hill, then retired to Harrison's Landing on the James to wait and see what could be retrieved from the wreckage.

Twichell was only voicing the thoughts of a multitude of grim men when he pondered "the 30,000 corpses we leave behind us" and asked for what purpose they had been sacrificed.

"I could not help a feeling of rebellion against the fate that forces the abandonment of ground that cost so much blood and was made so sacred," he mourned, staggered at the ruin of all his—and the Union's—hopes. ". . . When I think of how grand our army was last winter, and of how much it has since cost in men and money, and how little it has been made to accomplish, and of its present condition . . . I am persuaded that something or somebody is all wrong." [27]

CHAPTER XV

Backward from Richmond

Strongly entrenched at Harrison's Landing and backed by Federal gunboats on the James, the Army of the Potomac was in no immediate danger from the badly bruised Confederates. Richmond was still less than twenty miles away, although each of those twenty miles seemed to have lengthened enormously. There was time now to draw breath and ponder what should be done.

In a like position, there is little doubt about what Robert E. Lee or Stonewall Jackson would have done. They would have drawn up a new battle plan and attacked. But McClellan was immobilized by caution and he was also sulking over what he conceived as the shameful failure of the government to support him. True, in a ringing July Fourth order to the army he reaffirmed his intention to "enter the capital of the so-called Confederacy." But he did not say when or how this should be accomplished. His intention was predicated on the arrival of reinforcements sufficient to outnumber the vast gray horde which his active imagination and his spurious intelligence service led him to believe lurked over yonder in the swamps. Lincoln had learned to his sorrow that no matter how many reinforcements he sent Little Mac, Little Mac always believed the enemy got more men faster.

So the army sat down and waited. Sickles said goodbye to three men he had grown to like, the Comte de Paris and his brother and uncle, who were returning to Europe full of bewilderment at the failure of the campaign that had seemed so irresistible only a few weeks earlier.[1]

There was time now too to lighten the memory of slaughter and defeat with gay parties in which the convivial Sickles, along with the one-armed Kearny and the whiskey-loving Hooker, took a leading role.[2] Hooker, once so happy to shuck off Sickles, now regarded his subordinate with liking and respect. Fighting Joe had come with grudging surprise to the realization that the dapper politician from New York was always eager to lead his men personally where the battle was hottest.

But Sickles was careful not to go along with his division commander's loud-mouthed criticism of McClellan. He got along well with Little Mac, another good Democrat, and was aware that the commanding general still enjoyed the almost universal affection of the army, which was ready to blame its reverses on anything but poor generalship. While the Peninsula failure was a bitter pill for Sickles, his elastic nature rebounded with optimism. His brigade had been glorious even in retreat. He was in love with his brigade and his men felt the same way about him.

"Don't believe the exagerated [sic] reports of ill treatment which are circulated about Company A," Private Brannigan wrote his sister. "Gen. Sickles is the very man to treat his soldiers well, and returns in full their attachment to him." [3]

Sickles was now planning to get leave to return to New York, with several motives in mind. One of these, and undoubtedly the only one he stressed, was the need for recruiting. Hooker's division had done some of the hardest fighting of the campaign, the evidence being plain in the sorry condition of Sickles' own Excelsior Brigade, which had shrunk from 4500 men down to 2000 effectives.[4] The Union army at this stage of the war was a volunteer army, and while men had enlisted enthusiastically in the days when the defeat of the Confederacy was fondly imagined to be a three-months lark, the flow of volunteers had sagged with the sobering realization that rebel bullets could draw blood. The only way to get more volunteers was to go to city and hamlet and recruit them with a sort of medicine-show harangue, a business at which Sickles' platform dash could be effective.

Another consideration was the Congressional election coming up in the fall. Some of his Tammany friends felt that his battle exploits had all but erased the once indelible Sickles shame and that he should seek election to his old seat in the House. One of them, Henry Liebeman of New York, had written him suggesting that it would be advantageous if Mrs. Sickles would "visit the Sick and Wounded of your Brigade that are located in the City." [5] Teresa, still haunted by remorse, was eager to do anything she could, and she had impulsively accepted Liebeman's offer to escort her on a visit to the hospitalized soldiers. Then she had thought better of it and written him:

> Upon reflection I think it advisable for me to defer the visit proposed for today, until I hear direct from the General.
> He will write to me if he desires me to call.
> With many thanks to you for your kindness . . .[6]

Behind the genteel words lay her perfect understanding that while her husband might regain his reputation, she could never do so.

So there was politics for Sickles to consider—matters he could not properly appraise from the encampment on the James. Then too, nervous energy drove him. He was a mover, never a sitter, and a hero's role before the home folks might be pleasant. After a fortnight at Harrison's Landing he was off to Washington to ask permission to go on recruiting duty.

Every colonel and brigadier in McClellan's army would have given his lice-ridden shirt to quit the fever-racked camp, go back to his home bailiwick and drum up recruits, but this was a privilege accorded only to the lucky few. It was granted on a basis of an individual officer's record, his need for men, and possibly to some extent his persuasiveness and influence with the Secretary of War. On all those counts Sickles stood high.

"The General has a way of getting what he wants," [7] Twichell observed when he heard what was afoot. He was right. Mr. Stanton gave his permission. Late in July Sickles was on his way back home along with his friend Thomas Francis Meagher, whose Irish Brigade had likewise suffered heavy losses.

In New York he was delighted to learn that Horace Greeley had started a subscription to present him with a silver-mounted sword.[8] He sounded out his friends on the question of whether he should devote himself to politics or the military, two pursuits that held almost equal fascination for him. His own political position had been rendered confused by events which criss-crossed and obliterated party lines. A staunch Democrat, he was yet a supporter and admirer of the Republican Lincoln and was flat-footed for all-out prosecution of the war—a stand that took real courage because it angered many of his old Tammany cronies, among them Fernando Wood and Samuel Butterworth, both of them confirmed Copperheads who wanted peace at any price. Wood had further muddied the picture by making a trip down to the Peninsula and having several confidential chats with General McClellan. Sickles knew precisely what was in the wind. Wood was sounding out McClellan for the 1864 Democratic Presidential nomination.

Sickles threw himself into the recruiting drive with eloquence and plenty of backbone. He did not truckle to the advocates of peace. To his credit, he treated the war as a tragic necessity above mere politics. He defended McClellan and praised Lincoln. To a populace bewildered by the champions of peace, of partial war and total war, by the conflicting claims of Abolitionists, anti-Abolitionists, Peace Democrats, War Democrats, and Republicans, he sought to simplify the vital issues.

"Every man . . . can put implicit reliance in the good faith, the integrity, the intelligence, the patriotism, and the nerve of Abraham Lincoln," he told an audience at the Produce Exchange. ". . . I did not vote for him, but I will fight under his orders, and I will trust him everywhere, and pray for him night and day . . . All that the army has to say to the people is, 'Give us men and we will give you victories.' "

The reason victory had not come, he said, was that the South had enrolled for war on a whole-hearted scale unheard of in the North. "A man may pass through New York, and unless he is told of it, he would not know that this country was at war . . . In God's name, let the State of New York have it to say here-after that she furnished her quota to the army without con-scription—without resorting to a draft!" [9]

The general applied himself to recruiting as though victory depended on him alone. Possibly he overdid it at times. Chap-lain Twichell had now been granted leave, and Sickles rounded up him and a group of wounded and furloughing Excelsiors for a drum-beating enlistment rally before the city's volunteer fireman at the Seventh Regiment Armory. Twichell was to make one of the speeches, and he put some thought on what he would say but never got to say it.

"It all went off well except my speech from which I was luckily delivered by the prolixity of earlier performers," he wrote. "The General himself was in excellent wind and held out for a good hour and a half." [10]

With a few of his officers and men, Sickles made recruiting trips into upstate New York, going as far north and west as Dunkirk and Jamestown. He returned to the metropolis to be feted at the Winter Garden, where a performance of "The Hunchback" was given for the benefit of the Excelsior Brigade. Dressed to the nines as usual, he rose in his flag-draped box and gracefully acknowledged the cheers of the audience. With others, he addressed a mammoth rally at the Brooklyn City Hall, and when he came outside he found a large crowd waiting there, so he made a speech to them too. Unlike so many of his West Point colleagues, Sickles knew exactly what he was fighting for and was not afraid to put it in the record.

The war, he said, should be fought ceaselessly until the complete suppression of the rebellion. Possibly emancipation would result from it, but the war was not directed against in-stitutions or states. It was aimed solely to put down a lawless insurrection which "to this hour never had a pretext." [11] In fact, though by no means averse to the flowing bowl himself, he was inclined privately to place a large share of the blame for the war on liquor. "It was a Whisky Rebellion," he later told a newspaperman friend. "Whisky everywhere—in the committee rooms, private houses, at a hundred saloons. There never was a state that seceded that did not secede on whisky. The debate reeked with whisky. The solemn resolves of statesmanship were taken by men whose brains were feverish from whisky." [12]

What with one thing and another, Sickles managed to stay away from his brigade for more than two months, an interval that saw plenty of action in war-ravaged Virginia. The ill-fated Peninsula adventure had been given up as a failure, and McClellan and his army had been shipped back to Alexandria. Lincoln, about ready to give up on McClellan, had brought tough-talking General John Pope in from the West. Pope, who delighted in saying that his headquarters were in the saddle— "where his hindquarters ought to be," amended Lincoln—was given a patchwork army and was soundly defeated at Second Bull Run by Lee and Jackson. Pope was through almost before he got started, and to many pessimists it looked as though the Union was through too.

In desperation Lincoln created the office of general-in-chief and installed in it another Western officer, scholarly Major General Henry Wager Halleck, a man long on caution and detail and short on the crying need of the moment—a driving will to win. In equal desperation the President rescued McClellan from temporary eclipse and gave him command of all the forces around Washington. The victorious Confederates were crossing the Potomac and invading Maryland, and Little Mac seemed the only man handy who could organize the battered Union divisions into an army to strike at the rebels.

Hooker's division had returned from the Peninsula in time for a nasty engagement at Bristoe Station August 27th and had taken losses it could ill afford. The famous fighting division which had numbered 13,000 men at the beginning of the Peninsula Campaign was now drawing rations for less than

4000. It was left at Alexandria to refit and recuperate while McClellan marched his army into Maryland in pursuit of Lee.

"I regret exceedingly that Gen. Sickles was not with his brigade in the late battles," Twichell wrote a little anxiously. "I am sure had he anticipated such sharp work, so soon after our landing at Alexandria he would have slipped all other business for the time to lead us." [13]

Sickles, too, regretted his absence. His extended leave was not caused by concern for his own skin. It was simply a time when many irons in the fire resulted in the neglect of one. When he returned to duty early in October he had made his decision: for him the military, not the race for Congress.[14]

Hooker had accompanied McClellan as a corps commander, and when Sickles reached Alexandria he found himself elevated to the command of Fighting Joe's old division. Despite its sad depletion it was a high-spirited outfit with a combat record second to none. The brigadier was delighted. Within sight now was promotion to a major-generalship, the highest rank in the Union army.

Meanwhile McClellan had met Lee's outnumbered forces at Antietam and in the bloodiest battle of the war had all but shattered the Confederate army. It was a pity that he did not know this. Hobbled by caution and preoccupied with his own losses, he held an entire corps of three divisions out of battle and failed to order the last smashing attack which almost inevitably would have crushed the proudest army of the South. What might have been a turning point in the conflict became another tragic story of opportunity lost. While Little Mac meditated on what he conceived to be one of the most brilliant victories in all military history, the real victory eluded him as the valiant rebel remnant limped away across the Potomac unopposed. Lincoln, seeing the opportunity with his usual clarity, all but beseeched McClellan to pursue and strike a finishing blow. Little Mac felt he had done enough, and found all manner of fantastic reasons for sitting down with his army for a solid six weeks.

To Lincoln it was one of the supreme disappointments of the war. Somehow, while he was imploring McClellan to move, the busy President found time to go out with Generals Heintzelman and Banks and review Sickles' division. When Lincoln arrived he found that Sickles, always ready for a pleasantry, had provided for him a horse "richly caparisoned in the trappings of a general officer."

"Sickles, I am not going to take command of the army," the President protested. But he took the jest with good humor, complimented the men on their show, and went off to resume his worries about finding a leader for the Army of the Potomac.[15]

Sickles had once entertained a suspicion that the presence of his brigade at First Bull Run might have altered the outcome. Possibly he felt that way now about Antietam. Certainly he had no doubt at all that his division was the best in the army. He would not allow it to be outdone in any way. His jealous *esprit de corps* extended even beyond earthly considerations. When he learned that Chaplain Twichell was troubled because converts were few, and that seventeen had been baptized the day before in a rival division, he brushed aside the difficulty.

"Hell, is that all?" he snapped. "Detail forty men at once for baptism!" [16]

When McClellan finally shepherded his men across the Potomac on November 1st, Sickles received orders to join him. His division was near Manassas Junction when momentous tidings arrived: Little Mac had been relieved and replaced by his friend General Ambrose Everett Burnside, late commander of the Ninth Corps. Burnside was unusual not only for the grandly scalloping whiskers that were to become a household word. He was one of the few high-ranking officers of the Army of the Potomac who did not covet its command. While lacking the derring-do of Hooker, he possessed qualities Fighting Joe could have cultivated—namely, scrupulous honesty and unselfish devotion to the Union. Reluctantly accepting the command as a duty, Burnside speedily whipped up a plan of attack.

He proposed to concentrate his forces around Warrenton

as a feint, giving Lee the idea that he would be attacked at Culpeper or Gordonsville. While Lee was preparing against this maneuver, Burnside would force-march his army some forty miles down the Rappahannock, cross at Fredericksburg, and drive for Richmond. In a bid for greater efficiency he divided his army into three "grand divisions" under Generals Hooker, W. B. Franklin, and E. V. Sumner, each grand division comprising two army corps.

In the midst of this preparation, Sickles was pleased to receive official notice of his elevation to a major-generalship. He affixed the glittering twin stars to his shoulder straps and—since money still had a habit of slipping through his fingers—must have been cheered to know that his salary was now boosted to $445 a month plus forage for five horses.

Whatever Burnside's faults, he went to work in a business-like fashion and deserved a fate far better than he got. The first units of his army reached Falmouth, across the river from Fredericksburg, on November 17th, and the rest were close behind. Caught flat-footed by the ruse, Lee was miles away with his main army and Fredericksburg was held only by a light force. It would have been easy to cross, take the city, and head south except for one fantastically disastrous omission—lack of pontoons.

The Rappahannock was wide here and pontoons were essential. They had been ordered. Burnside expected them to be waiting for him, but someone had blundered along a line of army paper work and the pontoons were not there.

Pleading for haste, he sat down to wait for them. Not until November 25th did the first of them arrive, and in the meantime the enemy could be seen thickening to swarms across the river. Lee had divined Burnside's move and had plenty of time to counter it. The harassed Union commander saw all hope of a surprise crossing against light opposition fade. If he crossed now, he did so against the bulk of Lee's replenished army—a thought that made him pause to ponder other possibilities. But Burnside had an unhappy strain of stubbornness, and on December 11th he ordered the crossing, his plan virtually unchanged.

Under a tremendous artillery barrage, the army gained the opposite bank with inconsiderable losses, probably because the Confederates, well satisfied with their entrenched position in the heights beyond, were not too sorry to see them cross. After that came disaster.

Franklin, entrusted with the Union left, began an oddly restrained assault by sending Meade's division of the First Corps at the waiting Stonewall Jackson. Meade's men fought like heroes and even took some enemy positions, but without adequate support against a savage counter-attack they could not hold their gain and came flying back in disorder. Of the eight divisions in his command, Franklin inexplicably used only three in a situation where nothing but all-out assault could have been successful. Sickles' division, held in reserve, saw only light supporting action.

A couple of miles upriver, directly behind the town of Fredericksburg, the Confederate corps of General James Longstreet was beautifully placed on high ground commanding an open plain. Here Sumner, directing the Union right, sent wave after blue wave against a virtually impregnable position, and the carnage was terrible. Sickles' friend Meagher—a big man and an excellent target—did not feel quite up to leading his Irish Brigade that day. The brigade made a gallant but futile charge without him, and only 300 of its 1400 men got back in reasonably good condition.

Though the Federals lingered for two days more, the battle was over but for sporadic skirmishing. On the night of December 15th the Army of the Potomac retired across the river. Burnside's maiden attempt, which might have been brilliantly successful but for a matter of pontoons, was instead a catastrophe, and it had to be admitted that the commander had failed to mount a well-planned and effective attack. The Union had lost more than 12,000 good men in casualties, more than twice the rebel loss. Fredericksburg was a cruel blow to an army that had suffered much from mishandling and was to suffer more.[17]

With the army withdrawn to Falmouth to lick its wounds, there was vast dissension. Somehow, Burnside lacked the magic ability of McClellan to commit grievous errors and still retain the confidence of his men. While much of the criticism was motivated by sincere concern for the well-being of the army, it is doubtful that the ambitious Hooker was inspired alone by such noble sentiments. Fighting Joe was openly contemptuous of Burnside, even accusing the commander of cowardice. While some of his invective may have been whiskey talking, Hooker wanted Burnside's job, drunk or sober, and the effect of his ridicule was close to sabotage. Sickles, despite his admiration for Hooker's fighting qualities, must have been alarmed at his loose talk.

Around Christmas, two brigadier generals, John Newton and John Cochrane—the latter Sickles' old Tammany colleague in Congress—were in Washington on leave. They took it upon themselves to call on Lincoln and inform him that the army had utterly lost confidence in Burnside and that to proceed under his command would mean disaster.

While Lincoln was incensed at this tale-bearing, it confirmed other reports he had received and raised an issue he could not ignore. The President held Burnside in warm esteem, and yet it appeared that things were decidedly out of hand.

While the storm around the luckless commander's head was brewing, the Army of the Potomac was marking the holidays at Falmouth with something approaching peacetime zest. At Sickles' headquarters, soldiers had spanned the street between the staff tents with arches of evergreens adorned with Yuletide decorations. The sociable general invited all his officers to join him in a gala celebration on New Year's Day, 1863.

Brigadier General Joseph Revere, a New Jerseyite now leading Sickles' old Excelsior Brigade, went with a gay group of officers to the division commander's fir-festooned tent and found Sickles the soul of hospitality. A stone's throw away was the vacated house of a secessionist, and the major general had stocked it with hams, fowl, and other delicacies from Washing-

ton, not to mention a plentiful supply of liquor. On the piazza
music was dispensed by an orchestra of violins, flutes, an ac-
cordion, and "a man who chirruped like a bird." Twichell was
there with his chaplain colleague, Father O'Hagan, but they
did not stay long.

"Father O'Hagan and I . . . observed that rum was flowing
freely," Twichell commented, "and so, having made obeisance
to the General, we omitted the refreshments and retired to his
[O'Hagan's] quarters where we devoured a quiet dinner and
consumed some tobacco in peace." [18]

The party was gay enough to leave a lasting impression on
Regis de Trobriand, a colonel in the Third Corps and no blue-
nose. "General Sickles . . . did things in grand style," he recalled. "During the whole day he kept open house at his headquarters . . . The champagne and whiskey ran in streams. I
wish I could add that they were used in moderation; but the
truth is that the subaltern officers, attracted by the good cheer,
partook of them so freely that it was not to the honor of the
uniform nor to the profit of discipline. *Amicus Sickles, sed
magis amica veritas.*" [19]

On January 26th President Lincoln reluctantly removed
Burnside as commander of the Army of the Potomac and replaced him with Hooker. The President was painfully aware
of Hooker's failings, but he had fought well, was popular with
the men and with the public, and perhaps he was the man
who could find the elusive key to victory.

To Major General Sickles, the elevation of his close friend
Hooker was news as cheering as the election of Buchanan back
in 1856.

CHAPTER XVI

Barroom and Brothel

Joseph Hooker was a handsome, strapping, blue-eyed giant of forty-nine who had so many obvious faults that his appointment was a clear sign of the President's desperation. Everybody knew that Hooker was a tosspot and braggart. He lacked the cool steadiness expected of a man who was to lead a vast army into battle. Yet Hooker's record bristled with aggressive and successful combat achievements as a division and corps commander. His men swore by him. In camp he might be a troublemaker, but not once in battle had he made an important mistake.

Now, above all, success was the yardstick. Hooker's personal foibles could be forgiven if he could whip the disgruntled army into shape and make it win.

The weather was bad for war that winter, and the new major-general commanding the Army of the Potomac was not immediately required to live up to his *nom de guerre* of Fighting Joe. The army went into winter quarters at Falmouth, with the Confederates doing likewise just across the river at battered Fredericksburg. The opposing pickets worked out a gentlemen's agreement not to make life miserable by doing any shooting, and occasionally traded newspapers, tobacco, and coffee.

True, the rebels had the better of the chaffing that constantly went on between the Blue and the Gray. They were not forgetting that Jackson had cunningly made off with great stores belonging to the Union Generals Pope and McDowell, and they gleefully referred to Pope as their Commissary and McDowell as their Quartermaster [1] —quips for which the Yanks had no really adequate retort.

Hooker quickly scrapped Burnside's grand division set-up and returned to corps organization. He gave command of the First Corps to General John Reynolds; the Second to Darius N. Couch; the Third to Sickles; Fifth, Meade; Sixth, John Sedgwick; Eleventh, German-born Franz Sigel; and Twelfth, Henry Warner Slocum. Of the seven, only Sickles and Sigel were non-West Pointers, and Sigel had graduated from the military academy at Karlsruhe and fought in the revolution in Baden. Of the seven, only Sickles was new to corps command. In fact, he had commanded a division in only one battle in which he took little part.

"There were men about Hooker who believed in, and hoped to rise with him," [2] one observer later recalled. Sickles was in the forefront of these, and yet Hooker was too interested in victory to assign such an important command on the score of friendship alone. He had witnessed Sickles' fighting talents as a brigadier on the Peninsula and was confident that he was equal to the task. Perhaps it may be said that friendship did no harm. Hooker promoted Sickles on a provisional basis, for his appointment as a major general had not yet been confirmed by the Senate and corps command was definitely a two-star job. Some Senators had not warmed toward him. Once again that body displayed a "strong personal opposition" and refused to confirm the nomination until March 9th, after Lincoln had presented Sickles' name for a second time. [3]

In giving Sickles the potent Third Corps, the new commander passed over thirty-three-year-old Oliver Howard, a West Pointer who ranked Sickles. The one-armed general, who had a good battle record, complained to Hooker about this. Seniority was an important factor in the army, not to be overlooked without good reason, and Howard could have raised a sizeable commotion. Yet Hooker was strong enough on Sickles to retain him in command despite Howard's understandable chagrin, and the ex-divinity student had to be satisfied with division command for a while. This problem was later solved when Sigel, who ranked the commanding general himself and was disgruntled at not being given a larger command, was relieved at his own request. Howard was then given Sigel's Eleventh Corps, largely composed of German-Americans some of who spoke only rudimentary English.[4]

For his chief of staff Hooker chose Daniel Butterfield, the dapper little New Yorker who never saw West Point but had served in the state militia and had fought well under McClellan, Pope, and Burnside. Butterfield, who was only thirty-two, came from a wealthy family and also had the advantage of friendship with Secretary of the Treasury Chase and Senator Henry Wilson, chairman of the Senate committee on military affairs. Being interested in music, he had found fault with some of the army bugle calls and had originated one which later became not only army regulation but also known to every citizen capable of carrying a tune—"Taps."

In the light of what was to happen later, it was with ironical prescience that George Gordon Meade, the stiff and precise Pennsylvanian now heading the Fifth Corps, had decided reservations about two of Hooker's choices—namely, Sickles and Butterfield.

"I believe Hooker is a good soldier," Meade wrote his wife. "The danger he runs is of subjecting himself to bad influences, such as Dan Butterfield and Dan Sickles, who, being intellectually more clever than Hooker, and leading him to believe they are very influential, will obtain an injurious ascendancy over him and insensibly affect his conduct." [5]

Meade did not specify under just what heading Sickles and Butterfield should be classified as "bad influences," but clearly he had no high opinion of the two New Yorkers and regarded them as political wire-pullers.

But all this was beyond the ken of the ordinary soldier who had to face the bullets. To most of them Hooker was an inspiring figure who was long overdue at the top. After Fredericksburg, a feeling of futility had permeated the ranks and desertions had mounted to the alarming average of two hundred a day. Fighting Joe applied himself to rehabilitate his men by feeding and treating them well. In this he was successful, and in fact there was no reason why he should not have been since he had many weeks to concentrate on *esprit* and reorganization without having to worry about the enemy.

In this work the busy Butterfield, a man who fussed about such items as bugle calls, took an active role. He recalled that the lamented Kearny—killed in Pope's campaign—had distinguished the men of his division with a shoulder patch, and that the soldiers had seemed proud of this identifying symbol. Butterfield conceived the idea, routine today, of creating a shoulder symbol for each corps—a shamrock, a Maltese cross, a crescent —and with each division of the corps bearing the insigne in a different color. In Sickles' Third Corps the men were busy sewing a diamond on their uniforms.

During this period of army overhaul, there was time for ranking officers to shake Virginia mud from their boots. "General Sickles left for New York— Politics the order of the day!" Father O'Hagan noted in his diary.[6] The Catholic chaplain knew the foibles of his commander and commented on them in salty style. "Breakfasted with the General as usually on Sunday mornings," he wrote a fortnight later. "His rhumatism [sic]—though it prevented his coming to mass, did not affect his appetite not having reached the regions of his stomach." [7]

The army was drilling like mad, but among the officers the winter encampment of 1863 was notable particularly for its entertainment. With the army an easy day's ride from Washington, many officers' wives arrived to stay until the next big push should begin. Soldiers had to watch their swearing as they labored to make officers' tents and houses more luxurious. There was much whist-playing and punch-drinking of evenings, and dances were common. Distinguished guests—Senators, governors, ministers, Cabinet members—were continually dropping in, which inevitably meant a review of the troops and also gave the ladies an opportunity to appear in their flounciest crinolines.

Among the participants in this gayety was a remarkable young woman, née Agnes Leclerque of Baltimore, who now bore the title of Princess Salm-Salm. The princess had won renown a few years earlier as a circus rider, and was the recent bride of Vienna-born Prince Felix de Salm-Salm, a soldier of fortune who had cleared out of Europe only a jump or two ahead of some embarrassing obligations. Salm-Salm, who wore a monocle and spoke little English, had made effective use of his wife's charm in wangling a colonel's commission from New York's Governor Morgan, and now commanded the Eighth New York in the heavily Teutonic Eleventh Corps.[8] The Salm-Salms had a gay time that winter.

"Some of these festivals were indeed sumptuous," the princess wrote, "and I especially remember one given by General Sickles, in a hall improvised from canvas by uniting a dozen or more large hospital tents in a convenient manner.

"This immense tent was decorated inside and outside with flags, garlands, flowers and Chinese lamps in great profusion, and offered a fairy-like aspect. The supper laid under the tent for about two hundred persons, ladies and gentlemen, could not have been better in Paris, for the famous Delmonico from New York had come himself to superintend the repast, and brought with him his kitchen aides and batteries, and immense quantities of the choicest provisions and delicacies, together with plate and silver, and whatever was required to make one forget that it was a camp supper. The wines and liquors were in correspondence with the rest, and no less, I suppose, the bill to be paid." [9]

The new Third Corps commander was the most confirmed party-giver at Falmouth that winter. He now had his headquarters at the Fitzhugh house, a comfortable place abandoned by its secessionist owners and well equipped for hospitality. Here he gave a "grand supper" on March 1st strictly for the brass, with Hooker as the honored guest and none of those invited being of lower rank than brigadier generals. There were two exceptions, however—Chaplains Twichell and O'Hagan, for both of whom Sickles had a great liking.

The two men of the cloth, Protestant and Catholic, had an earnest consultation about this and reluctantly decided not to go. For one thing, they would feel ill at ease among so many generals, and for another, as Twichell put it, "there will be free drinking and we should be annoyed by solicitations to join in it." [10]

To Sickles, any unusual occasion furnished sufficient grounds for a party. When a captain in a Jersey regiment was married that March, it was the signal for an all-out soirée. "If [the groom] had been a colonel," observed Colonel de Trobriand, now one of Sickles' regimental commanders, "he could not have had more pompous nuptials. Generals were present in an imposing number. There was dancing, drinking, banqueting. The commanding general himself was present, full of gayety and life. Then succeeded a ball, given by General Sickles at his headquarters, where, as usual, there was feasting to the heart's content." [11]

The rigors of warfare were indeed being softened. According to the Princess Salm-Salm, however, the "unheard-of luxury" of such affairs as Sickles' gala Delmonico party caused no criticism among the rank and file. "The soldiers," she declared, "did not grudge the generals their luxurious habits." [12]

That is as may be. If the infantrymen and artillerymen had any complaints about all this splendor, they did not mention them to the princess. But in addition to drill, there were also occasional contests and entertainments for the ordinary soldiers —horse and foot races, greased-pole climbing, target competition, and the like. At one marksmanship contest, General Sickles rode up, "dismounted and taking a musket hit the target the first time trying." [13]

St. Patrick's Day was the event of a momentous celebration, and naturally the lead was taken by General Meagher's Irish Brigade, which boasted officers with such richly rolling names as Keough, O'Keefe, and Gallagher, who could attack a keg of whiskey with the same zest as they assaulted the enemy. According to one who was there, the brigade's drinking materials "comprised eight baskets of champagne, ten gallons of rum and twenty-two of whiskey." In the mixing of the punch, "Captains Gosson and Hogan were voted masters of ceremonies, in which they labored so diligently that before the mixture was complete both felt overpowered by their labors and had to be relieved from duty." [14] Tall General Meagher himself was a sight fit to gladden any Irish heart, clad in white hat, green cravat, a brown coat, and white velvet breeches, and fortified with potations that made him exceedingly gay—gay enough to forget momentarily that he had not yet been given the second star he felt he deserved.[15]

The events included a hurdle race, conducted in true Kilkenny style, with no one sparing the horses. One observer was Major General Hiram Berry, a Maine politician who led one of Sickles' divisions. Berry summed it up in this manner: "Result: Large lot of whiskey punch drank, mass was said by the priests, the races commenced, stakes for money large, accidents not a few, one man and two horses killed, two nearly so, many with arms broken, and much horse-flesh used up." [16]

The affair at least had the advantage of getting the surgeons in trim for more serious work. But it was not the soldiers as much as the officers who drew criticism for their goings-on that winter. Charles Francis Adams Jr., grandson of John Quincy and a member of one of the nation's most famous families, was a cavalry captain and he did not like the way things were going at all. To Adams, Hooker was a "drunken West Point military adventurer." [17] The memory of the Falmouth sojourn stuck in his craw so persistently that it came out in his autobiography, published more than fifty years later:

> . . . that was a period in its history when, so far as character was concerned, the Army of the Potomac sank to its lowest point. It was commanded by a trio, of each of whom the least said the better. It consisted of "Joe" Hooker, "Dan" Sickles and "Dan" Butterfield. All three were men of blemished character. During the winter (1862–3) when Hooker was in command, I

can say from personal knowledge and experience that the headquarters of the Army of the Potomac was a place to which no
self-respecting man liked to go, and no decent woman would
go. It was a combination of bar-room and brothel.[18]

Colonel de Trobriand, who was likewise there and was a shade
less conservative, made no mention of widespread whoring but
was disturbed by the abuse of liquor in camp. He mentioned
one regiment where "the soldiers were often disturbed in their
sleep by the obscene refrains and drunken cries from the tent
of the commanding officer." [19] But De Trobriand had liking
and respect for Sickles, his own corps commander, and gave an
illuminating opinion of him:

> Sickles was one of the striking figures of this war. More as a
> man than as a general officer; in many ways a typical American.
> He was gifted in a high degree with that multiplicity of facul-
> ties which has given rise to the saying that a Yankee is ready
> for everything . . .
> He has a quick perception, an energetic will, prompt and
> supple intelligence, an active temperament. Naturally ambi-
> tious, he brings to the service of his ambitions a clear view, a
> practical judgment and a deep knowledge of political tactics.
> When he has determined on anything, he prepares the way,
> assembles his forces, and marches directly to the assault. Ob-
> stacles do not discourage him. . . . he has many strings in his
> bow, if one breaks he will replace it by another.
> In him, ability does not exclude frankness. He likes, on the
> contrary, to play with his cards on the table with his friends and
> against his enemies . . .[20]

One of the strings in Sickles' bow was his friendship with
Lincoln, for whom he had sincere regard. When it was announced that the President would visit the camp in April with
Mrs. Lincoln and Tad, there was a great scurry to make it a
grand occasion, with ladies digging into trunks for their best
finery. Hooker made ready to receive the distinguished visitors
with troop reviews and proper ceremony, but was glad to leave

the entertainment part of it to Sickles, the acknowledged authority. Sickles suggested to the Princess Salm-Salm and a number of the other officers' wives that they treat Mrs. Lincoln as a queen and attend her in the guise of ladies-in-waiting. Fortunately, the ladies had better sense than the general and this atrocious idea was rejected.[21]

As Sickles told the story later, he was concerned at the President's extreme melancholy. He wanted to do something to take Lincoln's mind off the war, if only momentarily. After the chief magistrate had reviewed Sickles' troops, he repaired to the general's headquarters, where a line of officers' wives waited to be presented to him. Struck by what seemed to him an inspiration, Sickles proposed to these ladies that they encircle the President in a bevy so that he could not escape, and kiss him.

This idea was likewise rejected, except by the glamorous Princess Salm-Salm, who was among those present. On being presented, she stood on tiptoe, pulled Lincoln's head down, and managed to buss him fondly on the cheek.

The President took this nonsense with good humor. The highly jealous Mrs. Lincoln was not present, but young Tad was, and his mother soon heard about the kissing episode. It quickly became known that the First Lady was in a towering pet about it—furious at Sickles for proposing the idea and equally furious at her husband for being innocently on the receiving end. "It was known," as one observer wrote, "that Lincoln had been subjected to an unhappy quarter of an hour." [22]

Hooker, always ready for a joke, hit on an artful one when he appointed Sickles to accompany President and Mrs. Lincoln back to Washington as honorary escort.

"I joined the President and his family on the steamboat, at Acquia Creek," Sickles recalled. "All went well until supper was announced. Seated at the table in a private cabin, face to face with Mrs. Lincoln, I at once saw how much I was out of favor. I was not recognized. The President tried his best to put his good wife in better temper, but in vain; she evaded every overture, even the amusing anecdotes he related with characteristic tact and humor. Not a smile softened her stern features. At last Lincoln turned to me, exclaiming:

" 'Sickles, I never knew you were such a pious man until I came down this week to see the army.'

" 'I am quite sure, Mr. President,' I replied, 'I do not merit the reputation, if I have gained it.'

" 'Oh, yes,' rejoined the President. 'They tell me you are the greatest Psalmist in the army. They say you are more than a Psalmist—they say you are a Salm-Salmist.'

"This was more than Mrs. Lincoln could resist. She joined in the hearty laugh . . . and peace was restored." [23]

Peace was restored in the President's household, but late in April the army, after almost five months in camp, was on the move for war. The fun was over and the fighting was to begin. Joe Hooker had devised a well-conceived plan whereby he felt he would surely crush Lee's army. As a massive and secret maneuver got under way, Brigadier General M. R. Patrick, provost marshal general of the Army of the Potomac, took an uneasy look around and confided to his diary some apprehension that Hooker's rebuilding job might not be quite solid:

> . . . There is a curious state of things now in this Army— Confidence enough is felt in Hooker, I think, but not a great deal in some of his Corps Commanders . . . Sickles & the most of his crew, are poor—very poor concerns, in my opinion.[24]

CHAPTER XVII

The Enemy Must
Ingloriously Fly

Hooker's plan was based on deception and numerical superiority. He had some 120,000 men against Lee's approximate 65,-000. He would send Sedgwick's big Sixth Corps across the river below Fredericksburg, with Reynolds' First and Sickles' Third Corps lying in reserve. While Lee braced to meet this assault, the rest of the Union army would sneak up the Rappahannock, cross, and then advance on the unsuspecting Lee's rear. The Confederates would be caught between the hammer and the anvil, their fine entrenchments turned into a trap.

Meanwhile General Stoneman, leading the cavalry, would already be across the river, circling around Lee's rear and smashing his communications with Richmond. How then could the foxy rebel leader keep himself from being cut off, hemmed in, and destroyed?

Hooker had such confidence in his design, and was so determined to prevent leaks, that he kept it all in his own head. He did not divulge it to Lincoln, to Stanton, to General-in-Chief Halleck, nor to his own corps commanders. He issued orders for the preliminary movements, and the various units of the great army got under way without knowing the why or the wherefore. Some of the corps leaders—particularly Meade and Couch, whose opinion of the commanding general was already somewhat dubious, were annoyed at this demonstration of distrust.

Certainly Sickles, who always liked to know what was in the wind and usually did, must have been irked at the necessity of moving in the dark. But he was a loyal Hooker partisan and he obeyed orders. Under him in his first test in high command he had close to 19,000 of the best men in the Army of the Potomac, second in size only to Sedgwick's four-division Sixth Corps. His three divisions included Hooker's and Kearny's old outfits—proud fighters who felt with some reason that they could lick anybody if the terms were anywhere near equal. His divisional commanders were solid and proven: Hiram Berry, the man from Maine; David Birney, a Philadelphia lawyer; and Amiel Whipple, who had risen from captain to brigadier general in a year's time.

By April 30th the movement had progressed smartly. The corps of Meade, Couch, Slocum, and Howard had crossed the river, driven the enemy pickets and advanced east of the Chancellorsville crossroads. Sedgwick and Reynolds had crossed below Fredericksburg and were facing Lee's entrenched forces there with orders to make a demonstration but no real attack. Sickles had now been instructed to bring his corps around to join the others in the vicinity of Chancellorsville. Lee was neatly caught between the closing jaws of a vise.

Hooker was so exultant at the success of his maneuver that he seemed to forget that the fighting still had to be done. He sat down and penned an order to the army that was a little premature:

> It is with heartfelt satisfaction the commanding general announces to the army that the operations of the last three days have determined that our enemy must either ingloriously fly, or come out from behind his defenses and give us battle on our own ground, where certain destruction awaits him . . .[1]

Having issued this statement, Fighting Joe, the previously nerveless warrior, seemed to be assailed by a case of nerves. It was said that in order to keep a clear head to direct this massive maneuver, he had strictly eschewed liquor. Cold sobriety was a condition fairly unusual to him, and possibly it had a part in giving him the fidgets. It may be that Hooker and the Army of the Potomac would have been better off in this climactic moment if the general had a drink—a stiff one—under his belt. For the first time he had the awful responsibility of directing a vast army whose success was not only vital to him but to the Union itself. Hooker, who had sneered at McClellan's caution and Burnside's hesitation, now was overwhelmed by caution and hesitation just when those two qualities were fatal.

His entire operation had been predicated on smashing attack. Now, with Lee finally aware of the threat and turning to meet it, Hooker went on the defensive. He ordered his corps east of Chancellorsville to stop their advance, drop back to positions of the night before, and dig in. He would let Lee do the attacking.

This word came like a dash of cold water on Darius Couch, Hooker's second in command, and to the other corps leaders at the scene. Hearing Sedgwick's guns booming from Fredericksburg some ten miles east, they had tumbled to the scope and success of the maneuver which Hooker had kept so secret. Lee had been trapped and his army was in a parlous position. The usually sedate Meade was so delighted that he executed a heel-kick and let out a hip-hip-hurrah, until that incomprehensible order came through.[2]

Fall back? It seemed unthinkable. Anyone could see that the thing to do was to capitalize on this glorious opportunity, press on toward Fredericksburg and close the vise on Lee before he could take the initiative. Couch wondered if Hooker had lost his mind. He sent word asking that the present position at least be held, and Fighting Joe snappishly answered no. Fall back. Let Lee attack.

So the vise which was to close on Lee did not close but opened a little. The next move was Lee's to decide while Hooker supinely waited.

Early on May 1st, Sickles' corps marched up the river from its position opposite Fredericksburg, crossed the Rappahannock, and was at Chancellorsville shortly after noon.

"As we moved along the plank road in the afternoon," recalled a member of the 63rd Pennsylvania, "the infantry marched in the fields by its sides, which were higher than the road itself, to give free use of the main thoroughfare to the ambulances. General Sickles, surrounded by his staff, sat smoking his accustomed cigar, coolly surveying the passing of the troops and the situation on out front. The enemy, who had discovered the movement, opened upon us from numerous batteries and their shot plowed the ground around us and shrieked over our heads and through our ranks. Observing this, the general, without changing his own position, remarked in that peculiar deliberate tone of voice, 'Boys, I think the enemy see you—you had better take to the road.' " [3]

While Sickles' men bivouacked that night about a half-mile west of Chancellorsville, a historic conference was taking place at Confederate headquarters. Lee had left Early's division, plus an extra brigade, to hold off Sedgwick at Fredericksburg and had moved the entire remainder of his force—some 40,000 men —to face Hooker. Possibly he felt some contempt at Hooker's prompt abdication of the attack, but he was still in a nasty predicament. He had the choice of retreating between the open jaws of the vise, or taking the attack himself against greatly superior forces.

He talked it over with his strong right arm, Stonewall Jackson. Apparently the idea of retreat never entered into the discussion. It was merely a question of how the attack should be made. From Jeb Stuart, the rebel cavalry leader, had come word that the Union right, composed of Howard's Eleventh Corps, was none too well protected. Out of the conference came the decision to execute a maneuver that would have been foolhardy in any but expert hands, and against any but a clumsy adversary.

Lee, the trapped, would become the trapper. While he made a demonstration against Hooker's forces facing east, Jackson would march 30,000 men in a westward circle around the Union army at Chancellorsville and fall on it from the west.

Hooker's army on May 2nd formed a rough semicircle extending from the Rappahannock around Chancellorsville and off to the west, ending in a choked jungle aptly called the Wilderness. Meade held the left, his left on the river. Then came Couch, Slocum, Sickles, and Howard.

Birney's division of Sickles' corps had pushed out to Hazel Grove, some two miles southeast of Chancellorsville, leaving Berry's and Whipple's divisions in the rear. In the morning, Birney was astonished to receive reports from his pickets that a large enemy force was passing westward not far beyond his lines.[4] This of course was Jackson, doing the impossible. A native had shown him a brush-choked, little-used road by which he could circumnavigate the Federals if he was quick and lucky.

Sickles got out there in a hurry, his aggressive instincts aroused. It appeared to him that the enemy must be retreating. He sent word to Hooker and asked permission to attack.

Hooker, whose headquarters were now in the Chancellor house, the only sizeable structure in the hamlet, was puzzled. The enemy did not belong where Sickles had seen him. Was he retreating—or was he getting around the Union flank?

Fighting Joe gave Sickles permission only to "advance cautiously" and "harass" the movements of the enemy.[5] The once pugnacious commander now seemed satisfied to let his army become a mere gadfly buzzing around the Confederate forces. He also took the wise precaution to warn Howard, on the extreme right, to be on the watch against a flanking movement.

Sickles stretched his orders as far as he could. He had already sent forward his elite outfit, Colonel Hiram Berdan's Sharpshooters, two regiments made up of men from woodsy New England, Michigan, and Minnesota who could shoot the eye out of a squirrel.[6] Informing Slocum and Howard of his movement, he ordered Whipple's division up in support of Birney and pushed harder. By mid-afternoon there was warm skirmishing and several hundred rebel prisoners were taken, but that was all. What Sickles had been attacking was Jackson's rear guard, and the fighting faded out as Stonewall's column drew past with only minor losses.

Sickles was watching as a provost guard brought some of the prisoners in at Hazel Grove. "Who took those Johnnies?" he asked.

"I did, sir," grinned the provost officer by way of making a little joke.

"The devil you did," Sickles scoffed. "There's the Sharpshooters—they captured those men."

He talked with Lieutenant Thorp of the Sharpshooters, who had already questioned some of the prisoners. Thorp said the rebels claimed their troops were moving around to flank the Yanks on the right, and that things would be plenty hot before long.

"We'll take care of *them!*" Sickles snapped.[7]

But of course, prisoners could not be believed. They lied more often than not, taking delight in spreading confusion. And there was confusion enough in the Union camp so that no additions were necessary. Sickles was confident that the enemy was retreating and was itching to get after him. Hooker also had become convinced of the retreat but was not so itchy. He ordered his corps commanders to prepare to move early in the morning and sent word to Sedgwick to assail the rebel force at Fredericksburg with everything he had.

"We know that the enemy is fleeing, trying to save his trains," he informed Sedgwick. "Two of Sickles' divisions are among them."[8]

General Oliver Otis Howard's Eleventh Corps was still posted at Sickles' right in a veritable jungle around Dowdall's Tavern, two miles west of Chancellorsville. This heavily Teutonic outfit, officered by men with names like Buschbeck, Von Gilsa, and Schimmelpfennig, was somewhat disparaged by the rest of the army, which referred to them as the "Dutchies." Possibly Hooker himself was not too confident of them, and stationed them purposely in a position he believed would be well to the rear of the hot fighting. The Germans were disgruntled at what they considered the unfair treatment of their former commander, the revered Franz Sigel, and as a result they had little use for the one-armed General Howard,[9] so their morale may not have been of the best.

Young Oliver Howard was a little careless that day. He had been warned by Hooker to watch his flank, but he seems to have been lulled by a conviction that the enemy was on the run. That afternoon he received a frantic warning from one of his brigade commanders that the enemy was advancing in large numbers from the west. Howard well knew that this area, deep in the Wilderness, was so overgrown with brush, brambles, and second-growth trees that a rabbit would have trouble picking its way through. Impossible, he said. Some of the pickets must be letting their imaginations run away with them.[10]

It was nearing six o'clock, and many of the Germans were beginning to prepare supper, when Howard discovered that Stonewall Jackson was not one to be intimidated by undergrowth. Preceded by scurrying forest animals, a horde of rebels uttering their blood-curdling battle cry broke through the thickets and descended on the Eleventh Corps.

The corps was in anything but a position to receive an attack from that quarter. Caught by a hot enfilading fire in their flank, many of the men threw down their guns or messkits and fled. The jungle was a chaos of wild yells as a hail of bullets rattled through the trees and officers tried to reform their units and turn them to face the assault. Howard himself came riding out, a flag under the stump of his arm, to lead the defense in person and attempt to forestall the disaster for which his own unwariness was largely responsible. Some of the regiments did heroic work, taking firing positions and giving ground slowly while other panic-stricken units burst through their lines in a mad rush for the rear. But it was an unequal battle, with those of the Germans who stayed being overwhelmed and almost surrounded by gray-clad marksmen, and before long it turned into a rout.

When fugitives came streaming past his headquarters at the
Chancellor house, Hooker became aware that it was not the
enemy that was "ingloriously flying." He kept his head and soon
had Berry's division of Sickles' corps, as well as a division of
Couch's Second Corps, faced around to bolster the broken
Eleventh. Cannon were wheeled into new positions, and as it
grew dark the flame and the tumult was terrible.

A mile or so to the south, beyond Hazel Grove, Sickles with
his other two divisions was well-nigh cut off from the rest of
the army by the collapse of the Eleventh. So convinced was he
that the enemy was retreating that at first he could not believe
the report of the disaster. He believed it when fleeing remnants
of Howard's corps came racing across his rear, and pursuing
rebels collided with his outposts.[11]

The Third Corps gave some ground before order was restored.
Sickles had with him Brigadier General Alfred Pleasonton,
a cavalry officer, and Pleasonton in the nick of time got twenty-
two cannon unlimbered to blaze away at the oncoming enemy
with canister. The artillery fairly blew them apart, and by the
time they reformed and came again the bulk of Whipple's men
were ready for them.[12] There was fierce fighting as darkness
came and moonlight bathed the wilderness. There was confusion, too. Sickles, who had no time to think of sleep that
night, wanted to launch an attack to recover a few field pieces
that got left in the No Man's Land between the lines, but for
all he knew some units of Howard's men might be caught in
pockets among the enemy before him. An officer was sent with
a white flag to inquire whether the soldiers to the west were
Union or Confederate, and was promptly taken prisoner by the
rebels, who regarded this as no legitimate white-flag errand.[13]

After midnight the attack was made anyway, begun by a
booming artillery fire and climaxed by a headlong infantry
charge about which the Confederate General Lane reported that
"Sickles' command rushed upon us with loud and prolonged
cheering." [14] The endangered cannon were recovered and in

the wee hours the exhausted Yanks lay down for an hour or two of sleep.

At Chancellorsville, too, the Confederate assault had finally been stopped. Jackson's wearied men would have to wait until morning to finish their wrecking job on Hooker.

They would have to do it without Jackson. That night the immortal Stonewall was riding in the moonlight to inspect his lines, and was fatally wounded—shot in error, it was said, by his own men. His command went to Jeb Stuart, the hard-riding cavalryman.

In the night battle at Hazel Grove, Lieutenant Thomas J. Leigh, a young officer of Birney's division, had the misfortune to become separated from his regiment and was captured with a few of his men. He was questioned by Confederate officers who were in an exultant mood.

"We've got Dan Sickles' corps cut off," one of them said, "and we'll capture the lot of them."

They seemed to feel a special vindictiveness toward Sickles, undoubtedly because of his desertion of the Southern cause when war loomed. "We'll hang him, God damn him, when we catch him!" the Confederate snarled.[15]

Whether hanging was in the offing or not, Sickles was in an uneasy position with Birney's and Whipple's divisions at Hazel Grove. His communications with the main army at Chancellorsville were still open, but should the enemy succeed there on the morrow he would very likely be isolated. On the other hand, Hazel Grove, which was no grove at all but a high clearing, was an excellent position for artillery and for infantry defense. Sickles' presence there was a thorn in the enemy's side, for if he could hold it he stood squarely in the path of a possible junction between Lee's forces to the east and Stuart's on the west. As a further advantage, his artillery could pour a destructive flanking fire into Stuart's men assailing Chancellorsville.

But Hooker, the once aggressive Fighting Joe, was playing it safe. Early Sunday morning, May 3rd, he visited Sickles in person and looked over the position at Hazel Grove. Though Sickles urged the advantage of staying, Hooker ordered him to withdraw and join the main force at Chancellorsville. The withdrawal began at once, with the rebels sniping merrily and Graham's brigade having hot work covering the movement as the two divisions made their way back to Chancellorsville.[16]

While the Union army had been badly treated, its losses so far were not appreciably higher than those of the Confederates and Hooker still had the upper hand had he known it. His army around Chancellorsville outnumbered the separated forces of Lee and Stuart by some 30,000 men. He had two sturdy corps— Meade's and Reynolds'—in reserve, neither of which had done more than shoot at a picket or two.

But when Stuart attacked that morning, his men clearly had not been told they were outnumbered. They threw themselves into the assault with furious shouts of "Remember Jackson!" and the fighting was so hot that many veterans of Fair Oaks and Antietam said they had never seen the likes of it.

The rebels had promptly taken advantage of Sickles' withdrawal from Hazel Grove and planted thirty-one field pieces there. All thirty-one of them were now hurling shell into the Union lines. The Federals were likewise doing murderous work with a tremendous battery placed behind the infantry at Fairview, just west of Chancellorsville. Artillery fire soon set the underbrush ablaze, and luckless wounded of both sides screamed in torture as they roasted to death.

"The wounded are continually passing through our lines," Colonel de Trobriand noted. "One of them, half naked, is as black as a negro. He runs shrieking toward the ambulances. It is an artilleryman, wounded by the explosion of a caisson . . . Sickles goes by . . . with a smiling air, smoking a cigar. 'Everything is going well,' said he, in a loud voice, intended to be heard. Then, in a lower tone, giving me his hand, he whispered in my ear a congratulation and a promise. It would appear that I won a star in the fight by moonlight the night before." [17]

Although De Trobriand's star did not come as soon as he

hoped, that little conversation in the heat of battle was a typical Sickles touch of the sort that endeared him to his men. But for all his confident air, things were not going well. The men of Stuart were attacking with ferocity, with the Third Corps taking the brunt of it and suffering terrible losses. Hooker, who could have emerged from torpor with a smashing counter-attack, seemed dazed. His admirable master plan had gone awry somewhere and he could not adjust himself to an enemy who had not moved as he expected. He not only allowed but ordered the two corps of Meade and Reynolds—well over 30,000 men—to stand idle over toward the river at a time when their help would almost surely have carried the day.[18] Back at Falmouth, Lincoln had given Hooker a piece of sound advice: "In your next battle, use all your men." The warning went unheeded although Meade and Reynolds were all but panting to get into the battle.

So Sickles' Third Corps bled while 30,000 good soldiers lolled a half-mile away with their arms stacked. His trusted General Hiram Berry went down, slain by a sharpshooter's bullet. One of his brigadiers, Gershom Mott, was carried away wounded, and disorder mounted. Brigadier General Revere, leading Sickles' old Excelsior Brigade, was under the mistaken impression that he succeeded to the command of Berry's division—General Joseph B. Carr actually did—and Revere also felt that the enemy fire was too hot for mortal man to stand. While Sickles was occupied elsewhere, Revere led the Excelsiors and several other units in a move to the rear. The exultant rebels poured in, forcing a withdrawal of the rest of the line.

Deadly as the attack was, the bulldog Sickles had ordered his men to hold. When he learned of the defection his rage was towering. General Revere was relieved of command, his army career destined to be ended.[19]

Fairview was lost as the Third Corps retired closer to Chancellorsville, with a portion of the Twelfth Corps at its left doing likewise. The artillery in new positions was getting ready to blast away at the Confederates when a little band of New

Hampshire volunteers appeared from the left into the field of fire. Sickles put spurs to his horse and galloped over in front of his batteries.

"Hold on there, gunners!" he roared. "Those are my men!" [20]

At the Chancellor house, now close behind the lines, the bemused Hooker was leaning against a pillar on the veranda when a rebel gunner got the range. A solid shot struck the pillar, knocking the general insensible to the floor. For a time it was thought he had been killed.[21] Fighting Joe undoubtedly would have done good service to the Union cause had he died then and there, for Darius Couch, the steady general from New York State, would have succeeded to the command and Couch was fairly aching to get those idle men into battle.

Aided by libations of spirits, Hooker revived and continued in command, if such it could be called. Stuart's Confederate forces on the west had now circled around and made a junction with Lee's on the east so that shot and shell were pouring on the Federals from three sides. When night came they were still holding. The Third Corps had dealt out plenty of punishment while taking a ghastly pounding, one of the dead being young General Amiel Whipple, Sickles' second division leader to fall.

On the next day Hooker's humiliation was complete when Lee rightly decided that Fighting Joe had run out of fight. Lee left Stuart with some 25,000 men to continue a show of attack at Chancellorsville, and turned with the rest of his forces to hurl himself at Sedgwick, now advancing from Fredericksburg. All that day Hooker, still suffering from his wound, allowed his 75,000 men to be held by Stuart with a third that number. Generals Meade and Reynolds, with their 30,000 well-rested men, were still in the status of unhappy spectators.

Sedgwick became aware that something had gone wrong when he was met by a sizeable portion of the Confederate army. There was a bloody battle near Salem Church, and that night Sedgwick managed to withdraw across the Rappahannock at Scott's Ford.[22]

That same night, at midnight, there was a rather grim meeting of corps commanders in Hooker's tent. Hooker, with Butterfield at his side, put the question to be decided: whether the Army of the Potomac should stay and fight, or retire. Hooker and his chief of staff withdrew while the question was debated. Of the five generals present, Meade, Reynolds, and Howard voted to fight it out, while Couch and Sickles favored retirement.[23]

There was a reason why Couch and Sickles, both aggressive men, took this stand. Couch was filled with disgust at Hooker's sorry bungling and later made it clear that his vote simply reflected his unwillingness to expose a fine army to more of such mishandling.

As for Sickles, his Third Corps had lost 4119 men in killed, wounded, and missing, the largest percentage of corps loss in the entire army. During the talk he allowed himself to make a few critical remarks about his friend Hooker—not about the conduct of the battle but because of Hooker's step in placing the responsibility of advance or retreat on his corps leaders.[24] It was a feeling he need not have expressed, as it turned out.

In a rare display of humility, Sickles admitted that he might not know as much about military strategy as his West Point colleagues, but he made it plain that he was not taking a back seat to anybody in political matters. He pointed out that the Peace Democrats and Copperheads had made ominous gains in the last election. In the light of this growing peace sentiment, and not forgetting the danger of European recognition of the Confederacy, Sickles declared that the cost of defeat would be incalculable, and on this purely political ground he advocated a retirement.[25]

A little later, Hooker returned with Butterfield. Although the vote of the corps generals was three to two in favor of fighting it out, Hooker told them he would accept the responsibility of ordering the retirement.

The strapping Pennsylvanian Reynolds, lolling on a cot in the corner, was disgusted.

"What was the use of calling us together at this time of night when he intended to retreat anyway?" he growled after Hooker had left.[26]

Next day the Army of the Potomac surrendered its priceless bridgehead, surrendered its chance of defeating a numerically inferior Confederate force which itself had taken heavy losses, and retreated across the Rappahannock.

When he got the news in Washington, Lincoln was beside himself with shock and grief.

"My God," he groaned, "what will the country say? What will the country say?"

CHAPTER XVIII

Sickles Is the Man

The country had plenty to say. Among the loudest of the sayers was Bennett's New York *Herald*. Secretary of War Stanton, in an unguarded moment, sought to palliate the disaster by declaring that only one-third of the Army of the Potomac was engaged at Chancellorsville—a statement that was not true, since the number was closer to two-thirds. The *Herald* promptly exploited this blunder. If Hooker had stood off Lee with only one-third of his army, why had he not thrown in the rest of his men and won a victory? Hooker, the *Herald* snapped, had "signally failed," and went on:

> . . . simple justice to the brave army . . . demands his removal. Who, then, is the man to command the Army of the Potomac? . . . General Daniel E. Sickles is that man. Had his advance upon the enemy on Saturday been promptly and strongly supported by General Hooker, the stampede of the 11th Corps might have been avoided . . . In all the details of Saturday's and Sunday's operations the reader will perceive that General Sickles displayed that quickness of perception, that promptness in action, and that never-failing self-possession which distinguish the great commander. Against the possible objection that he has had no education at a military academy, we need only say that Julius Caesar, Oliver Cromwell, General Washington, General Jackson, General Scott and a host of other distinguished military chieftains of the past and present, may be placed in the same category . . . We therefore would call

the attention of President Lincoln to General Sickles as the man for this position, for he has shown in the recent nine days' campaign on the Rappahannock the skill and coolness of a great commander in the hour of action and the crisis of danger.[1]

There were other laudatory articles in the *Herald,* one of them crediting Sickles with "the coolness and skillfulness of a veteran of a hundred campaigns." [2] Truly, Bennett had executed a complete about-face and the two men were now fast friends. Sickles, who never failed to read the papers, could hardly have been anything but delighted at this sort of publicity. It was flattering to be mentioned in the same breath with Caesar and Washington. If he felt some reservations about his ability to lead the Army of the Potomac, it was the first time in his life that his ambitions had been curbed by a feeling of incompetency. Self-doubt was something that never plagued him. But for all his ambition, Sickles had a deep-running sense of comradeship and loyalty that could not be submerged even by his inordinate hunger for advancement. Hooker was his friend and he stood by him.

The Chancellorsville fiasco had blown up dark squalls of criticism in the North, and Hooker was now on the receiving end of the same sort of vituperation he had once so enthusiastically aimed at McClellan and Burnside. "Every body is feeling badly," General Patrick noted in his diary, "& Hooker & Butterfield are attempting to punish the newspapers for telling the truth," adding two days later, "I have had telegraphic dispatches of all sorts during the day and one requiring all *Heralds* brought to the Army to be burned, on account of abusive Editorials of Gen. Hooker and Dan. Butterfield—Butterfield ordered them burned . . . There is a feeling of universal disgust among the Officers as to the Management of Gen. Hooker . . ." [3]

Possibly, as the newspapers blazed, Fighting Joe achieved a more charitable view of the shortcomings of his predecessors. If so, he was hardly a good loser. He blamed his defeat on Stoneman, whose cavalry raid had misfired. He blamed it on

Sedgwick for failing to press on from Fredericksburg. He blamed it on the Eleventh Corps' rout, and on the cannonball that knocked him flat, and even claimed he had not received wholehearted support from some of his corps commanders. He blamed it on anything and anybody but the person solely responsible—Joe Hooker.

After the humiliated army returned to its camp at Falmouth, the commanding general, if he kept up with the news, was well informed of a fairly unanimous editorial agreement that he should be replaced, whether by Meade, Reynolds, Couch, Sickles, or someone else—almost anyone else. In New York, the lawyer Strong gave ear to a rumor that Sickles was to succeed Hooker, commenting, "A very doubtful improvement, but there are judicious men who rate Sickles very high." [4]

There were also some who did not. Young Captain Charles Francis Adams sounded off like a man with a bellyful:

> Sickles, Butterfield and Hooker are the disgrace and bane of this army; they are our three humbugs, intriguers and demagogues. Let them be disposed of and the army would be well satisfied to be led by any of the corps commanders.[5]

At Falmouth, the army returned to its old routine of watching Lee across the way and attending to other matters. For one thing, Brigadier General Revere was brought up before a court-martial on charges preferred by Sickles, who said Revere "shamefully led to the rear the whole of the Second Brigade and portions of two others, thus subjecting these proud soldiers for the first time to the humiliation of being marched to the rear while their comrades were under fire." [6] Sickles testified angrily against his subordinate, and Revere was dismissed from the army —a sentence Lincoln later softened by allowing him to resign.

Sickles' impulsive friend Meagher, whose hard-fighting Irish Brigade had taken such losses that it was now down to a mere 400 men, wrote Stanton for permission to go home and recruit more men. Stanton did not deign to reply, and Meagher resigned his commission in a huff.[7]

In truth, the army was considerably reduced in numbers not only by casualties but also by the departure of several thousands of soldiers whose enlistment period was up. Conscription was now in force and the depleted ranks were theoretically to be filled by drafted men, but the draft was not working smoothly as yet. Although Sickles was among those who felt that officers should be permitted to leave the army for recruitment work, he was doing anything but quitting. He had won new laurels at Chancellorsville, he was a corps commander, and it may be that he envisioned even higher position as a possibility.

If so, he made no effort to climb at the expense of Hooker. In his official report on the battle he went rather needlessly out of his way to praise the commander, remarking, "It is impossible to pass over without mention the irrepressible enthusiasm of the troops for Major-General Hooker, which was evinced in hearty and prolonged cheers as he rode along the lines of the Third, Eleventh and Twelfth Corps." [8]

Nor did he fail to take this opportunity to deliver an official reminder that his own men had fought nobly, writing with pardonable pride, "As long as the history of this war shall be read, conspicuous upon its pages will be the record of the achievements and the sacrifices of the Third Army Corps in the battles of the Wilderness and of Fairview." [9]

General Pleasonton, a firm friend of Sickles, agreed on that score and also felt that the Third Corps commander himself deserved high praise. He wrote Sickles: "In concluding this report, general, you will pardon me for expressing to you the admiration excited by the resources with which you met every difficulty on that trying occasion [Hazel Grove], and I can frankly assure you the courteous politeness and easy composure so conspicuous in all your actions inspired confidence in all around you." [10]

At length it became apparent that Hooker, despite his blunders and regardless of the criticism, was to be retained in command. The Army of the Potomac, as Meade pointed out, already looked ridiculous enough because of its policy of changing commanders after every lost battle. But Darius Couch had had all he could stomach of Hooker, and he asked to be relieved and was. His post as leader of the Second Corps was given to General Winfield Scott Hancock, a handsome Pennsylvanian renowned for his talents at fighting and cussing.

Among the post-mortems of defeat, there developed a minor difference between Generals Hooker and Meade over the question of just how Meade had voted at the midnight council near Chancellorsville. Hooker, still smarting in ignominy, was trying to slough off a portion of it by claiming that his corps commanders had favored retreat. Meade, a stickler for correctness who wanted his true thoughts on the record, sent notes to the other four commanders who had been present, asking them to give their impression of his remarks at the council. Sickles replied to Meade in part:

> You expressed the opinion that General Hooker should attack the enemy; that a retrograde movement . . . had become impossible. This opinion afterwards yielded somewhat to other considerations; among these were our deficiencies in supplies; our imperilled communications; the hazards of a general engagement with an enemy whose forces we could not estimate . . . At the close of the discussion, my impression was that your original preference appeared to have surrendered to the clear conviction of the Commanding General of the necessity which dictated his return to the North bank of the Rappahannock . . .

Meade, who had made it clear to others present that he wanted to fight it out, must have been distressed to learn that Sickles had gained the opposite opinion. In the same mail Sickles sent a copy of Meade's note and his own reply to James Gordon Bennett of the *Herald,* along with a letter to Bennett marked "private":

> For your perusal and information—not for publication at present—I enclose some correspondence between Major Genl

Meade & myself & Gen. Hooker about the Council of War on the
night of the 4th—that eventful Council which was contrived in
the "Wilderness" and deliberated in the Storm and brought
forth the Monster retrograde movement . . .[11]

The letter went on to urge renewed efforts against the rebellion and make some pointed critcisms of the government in
failing to put teeth in conscription so that regiments which
"are mere skeletons" might be filled. The propriety of relaying
another general's personal letter about a fairly confidential
army dispute to the publisher of the nation's biggest newspaper
may be questioned. Sickles' motive in doing so is not entirely
clear, since the controversy was of little importance, but apparently he wanted to keep on close terms with Bennett, to
defend Hooker and to let the publisher feel he was getting
"inside" information.

Be that as it may, Sickles felt enough campaign fatigue so
that early in June he took leave and returned to New York.[12]
While he was being feted by the Board of Councilmen in the
metropolis, the Confederate Army of Northern Virginia was
already on the move. Lee was now resolved to carry the war
into the North.

As the rebel army marched through the Blue Ridge and down
the Shenandoah, Hooker's men followed along a shorter arc east
of the mountains, keeping between the enemy and Washington.
There were some bloody cavalry engagements along the route,
that arm of the Federals now being under Pleasonton, and
young Captain Adams was in the thick of it with his squadron.
Adams erupted in disgust at the army's leadership in a letter
to his brother:

All whom I . . . see seem only to sadly inquire of themselves how much disaster and slaughter this poor army must go
through before the government will consider the public mind
ripe for another change. Meade or Reynolds seems to be the
favorite for the rising man and either is respectable and would

be a great improvement on the drunk-murdering-arson dynasty
now prevailing of Hooker, Sickles and Butterfield.[13]

As the opposing armies marched northward and a major battle
grew steadily more imminent, the signs were increasing that
Hooker once more was losing his grip. At Chancellorsville he
had been given bitter proof of the cunning and enterprise of
Lee. Possibly the thought preyed on him. If he could not defeat
Lee at Chancellorsville with all the odds in his favor, what
would happen in the next battle? He began to magnify the size
of the enemy army.[14] His dispatches to Lincoln grew more
querulous, demanding, and even insolent. He topped it off with
a telegram insisting that the impossible was expected of him and
ending with the "request that I may be relieved from the position I occupy."

Perhaps Hooker regarded it as incredible that commanders
would be changed at this critical point, and hoped by his threat
to get concessions in the way of more reinforcements. If he was
bluffing, his bluff was called. Lincoln was finished with Hooker.
Early on the morning of June 28th, an officer from Washington
aroused General Meade in his tent near Frederick, Maryland,
and told him he had bad news for him—he was the new commander of the Army of the Potomac.

There is no evidence that Lincoln was impressed enough by
the military advice of the New York *Herald* even to consider
Sickles for the post,[15] or that Sickles' good friend Stanton urged
his elevation. The gravest hour of the Union was approaching
inexorably, heralded by the pounding of horses' hooves and the
footfalls of almost 200,000 men marching northward. Entirely
apart from the question of army seniority, Lincoln, with all
his admiration for Sickles' fighting qualities, must have had
doubts as to the New Yorker's fitness for top command.

It happened that Sickles, his leave over, rejoined the army
at Frederick on the very day of Hooker's removal. To him, the
eclipse of his friend was "a misfortune to the army" [16] and a

personal misfortune as well. No more would he mingle on terms of amiable familiarity with the commanding general. The boss now was Meade, whom he considered tiresome and stuffy, and who regarded Sickles with reservations of his own.

Up ahead about thirty-five miles was a Pennsylvania town no one ever heard of before. Gettysburg.

CHAPTER XIX

"This Is a Good Battle-field"

General George Gordon Meade was a fifty-three-year-old regular army man whose careworn, pouch-eyed expression made him look like a nervous pedagog and belied the fact that he had shown great personal valor at Fredericksburg and elsewhere and had been severely wounded on the Peninsula. Meade was the sort who could go out and get wounded without making it appear particularly spectacular or heroic. A religious man, he was a model of rectitude, devoted to his family. He was given to worry, so that occasionally when too many troubles beset him he would fly into tantrums. Behind his back he was known as the Old Snapping Turtle. While he had none of the color and magnetism of Hooker or Sickles, he had proved himself a solid soldier in lesser commands and had the respect of the men and most of his general-officer colleagues.

There were exceptions, of course. He did not enjoy the whole-hearted admiration of Sickles, who later said he "apprehended that disaster might result" [1] from Hooker's removal. Nor was spruce young Daniel Butterfield, Fighting Joe's chief of staff, inclined to revere the man who had replaced his crony. During the previous winter, Butterfield had been overjoyed at promotion to command of the Fifth Corps, only to be cast into despair when Meade "bumped" him out of the post on the strength of seniority [2] —a bitter blow to the little dandy from Utica and possibly one that still rankled.

So, as the army marched toward a fateful field, all was not

quite *en rapport* between the general commanding on the one
hand and his Third Corps commander and his own chief of staff
on the other. Meade would have been happy to rid himself of
Butterfield. In fact he tendered the post to Andrew Humphreys,
who was now leading Sickles' second division. But General
Humphreys, known by his friends as a "fighting fool," liked
combat better than staff work, and he decided he would be
more useful at the head of his division. Butterfield was kept on
for the time being—a decision Meade was later to regret.

The Old Snapping Turtle was faced with too much of a crisis
to waste time on details. Gratified as he was at the honor of top
command, he seized it gingerly. He was haunted by self-doubt.[3]
He had considered Hooker a "good soldier"—and look at what
Lee had done to Hooker at Chancellorsville! A man might be
ever so foxy in his handling of 10,000 or 20,000 men, but let him
be saddled with sole authority over the fates of nearly 100,000
men and none could tell whether the weight would bend or
break him.

In taking command at this frightening moment, Meade was
shouldering a duty enormously magnified by the pressure of
time. He had to protect Washington and Baltimore, he had to
unify seven army corps whose reaction to Hooker's removal
might not improve morale, he had to seek out a fast-marching
enemy and beat him—and he had to do all this with speed.
Maybe only a few days would tell the tale of victory or disaster.
The Confederates were now well into Pennsylvania, and Governor Curtin of that state was in a frenzy. In Harrisburg and
Philadelphia, green militiamen were being handed muskets they
scarcely knew how to shoot, and nervous citizens were preparing
to flee. For the first time the war had come to the Keystone State,
the heartland of the Union. If the Confederates could win here,
then the game might be all but over.

A dashing and aggressive commander might well have been
shaken at the prospect, and Meade, for all his tactical ability,
was not that. Caution ruled him as he hurried his army forward
with orders that showed his own uncertainty. Feeling that Lee

was bound to attack, he contemplated taking a strong defensive position along Pipe Creek in northern Maryland. Yet he sent a division of cavalry under John Buford, and his First and Eleventh Corps into Pennsylvania to find the enemy, presumably not just to watch him.

As the army marched, Meade on June 29th administered a polite rebuke to Sickles:

> I am directed by the commanding general to inform you that the train of your corps is at a stand-still at Middleburg, and delaying, of course, all movements in the rear. He wishes you to give your immediate and personal attention to keeping your train in motion.
>
> Very Respectfully, &c
> S. Williams
> Asst. Adj. General [4]

Never one to relish criticism, Sickles must have been nettled at this suggestion that his slowness was holding up other units. Next day came another little stinger:

> The commanding general noticed with regret the very slow movement of your corps yesterday. It is presumed you marched at an early hour, and up to 6 P.M. the rear of your column had not passed Middleburg, distant from your camp of the night before some 12 miles only. . . . The Second Corps in the same space of time made a march nearly double your own. [5]

On the evening of June 30th, Sickles made his headquarters in a farmhouse just east of Emmitsburg, Maryland, while his corps went into bivouac in the fields. The men had been marching steadily and hard for three weeks, a strain on leather as well as muscle, and some of the soldiers were barefoot. [6] To the tired fighters there was one compensation—they were in beautiful rolling country never heretofore touched by the conflict, friendly country where the citizens cheered them and gave them flowers, fresh bread, and cakes.

Early on July 1st, Sickles sent his senior aide, Major Henry Tremain, galloping off to find General Reynolds of the First and get whatever orders Reynolds had to give. Meade had placed Reynolds in command of the left wing of the army, comprising the First, Third, and Eleventh Corps, and all Tremain knew was that Reynolds was somewhere off to the north.

Tremain rode along, asking questions of the natives. As he neared Gettysburg he heard the rumble of cannon, and after that he merely had to follow the sound. Buford, the pugnacious Union cavalryman, had encountered a Confederate column heading toward Gettysburg from the west and was welcoming them with canister and musketry. Tremain found Reynolds near the theological seminary to the west of the town. The general had ridden up in advance of his troops to size up the situation.

"Tell General Sickles I think he had better come up," Reynolds said to the aide.[7]

Tremain rode south again and in due time reported to Sickles with this message. Sickles was in a quandary, for he had been ordered by Meade to hold his position at Emmitsburg, and now Reynolds directed him to proceed to Gettysburg. He sent another courier off to Reynolds and paced the porch of the farmhouse, chewing a cigar as he waited. Sometime later, a dispatch rider galloped up, his horse dripping lather. He handed Sickles a note: "General Reynolds is killed. For God's sake, come up. —Howard." [8]

Events had been rushing to a climax at Gettysburg to force Meade to give battle at a spot he had not contemplated. Reynolds, a spirited commander aroused at seeing his native Pennsylvania invaded, had appraised the layout and decided to fight it out right there. He had hurried his First Corps up to support Buford, and had given the advance units of A. P. Hill's Confederate corps a licking. But more of the gray-clad troopers came on—there seemed to be an endless amount of them. A sharpshooter's bullet penetrated Reynolds' brain, and the gallant general's body was borne away on a blanket swung between muskets. Oliver Howard had brought up his Eleventh Corps to take command as the senior officer present and to get set for an assault from another Confederate corps—Lieutenant General Richard Ewell's, just in from the direction of York. Ewell's men had attacked with such fury and numbers that Howard's corps was forced to retire through the town, losing a good many men in so doing. In the battle, Ewell was shot through the leg, a wound that did not even make him wince since the leg happened to be a wooden one, a memento of Second Bull Run.[9]

So now Howard was hard pressed and pleading for help, and Sickles, with explicit orders from Meade to hold Emmitsburg, was in a dilemma. He resolved it by leaving two brigades under General Graham at Emmitsburg while he led the rest of his corps post-haste toward Gettysburg.[10] They marched that hot evening through lush, well-kept farming country vastly different from denuded Virginia, with wheat almost ready to thresh and fruit growing heavy on the boughs. Tremain, riding on ahead, saw three farmers sitting on a fence and asked them what was happening at Gettysburg.

"Our men's a-getting it, I guess," one of them replied.[11] Perhaps this was a natural assumption after the way they had been a-getting it at Chancellorsville, Fredericksburg, and beyond.

Sickles' Third Corps, which had numbered more than 19,000 men before Chancellorsville, had been reduced by casualties, illness and the departure of men whose enlistment time was up, to slightly less than 12,000. Instead of three divisions he now had two, one led by Major General Birney, who had won his second star on Sickles' recommendation for his good work at Chancellorsville, the other by the battle-loving Humphreys. Though diminished in numbers, the corps' morale was high. It was proud of the added prestige it had won in the Wilderness and Fairview, proud of its commanders and quite ready to follow them anywhere.

Some of the indomitable confidence and cockiness of Daniel Edgar Sickles had filtered down through the echelons and into the ranks of this combat-proven Third Corps. A sixteen-year-old fifer from Boston named C. W. Bardeen who had enlisted before he was dry behind the ears, was to speak glowingly of Sickles for the rest of his life.[12] In the Third Corps were soldiers from New York, New Jersey, Pennsylvania, Massachusetts, New Hampshire, Maine, Michigan, and Rhode Island, and there was prideful agreement among them that their outfit could fight like no other. Few if any of the 11,000-odd had the slightest doubt about Major General Sickles' ability to lead them with valor and military skill into whatever was to come.

If any of the higher officers had reservations about Sickles' wisdom and tactical soundness, it was Brigadier General Andrew A. Humphreys, the dashing West Pointer who led the Second Division. Humphreys, a good friend of Meade who had been offered the chief of staff's post, may have been aware of Meade's misgivings about Sickles. If so, he did not let it affect him in the least, for he was to cover himself with glory following orders given him by the New York politician who had never studied military theory on the banks of the Hudson.

The road to Gettysburg crossed the Pennsylvania state line only a mile north of Emmitsburg and wound onward in a generally northeasterly direction toward the seminary town fourteen miles away. It was the first time many of the soldiers had been in Pennsylvania. They liked the looks of the country as well as the pretty girls who waved at them. After dark, a group of Excelsior men saw a light in a farmhouse and strode over to see if they could get some home-cooked food. They looked in and were startled to see a party of rebel artillerymen seated at the dining room table stowing away beef and potatoes with enthusiasm. Clearly the Confederate positions were not far distant. The Excelsiors sneaked away, deciding to make their hard-tack do.[13]

The rumble of artillery from the northeast had become desultory now, and by the time the first units of Sickles' corps reached Gettysburg that night, the day's fighting was over. The town had been lost to the rebels, with the Federal First and

Eleventh Corps falling back to strong positions on Cemetery Hill overlooking the village. Tired infantrymen were sprawled among tombstones, wryly joking about a sign that promised a five-dollar fine to anyone firing a gun within the limits of the graveyard. Meade had not yet arrived, General Slocum of the Twelfth Corps being in charge as the ranking officer present. Sickles sent a dispatch to Butterfield asking if his remaining force should be brought up from Emmitsburg, and ending with the observation, "This is a good battle-field." [14]

When Meade reached the field late that night, he was a man burdened down by the responsibility that faced him after only three days in command. It appeared now that there would be a battle at Gettysburg, a place neither he nor his adversary, the peerless Lee, had chosen deliberately. On its result would hang issues momentous enough to chill the blood. Defeat for the Army of the Potomac here might mean an assault on Washington, recognition of the Confederacy by foreign nations, utter discouragement in the North, the final end of the Union. The stakes were not merely high. They were crucial.

With him Meade had brought his staff engineering chief, young, ascetic-looking Brigadier General Gouverneur K. Warren. Behind him at Taneytown he had left his chief of staff, Butterfield, a man he did not altogether trust and whom he had once labeled, along with Sickles, as a "bad influence." Butterfield's job was to speed along the remaining units of the army and get them to Gettysburg in time to brace for the clash—work enough for any man, and yet Meade was probably glad to shake off his dapper staff chief and rely on Warren, whom he liked, as his right bower. The commanding general had been acting like anything but a man who sought a collision with the enemy. His dispatches to Washington showed a hesitancy and caution that seemed to increase as his army neared the foe, and he had delayed unaccountably in reaching the field and taking personal command. But now he was there, and appeared to have steeled himself for the ordeal—a pitched battle with Robert E. Lee and the Army of Northern Virginia. Meade stayed up most of the night taking stock of the situation and meditating an attack on his right.

When dawn came, Meade found a field at his disposal that was in many respects admirably suited for defense. At his right was steep Culp's Hill, where Slocum and his Twelfth Corps were solidly established. To the left of this was Cemetery Hill, over-looking the town, a height occupied by the somewhat battered First and Eleventh Corps. Curving to the south from this eminence was the long line of Cemetery Ridge, which lost in elevation as it approached a rugged, boulder-strewn hill known as Little Round Top. Still further south was the even higher Round Top itself, whose peak was almost a half-mile from its smaller namesake and was therefore beyond effective rifle range. From Culp's Hill to Little Round Top was an uninterrupted curve of high ground roughly in the form of the letter J, about three miles in length, which offered good positions for infantry and artillery. Here, as Sickles had said, was a "good battlefield," if the enemy could be prevented from outflanking it.

Nature, of course, could hardly be expected to arrange the terrain in every detail according to a commander's wish. It was true that that part of the ridge nearing Little Round Top was not as high as the rest, was dotted in places with trees and brush, and might be less easily defended.

It happened that this was the very section of the ridge assigned to General Sickles and the Third Corps.

At eight o'clock on the morning of July 2nd, one of Meade's aides arrived at Sickles' headquarters to see how the corps was faring. Sickles, who had been up most of the night, was asleep in his tent, but was aroused. He said that his corps was not yet posted and that he was in some doubt as to where he should go. The aide, who was Meade's son, rode back to the command-ing general and informed him of this. Meade sent him back post-haste to tell Sickles that he was to prolong the line along the ridge already formed by the Second Corps. He was to place his right on the Second Corps' left, and his left on Little Round Top.[15]

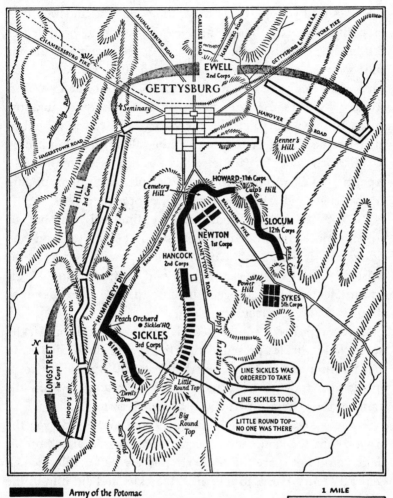

Army of the Potomac
Army of Northern Virginia

1 MILE

Sickles told young Meade he was now moving and would be in position shortly. Then the New Yorker who had written Butterfield "This is a good battle-field," took a long look around and became less and less satisfied with his own part of it.[16] Parts of his line were low, strewn with boulders, or had visibility reduced by trees. He later described it as "unfit for infantry, impracticable for artillery." [17] Moreover, he saw ground slightly higher some 2000 feet in front of him, along the Emmitsburg Road which roughly paralleled his position. He envisioned a repetition of Chancellorsville, with Lee planting dozens of guns on that ridge and raking his corps with hot metal.

He got his two divisions into the line assigned, but by eleven o'clock his misgivings were strong enough to send him riding to Meade's headquarters almost a mile north at the Leister house. Exactly what Sickles said to Meade, and Meade said to Sickles, became fogged because the two later disagreed about it, but a few facts stand out.

Meade repeated his instructions as to the position Sickles was to hold. Sickles protested that there were disadvantages in that position and inquired whether he could dispose his corps on his own judgment. Meade replied, "Certainly, within the limits of the general instructions I have given to you." [18]

Sickles asked Meade if he would come and look over the ground, but the commanding general, fearing an attack on his right, could not spare the time. He told his staff artillery chief, General Henry Hunt, to return with Sickles and aid him in the placing of batteries.

When the two men rode back together, Sickles pointed out to Hunt a movement he had been contemplating. He proposed to move his line forward to occupy the ridge along the Emmitsburg Road—ground he was convinced Lee would exploit unless the Federals got there first—and he asked Hunt if he would authorize the move in Meade's name.

Hunt knew better than that. He was not going to usurp the authority of the commanding general. He could see advantages as well as drawbacks to Sickles' proposed position, but he told the New Yorker that such an order would have to come from Meade himself.[19] Then Hunt rode off to inspect battery positions elsewhere.

Meanwhile, through a misdunderstanding Meade had allowed Buford's division of cavalry, which was badly used up, to retire. Meade was under the impression that other cavalry was available—an error, for the rest of the horse was violently engaged with the Confederate Stuart off the Union right. This peculiar slip did not seem to upset Meade overmuch when he learned of it, for he appeared convinced that the main rebel attack would come on his right. It left the Union left flank—Sickles' flank—unprotected by cavalry.[20]

Off on Sickles' left, General Birney was as uneasy about the situation as his chief. With Sickles' permission, Birney sent out eagle-eyed Colonel Berdan with a hundred of his Sharpshooters and the 3rd Maine regiment to find what the enemy was doing. Berdan moved with his men across a peach orchard —soon to gain such sanguinary fame that it became capitalized —and across the Emmitsburg Road. The sun was higher, it was growing hotter by the minute, and the men were sweating as they moved forward with caution. Near a farmhouse beyond the road they met a barefooted boy, a staunch Union lad.

"Look out!" he warned. "There are lots of rebels in there, in rows." [21]

Berdan's men were skeptical. They pushed westward into the woods and found them posted with rebel pickets. The Sharpshooters and Maine marksmen began blazing away and soon had a warm little skirmish on their hands. They drove the pickets back some 300 yards when, near Pitzer's Run, they almost collided with three columns of enemy infantry moving toward the Union left. Things quickly grew too uncomfortable for Berdan and his 300 men, and within twenty minutes they had to retire, having lost sixty-seven of their number in killed and wounded.[22]

When this encounter was reported to Sickles, along with the news of a heavy enemy movement toward his left, his concern grew apace. The rebels, he felt sure, were sweeping around in concealment to assail him in large force, and soon they would seize that inviting high ground across the valley to his front and rake him unmercifully—unless he occupied it first.

Sickles hesitated no longer. He ordered the forward move that was to go down in history as Gettysburg's colossal blunder, or as the maneuver that saved the day and the Union, depending on the point of view. With battle flags flying, Humphreys' division marched across the valley and up the incline almost to the Emmitsburg Road. Birney's division moved forward and to the left, taking a line almost at a right angle to that of Humphreys. The Third Corps now formed an extended V. Birney's new line began at rock-strewn Devil's Den, a quarter-mile in front of Little Round Top, and joined Humphreys' at the hill on the Emmitsburg Road where the peaches grew.[23]

This maneuver had observers on Cemetery Ridge pop-eyed. General John Gibbon, astride his horse alongside of Hancock, wondered if there had been an order for an advance which the Second Corps somehow had missed.[24] Colonel Frank A. Haskell, a Wisconsinite on Gibbon's staff, had a low opinion of Sickles but had to admit "It was a magnificent sight to see those ten or twelve thousand men—they were good men . . . sweep steadily down the slope . . . toward their destined position." Magnificent it was, but in Haskell's opinion foolhardy: "I suppose the truth is that General Sickles thought he was doing for the best . . . But one can scarcely tell what may have been the motives of such a man—a politician, and some other things, exclusive of the Barton Key affair—a man after show and notoriety and newspaper fame and the adulation of the mob." [25]

Without question, General Sickles thought he *was* acting for the best, though he was going against Meade's orders. He felt rightly that he knew the ground better than Meade and was apprised of enemy operations that the commander seemed to ignore. He was resentful that Meade was so infernally preoccupied with guarding against an attack on his right that he dismissed the left as of minor consequence. The Third Corps leader—and his trusted General Birney—were both seriously concerned about an enemy maneuver Meade underestimated. Sickles had been guilty of many a foolish impulse in his day, but the change of position was not impulse. It was the fruit of careful deliberation. He had pondered this move for hours, harassed by his growing belief that he would receive the brunt of the onslaught, and he had made it after at least one futile effort to persuade Meade to look over the ground in person.

The forward move was made with the best of intentions, in the conviction that it would offer greater safety to the Third Corps and the whole army. Its wisdom was another matter entirely. While Sickles gained tactical advantage in some ways, he lost it in others. His corps was thrust out far ahead of the rest of the army, unsupported at either end. There was a half-mile gap between his right flank and the left of the Second Corps, back on Cemetery Ridge.[26] His center formed an angle at the orchard so that judiciously-placed enemy artillery could enfilade his lines both ways. Furthermore, in his original line Sickles had covered slightly more than a mile of ground and had been spread out quite thin. Now, occupying a line almost twice as long, his lack of depth was greatly magnified.

Worst of all, Little Round Top, soon to be recognized as the key to the whole Union position, was left without a single fighting man on its rocky height.[27]

But the Devil's Den offered excellent defensive cover, the high peach orchard was soon bristling with armament, and Sickles and most of his men were quite pleased about the change. Sickles set up his headquarters at the comfortable Trostle farmhouse, from which he could see both extensions of his line. Some of Humphreys' men on the right ran into a rare piece of luck. They found a pretty miss named Josephine Miller at the Rogers farmhouse who set to work baking biscuits for them.[28]

Noon was past, and by 3:30 everybody was wondering why it took the Confederates so long to begin the day's work. Then, with the ominous gradualness of a gathering summer storm, Sickles' pickets to the south of Birney's line were driven back by increasing numbers of rebels. Southern cannon began speaking more insistently. The long-awaited attack was finally beginning,[29] and Meade rode up to see what was brewing.

He must have been astonished at what he saw, but according to one witness the Old Snapping Turtle did not snap.

"General, I am afraid you are too far out," he said to Sickles.

Sickles made it politely plain that he did not agree. The line he was holding, he said, was a strong line and the best one, and he was confident that with adequate support he could defend it. "However," he added, "I will withdraw if you wish, sir."

"I think it is too late," Meade said. "The enemy will not allow you. If you need more artillery, call on the reserve. The Fifth Corps—and a division of Hancock's—will support you." [30]

Meade's last words were jerked out as his horse reared in terror at the report of a cannon nearby and bolted away, out of hand. For several seconds the commanding general of the Army of the Potomac was astride a crazed animal as willing to carry him into the Confederate lines as anywhere else.[31] Then he got his steed under control and was off to bring up support for Sickles—support which soon would be desperately needed.

For now Hood's and McLaws' divisions of Longstreet's corps catapulted themselves furiously against Birney's extended line, and the hot summer air shivered with rebel yells, staccato musketry, and the thunder of artillery.

CHAPTER XX

Never Call Retreat

Birney's seasoned veterans met the assault with coolness and valor, fighting from behind boulders, trees, and stone walls. But this was a charge that meant business. Longstreet's Confederates were swarming in like bees. At the right, in the orchard salient, Graham's brigade was solidly dug in and backed by thirty belching guns. In the center, De Trobriand's brigade had twelve howitzers behind it as the men crouched in a knee-deep wheat field edged by trees. On the left, protected by a six-gun battery, General J. H. H. Ward's brigade fought in wild, boulder-strewn terrain ending in the fantastic rock formations of Devil's Den, overlooking sluggish Plum Run.

Ward took the first shock, but in a few moments the yelling brigades in gray hit the whole line with fearful impact. General Sickles' expectation of mass attack on his position was proven violently correct. Longstreet had done exactly what Sickles had thought he would do—wheeled around and come in from the south. Humphreys' division along the Emmitsburg Road was unoccupied at the moment, with Birney taking it all. Birney's men had fought every step of the way at Chancellorsville and if anything they were tougher now. A good many of them being Pennsylvanians, they battled with an added fury in defending their home ground, and charging rebels were falling like autumn leaves. Yet more came on. It soon was apparent that the Third Corps was heavily outnumbered.

"The Confederates appeared to have the devil in them," [1]

De Trobriand observed. He was sweating in his efforts to keep his sagging line intact. Soon he was forced to send a regiment to the aid of Ward, who was in danger of being turned. De Trobriand had not approved of Sickles' forward move, which he described as a step showing "more ardor to advance to meet the fight than a nice appreciation of the means to sustain it," [2] but he fought like a Trojan to sustain it.

His thoughts then were sombre: "Hold on there, hard and firm! There is no reserve." He had only three regiments left—thin regiments which grew thinner before his eyes as enemy bullets took their toll—and when an aide of Birney came to plead for another regiment, De Trobriand had an unanswerable answer: "Tell General Birney that . . . far from being able to furnish reinforcements to anyone, I shall be in need of them myself in less than a quarter hour." [3]

Birney, reduced to switching regiments from one spot to another wherever the attack was about to break through, sent an urgent appeal to Sickles for help.[4] Sickles hurried over Burling's brigade from Humphreys' division on the double. Sickles in turn was imploring Meade for reinforcements, and Meade was working to get them up. It was a time of such extremity that minutes might make the difference between holding and collapsing in rout.

About this time, young General Warren went over to Little Round Top to see what was doing there. He was horrified to find it unoccupied except by a couple of signalmen. There was nothing in the world to prevent the Confederates from gamboling up the hill like picnickers. When they got it—and planted batteries on it—the whole Union line along Cemetery Ridge, as well as Sickles' advanced position, would be at their mercy. To pile crisis on top of emergency, Warren saw a column of rebels approaching from the west.

Warren forgot all about a general's dignity and sprinted down the east slope of the hill like a rabbit. He came upon a regiment of the Fifth Corps, the 140th New York under a handsome young West Pointer, Colonel Patrick O'Rorke. O'Rorke was marching around the hill to reinforce Sickles. He had no authority to leave his own division, and was under no compulsion to obey General Warren, but there was an expression in the general's face that clearly said this was no time to debate the niceties.[5]

"I'll take the responsibility!" Warren yelled. "Come on!"

O'Rorke came on the run. So did Lieutenant Charles Hazlett, heading the brigade artillery. The slope of Little Round Top was too rugged for horses, so Hazlett got his cannon up there by sheer, back-breaking manpower. O'Rorke's infantrymen reached the summit in time to see a swarm of howling Confederates racing up the west slope. Gunfire rattled like hail, and men began to fall. Hazlett's artillerymen were winded and drenched with sweat, but they dragged their pieces to the top. They unlimbered them and began to spew out canister. The Confederates might have taken the height without a shot and personally altered history had they been five minutes earlier Under this withering volley they faltered in their charge and took cover. O'Rorke and Hazlett were both killed, as were many other valorous men, but by the grace of General Warren and a regiment of heroes the all-important hill was held until reinforcements came and the crisis was past.

Down on Sickles' front, the crisis was anything but past. Birney's division, a third of its men lying in their own blood, was giving ground under a torrent of fire. By now Humphreys' division along the Emmitsburg Road was catching it as fiercely from A. P. Hill's Confederates. Sickles' aides were using up their horses in frantic dashes to make pleas for help. Graham's men in the peach orchard salient gave way before a charge by rebels under General Barksdale—the same Barksdale who had lost his wig in that peculiar Congressional tussle four years earlier. Graham himself was wounded and captured, and Barksdale this time lost more than his wig. He was killed. A brigade of Fifth Corps men under General James Barnes came to Birney's aid and found the field an inferno. Barnes, it was said, cried, "It is too hot, my men cannot stand it," [6] and withdrew

them—a charge later denied by Barnes. A brigade from the
Second Corps under General Samuel Zook hurried in to fill
breaches in the line, and although Zook was killed almost immediately, his men staved off disaster for a time. Altogether,
Meade drew units from the First, Second, Fifth, Sixth, and
Twelfth Corps to bolster Sickles' buckling line, but almost half
of Lee's entire army was attacking there.

Private Brannigan, in the thick of it, tried to describe it.
"Fighting, dying, [we] yielded the ground inch by inch, foot
by foot," he wrote, "until all organization ceased and the
corps [was] now a rabble, and yet so terrible a one that the
force driving us were in almost the same condition." [7] Colonel
Haskell, viewing the carnage from Cemetery Ridge, described
it in one sentence:

"What a hell is there down that valley!" [8]

On reflection, Haskell had a strong feeling that this wholesale mayhem was caused solely by Sickles' forward move. "Oh,
if this corps [the Third] had kept its strong position upon the
crest," he mourned, "and supported by the rest of the army
had waited for the attack of the enemy!" [9]

General Sickles, who had ridden off through cannon fire to
examine his lines and talk to Birney and Humphreys, returned
to the Trostle place, remaining on his horse to watch the battle.
Hostile metal was whistling dangerously close, but he seemed
oblivious of personal danger. Though he must have been in a
fever of anxiety for his shattered corps, he gave orders to aides
"in an easy, quiet tone without any excitement," [10] and he seems
never to have entertained the thought of retreat.

It was nearing 6:30, and the fiery sun was lowering off over
the Confederates' lair on Seminary Ridge, when one of those
vagrant cannonballs did not whistle by. It struck the general
on the right leg and left it hanging in shreds.

As he fell from his horse, a couple of soldiers ran to his aid.
They carried him over to the wall of the nearby Trostle barn.
He seemed only moderately upset, and was cool enough to
direct one of the men to buckle a saddle strap tightly over

the thigh as an improvised tourniquet.[11] Major Tremain returned from an errand at this moment and was filled with
concern to see the leader for whom his affection had grown
since the Peninsula days lying white-faced and bleeding.

"General," he exclaimed somewhat unnecessarily, "are you
hurt?"

Sickles was still thinking of the Third Corps. "Tell General
Birney he must take command," he said in a clear voice.[12]

A stretcher was brought up and the wounded man lifted onto
it. Despite his pain and shock, Sickles was not one to allow
this moment to pass without making full use of its dramatic
value. Being informed that a rumor had gone around that he
was mortally wounded, he requested a stretcher bearer to remove a cigar from a case in an inside pocket and light it for
him.[13] He was carried away with the Havana projecting jauntily
from his mouth, a sight that impressed Colonel William Doster
as he passed by and made him reflect, "This is giving the 'solace
tobacco' a new meaning." [14]

But he was a badly wounded man, and losing blood despite
the strap around his leg. A little to the rear he was transferred
to an ambulance with a medical aide who poured brandy down
his throat in liberal quantities—the routine Civil War method
of counteracting shock. Tremain likewise got into the jolting
wagon for, as he later wrote, "I thought the end had come," [15]
and he did not want Sickles to expire without a friend near him.
Twichell and O'Hagan, the two chaplains, rode up and joined
the cortege, sadly prepared to speed his soul into eternity.

The Third Corps field hospital behind the lines was a ghastly
huddle of tents near Taneytown Road where shrieking wounded
were being brought in by the score to lie in agony or uncon-
sciousness while they waited the ministrations of a sweat-grimed
and hopelessly undermanned staff of surgeons whose arms were
bloodied up to the elbows. Amputations made up by far the
largest percentage of their work. The number of severed arms
and legs in baskets beside the operating tables was already
large by the time Sickles arrived. Since he was a major general

he received the immediate attention of Dr. Thomas Sim, the corps medical director. It was growing dark inside the hospital tent. Candles skewered on bayonets furnished a flickering light while chloroform was administered and Dr. Sim sawed the general's maimed leg off well above the knee.[16] The severed leg of General Sickles was too important an object to be tossed away with all the rest. It was wrapped up and preserved for whatever disposition Sickles might later want to make of it, if he lived.

Meanwhile, the Third Corps had battled with desperate valor and yet had absorbed a beating so brutal that even Chancellorsville seemed routine by comparison. In one of Humphreys' regiments, the commanding colonel was shot, a major took command and was instantly wounded. The command then devolved on a captain, who was killed, as were several other officers, and in the end a corporal found himself the ranking officer.[17]

Altogether, of its less than 12,000 men, the corps in four hours had lost 4211 in killed, wounded, and missing.[18] The loss included many seasoned officers who were virtually irreplaceable. Units of other corps coming to the Third's aid had also taken dreadful punishment. So had the enemy.

Sickles' men had done themselves proud, but they could not contain 30,000 of Longstreet's and Hill's hard-charging marksmen. The extended line had finally been withdrawn over a shell-torn field on which the Confederates came within an ace of breaking through and causing a rout. But in the end the Union reinforcements held—and they held along the very line on Cemetery Ridge that Meade had asked Sickles to occupy in the first place. The rebels, bady hurt themselves, would wait for another day to see if they could smash through to victory.

The Union men were bone-weary as they bivouacked that night, but not too weary to discuss that astonishing forward move made by General Sickles. While the arguments were pro and con, the feeling of Colonel Haskell of the Second Corps was decidedly con. He commented about Sickles:

"I hope the man may never return to the Army of the Potomac, or elsewhere, in a position where his incapacity, or something worse, may bring fruitless destruction to thousands again." [19]

CHAPTER XXI

Tell It to Lincoln

In the morning, while the two armies were preparing to resume the struggle, elaborate arrangements were made to get Sickles to more comfortable quarters in Washington. There was a railroad to Gettysburg, but it was firmly in the hands of the Confederate General Ewell, a man who also had only one leg. The nearest usable rail point was at Littlestown, twelve miles southeast, and the patient would have to be carried in a stretcher every step of the way.

He left with a formidable escort of forty infantrymen, to serve not only as relief stretcher bearers but also as guards, for the trip would be made through country not entirely free from Confederate horse. With him also went his three aides-de-camp; Dr. Sim and a medical aide; Lieutenant Colonel James Rusling; two wagons containing rations and hospital supplies, and a small squadron of cavalry for courier duty.[1] It was costing the hard-pressed Army of the Potomac about the equivalent of one of its more depleted regiments to get the Third Corps commander on his way. Though he had been given an opium pill or two, Sickles was in some pain as he gave instructions to his four bearers on how to carry him with a minimum of jolting—those on the left to place the left foot first, those on the right, the right.

"And don't let me fall," he said wryly. "It would be the last of me." [2]

They made four miles that day, with a veritable thunder of

cannon coming from the rear, when Sickles could stand it
no longer and the party put up for the night at a farmhouse.
But in the morning he arose early and—mark this well—he
shaved.[3]

One of his couriers brought him the glad news that Meade's
army had hurled back the last-ditch charge of Pickett, to send
the Confederate tide, flowing strong ever since Antietam, on
the ebb. At Littlestown a train was waiting for him and other
wounded, arranged for by that genius of army transportation,
General Herman Haupt.[4] Sickles' stretcher was placed across the
backs of two seats, and that was the way he rode with 1500 war-
mangled men to Washington along with Dr. Sim, Tremain,
Rusling, and the other two aides.[5] They reached the capital on
Sunday, July 5th, to find the city, recently fearful of capture,
aflame with enthusiasm over the glorious victory at Gettysburg
—the first time the activities of the Army of the Potomac had
been productive of anything but despair for nigh to a year.

Placed in lodgings on F Street, Sickles was attended by Dr.
Sim, Rusling, and the three aides. What with his harrowing
trip, he was in a weakened condition and was approaching the
crisis that would tell whether he would live or die. Modern
asepsis was unknown at the time. Wounds were packed with lint
scraped from cloths often germ-laden, so that infection was the
rule rather than the exception and post-operative mortality was
enormous, the wonder being that there were any survivors.[6]
The general was in such a shaky state that Dr. Sim refused to
allow him to be lifted into a bed. He stayed on his stretcher in a
bedroom. Orders were that he was to see no one.[7]

He was lying there late that afternoon when an aide entered
and announced his Excellency the President. The order to
see no one went by the boards. Lincoln walked in with his
son Tad, shook hands gravely with Sickles, asked him about his
wound, then adjusted his awkward length to a chair and got
down to the subject uppermost in his mind—Gettysburg. He
had been following Meade's dispatches anxiously. Already he
was haunted by doubts that the cautious Old Snapping Turtle

would pounce on the beaten and retreating Lee and finish him off as he should have been finished at Antietam.

Pitifully weak though he was, and perfectly aware that he might die, there was no man in the world Sickles would rather have seen at that moment than the President. He well knew that Meade might have some unpleasant things to say about his forward move at Gettysburg. On his own part he had a bone to pick with Meade. Sickles regarded his Third Corps with an almost paternal pride and affection. The corps had taken bloody punishment out there in the now capitalized Peach Orchard and Wheat Field and many of its finest men would never again answer rollcall, for which he was inclined to place blame on Meade rather than himself. Dan Sickles could carry himself coolly amid shot and shell, and could light a perfecto while his shattered leg was spouting blood, but his courage was not of the sort that could gracefully admit error.

"Sickles, recumbent on his stretcher, with a cigar between his fingers, puffing it leisurely, answered Mr. Lincoln in detail, but warily, as became so astute a man and soldier," recalled Colonel Rusling, who was present, "and discussed the great battle and its probable consequences with a lucidity and ability remarkable in his condition then . . . Occasionally he would wince with pain, and call sharply to his orderly to wet his fevered stump with water. But he never dropped his cigar, nor lost the thread of his narrative . . . He certainly got his side of the story of Gettysburg well into the President's mind . . ." [8]

"His side of the story of Gettysburg" ought to be italicized and underlined. Even Rusling, the Third Corps quartermaster and an admirer of Sickles, well knew there were two sides to that story and that the crippled general was concentrating on *his* side. Had not Lincoln been a shrewd judge of character, expert in allowing for prejudice, undoubtedly he would have departed with a fixed impression that Sickles was in great part responsible for the victory at Gettysburg and that Meade was a timorous incompetent who was lucky to have good men under him. Sickles would never say such things bluntly, but he was a master at getting an impression across by skilful indirection. He could convey this idea with the sincerity and solemnity of a man who did not know whether he would live or die, since he believed in it firmly himself. He would always believe in it until he died, and there was a measure of truth in it.

Henry Wikoff, who called repeatedly, likewise heard the Sickles version of the battle and must have communicated it to his paper, the New York *Herald*. Likewise Secretary Stanton. Likewise James T. Brady and General Thomas Francis Meagher, who came all the way from New York with several other friends to bring delicacies and sit at the side of the bedridden hero.[9] Brady heard something else. Sickles wanted to do something for the wounded of the Third Corps, and was starting with a contribution from his own purse. Could Brady help? Brady did. He went back to New York, made a stirring speech at the Stock Exchange and gathered in a fine subscription which was duly sent to General Birney for distribution.[10]

His beloved Third Corps, in truth, was much on Sickles' mind. The town was seething as always with rumors about the army, and one of them must have disturbed him, for Lincoln on July 10th thoughtfully took the trouble to dispel the general's apprehension:

> My dear General:
> I understand you are troubled with some report that the 3rd Corps has sustained a disaster or repulse. I can only say that I have watched closely, and believe I have seen all the despatches at the Military Telegraph office up to a half hour ago . . . and I have heard of no such disaster, or repulse. I add that I do not believe there has been any such.
>
> Yours truly,
> A. Lincoln [11]

Lincoln had indeed been watching the telegraph. If anything his complaint was that, far from meeting any "disaster or repulse," the Army of the Potomac had been following the retreating Lee at too safe a distance. Through General-in-Chief

Halleck he had been exhorting Meade to press forward and administer the *coup de grace:* "You have given the enemy a stunning blow at Gettysburg. Follow it up, and give him another before he can reach the Potomac . . ." [12] But Meade, who had fought so sagacious a battle at Gettysburg, had succumbed once more to timidity. Affrighted at his own losses and fearing defeat at the hands of the limping Confederates, he allowed them to cross the Potomac on July 14th virtually unopposed. The enemy, caught in a net, had slipped away and with him had vanished another precious opportunity to shorten or end the rebellion.

"The greatest disaster of the war!" Lincoln groaned to Sickles while visiting him next day. [13]

It is doubtful that Sickles came to the defense of Meade. Possibly even then, seeing the President's impatience with the excessive caution of the commander, Sickles was contemplating a flank attack on Meade aimed at restoring his old friend Hooker. The second battle of Gettysburg was brewing. When the clash came the cigar-smoking general would be ready with a tactical maneuver quite as astonishing as the one he made into the Peach Orchard.

Meanwhile, he was getting the best of care. By order of Secretary Stanton, Dr. Sim stayed with him along with several medical aides and orderlies. The faithful Major Tremain was there to attend to official routine, seconded by two younger staff aides, Captains Moore and Fry. Messages of sympathy were pouring in by the hundreds, and the three staff officers were kept busy answering them. Possibly Sickles was a crotchety patient at times, for Tremain wrote in some desperation, "To come from active field service, and remain about a sick room is awful to me . . . I must seek some change somewhere before many weeks." [14] In addition to his pain and the oppressive Washington heat, the general was suffering from occasional attacks of nervous anxiety which he blamed on the after-affect of the chloroform administered him. [15]

Still, he had buoyance enough to ponder the question of what to do with that right leg that used to be a part of him. He hit on a solution with a characteristic Sickles touch of gothic humor. He had the leg placed in a miniature coffin and sent to the Army Medical Museum, founded the previous year. It was said that for years afterward he took pleasure in escorting friends there to pay due respect to the leg.[16]

Improving rapidly after mid-July, he enjoyed several further visits from Lincoln and was pleased at the President's invitation that he convalesce at the Soldiers' Home, where the Lincolns were summering.[17] This offer of hospitality Sickles regretfully refused. He now had a pair of government-issue crutches which he began experimenting with gingerly in his room. He was anxious to get back to New York. This was an idea Dr. Sim stoutly opposed at this early date, but the will of his patient was set. On July 22nd Sickles clumped into the White House on crutches to pay Lincoln a farewell call, then set out for home with an entourage including Dr. Sim, Captains Moore and Fry, and several others.[18]

Although the trip was made by short stages, he was haggard when he arrived in Jersey City next day. He was met there at the dock by a revenue cutter that had been placed at his disposal and was crowded with a group of his closest friends, including Brady and Meagher. Weak as he was, the general could not resist an impulse that was to become second nature with him—to display with pride the absent leg and pinned-up trouser. He insisted on walking with his crutches to the waiting boat. He winced with pain and several times had to be aided by an orderly when he seemed about to fall, but he made it to the deck amid the cheers of the onlookers. Cheers were something Sickles frankly enjoyed, even at the cost of agony. This stubborn effort so exhausted him that he was not able to enjoy to the full a rich offering of game and wines served aboard the vessel as it steamed upriver to his home on the Hudson, with the eloquent Brady presiding as toastmaster.[19]

Where was Teresa during this splendid ceremony? Where was Laura Sickles, now a pig-tailed girl just short of ten? The accounts of the day do not say; the newspapers were in apparent agreement that Mrs. Sickles was not a fit subject for mention in their columns.

New York was still shaken by vivid memory of the bloody Draft Riots only a week earlier, but the Board of Councilmen hastened to tender the city's thanks to General Sickles and order a gold medal struck for him.[20] Sickles took time to rest and to write Secretary Stanton about his future employment:

> It will not be long before I shall be ready for work again—Can you not then give me a Command? If you send a Column to operate in Texas that is a service I would like very much—Make it a Department & let me take my old Corps with me & Depend upon it I would do no discredit to your Choice & Texas should be reoccupied & held securely—It is there the French will turn up if Louis Nap. adheres to his Mexican or rather American policy—the South would Cede all they have West of the Mississippi as the price of recognition & this would be a tempting bit—Now it could be plausibly said they hold undisturbed possession of Texas & could give Colorable title—Send me down there to thrash Magruder and Watch the French on the banks of the Rio Grande.
>
> Meanwhile please do not permit Gen. Meade to break up my corps—which I hear he contemplates.[21]

Sickles' experience as a diplomat and with the House Foreign Affairs Committee made him acutely aware of international implications which more insular generals might overlook. Louis Napoleon had installed his puppet Maximilian on the throne in Mexico, and to Sickles the government had not only the duty to put down the rebellion but also to prevent the French from taking advantage of the American struggle to nip away at Texan territory won at bloody cost from the Mexicans. Also, he was keeping in close touch with General Birney and other Third Corps officers and had heard the appalling rumor that Meade was thinking of dissolving the corps and incorporating its shattered remnants into other commands.

Torso engraving of Brigadier General Daniel E. Sickles,
standing with arms folded, sash over shoulder
and epaulets 1861-1862. *GNMP*

Brigadier General Daniel E. Sickles. *GNMP*

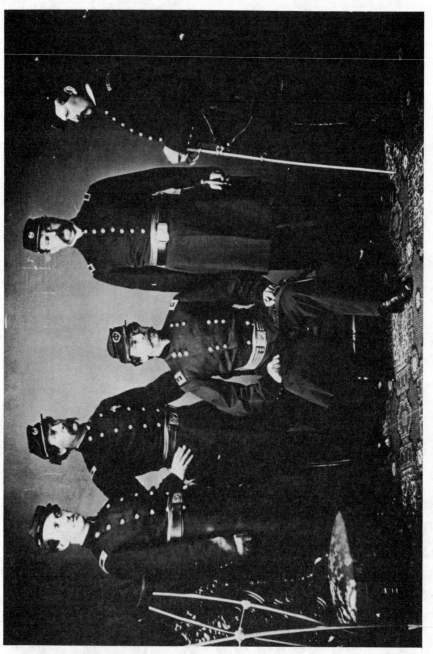

Major General Daniel E. Sickles and the 3rd Corps Staff. *GNMP*

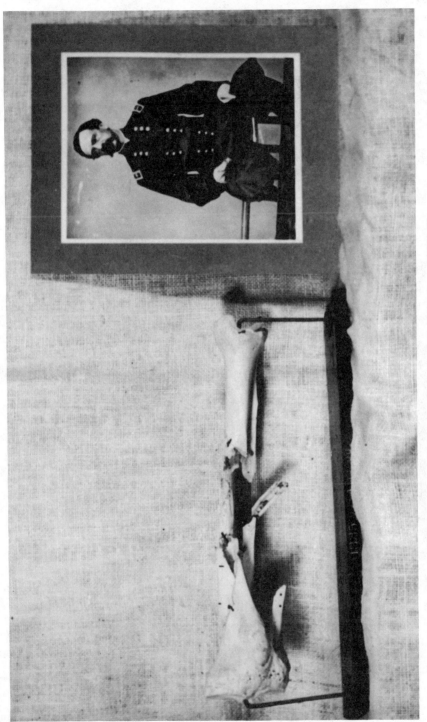

The leg bone of General Daniel E. Sickles. *GNMP*

Engraving of Major General Daniel E. Sickles.
MOLLUS / Mass. Comm. / USAMHI

FROM A PHOTOGRAPH, COPYRIGHT, 1902
BY J. E. PURDY, BOSTON

MAJOR GENERAL DANIEL E. SICKLES, U. S. A. RETIRED
COMMANDER MEDAL OF HONOR LEGION
ELECTED NOVEMBER 7TH, 1902

Major General Daniel E. Sickles USA- retired Commander
Medal of Honor Legion 1902.
MOLLUS / Mass. Comm. / USAMHI

Generals Sickles, Carr and Graham at Trostle Farm, site where General Sickles lost his leg 1886.

39th Annual Reunion Army of the Potomac, Antietam Maryland
September 16th and 17th, 1910.
MOLLUS / Mass. Comm. / USAMHI

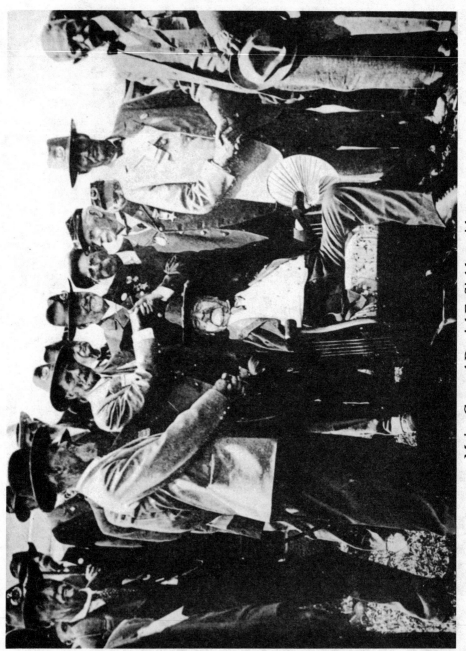

Major General Daniel E. Sickles with

General Daniel E. Sickles at his headquarters at the Rodgers House site during the Fiftieth Anniversary of the Battle of Gettysburg. Seated in chair and surrounded by veterans and guests, under locust tree in front yard 1913. *GNMP*

There was logic in this, since the corps had lost about thirty-five percent of its men to Longstreet's bullets at Gettysburg and was now down to hardly more than division strength. But to Sickles, no amount of logic could justify such a move. The Third Corps was bone of his bone, his proudest possession, the product of his own personality and leadership, a body of men linked to him with ties cemented over many campfires, long marches, and furious battles. Meade break it up? The mere suggestion made him bristle, intensifying a hostility already active enough.

Secretary Stanton replied with warm regards but pointing out that there was little use in naming Sickles to a new command until he was fully recovered and physically able to take the field. Sickles came right back with a request that his friend Charles Graham, wounded and taken prisoner in the Peach Orchard, not be forgotten:

> . . . Pray do all you can to Expedite the Exchange of Gen. Graham—I am afraid of losing him—his health is delicate and I dread the Effect of Confinement & privation upon his Constitution—too proud to accept a parole when proffered at Gettysburg he cannot survive the brutal incarceration imposed by Winder and Letcher at Richmond—Rescue him if possible for he is a brilliant officer.[22]

Sickles' concern for his friends was exceeded only by his own urge to get back into combat. To one of his Third Corps generals he wrote on August 1st: "I shall rejoin the corps the very first day my strength will permit. My stump at present is very painful when a storm approaches, or during its progress. This will not last long. It has not yet shrunk to its natural size, so that I can be measured for an artificial leg; nor has it acquired sufficient hardness to enable me to ride in a carriage faster than a walk over any but a park road . . . I expect to be with you, for a trial at least, between the 15th and 20th of August." [23]

This estimate was wildly over-optimistic. Though he benefited from the tender ministrations of Teresa, proud of the husband who was hailed as a hero of Gettysburg, a leg amputation under the medical conditions of the day was an ordeal from which recovery would be both painful and slow.

On August 11th he fled the heat of New York and left for Lake George, hoping that the bracing Adirondack climate would speed his recovery.[24] With him still were young Captains Moore and Fry, ready to lift the crippled general in and out of trains and carriages and to surround him with an atmosphere of military smartness and respect. For them, this junket into the vacation-land of the wealthy must have been a dream assignment after months of tent life, hardtack, and battle tension, even if the patient could be snappish at times.

The luxury-loving Sickles put up at swank Fort William Henry Hotel and created a sensation among moneyed guests whose previous exposure to the rigors of war was largely confined to newspaper headlines. To have a genuine, gilt-edged, one-legged hero in their midst, with two stars on his shoulders, added just the proper dash of vicarious martial thrill to a porch-sitting vacation.

Was the general content with porch-sitting? Far from it. He rolled tenpins on the green. He played billiards, clumping around the table with his new crutches. "He has been hunting or fishing almost every day since his arrival here," reported the New York *Times* correspondent. ". . . The General has shot two deer."[25]

Sickles seemed determined to prove just how active a man with one leg could be. He thoughtfully sent the head of a buck he had shot to Lorenzo Delmonico,[26] the New York restaurateur who doubtless was still wondering whether the government would pay the debts incured in provisioning the Excelsior Brigade back in the trying days when the brigade was an unclaimed orphan.

The hotel took cognizance of its distinguished guest by holding a grand soirée in his honor. Sickles was unable to join in the dancing, of course—a handicap he was to lament for the rest of his life, for he loved to pirouette with a beautiful woman on his arm—but his presence could never go unnoticed. Serenaded after the dance by an admiring throng, he gave a speech in which, among other things, he touched on the eternal chasm separating those who fight wars and those who stay at home, or at such luxurious resorts as the Fort William Henry Hotel:

> Although New York has sent almost 200,000 men to the field . . . yet in this state we have only a dim appreciation of war . . . When the day comes—not far distant, I believe—for magnanimity and justice and conciliation, the army will prove that they who are fearless in conflict are generous in victory. Like the soldier in "The Lady of Lyons," we may exclaim, "It is astonishing how much we like a man after we have fought with him." . . .[27]

This was something more than a sugary oratorical confection whipped up to please the summer crowd. It was touchy talk. Sickles as usual knew what he stood for and was not afraid to say it. In preaching "magnanimity and justice and conciliation" toward a defeated South he was taking a flat-footed stand on the hottest issue of the war—a stand alongside that of Lincoln and bitterly opposed by hard-shell Republican radicals who swore that rebel leaders should be hanged and the South treated precisely as a conquered enemy nation when and if it was conquered.

For Sickles, a holiday was merely an opportunity to find new ways of being busy. One of his chores was to give his attention as attorney for William McGarrahan to McGarrahan's claim to title of certain lands in gold-rich California. This was a case he had taken at the request of his friend Meagher in 1858, and the matter was still unresolved.[28] Since the wresting of California from Mexico, the question of who held title to lands which might make a man rich was a feverish one, so that some of the quarrels still awaited judgment. Meanwhile Sickles had acquired part ownership of McGarrahan's disputed land and thus had more than a lawyer' interest in it. From Saratoga

Springs he wrote to the President asking his personal intercession in the case, admitting it "is to myself one of great importance in a pecuniary point of view." [29] He got a polite brush-
off in reply:

> Your note and brief about the California land claim are re-
> ceived. The question presented is a property question, with
> which I do not think I should meddle as a volunteer. It will
> save me labor, therefore, if you will point me to the law which
> assigns any duty to the President in the case. This done, next
> send me a reference to the treaty and all the statutory laws
> which bear upon the case. Yours truly,
>
>   A. Lincoln [30]

The President was quite properly side-stepping any involve-
ment in ticklish property quarrels which he felt were problems
for his Attorney General and Secretary of the Interior, but
Sickles was not an easy man to brush off and Lincoln would
hear of it again.

Feeling improved but still impatient at the slowness of his
leg to heal, the general left the resort on September 17th and
spent ten days in New York, where he was happy to learn that
his efforts on behalf of General Graham had been successful.
Graham was being sent north in a prisoner exchange.[31] In his
home city Sickles once again was the recipient of enough honors
and fetes to weary him. He had indeed come a long way since
the black days of 1859. Even the lawyer Strong, who frankly de-
tested him, commented with wonderment: "I suppose Sickles,
with his one leg, among our best volunteer officers. His recupera-
tive powers are certainly wonderful. Four years ago he was a
ruined man in every sense, a pariah whom to know was discreditable." [32]

Moving on to Washington, he stopped en route in Philadelphia, where he was greetly warmly by his old friend Daniel
Dougherty. Dougherty refused to let the crippled general pass
through the city without making an occasion of it. Sickles was
serenaded by Birgfeld's band at the Continental Hotel, where

Dougherty gave an address of welcome and praise, thanking him for the heroism and sacrifice which had saved Philadelphia from rebel occupation and driven the invader from Pennsylvania.

Amid "deafening cheers," Sickles struggled out on the balcony with his crutches and gave the felicitous sort of speech that came so easily for him. He heaped laurels on the many Pennsylvania-born soldiers who had fought and died at Gettysburg, and reserved heartiest applause for his own subordinate, General David Birney, the Philadelphian who had held the line from Peach Orchard to Devil's Den. Sickles even made brief mention of himself:

> Although I am now suffering some little inconvenience, owing to a casualty that occurred in a recent battle, let me tell you and the world that I am proud of that sacrifice.[33]

Possibly some of the listening Philadelphians wondered why Sickles made no mention of George Gordon Meade, the Philadelphian who led the army that had rolled back the Confederate tide. For all his desire to please his listeners, Sickles would not praise the general he cordially disliked and regarded as unfit.

Moving on to Washington, Sickles worked energetically to settle the California land case. Not at all rebuffed by the President's letter, he saw Lincoln about it, explaining that he merely wanted him to authorize the Secretary of the Interior to act on it without interference from the Attorney General.[34] He likewise called on Interior Secretary Usher several times, but the case was still in the air on October 18th when he went down to Fairfax Station, Virginia, to pay a little visit to General Meade.

This was a mission both triumphant and painful. It had been noised about in the papers that the soldiers of the Third Corps were preparing to give their crippled ex-commander a royal greeting and had collected more than $5000 with which to make him a gift [35] —a prospect that could scarcely do any-

thing but please him. But then there was the unpleasant necessity of seeing Meade and asking that he be allowed to resume
command of the corps.

While Sickles never hesitated to ask a favor of a friend,
it galled him to be forced to approach an enemy with hat in
hand. His attitude toward Meade, long tinged with dislike, had
darkened since Gettysburg. It was an enmity between opposites,
between men who rubbed each other the wrong way, for Meade
had always been at least superficially polite and had not even
administered a sharp rebuke when he discovered Sickles' unauthorized forward move. In his official report on Gettysburg
he had been surprisingly restrained in mentioning Sickles, saying merely that the New Yorker had advanced his corps "not
fully apprehending instructions." [36]

This was just the kind of criticism fit to make Sickles' blood
boil. If he took pride in anything, it was in his quick intelligence. He was enraged by any suggestion that he had mis-
apprehended instructions, which seemed to mark him as a bungling subordinate. Who was the bungler at Gettysburg? Why,
it was Meade himself. Sickles was perfectly convinced that his
own forward move was the maneuver that had saved the field
by absorbing the shock of Longstreet's attack and giving the
misguided Meade time to bring up reinforcements.

To heighten his choler, there were rumors that Meade had
said he would have court-martialed Sickles had not the loss of
his leg taken him out of action.[37] In the man who had been
toasted in New York, Lake George, and Philadelphia as "the
hero of Gettysburg" and felt the accolade fairly won, this talk
of a court-martial aroused fury.

So the encounter between the two generals at Fairfax Station
was no back-slapping reunion. Scrupulous politeness was observed. They smiled, shook hands, and Meade inquired about
Sickles' leg and general state of health. Sickles thanked Meade
for his solicitude and said he was feeling like a new man, which
he decidedly was not.[38] He admitted he was perhaps not yet
quite up to a full campaign, and finally popped the climactic

question: Could he have his corps back, if only for the next major battle?

Meade was firm on this point. The answer was no. He did not come out with the blunt truth and say he distrusted Sickles and did not want him back under any circumstances. He pointed out that Sickles was still in a state of convalescence and far from ready for rigorous field duty. A man who moved painfully on crutches and could not sit a horse was about as ready to take up foot-racing as to lead a corps into battle. Meade cited the case of the Confederate General Ewell, who had lost a leg at Second Bull Run and had recuperated for nine months before resuming his command.[39]

It was a bitter blow to Sickles even though he was painfully aware of his own incapacity. Possibly he reflected that had his friend Hooker been commanding general, Fighting Joe would have slapped him on the back, brought out the whiskey, and roared, "Stay with us as long as you're able."

But the sting of Meade's refusal must have been partly alleviated by the uproarious welcome given him by his old Third Corps. In truth, the men who wore the diamond patch had become heartily disgruntled with events since Gettysburg. For one thing, the army under Meade seemed to be engaged in watching Lee rather than actively pursuing him, and had actually been forced into a "tactical retreat" at Centerville. For another, the Third Corps command had gone to General William French, described in candid terms by Colonel de Trobriand as "a large man with a red nose, a flushed face, a bald forehead, a dull look. Near him, a glass and a bottle of whiskey appeared to be on the table *en permanence*." [40]

The spirit of the men seemed epitomized in De Trobriand's lament, "Poor Third Corps! Your best days were over." [41] They had a wry little joke about that among themselves. They called the corps as it had existed under Sickles "The Third Corps as we understand it." When the crippled general appeared to review them, they let out all the stops. On behalf of the corps, General Birney presented Sickles with a fine barouche drawn by four matched horses—a gift toward which privates, noncoms, and officers had contributed.[42] When he climbed into the glittering equipage with Birney and rode down the ranks, the ovation was thunderous.

"One prolonged and tumultuous cheer greeted him along the lines wherever he appeared," wrote one soldier witness, "and nothing but his disabled and weak condition prevented the 'Diamonds' from taking him out of his carriage and bearing him aloft on their shoulders through the camp. A braver soldier was not to be found in the army." [43]

After the review was over and the two generals retired to Birney's tent, a throng gathered outside to rend the air with cheers. "It must be acknowledged," De Trobriand conceded, "that this reception was not only a manifestation in honor of the old corps commander, but also a protest against the successor given us." [44]

The Third Corpsmen left no doubt that they would have preferred their disabled general above anyone else to command them, whether he was gloriously right or monstrously wrong in ordering that move into the Peach Orchard which had cost more than 4000 of their numbers.

Right or wrong . . . which was it? It was an argument that would go ringing down through the years with all manner of heat and bitterness, theorizing and speculation, but with never a definite answer.

Technically, of course, Sickles was wrong. In moving his corps forward, he went contrary to Meade's express order and also failed to report his move, leaving Meade ignorant of the new position of his left wing. A commanding general might as well go fishing if his corps leaders are to be allowed to choose ground of their own liking without regard to the rest of the army. Sickles' error in command is clear as crystal.

But a stretching of orders may be forgiven or even applauded if it results in decided advantages such as Sickles claimed his maneuver produced. Had Sickles taken the line along the ridge Meade ordered, and had Longstreet attacked there with the same headlong fury, it is possible that the Confederates would have broken through not merely into Sickles' rear but into the entire Union rear and that disaster would have been the result.[45]

General Meade could have used a little of the Sickles dash. General Sickles might have profited with a modicum of the Meade caution. Mistakes there were on both sides, Blue and Gray. But when the massive collision came, Sickles' men covered themselves with glory, Meade fought a magnificent defensive battle, and when it was over the field was won for the Union. It would have been pleasant if it were left at that, with an end to recriminations. Actually, the recriminations were only beginning.

General Sickles, back in Washington, was already contemplating his next move—to have Meade removed from command in disgrace.

CHAPTER XXII

Certain Grave Charges

"I met General Sickles at the President's today," wrote Secretary of the Navy Gideon Welles on October 20th. "When I went in, the President was asking if Hancock did not select the battleground at Gettysburg. Sickles said he did not, but that General Howard and perhaps himself, were more entitled to that credit than any others. He then detailed particulars, making himself, however, much more conspicuous than Howard, who was really used as a set-off. The narrative was, in effect, that General Howard had taken possession of the heights and occupied the Cemetery on Wednesday, the first. He, Sickles, arrived later between 5 and 6 P.M., and liked the position. General Meade arrived on the ground soon after, and was for abandoning the position and falling back. A council was called; Meade was in earnest; Sickles left, but wrote Meade his decided opinion in favor of maintaining the position, which was finally agreed to against Meade's judgment.

"Allowance must always be made for Sickles when he is interested, but his representations confirm my impressions of Meade, who means well, and, in his true position, that of a secondary commander, is more of a man than Sickles represents him,—can obey orders and carry out orders better than he can originate and give them, hesitates, defers to others, has not strength, will, and self-reliance." [1]

These observations of the Navy Secretary, while betraying some confusion as to the complicated progress of events at Get-

236

tysburg, reflected Welles' uncommon discernment about people. They also showed that Sickles was wasting no time in gaining Lincoln's ear and continuing the indoctrination he had begun when the President visited him as he lay sick and feverish in his bedroom shortly after the battle.

Rejected by Meade, Sickles was a general without a command. His next step, had he followed ordinary routine, would have been to call on General-in-Chief Halleck, known as Old Brains, and see if he had some post for him in which a missing leg would make no difference. But Sickles had no love for Halleck, who despised Hooker, was a friend of Meade and therefore was an enemy of Sickles. Furthermore, the crippled general was not inclined to consult an underling when he could go to the very top. He avoided Halleck and saw President Lincoln and Secretary Stanton, the two men who were running the war and could with a word give him a command—and could also listen to his opinions on Gettysburg.

In his handicapped condition, Sickles was no easy man to find a post for, particularly since his pride would not allow him to accept any minor assignment. Weeks passed as he lingered in the capital, chafing at his forced inactivity. He turned his attention again to the McGarrahan case. He had time also to impress on his friends in the Senate and House and in other official positions what he regarded as the real inside story of Gettysburg. His eagerness to present his side was spurred when General Halleck came out with his official report on the battle. In it Old Brains held short shrift for Sickles, writing: "General Sickles, misinterpreting his orders, instead of placing the Third Corps on the prolongation of the Second, had moved it nearly three-quarters of a mile in advance—an error which nearly proved fatal in the battle." Halleck further showed exactly where he stood on the question when he added, ". . . to General Meade belongs the honor of a well-earned victory in one of the greatest and best-fought battles of the war." [2]

Sickles seethed. This was a direct contradiction of his own version, which had it that Gettysburg was won in spite of

Meade's deplorable incapacity and only by virtue of fast and heady work on the part of some of his corps commanders, notably Sickles. It was easy for him to imagine that Meade and Halleck, West Pointers both, had got their heads together to smear and discredit the only non-West Pointer who led a corps at Gettysburg. It was easy to conclude that he was the intended victim of a plot inspired by personal and political animosity.

Sickles, who never did anything by halves, had forsworn political office and plunged into the military with whole-hearted dedication. He was fiercely proud of his two stars and of his combat record, and anyone who questioned his sagacity as a corps leader touched his pride where it was tenderest. A plot against him? Well, two could play at that game. Sickles was a seasoned navigator of the tricky political cross-currents swirling in Washington, and knew as well as anyone how to maneuver an enemy into an eddy that might sink him.

The Sickles-Meade-Halleck fracas was already stirring a buzz of speculation among upper-echelon officers. In camp down in Virginia, Brigadier General Patrick set down in his diary:

> Col. Sharpe came down [from Washington] yesterday After-noon . . . He tells me that Sickles openly announces his inten-tion to fight the battle with Halleck, who has made more serious & damaging charges against him than Meade did. He will ask for, either a Court of Inquiry, or a Committee of Investigation in Congress. It is probable that he will succeed in flooring both. He is all powerful at the White House & is the Gallant of Mrs. Lincoln, going there at all times, Although the President is sick —too ill to see persons on business, he (Sickles) is said to call on him at any time . . .[3]

Sickles was going to fight the battle, without a doubt, but no court of inquiry or special committee was necessary. In the already constituted Joint Congressional Committee on the Con-duct of the War he had a handy instrument for laying these base canards of Meade and Halleck and proclaiming to the nation what he felt was the truth about Gettysburg.

This committee, founded early in the war as a Congressional

watchdog over battlefield activities, had kept a constant and critical scrutiny on the Army of the Potomac for two reasons. That army's operations more often than not had been attended by a singular lack of success, and it was invariably located handy to Washington—too handy for comfort, in fact, for if the Army of the Potomac was nearby, so was Lee. The strongest figures in the committee were Senators Benjamin Wade of Ohio, its chairman, and Zachariah Chandler of Michigan, both of them able men and violently radical Republicans.

Under Wade and Chandler, the committee had frequently sniped at Lincoln's policies. It scorned the President's view of the war as a regrettably necessary method of recementing the Union with as little bitterness as possible. In its opinion the purpose of the war was to inflict punishment, to drive the devils of "treason" and slavery out of the South, and to do it with the mailed fist. It called for the blood of secessionist leaders as traitors, demanded voting and social equality for the slaves, and would have the seceded states do long penance before being granted readmission to the Union.[4]

The Messrs. Wade and Chandler were not forgetting how they had writhed under Southern effrontery during the Dixie-loving Buchanan administration. Now that they were in the driver's seat they were out to even the score, or maybe gain a little.

Unhappily, their animus sometimes obscured reason and justice. To press a punitive war, the committee wanted punitive-minded commanders and was hot for purging the army of those generals who merely fought—who did not burn with the urge to subjugate. It was dedicated to the proposition that a general had better be "right" politically—that is, have the properly vindictive attitude toward the South—and after that could come the less important considerations of military skill and efficiency. The committee was fond of General Hooker despite Fighting Joe's fiasco at Chancellorsville, because he was an advocate of toughness. It despised Generals Meade and Halleck as soft, conservative exponents of the Lincoln line of conciliation.

It is quite likely that the committee would have ambushed Meade even had not Sickles been on hand to furnish evidence against the commander. But Sickles was not the sort to let events take their own slow course if he could give them a push. True, he was a Lincoln man, opposed to the committee's partisan spleen. Still, in the committee he had a powerful, ready-made meat-axe to swing at the heads of those he felt were maliciously seeking to paint him as a bungler in order to hide their own gross incompetence. Undoubtedly, during that fall and winter he had a few private tête-à-têtes with Senators Wade and Chandler.

While a storm began to brew over the head of the unsuspecting Meade, Sickles lingered in Washington awaiting the assignment that was so slow in coming. He was a welcome guest at the impressive Stanton home on K Street. The White House also continued to hold an irresistible fascination for him, and as always he paid frequent calls there. One day in mid-December he crutched himself into the President's house in the company of Senator Ira Harris of New York. At the time, a stout-hearted little Confederate was a guest at the White House in the person of Mrs. Emilie Todd Helm, younger sister of Mary Todd Lincoln.

Kentucky-born Mrs. Lincoln's family was one of those which had been tragically torn by the rebellion, with most of its members on the Confederate side—a fact not lost on the President's enemies, many of whom considered the First Lady a rebel spy. She had lost three brothers in the Confederate service. Her sister Emilie's husband, Ben Hardin Helm, had commanded a Confederate brigade in the division of General John C. Breckinridge, Vice President under Buchanan, and young General Helm had been killed at Chickamauga in September. Now Lincoln had arranged passage through the lines for Mrs. Helm. The meeting between the young widow and the First Lady was a poignant one. The fact that the secessionist Emilie Helm was a White House guest had been kept quiet,[5] but Sickles, who had called a few days earlier, was aware of it. He paid his respects to Mrs. Lincoln and Mrs. Helm, then turned to the younger woman.

"I told Senator Harris that you are at the White House, just from the South," he said, "and you could probably give him some news of his old friend, General Breckinridge."

Mrs. Helm shook her head. It was three months since her husband had been killed while fighting under Breckinridge, and she explained that she had no idea of what might have happened since.

Senator Harris, an uncompromising rebel-hater, fixed her with a steely eye and began asking pointed questions about conditions in the South, which Mrs. Helm evaded. Nettled, Harris could not resist an unkind thrust.

"Well, we have whipped the rebels at Chattanooga," he said triumphantly, "and I hear, madam, that the scoundrels ran like scared rabbits."

The young widow flushed, but she was ready with a spirited parry. "It was the example, Senator Harris, that you set them at Bull Run and Manassas."

Perhaps the Senator felt he had met more than his match. He switched his attack to Mrs. Lincoln.

"Why isn't Robert in the army?" he demanded. "He is old enough and strong enough to serve his country. He should have gone to the front some time ago."

Mrs. Lincoln bit her lip. Since the death of her little son Willie she could not bear to think of the enlistment of her eldest boy Robert, who was now a student at Harvard.

"Robert is making his preparations now to join the army, Senator Harris," she replied. "He is not a shirker as you seem to imply, for he has been anxious to go for a long time. If fault there be, it is mine, I have insisted that he should stay in college a little longer . . ."

Harris was unimpressed. "I have only one son and he is fighting for his country," he growled. He turned to Mrs. Helm. "And, madam, if I had twenty sons they should all be fighting the rebels."

"And if I had twenty sons, Senator Harris," Mrs. Helm snapped, "they should all be opposing yours."

The conversation at an impasse, Sickles and Harris took their' leave. Then Sickles clumped back alone. He wanted to see the President.

Lincoln was feeling unwell and was resting, but the general was ushered in to see him. Sickles related to him the colloquy between Harris and Mrs. Helm. The President's eyes twinkled at the report of Emilie Helm's swift ripostes. "The child has a tongue like the rest of the Todds," he chuckled.

Sickles saw nothing humorous about it. "You should not have that rebel in your house!" he said angrily, slapping the table with his hand.

This was meddling beyond the point which the easy-going President could allow. "Excuse me, General Sickles," he said quietly, "my wife and I are in the habit of choosing our own guests. We do not need from our friends either advice or assistance in the matter." Then he softened the reproof with a smile. "Besides, the 'little rebel' came because I ordered her to come, it was not of her own volition." [6]

The one-legged general made himself very much at home at the White House, but ordinarily he was the soul of good humor and courtesy. He was attentive to Mrs. Lincoln, who regarded him as a warm friend and possibly also remembered with gratitude his good work in smoothing over the Wikoff news-scoop uproar almost two years earlier. During the final months of 1863 he was a frequent guest of the Presidential couple, both at the White House and at the theater. Now forty-four, he looked years younger, slim, handsome, always faultlessly uniformed, with the empty right trouser leg—symbol of wartime sacrifice—somehow very much in evidence. The Lincolns found him a diverting companion, a man of easy charm and ready conversation that rippled with theatrical allusion and humorous anecdote.

While Sickles took a keen delight in White House society, it is doubtful that he limited himself to small talk. It was irksome as well as unsafe for him to remain without a command in the field. Washington tea-party generals often found themselves gradually divested of any authority save at the buffet table, a fate he did not wish to court. Lincoln—and probably the First Lady as well—must have heard a good deal from Sickles about his perfect fitness to resume command of the Third Corps, the outfit he conceived as so much his own that it was very nearly outrageous for anyone else to lead it.

This was a favor the President could not grant in the face of Meade's hostility. Sickles was still unassigned, still chafing at his unemployment, when he returned home to New York for the holidays.

In New York, he took a suite at the Brevoort House on lower Fifth Avenue, leaving Teresa and Laura at the uptown house on Ninety-first Street. His relations with Teresa were not of the happiest, but he had two other good reasons for separating himself from his family. With the difficulty he had in getting around, he wanted to be near his friends and political associates in the city. Also, he was being fitted for an artificial leg.

From the hotel he dashed off letters with his customary ease and grace, the President being the recipient of some of them. Among other things, he suggested to Lincoln that he stimulate recruiting by issuing a congratulatory order to soldiers who re-enlisted.[7] But first and foremost, after six months out of active army service he itched for something to do, and on this subject he addressed the President on January 27th:

> "The Times" of today mentions a rumor that I am to be assigned to the Command of the Dep't. of Washington—I hope there is good foundation for the statement—I can be useful in that post. Stationed at Washington, with duties ostensibly Military & appropriate to my rank and in a position where I can Communicate easily with the influential people who will be in Washington this year—I can be most useful in the other aspects about which we have Conversed.
>
> There is another field in which valuable service could be rendered by an officer of rank and ability—occupying half of his

time at the Capital & the remainder South. A Military Commissioner, giving his whole attention to the subject, could Contribute powerfully to increase and organize the elements of disaffection toward the rebel authorities in North Carolina, Georgia and elsewhere—and at the same time Contribute largely to the work of reconstruction in Arkansas, Louisiana, Mississippi & Tennessee. The Commissioner should be a man of tact & Address—well acquainted with the Southern people—their press, Clergy, politicians, & business men—familiar with political movements and the Military situation and the Characters of the Military and political leaders at the South, and the motives which influence them.

It seems to me that *now is the very time* for such a Mission—there is so much discontent at the South—so much hostility to the Richmond government . . .

This month I have devoted to learning the use of an artificial limb—in which I have been quite successful—I can walk without crutches, my health is so far reestablished as to make me anxious for employment.

Very respectfully
D. E. Sickles
Maj. Genl.[8]

If the powers in Washington could not think up a suitable assignment for him, it was not because Sickles did not help. He was suggesting himself, as an officer of rank, ability, tact, and address as the very man for the mission he outlined. Also, he was describing just the sort of post—half of the time in Washington, the other half moving about the South—that appealed to his restive, inquiring spirit. It may be that the busy President wished that Sickles would not bother him quite so much, cognizant though he was of the general's uncommon abilities. In any case, the letter seemed to strike Lincoln with an idea, for only two days later he telegraphed Sickles:

Could you, without it being inconvenient or disagreeable to yourself, immediately take a trip to Arkansas for me?

A Lincoln [9]

A "trip to Arkansas" was not precisely the sort of thing Sickles had in mind, but he could not be cavalier in laying down requirements for the chief executive. He telegraphed his acceptance, and followed with a letter whose last paragraph tactfully hinted that his heart was not in Arkansas:

> My first wish is to resume Command of my Corps—next to that, the Command at Washington—but I shall be entirely satisfied to undertake any duty in which you think I can be most useful to the Government,—whether in the field, or at Washington, Arkansas or elsewhere.[10]

A week later he hurried off to the capital, where he must have explained to the President the importance of his remaining long enough to testify before the Committee on the Conduct of the War. Fireworks, he well knew, were soon to crackle in Washington, and he expected to furnish some of the loudest explosions. While these other matters came to a head, he was once more the intimate of the Lincolns. On February 20th he received a note from the comma-loving First Lady, reading in part:

> . . . We have never had so distinguished & brilliant a matinée, as that of to day, you must have been indisposed or I am sure you would have favored us, with your presence—The President, is a little better to day, was able to visit the "blue room"; to night, I will try & persuade him, to take some medicine & rest a little on the morrow—Do not fail us tomorrow eve to dinner, at 6½ o'clock. Sincerely yr friend,
>
> M L[11]

Meanwhile, General Meade was campaigning in Virginia quite unaware of any sinister maneuvers in his rear. He was not ignorant of Sickles' animosity. A little earlier Meade had written his wife:

> I understand there is a bitter article in Wilkes' *Spirit of the Times* asserting that Hooker planned the campaign of Gettys-

burg, and that Butterfield wrote all the orders for the movements, in accordance with Hooker's plans. I furthermore hear
that General Sickles asserts that Hancock selected the position,
and that he (Sickles), with his corps, did all the fighting at
Gettysburg. So, I presume, before long it will be clearly proved
that my presence on the field was rather an injury than otherwise.[12]

Meade penned this with no more than fleeting annoyance.
It was not until later that the realization dawned on him that a
well-organized movement was afoot to disgrace and ruin him.
On March 6, 1864, he wrote his wife:

When I reached Washington I was greatly surprised to find
the whole town talking of certain grave charges of Generals
Sickles and Doubleday, that had been made against me in their
testimony before the Committee on the Conduct of the War.[13]

CHAPTER XXIII

The Campaign
of General Historicus

The Joint Committee on the Conduct of the War comprised three Senators and four Representatives, but largely reflected the violent prejudices of its two whip-cracking leaders, Senators Wade and Chandler. Among other things, the committee had strong suspicions of West Point, which it regarded as an institution flirting with treason in its neutral attitude toward slavery and Southern intransigence.[1] Senator Wade, the chairman, was hiding a dagger or two behind his back as he smiled and extended a friendly hand to the West Pointer Meade. When Meade arrived in Washington, Wade met him with great cordiality and assured him that there were no charges against him, adding that the purpose of the hearings was to compile a "sort of history of the war."[2]

The Senator's history of the war had a few secret pages in it. He did not mention that only two days earlier he had gone with Chandler to Lincoln and demanded the removal of Meade on the ground that he was incompetent. This the two radicals had done on the strength of the testimony of Sickles, Doubleday, and one other general opposed to Meade, before any opportunity had been given the commander to testify in his own defense—a fair gauge of the double-faced tactics of the Messrs. Wade and Chandler.[3]

Perhaps Wade could not be expected to be frank enough to

say that the chief aims of his committee were to smear and remove General Meade and General-in-Chief Halleck and to restore the command of the Army of the Potomac to Joe Hooker —a West Pointer, it was true, but one who had been sufficiently brain-washed to suit the radicals. This, on the face of it, was more than a little ridiculous. To replace Meade, who had won the nation's climactic battle at Gettysburg, with Hooker, who had come such a cropper at Chancellorsville, did not seem to fall within any known interpretation of military logic. But the committee was quite willing to twist logic to conform to politics. It set out to do it by attempting to prove, or to create the illusion of proving, five main points:

1. That Hooker's fiasco at Chancellorsville was not due to any lack of generalship on his part but was traceable to circumstances beyond his control, among them a conspiracy on the part of some of his corps commanders to thwart him.

2. That General-in-Chief Halleck did all he could to hamstring Hooker, but cooperated warmly with Meade.

3. That Meade had no battle plan before Gettysburg, but merely followed the campaign mapped out by Hooker and imparted to Meade by Butterfield, so that in a sense Gettysburg could be marked down as a Hooker victory.

4. That once engaged in Gettysburg, Meade planned to retreat, and was only prevented from doing so because in spite of him his army became too hotly involved to withdraw.

5. That after Gettysburg, the enemy was utterly prostrate and low in ammunition, and Meade's failure to pursue and attack him threw away a golden opportunity to smash Lee's army.

Only on this last count did the committee have a strong and logical argument. Meade indeed had lost a precious opportunity. He had shown himself lacking in the iron determination necessary to lead a force of the size of the Army of the Potomac. A better general was wanted, assuredly, but it took a queer sort of mentality to find him in Hooker. The man who would drive the enemy grimly on and on without rest—Grant—had not yet had time to get under way in his augumented command.

Significantly, the first witness to be called before the committee was Sickles. Questioned by Senator Wade, the New Yorker could find no fault at all with Hooker's tactics at Chancellorsville. Unfortunately, the battle had been lost, but not through any failing of Hooker. He praised Fighting Joe's generalship, vouched for his sobriety, and blamed the disaster chiefly on the "giving way of the Eleventh Corps" [4] and to the failure of some of his corps commanders to give him loyal support.

". . . I think there were many officers in his command decidedly hostile to him," Sickles testified, "which seriously impaired the efficiency of their cooperation, and militated against General Hooker's success." [5]

This was a point Senator Wade and his colleagues were to belabor incessantly with complete failure to appreciate the howling irony of the charge. Before succeeding to the command, Fighting Joe had all but fomented open mutiny against both of his previous commanders, McClellan and Burnside, a fact that was conveniently ignored. But it was when the questioning turned to the leadership at Gettysburg that the fur began to fly.

Sickles declared that on the morning of the second day at Gettysburg he went to Meade's headquarters and asked for orders. Meade, obsessed with his notion that an attack would come on his right, refused to take seriously Sickles' insistence that an assault was brewing at the other end of the line, and did not even bother to give him any orders.

". . . And I was satisfied, from information which I had received," Sickles went on, "that it was intended to retreat from Gettysburg." [6]

This was a bombshell—the first intimation that Meade, who had won the nation's plaudits for his victory, had actually intended to retreat. Sickles tossed in the accusation gratuitously.

He did not say *where* he got his information, nor did he specify what evidence he had to support it. His statement that Meade refused to give him any orders suggested that the commanding general queerly preferred to let the Third Corps remain in bivouac and drink coffee rather than prepare for battle—an incredible claim that was to be contradicted by other witnesses.

"I determined to wait no longer the absence of orders," Sickles continued, "and proceeded to make my dispositions on the advanced line, as it is called. I took up that position, which is described in the report of General Halleck as a line from half to three-quarters of a mile in advance, as he says, and which, in his report, he very pointedly disapproves of, and which he further says I took up through a misinterpretation of orders. It was not through any misinterpretation of orders. It was either a good line or a bad one, and, whichever it was, I took it on my own responsibility, except so far as I have already stated, that it was approved of in general terms by General Hunt, of General Meade's staff, who accompanied me in the examination of it." [7]

In his efforts to discredit Meade and justify himself, Sickles was ready to punish fact when the punishment seemed helpful. In describing his advanced position, he said without batting an eye, "Fortunately, my left had succeeded in getting into position on [Little] Round Top and along the commanding ridge to which I have referred; and those positions were firmly held by the Third Corps." [8]

Actually, the Third Corps' new line ended at Devil's Den, a good quarter-mile from the hill, and at no time during the battle did the corps occupy or defend that height. Nor was Sickles' statement that "those positions were firmly held" an entirely accurate description. For all its desperate valor in the face of heavily superior enemy forces, the Third Corps had finally been driven back in confusion and the broken line had been patched with other units.

But Sickles on the witness stand was a man thoroughly at home, a persuasive pleader firmly convinced of his own righteousness. By telling the truth, and even admitting an error or two on his own part, he could have built a strong case for himself. But error was something he refused to admit, and besides such a course would not have fitted in with the committee's intention, the destruction of Meade.[9] Sickles' testimony limned a picture of Gettysburg as a battle won despite the crippling handicap of a commanding general who did just about everything wrong.

Next witness! This was Major General Abner Doubleday, who had led a division of the First Corps at Gettysburg and was the inventor of a game known as baseball, which soldiers liked to play when they had the leisure. Doubleday, who had no idea that his future fame would rest more solidly on the pastime he had devised than on his generalship, had done a slow burn ever since Gettysburg. For a few hours on the first day of the battle he had succeeded by seniority to the command of the corps on the death of General Reynolds and had done some warm fighting although the corps had been forced to retreat. Then what happened? By order of General Meade, Doubleday was replaced as commander of the corps by General John Newton, whom he ranked, and was relegated to division command again. This was a humiliation Doubleday could not forgive.

Perhaps he did not know that General Hancock, on reaching the field, had sent a dispatch to Meade mentioning that "Doubleday's command gave way." [10] Doubleday brooded over his own replacement, and also the fact that Meade had given Hancock command of the field on the first day although General Howard ranked *him,* and came to the conclusion that Meade's motives were unworthy. "I thought this was done as a token of disapprobation at our fighting at all that day . . ." he told the committee, and went on:

I think General Meade thought a couple of scapegoats were necessary; in case the next day's battle turned out unfavorably, he wished to mark his disapprobation of the first day's fight. General Meade is in the habit of violating the organic law of

the army to place his personal friends in power. There has always been a great deal of favoritism in the Army of the Potomac.
No man who is an anti-slavery man or an anti-McClellan man
can expect decent treatment in that army as at present constituted.[11]

Doubleday, a general in the sulks, did not explain the
clairvoyance that enabled him to read Meade's thoughts and
motives. It did not seem to occur to him that Meade might
have had honest doubts about his capacity to lead a corps,
especially after that word from Hancock that his command gave
way. He was an angry man, and years later he was to admit
he had spoken too harshly of Meade. But in 1864 he was saying
exactly what the committee wanted him to say.

The embattled Meade, assaulted on one flank by Sickles and
Doubleday, now was hit by a surprise attack on the other by a
masked enemy. On March 12th, at the very time that Meade was
testifying before the committee, an anonymous article about
Gettysburg signed "Historicus" appeared in the New York
Herald. It was so critical of Meade and so complimentary to
Sickles as to approach burlesque. It told of Sickles' arrival
with his corps at Gettysburg, and the enthusiastic greeting
given him by General Howard—"Here you are, General, always
reliable, always first!"—and went on to blast Meade for dis-
regarding "the repeated warnings of that sagacious officer, General Sickles . . ."

Historicus, whoever he was, seemed in perfect rapport with
Sickles, even in the realm of misinformation. Historicus warmly
commended Sickles for his prescience in seeing the importance
of Little Round Top, failing to mention that the general neglected it entirely. Apparently Historicus was working on the
theory that if an untruth is repeated long and loudly enough, it
becomes truth. His main charge against Meade was considered
shocking enough to italicize:

It has since been stated, upon unquestionable authority, *that
General Meade had decided upon a retreat, and that an order*

to withdraw . . . was penned by his chief of staff, General
Butterfield, though happily its promulgation never took place.

Busily on the aggressive, Sickles had been in correspondence
with his old comrade, Daniel Butterfield. Since being wounded
at Gettysburg, Butterfield had taken a painful skid downward
in the scale of command. After his recovery he had joined
Hooker under Sherman in Tennessee and wound up as a division commander—a bitter comedown for the peppery little
dandy who had led a corps at Fredericksburg and had been chief
of staff of the mighty Army of the Potomac for six months.
Butterfield, the Hooker crony, was no admirer of Meade. His
dislike was whetted by Meade's move in replacing him as chief
of staff, by a report Meade wrote which Butterfield felt reflected on him, and by his present discontent. Possessed of this
prejudice, as much as the fact that as Meade's chief of staff he
was privy to much that went on at Gettysburg, he was a valuable
man for the committee to question. On February 30th, Sickles
addressed a note marked *Private* to Senator Chandler, right
bower of the head-hunting committee:

My dear Senator:
    Butterfield is at Willards—He has not received permission
from Genl Halleck to come here & apprehends it will be refused—Allow me to suggest that, as in Birneys Case, he be subpoenaed regularly—He comes now only by *request* from Senator
Wade.
    It is very important that you have Brig. Genl S. Williams Ast.
Adjt. Genl Army of the Potomac here *with all orders & Communications* bearing on the Gettysburg Campaign—*original*
drafts & *Copies* as received at Head Quarters—this is *all important* for you to have before you *when Butterfield is Examined*—
Then you will get the *real history* of the Campaign.
                                            Truly Yours
                                            Sickles [12]

So Butterfield was regarded as such a vital witness that he
sneaked into town secretly and special steps had to be taken

to make his appearance there within regulations. All this has the conspiratorial air of low-grade melodrama. And Butterfield, when he appeared as a witness, proved to be the biggest blunderbuss aimed at Meade's head.

The little New Yorker painted a contemptuous picture of Meade when that general was ordered to replace Hooker in command. According to Butterfield, Meade appeared dazed. He did not know what to do. He seemed to have no plan. He was so helpless that Butterfield took pity on him and briefed him on what Hooker's plans were, and Meade thankfully seized on them and adopted them almost without change as his own.[13]

Personal enmity was coming to the fore now with a vengeance. Butterfield went on to tell of his arrival at Gettysburg on the morning of July 2nd, to be greeted by Meade.

"General Meade then directed me," he said, "to prepare an order to withdraw the army from that position." [14]

Here was the gravest charge against Meade—an effort to wrest away from him his proudest achievement, the victory at Gettysburg, and make it appear that the victory had been won against his wish to retreat. Butterfield went into considerable detail about that retreat order. He grudgingly admitted that Meade "may have desired it prepared for an emergency, without any view of executing it then, or he may have had it prepared with a full view of its execution." [15]

An astonishing tempest in a teapot, the retreat order. There was no doubt that Meade asked Butterfield to prepare it, and that it was designed only for possible use in an emergency. Meade would have been a sorry general had he not taken steps to assure an orderly withdrawal should it become necessary, even though he intended to fight and hoped to win. Once he arrived at Gettysburg every action and order of Meade was proof of his intention to dig in for an all-out battle there. Yet the committee was determined to emblazon the precautionary withdrawal order as a badge of cowardice and shame.

Butterfield had a good deal more to say, and so did many others. In all, there were eighteen general-officer witnesses who testified before the committee on Meade alone and their testimony filled some 229 pages of fine print. The committee, of course, held the whip hand in setting the direction of the inquiry by the questions it asked, and often showed its bias by asking leading questions which called for answers derogatory to Meade or Halleck. While it did not have the effrontery to call only witnesses antagonistic to Meade and Halleck, it was able to control the questioning so that the enemies had more to say than the friends.

General Meade, however, was allowed to talk at length. Although by this time he well knew that the Committee on the Conduct of the War was not so much a disinterested fact-finding body as it was a wrecking crew, his testimony was restrained and factual and he made no accusations against anybody.[16] It was not until he read the Historicus article that he exploded in righteous rage. He enclosed a clipping of the article in a communication to Secretary Stanton, asking an investigation of its authorship and a court of inquiry, saying, "I cannot resist the belief that this letter was either written or dictated by Maj. Gen. D. E. Sickles." [17]

Stanton, though he was Sickles' friend, seemed to be taking no sides in the matter. He passed the letter both up and down —to President Lincoln and to General-in-Chief Halleck—for action on Meade's complaint. Halleck was first to reply:

> The Secretary of War has shown me your letter in regard to the communications in the *Herald* signed "Historicus." I have no doubt that and other articles of the same kind in the New York papers were written or dictated by General Sickles; nevertheless, you will not be able to fix on him the authorship, and nothing would suit him better than to get you into a personal or newspaper controversy. He would there be perfectly at home, and, with his facilities for controlling or giving color to the New York press, would have greatly the advantage. My advice would be to ignore him entirely in this controversy, unless he makes himself officially amenable, which I think he is too shrewd to do. He cannot by these newspaper articles injure your mili-

tary reputation in the slightest degree. Indeed, I think that any attacks from him will have the contrary effect.[18]

Perhaps Old Brains lacked some of the qualifications for a successful general-in-chief, but this letter—aside from its dubious last statement—showed him keen in his judgment of the men and issues involved. Lincoln had the same advice to offer, but based it on the consideration that always loomed largest in his mind, the successful prosecution of the war. He wrote Meade in part:

> . . . It is quite natural that you should feel some sensibility on the subject; yet I am not impressed, nor do I think the country is impressed, with the belief that your honor demands, or the public interest demands, such an inquiry. The country knows that at all events you have done good service; and I believe it agrees with me that it is much better for you to be engaged in trying to do more than to be diverted, as you necessarily would be, by a court of inquiry.[19]

Meade, although deeply wounded by the assaults against him, apparently realized that he could not joust against a newspaper phantom. But after Butterfield testified and depicted him as a nincompoop so helpless that he had to beg for his predecessor's campaign plans, and worst of all, a faint-heart who wanted to flee Gettysburg, Meade could stand it no longer. He had to fight these charges in the only arena available to him—the meeting room of the Committee on the Conduct of the War. He asked leave to appear again. On April 4th, he stood before the little group of legislators who were so polite to him and so determined to have his scalp, and said in part:

> I utterly deny, under the full solemnity and sanctity of my oath, and in the firm conviction that the day will come when the secrets of all men shall be made known—I utterly deny ever having intended or thought, for one instant, to withdraw that army, unless the military contingencies which the future should develop during the course of the day might render it a matter of necessity that the army should be withdrawn.[20]

He did more than swear a solemn oath. He produced evidence in the form of orders to units of his army which proved preposterous any idea that he intended to retreat except as a last resort. Unfortunately, Meade had no newspapers at his beck and call and his evidence did not get the publicity it merited. By a remarkable coincidence, once again on the same day Meade testified, General Historicus mounted his second front-page assault in the friendly terrain of the New York *Herald*. His timing was unerring even if his facts were shaky.

Historicus' first effort had aroused a storm of angry criticism, some of which the *Herald* published. One of the letters, signed "Staff Officer of V Corps," hit the nail squarely on the head when it said the first article was "manifestly intended to create public opinion" and added that the intention of the writer was to "bolster one officer at the expense of others." [21]

Historicus could hardly allow such challenges to go unanswered. Besides, he was intent on getting his peculiar propaganda before the public as often and as strongly as possible, well knowing that many undiscerning readers would accept it as fact. He pounded his points home again, writing in part:

> . . . Instead of being occupied with the steady advance of the enemy, General Meade was entirely engrossed with the plans for a retreat . . . just at the moment the general order for retreat was prepared the cannon of Longstreet opened up on our left wing, under Sickles.
> . . . I defy my assailants to deny that the invincible resistance of the Third Corps under Sickles . . . saved the army.
> . . . Yet General Meade still commands this noble army . . .[22]

Meade writhed under the lash. "It is hard that I am to suffer from the malice of such men as Sickles and Butterfield," [23] he wrote his wife. It did him no good to note that Historicus, in his second salvo, had included part of a personal letter from General Birney which could have been sent to no one but Sickles, and which indicated that General Historicus and General Sickles would cast the same, identical, one-legged shadow.

Meade had made errors of indecision and excessive caution, but he deserved no such torment as this.

True, while Historicus was a busy and vindictive fellow, he did not control all the press. Here and there the quiet voice of reason and fairness spoke up. The *Round Table*, a New York newspaper unfortunately of small circulation, had this to say:

> . . . one thing is certain, that the fact that General Sickles lost a leg in the engagement saved him from removal from the army. We honor General Sickles for . . . [his] untiring energy and personal bravery . . . But we cannot blink the fact that General Sickles is quite as much a politician as a soldier. We know that he has accomplished more by personal address, adroitness and cunning management of newspaper correspondents, than by actual display of military ability . . . He is not a man to forget a fancied slight or to lose an opportunity of resenting it. In view of this, we are at no loss to account for his hostility to General Meade . . .[24]

The hearings before the Committee on the Conduct of the War dragged on deep into April. When they were finally finished, the committee, with the aid of General Historicus and other interested parties, had laid down a blistering barrage of whispers, rumors, newspaper publicity, and weighted testimony, all aimed at the head of General Meade. The question was, would they get their man?

They did not. Senators Wade and Chandler demanded of Lincoln that he remove Meade, suggesting that Hooker was the man for the command. Lincoln refused. Whatever his doubts about Meade, he wanted no more of Fighting Joe. Besides, he now had a new general to run the whole shebang—a fellow named Grant.

Meade was bowed and bloody, but by the grace of Abraham Lincoln he continued in command of the Army of the Potomac, victor of the second battle of Gettysburg as he was of the first.

CHAPTER XXIV

A Better General

While all this shouting was going on, a stocky, untidy-looking man arrived in the capital at Lincoln's request for the purpose of having three stars affixed to his shoulder straps. He was Ulysses S. Grant, the Westerner everybody had been talking about, victor at Donelson, Vicksburg, and Chattanooga and now the first lieutenant general since Washington. He was to lead all the far-flung Union forces, with Halleck under him as chief of staff. The President hoped he would be able to do something about that most mishandled of all armies, the Army of the Potomac.

Grant was one of those unusual generals who had spent all their time fighting, so his face was new in the capital. Washington buzzed about this "unconditional surrender" fellow. His arrival touched off a current of enthusiasm that was partly due to his victories and partly a reflection of the hope that here at last was the better general, the man who would bring an end to the war that was bleeding the nation white.

When Lincoln gave a levee for Grant at the White House in March, the new lieutenant general was embarrassed at all the fuss made over him. He had to stand on a sofa so that the crowd could get a full-length view of him, and had his hand pumped until it was all but bloody. Sickles was there, of course, and when he was introduced to Grant by Stanton, he had his usual felicitous greeting ready.

"Besieged by friends, even you must surrender, General," he said.

Grant, though never known for repartee, surveyed his sore arm ruefully and got off a riposte that for him was a sparkler:

"Yes, I have been surrendering for two hours until I have no arms left." [1]

To think that Sickles would let slip this chance to get the ear of the new military chief would be to underestimate his aggressive opportunism. He was still thinking of his cherished Third Corps, still hoping to lead his old troops into battle, and Meade's plan to absorb the corps into other units incensed him. To Grant he protested the move and begged him to intercede and save the Third Corps from dissolution.

Grant's answer was no. He was allowing Meade to handle the affairs of the Army of the Potomac, and if Meade said it was best to regroup his forces, it would be done.[2] Furthermore, this man Grant was a person who made a decision, stuck to it and could not be budged by cajolery no matter how eloquent or forceful. To Sickles this was a disappointment of the bitterest sort. The first meeting between these two men who were to be linked intimately in later struggles was an unhappy one for the New Yorker.

But they parted friends. Sickles had an uncanny knack for pressing a point to the very limit, and then, if he was still refused, to accept it with grace and charm.

In April Sickles left on his mission for the President, probably glad to quit the smouldering ruins of the Meade investigation. While his tactics had been less than guileless, he was a man who could convince himself of the purity of his motives. Meade, he felt, was the bane of the Army of the Potomac and his removal would have been a service to that army and to the Union.

Well, he had failed to scuttle Meade—Lincoln would regret standing by that bungler!—so now he was off to the South with a staff of five, including Major Tremain. His orders meanwhile had become more complex than merely making a "trip to Arkansas." He was to proceed first to Nashville on a confidential assignment that was not officially disclosed but whose purpose Sickles admitted years later to a newspaper reporter. Tennessee, never a whole-hearted member of the Confederacy, was now largely occupied by Federal troops and Andrew Johnson was sitting in Nashville as military governor. Johnson, the proud plebeian and fanatical slavery-hater, had little mercy for those of his fellow Tennesseans who had sinned by embracing secession. There had been complaints that his administration was unduly harsh. Sickles' object was to see if Johnson could be tactfully checked so that his government would conform with Lincoln's conciliatory policy toward defeated peoples.[3]

This accomplished, Sickles was to make a complete circle by land and sea around the edge of the shrinking Confederacy, stopping at military posts en route to see how reconstruction was progressing in Union-occupied areas and what success Lincoln's amnesty proclamation was having in inducing Confederate soldiers to desert.

Since Sickles had known Johnson in Congress and was on friendly terms with him, his sojourn in Nashville was a pleasant one. In the midst of state affairs he did not neglect the amenities, arranging an excursion to the Hermitage with Johnson and writing, "The Carriage will Call for you at the time you name." [4] Nor did he miss this opportunity to journey down into northern Georgia where his old sidekicks Hooker and Butterfield were fighting under the fiery Sherman. He stayed to witness the assault against the rebels at Resaca, and enjoyed a few days of camp life with his old comrades.

Here were three intimates who spoke each others' language and were unanimous in a hearty detestation of General Meade. Both Hooker and Butterfield were discontented men who felt themselves undeservedly shunted into subsidiary commands. Hooker was grumbling as openly as ever, with Sherman now the target of his wrath. The far more sagacious Butterfield was cautioning Hooker to desist in his criticism,[5] and at the same time Butterfield was pulling strings to be given a corps—a command that failed to materialize, disappointing him so sorely that he was soon to resign and go home.

Sickles reported enthusiastically to Lincoln on Sherman's smashing campaign, not forgetting to hand plaudits to Hooker and Butterfield for their work.[6] On May 18th he was on his way to Memphis, where another ex-Congressional colleague, General Cadwallader Washburn, was the Union commander.

Memphis at the time was swarming with Northern war profiteers seeking to lay their hands on Southern cotton. The South was glutted with cotton that could not be shipped out owing to the blockade, while in the North it was almost unobtainable and therefore priceless. Southern profiteers were likewise lurking in the wings, ready to make any sort of illicit deal to obtain foodstuffs and supplies so desperately needed in the Confederacy. The stakes were large and bribes were common, with many an officer lining his pockets by his willingness to look the other way. Memphis was said to be such a ready source of supply to the beleaguered Confederates that they deliberately refrained from attacking the city.

General Washburn had ordered a stop to this, but when Sickles looked over the situation he believed that all trade with the enemy should be forbidden right from the top, by Presidential decree. He so informed Lincoln, writing in part:

> The effect upon our Army and Navy cannot be other than injurious, when they see a vast trade carried on with our enemies. This intercourse enriches a mercenary horde, who follow in the rear of our forces, corrupting by the worst temptations those in authority, giving aid and comfort to the enemy, and relieving that extreme destitution of the insurgent population, which would otherwise operate as a powerful inducement towards the restoration of tranquility and order.[7]

Sickles' next stops were at Helena, Arkansas, and New Orleans. He was now deep in conquered enemy territory, watching the first feeble efforts at self-government under the Union of areas wrested from the Confederacy. He had good opportunity to see the problems of reconstruction at first-hand among people buffeted by war and defeat, many of them still bitterly hostile toward the conquerors and far from convinced that their cause was lost—an experience that was to be useful to him later.

And as always, he was ready and willing to make a speech at the drop of a hat. In New Orleans he was received with great honor when he visited the constitutional convention with the local commander, General Canby. Both were called on for speeches. It is written that "General Canby responded very briefly, and General Sickles more at length." [8]

Leaving the Crescent City and traveling on Navy vessels, he visited the Union-held Pensacola navy yard in Florida at the time that Sherman, to the north, was pushing his massive drive on Atlanta. Thence around Florida and a stop at Union-held Charleston Harbor, the cradle of secession back in '60. He returned to Washington early in August to visit the President and give him his verbal impressions of the journey.

Characteristically, Sickles had spent money lavishly on the trip to an extent considerably exceeding his army pay. He reminded the President of this in a note asking Lincoln to sign an allowance order:

> . . . May I request that you sign and send me the enclosed order to my address—Brevoort House—New York—It is a proper and customary allowance to officers not serving with troops and although inconsiderable in amount will help to reimburse me for a portion of the expense of my tour . . . [9]

Then he returned to New York to await further orders—to await with keen anxiety the word from Washington that would send him back to action again.

Meanwhile, the throes of civil war could not keep the North from girding for another Presidential election, with politics not as usual but far more bitter. The Republicans had renominated Lincoln, and surprisingly had named Andrew Johnson as his running mate—the same Johnson with whom Sickles had enjoyed a whiskey punch or two down in Nashville. The

Democrats, dominated by Copperheads and peace men, had gathered in Chicago, called for action to put a speedy stop to a war which they described as a "failure," and nominated General McClellan and George Pendleton—the identical Pendleton who was a brother-in-law of the late Philip Barton Key.

The Democrats should have taken a long look at their candidate before nominating him. Little Mac, for all his certainty that he could save the country from Lincolnian ruin, was no Copperhead. He accepted the nomination, but he did so with a letter that made Democratic leaders tear their hair.

"No peace can be permanent without union," he wrote. "I could not look in the face the gallant comrades and tell them that their labors and the sacrifices of so many of our slain had been in vain; that we had abandoned the Union for which we so often periled our lives."

This was queer talk after the convention had jettisoned the Union in favor of quick peace. The Democrats were in the painful position of the man who rode off in opposite directions. They had a platform demanding peace, and a candidate calling like Lincoln for war to restore the Union—two ideals difficult to reconcile with any recognizable logic. Confusion reigned in the Democratic ranks. In New York, Tammany flew apart in violent schism, with the greater proportion of the faithful strong for McClellan, logic or no.

Who was Sickles for? Though he still called himself a Democrat, by this time he was heavily suspect among the sternest braves of the Wigwam because of his championing of Lincoln. In a letter to the Democratic Union Club of New York he began with a bit of bland nonsense.

". . . Since entering the army," he wrote, "I have not been inclined to take a prominent part in political affairs. When I became a soldier, I ceased to be a politician."

That statement had better be charitably passed over. As long as he lived, Sickles would never cease to be a politician. But he quickly moved from polite inanity to solid sense, and in so doing displayed the old Sickles courage.

He was in enthusiastic accord, he went on, with "Genl Mc-Clellan's admirable letter of acceptance—rather than the Chicago Resolutions—the promulgation of which will forever be regarded as the most disgraceful event in the history of the Democratic Party. If the Convention were again Convened and Gen McClellan's letter adopted as their manifesto, the honor and the fortunes of the country would be vindicated—and the means of an early and honorable peace truly strengthened." [10]

On the all-important, overriding issue of the day—war or peace, union or disunion—he saw clearly with Lincoln. He was unconditionally for pressing the war until the Union was reestablished, even though this stand caused him to be labeled as a traitor by Copperhead members of Tammany.

Indeed, Sickles seemed to have two different sets of principles, so easily demountable that they could be exchanged like a shirt. To his friends he was little short of an object of veneration. Major Tremain, who had served as ADC under him for more than two years and knew him in all his moods as well as any man, was devoted to him.[11] His former comrades of the Third Corps, which was no longer in existence as a corps, missed him sincerely. Gershom Mott, who had served as a brigadier under Sickles and was now in Butler's Army of the James, wrote of the untimely death of General Birney, a victim of disease hastened by the privations of campaigning, and added:

"I feel as if almost left alone down here of the old Corps, and often think of the pleasant times when we were all together. Can you not come down and see those of us who are left? It would afford me a great deal of pleasure to have you do so." [12]

Sickles would have liked that, but he had been struck by a much bigger idea. He wanted to reconstitute the Third Corps and take it into the field under his own command. The break-up of the corps despite his energetic protests was a bitter pill for him to swallow, and in fact he had not quite swallowed it. On September 1st he broached his favorite subject once more in a letter to Lincoln:

. . . I am Confident that with proper and sufficient facilities
I could reorganize and fill up my old Army Corps (3rd) with
new Regiments, made up partly of veterans and the remainder
of volunteers, which would replace the Regiments that have
gone out of service. There is one division of my Corps now left
in the field—it would not be necessary to disturb this until I had
completed the two new divisions, with the local aid & cooperation I could command. A very large number of men could be
obtained who would not otherwise enter the service . . .[13]

The idle general was vastly unhappy in his idleness. He
had passed by a chance for political office in the belief that
his military star was rising, and instead it had sunk dismally.
Now he, like Hooker and Butterfield, was lost in a backwash
while other names pressed forward the Union flag and other
names appeared in the newspaper headlines. There was real
pathos in Sickles' pleas that he be given back his old command.
He felt he could do good work with it, and very possibly he
would have. If granted, his request would have meant a large
financial sacrifice, for as a lawyer he could earn many times a
major general's salary. Money, which meant so much to him,
stood a poor second to pride, action, and glory. There was
nothing he yearned for quite so powerfully as to lead his men
into Richmond and take a dominant, personal role in the destruction of the Confederacy—a dream of triumph that was to
remain only a dream.

Although he did not know it, his fighting days in the military
sense were over. Somehow, the idea no longer seemed prevalent
that General Sickles was essential for the successful prosecution
of the war. Possibly Lincoln, for all his respect for Sickles' discerning grasp of the larger issues, was a little unsure of a Hooker
partisan who would refight Gettysburg in the newspapers and
sic the radical Committee on the Conduct of the War on Meade.
In any case, the men in the field were now doing pretty well
without Sickles, with Atlanta in Union hands and Grant besieging Petersburg.

Sickles lingered in New York, restive, impatient. The summons he was hoping for did not come.

With his love for being in the vortex of any political turmoil, it must have taxed all his considerable will power to stay strictly out of the Presidential hustings until the tag end of the campaign. When he was invited to address a mammoth rally of Democrats for Lincoln on November 1st at Cooper Institute, he could not resist. Along with General Dix and other outraged Democrats he tore into the Chicago platform as an "act of degradation" and sounded the tocsin for the Republican Lincoln. The issues were clear and momentous, and he drove them home:

> . . . In this country there are a great many people who would rather stay at home than go to the front. There are a great many people who do not like to pay taxes and who find high prices a grievous burthen and who are disposed at all times to count the cost of everything, including national honor and national perpetuity. All these people . . . are accommodated by the Chicago platform. Every sneak in the republic who wants a hiding place can get under that platform. (Cheers and laughter.) No man, not even its candidate, has the courage to stand upon it. (Cheers and laughter.) . . . We know that the great mass . . . who desire the perpetuation of our nationality, and who are willing to make sacrifices to preserve our country . . . desire the re-election of Lincoln. (Great cheering.) [14]

So election time came, and the Lincoln-Johnson ticket was overwhelmingly victorious. Little Mac had lost his last campaign, this time not through caution. Would Lincoln, now safely installed for another four years, have time to turn his attention to such lesser matters as an assignment for a major general who had lost his good right leg at Gettysburg?

Still the summons did not come.

With Atlanta behind him, the destroyer Sherman was wheeling his army in an inexorable march to the sea, outstripping lines of supply, living off a hostile country, essaying the impossible and succeeding at it. The shriveled Confederacy was caught in a giant nutcracker, Grant at the north and Sherman at the south, both squeezing hard. Peace agitation in the North was all but silenced now, with the promise of victory looming like a rainbow. The papers were full of Grant, Sherman, Sheridan—yes, even of Meade. Not one word of Sickles.

For the forgotten general this was one of the most forlorn periods of his life. Events were careening, and he had no part in them. His position on the shelf was so mortifying that he had a recurrence of the nervous malaise that troubled him after Gettysburg, and he was forced to consult a physician, who prescribed a tonic.[15] On December 9th he wrote the President:

> My dear Mr. Lincoln:
>   I beg respectfully to remind you that I am still unassigned. Fully restored to health, as competent as ever for active duty, and anxious for employment, I hope to be spared the humiliation of being dropped from the rolls among the list of useless officers under the resolution now before Congress. Relying on your justice, I beg to commend my position to your kind consideration & remain, dear Sir,
>
> > Your friend & servant
> > D. E. Sickles
> > Mj. Genl.[16]

This was a plea that was close to anguish. The President read it and could not find it in him to ignore it. He called Sickles to Washington.

CHAPTER XXV

O, Captain, My Captain!

When he reached the capital, Sickles was disappointed to learn that the President and Secretary of War had not found a place in the army for him. Lincoln had something else in mind. He was turning the general over to Secretary of State Seward to embark on a special diplomatic mission.

This mission, a confidential one, had two purposes. Sickles was to go to Panama and Colombia to seek permission of the Colombian government (then in control of Panama) for the colonization of freed American negro slaves, who were becoming a social problem; and to petition for the free passage of American troops across Panama, which recently had been interdicted.[1]

Undoubtedly he made a last futile plea for the restoration of his Third Corps. But the old corps was now definitely dead. At any rate the South American mission was one of prestige carrying the promise of adventure and above all, action, which was about as essential to him as the breath of life. In January, 1865, he sailed from New York, with Teresa, Laura, and the Chevalier Wikoff waving goodbye.

That Sickles and Wikoff had been discussing—and possibly pulling a few wires—in regard to the composition of Lincoln's Cabinet for his second term, is evident in a letter Wikoff wrote the general shortly after his departure. In it Wikoff mentioned the possibility of General Nathaniel Banks being given the post as Secretary of War, and went on, "If Mrs. L. is the only impediment to Banks' going into the Cabinet, then I consider him there already, for I could surely [affect?] her scruples." [2]

To Wikoff, intrigue was as involuntary and vital a function as metabolism. There was some talk that Stanton might resign his post, and if this should be the case, Wikoff and Sickles were apparently exercising their influence to swing the office to Banks, a friend of Sickles. But undoubtedly Sickles hoped his old ally Stanton would stay, for the two had already discussed important work in South Carolina for the general when the war should be ended.

As for the Chevalier, even in the midst of scheming he had time for compassion. In the same letter he went on, "Terese was wonderfully affected by your departure—the tears were streaming down her face the whole time she remained on the Pier. She was full of sad presentiments. Her habit is to conceal her feelings & they must be deeply tried to escape in tears. Laura, too, was crying, the first time I have ever known her to do so." Wikoff ended the letter: "Write fully and often to Terese."

Arriving in Panama with his small staff of subordinates, Sickles heard considerable talk about the possibility of building a canal across the isthmus—an idea he filed away in his retentive memory. To get from Panama to Bogotá, Colombia's capital high in the Andes, was in itself an adventure. It meant a 500-mile boat trip up the Magdalena River, a stream navigable only in the rainy season. Whether Sickles took time to write "fully and often" to Teresa is not known, but as always he addressed affectionate letters to his parents.

In a reply to one of them, George Sickles admitted curiosity about his son's mission, whose purpose had not been disclosed even to him, and went on, "We were much pleased with your description of your Journey from Panama, and particularly with the description of the Port of Carthagena—its defences, walls, ordnance and works generally . . . Laura visits her Grandmother as a general thing on Saturday . . . Occasionally Laura stops overnight . . . The Gentlemen in the office send their compliments." [3]

Sickles pushed his projects energetically in Bogotá, hoping to return home in time to have a hand in the finishing of the rebellion. His working knowledge of Spanish was helpful, and he got along well with President Murillo, who had been Colombian minister in Washington when Sickles was in Congress [4]—another instance of his uncanny knack for finding friends wherever he went. He was successful in getting permission for the passage of troops across Panama and was making progress in his negotiations for negro colonization.[5] On May 2nd he was able to write Stanton:

> I have arranged satisfactorily all the business entrusted to me by the Sec. of State, and shall return to Panama by the next Steamer, which leaves Carthagena on or about the 1st of June. Unless other orders from the State Dep't meet me in Panama, I shall have the honor to report to you for duty, before the 1st of July. I trust you may then have occasion to employ me usefully in the field. You and I burnt the first powder in this war, on our side, and so I wish to be with you, "in at the death" of the rebellion. I pray you not to forget the South Carolina programme you have so long had in Contemplation for me. The news of the fall of Charleston and Columbia and Wilmington &c &c all came in by the last Mail. In this happy land they have only one Mail a Month from over the Sea,—and sometimes that fails to get over the Mountains;—this has lately happened, so that our dates from Washington are not later than 12th March. But when a Mail does arrive, we enjoy the feast as much as a traveller who Crosses the Great desert enjoys the first gushing spring he finds at the road-side.
>
> . . . I am happy to see the announcement that you will remain at the head of the War Department;—nothing will occur, I trust, to Constrain you to leave that post, until
>
> > "War's redeeming work is done,
> > Fought the fight, the Victory Won"
>
> . . . I shall have the pleasure to report in person to you, standing on *two* legs. In this Climate I have made gratifying progress in the use of my artificial limb, riding . . . over the

most difficult Mountain roads, on Peruvian and Granadian horses and on all sorts of Mules,—I venture to believe that Gen. Meade even would not now doubt my ability to ride far enough to the front to "post a battery" or make a reconnaissance" . . .⁶

So, on May 2nd, 1865, Sickles was still pleading with Stanton for a chance to "get in at the death" of the rebellion and warranting his physical fitness for field service. But the fight was already pretty well fought and the victory won. General Lee had surrendered on April 6th, although the news was a bit slow in reaching Bogotá. It came days later, and as Sickles himself described it:

> . . . It was here, in a remote foreign capital . . . that I received intelligence from our consul at Santa Martha, of the surrender of General Lee to General Grant. I lost not a moment in going to the palace of President Murillo . . . he summoned his Cabinet, and measures were at once taken to announce and celebrate this decisive victory and the peace it foreshadowed.⁷

For Sickles, the glad news was salted with regret. The war in which he had wagered his whole career and fortune was all but over without his help. Men in blue were parading the streets of Richmond, and he was in a "remote foreign capital" on an errand no one knew or cared about. He might as well have been on another planet.

But the enthusiastic Colombians were delighted to learn of the imminent ending of the war among the Yanquis. Bogotá was jubilant with parades, band music, and a banquet given by President Murillo to the diplomatic corps. "It is my best recollection," Sickles later commented, "that I was embraced that afternoon by 199—men!" ⁸

Pleasant as these celebrations were, he was in a sweat to get away, to get back home where an era was ending and a new one was to begin, a new union of the states which he well knew would find its launching marred with bitterness and strife and military occupation. In Bogotá, which had neither railroad nor telegraph, he was isolated from events which he knew must be moving at breakneck speed. How many other momentous things might be happening while he was marooned in this equatorial fastness? He had plans of taking a key role in the reconstruction of the South, but for all he knew, all the key roles might be assigned elsewhere while he parleyed in the Andes.

Sickles completed the loose ends of his mission with all speed. Late in May he began his journey to the coast via the shallow Magdalena. When he reached Honda, only sixty miles on his way, he was handed another dispatch which had made its tortuous way up the river by canoe. This one must have made the general's eyes pop.

President Lincoln, it said, had been murdered by an assassin as part of a plot to kill the victorious Union leaders. Secretaries Seward and Stanton had likewise been mortally wounded—Seward in a place that had seen violence before, the remodeled Club House where Key had died.[9]

The report about Stanton was untrue, of course, and Seward was to survive despite severe wounds, but Sickles did not learn of this until later. As far as he knew, the three topmost leaders of the government—all of them his friends—had been slain, and Washington must be in a condition nigh to chaos. No boat ever moved so sluggishly as the one which bore him down the Magdalena toward Barranquilla, where he still had a long ocean voyage ahead of him. The general had need of his nerve tonic now. History was being made in the capital while he was walled in by jungle 2500 miles away.

CHAPTER XXVI

People Are Too Pragmatical

During those first feverish days after the murder of Lincoln, Secretary Stanton all but took over the reins of government while some of the more nervous officials kept discreetly indoors in the fear that killers were still stalking the streets.

It was Sickles' fate to miss much that was stirring and tragic. By the time he reached New York, where he presented the Central Park menagerie with several crates of wild animals brought from South America,[1] the long, sad ceremonies for the dead President were a memory. The killer Booth—an acting fellow the theater-going Sickles had seen in less homicidal roles—had been shot, his accomplices captured and tried. Jefferson Davis was a prisoner, and there was hanging talk. After four incredibly valorous years, the Confederacy was dead, the South a morass of poverty, despair, and ruin.

Courageous, pig-headed Andrew Johnson had been elevated to the Presidency by Booth's bullet, and Senator Wade was saying, by God, there would be no trouble now in running the government [2]—meaning running it as Wade wanted it run, with a bull whip. Things had happened so fast that Johnson's unwisdom in getting a little drunk at his own inauguration as Vice President, and embarrassing the assemblage with a maudlin speech, was all but forgotten. Now that he was in the White House, the self-educated, secession-hating ex-tailor could be expected to be as unpitying toward the sinning South as any radical might wish.

Sickles arrived in the capital early in July, all but breathless in his haste to take part in councils that would dictate the destiny of the nation and also have something to do with his own future. Stanton had long ago discussed with him the job of "reconstructing" South Carolina, but now there were squads of major generals temporarily unemployed and seeking posts of importance. It would be a pity if one of them got in ahead of him.

Now he could be glad about those pleasant juleps he had had with Johnson down in Nashville. The Executive Mansion was occupied by the fourth consecutive President with whom Sickles was on gratifyingly familiar terms.

With considerable reason, Sickles felt that he was better qualified than most generals for a key post in the reconstruction of the South. He had political, diplomatic, and Congressional experience behind him. As a pre-war Democrat in Congress he had been a crony of Southern leaders, some of whom now survived and were courageously trying to restore a species of order to their stricken homeland.[3] In his mission for Lincoln when he circled the Confederacy, he had seen the first efforts of reconstruction at work in Tennessee, Arkansas, and Louisiana. A quick learner, he knew much about the South and its problems.

All questions of temperament aside, Major General Sickles had a sound background for the job of bringing order to chaotic South Carolina, and he got it. In September, 1865, he journeyed to Charleston and set up his headquarters in a fine house on Charlotte Street, the capital city of Columbia having been left in ruins by Sherman's men.[4]

So here he was at the fountainhead of the rebellion, the place where the Hotspurs had been hottest back in '60 and '61, the city of wealth and pride and social glitter that had gone delirious with joy when Fort Sumter, out in the harbor, had been forced to surrender.

Things were different now. Charleston lay partly in rubble from Federal artillery. Its once teeming harbor was quiet. Most of its shops were closed, with business near a standstill. Here and there were knots of idle Confederate veterans, some of them maimed, still wearing their ragged gray or butternut for want of other clothing—valiant ghosts of a cause that was lost. And there were the negroes, reveling in their new freedom but not knowing quite what to do with it, loitering about and wondering when Massa Grant, the deliverer, was going to set them up with forty acres and a mule.

Things were mournfully different. Out beyond the city, the crops that summer had been poor, since many of the slaves felt that emancipation meant they should cast toil behind them and go on a holiday. Stark hunger was stalking the land. Refugees wandered abroad in the naive hope that conditions might be better fifty or a hundred miles away. The master of a plantation who once owned black people by the score, was now apt to be found alone out beyond the stable trying to salvage a few turnips, while the mistress did a washing with unskilled hands. The wealth of this rich state, along with so many of its youth, had been poured out at Antietam, Gettysburg, Spotsylvania—a hundred battlefields where courage, in the end, had proven not enough.

All these things and more were the visible signs of an aristocratic way of life that had collapsed in anarchy and would never rise again. Maybe in time the fragments of this shattered society could be fitted together in some new way that would work, but until that was done the suffering and chaos and bitterness would be beyond telling.

Sickles' work began auspiciously when he was visited by a committee of leading Charlestonians who offered their cooperation. He told them, and told the local board of trade, that he was there to help them.[5] He had heard of the ruin left by war, but when he saw it with his own eyes his heart was touched. He had repeatedly preached the need for magnanimity toward the South when the conflict was ended, and now he had an opportunity to carry magnanimity into action.[6] He attacked the first enemy, hunger, by distributing rations by the thousands. At the same time he had to warn the recipients that this was no bottomless cornucopia that could be enjoyed in idleness. Able-bodied men and women were informed that they must go to work. Illiterate negroes, under the innocent delusion that freedom meant no more labor, discovered to their puzzlement that their liberation did not signify a farewell to toil.

In his efforts to put idle people to work, untended plantations in operation and to grease the rusty gears of commerce, Sickles worked closely with the provisional governor of South Carolina —inevitably an old friend. He was none other than strapping James L. Orr, the former Congressman and Speaker of the House who had occupied the Stockton Mansion before the Sickleses. There was no question as to who was boss. Major General Sickles, with 7000 soldiers under him, held the power of an absolute monarch. Yet he and Orr worked together with a unity of purpose that gratified the Carolinian.

The results were gradual but encouraging. Civil officers were elected and some semblance of order restored. When General Grant visited Charleston that winter on a tour of the South, he was pleased at the progress he saw even though a mere beginning had been made.

The sociable Sickles made Grant's visit the occasion for a splendid dinner he gave at his home in honor of the commander. In a typical touch of diplomacy, he used the affair as a device to woo the friendship of prominent Carolinians—former rebels all—whose cooperation was needed in the rebuilding of the state under the Union. Among those he invited were Orr, Magraw, last of the rebel governors of South Carolina; Trescot, who had been a Confederate diplomat; and former governor Aiken.

Aiken, once a wealthy planter, was now impoverished. He came to Sickles in considerable embarrassment, saying that much as he wished to meet General Grant, he did not own a proper dinner coat and was fearful the general would think he was not showing respect if he came unsuitably attired.

Sickles well knew that Grant was the last man in the world to be punctilious about dress. "Come in your old suit," he said. "The general will understand." [7]

While die-hard secessionists were anything but ready to swear undying amity for their Northern conquerors, the more intelligent of them recognized their defeat as a *fait accompli* and were anxious to re-enter the Union on the best terms possible. But as time wore on, they became increasingly alarmed at the temper of a Congress in which Dixie-hating radicals were gaining control. In Congress were some determined men—preeminent among them Sumner in the Senate and Stevens in the House —who had had little or no contact with plantation slaves. The freed Southern negro, they said, must now be granted full equality, including the right to vote. Whether motivated by malice or naivete, the legislators were never forgetting that this step was perfectly contrived to make Republicans of the emancipated slaves and give the party a brand-new voting majority in a South where all whites were Democrats.

To white Southerners, this was the crowning enormity. The great majority of freed slaves, through no fault of their own, were illiterates who had trouble enough signing an X and had not the slightest conception of government. They were assuredly not ready for the franchise.

In South Carolina, where there were forty-one black men to every thirty whites, white men were aghast at the prospect. They visualized the proud Palmetto State with a black governor sitting in Columbia and a black legislature ruling in halls hallowed by Calhoun and Hayne. The awful realization dawned on them that this "reconstruction" business did not involve merely a temporary swallowing of pride, a period of penance, and then a full-fledged return to the Union. It meant that negro equality—which in South Carolina actually amounted to negro supremacy—was being rammed down their throats.

This they could not abide. Since they had no voice in the matter, they fought it in the only way open to them, by stealth. Negroes were quietly warned to "keep in place." Some did not, and there were killings.

Daniel Sickles, in his efforts to persuade white Carolinians that Congress meant their ultimate good, was handed an impossible assignment because Congress meant no such thing. Tension grew. The general, while he understood perfectly the Southerners' fears of negro dominance, became impatient with the rigidity of the whites—an impatience that came out in a letter to Stanton:

> . . . A few months residence in the South dispels many illusions. If Contact with Negroes Cures Negro-Phobia, intercourse with rebels makes radicals. Mr. Sumner would not be in a hurry to confer Negro suffrage if he could see the plantation Negroes and thus Comprehend how hopelessly they lack Capacity for political franchises . . .[8]

But the seeds of hatred, sown deep, were bearing their fruit. The carpetbaggers came, determined to make solid Republicans out of bewildered ex-slaves. They held meetings and impressed upon the negroes that they were as good as the whites and perhaps a little better. Some of the Union soldiers, disgruntled at the hostility displayed toward them by the whites, maliciously encouraged negroes in acts of effrontery and insult. Threadbare patricians were being jostled and sneered at in the streets by blacks who were once their humble property.

So the fight of the whites against the "negro menace" went underground. There were secret meetings behind locked doors, secret rides of avenging posses. In Newberry, northwest of Columbia, a negro barber named Amos Wesley allowed his freedom to go to his head and was studiously contemptuous of the whites. One night a party of "Regulators" disguised as blacks rode up to Wesley's house, walked in and killed him in the presence of his wife and family. They rode away and no arrests were made although the sheriff (white) and the constables (also white) knew exactly who had done this job of regulating.[9]

In June, 1866, Sickles was given command of the Department of the Carolinas, embracing both North and South Carolina, and his problems were thereby doubled. He was responsible for order and security among some two millions of people although

his original force of 7000 officers and men had been depleted
through the muster-out of volunteers.

The general was getting his back up about the hostility of the
whites and the increasing activity of their secret nocturnal raid-
ers, known as Regulators. In several instances the Regulators
murdered Union soldiers who had angered them—a circum-
stance bound to excite the volatile Sickles temper. In the Beau-
fort district of North Carolina occurred one of many incidents
showing how the law could look the other way. Two negroes
regarded as offensive were slain by a hooded band of whites.
The usual coroner's jury met, and among the jurors were several
of the Regulators who had assisted in the slayings. With straight
faces these gentlemen joined in a verdict that the victims came
to their death by means unknown.[10]

The mission of General Sickles, which had set sail so amicably
with dinners and speeches, was encountering choppy waters.
The Carolina whites, in their subtle resistance, were not expressing direct protest against the military commander. They were
protesting against a Congress in Washington that was still hag-
gling over the degree of punishment to be meted out to the
South—a Congress in which the radicals were now in the saddle
and were intent on grinding "rebels" under the heel.

But the general's rule was being challenged, and he struck
back. In towns where officials were winking at a reign of terror
over the blacks, he instituted martial law. He warned sheriffs
and other officials that unless they enforced the law they would
be removed from office. He sent a squadron of cavalry to three
western counties of South Carolina where violence against negroes was rampant, and arrested a number of prominent citizens. He forbade the carrying of firearms—even by the police—
and a man found with a gun was liable to be tossed into Castle
Pinckney. He prohibited meetings of men who had served in
the Confederate armies.[11] He abolished discrimination against
negroes in public conveyances, fining a ship's captain $250 for
refusing to take a mulatto woman as a passenger.[12]

The kid gloves were now off with a vengeance. There were

indignant protests, some of which reached the ears of President
Johnson in Washington.

Being President had done something to Andrew Johnson.
The "poor white" Tennessean who had fought secession from
the start, endured exile because of it, and loathed slavery and
the planter class, had lost his malevolence. The old rebel-hater
had gone soft. He had come to understand that hatred was a
permissible and even necessary sentiment as long as war continued, but now that it was ended something else was needed. The
responsibilities of his office had broadened Johnson. He was
moved to pity for the prostrate South, and in his far-sighted
awareness that the time for generosity and helpfulness had come
he had begun to approach the stature of Lincoln. Unhappily, he
was a stubborn man with no genius for diplomacy or persuasion.
His turnabout aroused fury among the radicals in Congress who
had counted on his help in keeping the South under the heel
for years. Johnson used to talk tough, they said, but look inside
him now and what did you find? Nothing but a Copperhead, a
traitor.[13]

The former tailor who, it was sneeringly said, still sat cross-
legged occasionally in the White House, tried to steer a moderate course despite venomous abuse. When he heard complaints
from the Carolinas, he recalled that Sickles was known as a headstrong fellow and decided it might be better to have a milder
commander there. Still, he did not want to incur Sickles' resentment. The general had powerful friends in Grant and Stanton,
and Johnson was painfully aware that he needed all the political
allies he could salvage. So, in the summer of 1866 he offered
Sickles the post as minister to the Netherlands.

Sickles did not rise to the bait. For one thing, the salary was
modest. For another, the job would take him out of the country,
away from political councils and away from the possibility of
advancement to more important posts. Before making any decision he wanted to know whether Grant was behind the move.
He wrote Grant inquiring whether the general-in-chief was satisfied with his performance. Grant replied that he was perfectly

satisfied and would regret to see Sickles replaced.[14] Sickles thereupon refused the post, writing Stanton:

> . . . I have written to Mr. Seward declining the Mission to the
> Hague. The place is too far inferior in rank and Consideration
> to my present employment. The Salary is altogether inadequate.
> Deduct, say $3,500 a year for my family which always remains
> at New York only $4000.00 would be left for an official Establish-
> ment at a foreign Court—a sum I well know by Experience to be
> insufficient to maintain a respectable Establishment. If appointed
> to St. Petersburg, Madrid, Florence, Berlin or Paris I could ac-
> cept. Otherwise, when my services are no longer required in the
> Army I shall prefer private life and remunerative briefs . . .[15]

The general's father was now several times a millionaire, having made killings in real estate, but old George Sickles had evidently long since decided that to give money to his spendthrift
son was an investment in which more margin was always needed,
with never a dividend. Sickles had to struggle along on what he
made, no easy task in view of his expensive habits. He even
had to turn down a request of his New York friend Henry
Liebeman for a loan, writing him, "I have no income beside my
pay, which is barely sufficient to meet demands I Cannot disregard." [16]

So he declined the Netherlands post and remained at Charleston, with Teresa and Laura living in New York. This was an
arangement that had been followed ever since the Key scandal.
For seven years Sickles had been away from home far more often
than not on assignments military or official. On many of them
he could easily have taken his family with him, but not once
did he do so. His policy of leaving Teresa at home was not motivated by cruelty or neglect. He and she were merely accepting
an accomplished social fact, knowing that Teresa would forever
be an outcast and would be exposed to endless snubs and torment were she to be so rash as to essay a new entrance into
society.

Teresa stayed at home, where she at least had the friendly cushion of her family and a few intimates who would keep her from absolute quarantine. Down in Charleston, Sickles did not resign himself to loneliness. The general was now forty-seven and had only one leg, but he was still the accomplished rake. However, the days when he would consort openly with women of uncertain reputation were over. He had come to the realization that a man in politics had better be discreet.

In the course of his duties, Sickles had to visit the South Carolina capital at Columbia occasionally. One of his ladies of the moment there was one Allie Grant, who lives for posterity only in a letter she addressed to the general in which one can read fully as much between the lines as in them:

> . . . I was inclined to call and see you again while you came up here, but some of the Delegates were talking already about my first visit and I thought it would be best to stay away. People are generally too *pragmatical* in Columbia. I passed you several times face to face in the street, once I came very near stopping and speaking to you . . . Columbia is awfully dull and I do wish I was down in Charleston.[17]

The bored Miss Grant ended with "Good night and Pleasant Dreams, Resp., Allie Grant," and added a startling postscript: "I think you had better come to Columbia for a while, and I will let you see me, not in *disguise* tho."

Just what the lady meant by that may or may not be clear. But if the general was occupying his leisure with fast women, he was also accomplishing constructive objects. He received, for example, from one Jane Petigru a note whose single sentence breathes gratitude:

"General Sickles, you have been so kind to me from the very first of your coming here, what I would do without the help of the two Rations a day I can not tell." [18]

But unfortunately the Congress in Washington was motivated by anything but sympathy. The radicals, now in control, were energetically rubbing salt into the wounds of the South and giving no sign of allowing the defeated states to govern themselves. Small wonder that Sickles could write Stanton:

> . . . The Southern people yield to the United States only a reluctant, Constrained, sullen . . . allegiance. The Southern people could not be relied upon a day, if we were at War with a formidable Military and Naval power. In my Department I have not yet seen the American flag raised by a Carolinian. If it floated over a Dwelling, or a Hotel, or a Shop, the population would avoid the place as they would shun a pest house filled with lepers . . .[19]

The war was finished, but it would take a century to finish the hatred. Winter came to the Carolinas, and with it came privation, disease, and increasing bitterness. The general had his troubles. He also had unfinished business to attend to. Now that summer was over, his men could return to the job of giving decent burial to the dead of Sherman's conquering army, some of whom still lay in hastily-improvised graves.[20]

Early in February, 1867, Sickles made a hurried trip to New York. Teresa was dead.

CHAPTER XXVII

Letters Edged in Black

"The lady, who had but attained her 31st year, had been for some time in failing health," recorded the New York *Herald*. "A recent cold, slightly increased from time to time, took deep root in her constitution, and resulted in the melancholy catastrophe of her premature death."

The funeral was held at St. Joseph's Church on February 9th, four days after her death. One of the pallbearers was James Topham Brady, a sincere friend even though he had been forced to deal rather harshly with the lady when he was defending her husband for the murder of Key back in 1859. Among the others were four generals of the army—Alfred Pleasonton, Gordon Granger, Charles Graham, and Henry Tremain, the latter Sickles' old aide-de-camp.

"The afflicted husband," the *Herald* went on, "accompanied by his young daughter, his parents, now advanced in years, and Mr. and Mrs. Bagioli, parents of the deceased lady, occupied seats near the altar." After chanting the Catholic service, the Reverend Father Farrell came forward and delivered "a most earnest and impressive address," alluding "in words of touching tenderness to the deceased." [1] The church had been one of Teresa's few refuges during her eight-year penance, and now it was her last refuge.

In death, That Woman of the Key scandal achieved a semblance of public recognition she had not known since 1859. St. Joseph's that day was crowded with mourners, many of whom had not spoken to Teresa since the "Washington tragedy." Not so Henry Wikoff, who was there and who undoubtedly wrote the *Herald's* account. Wikoff had been one of the few to remain friendly when others turned away.

Sickles, it was said, was bowed with grief. Despite all the Fannie Whites and Allie Grants in the life of this determined profligate, there was only one Teresa, linked with him since childhood in gayety and triumph and the blackest depths of ruin. Possibly he was not unconscious of blame that she died in unhappiness when she should have been entering the fullness of life.

Sickles was still lingering in New York on February 26th when he addressed to President Johnson a letter on black-bordered paper:

My dear Mr. President

The vacancy made in the grade of Brigadier General in the Army, by the recent resignation of Gen'l Rosecrans, opens the way for a promotion I venture to ask at your hands. For my Military record and professional qualifications I feel authorized—or rather justified—in referring to the Secretary of War & the General in Chief of the Army.

Not desiring Civil office, I Confess my ambition to deserve and attain a rank in the permanent Military Establishment Corresponding to the grade I reached as a Volunteer officer by service in the field during the War for the suppression of the rebellion.[2]

Having pressed his own case, Sickles was off to Washington to use his influence in behalf of his friends, among them Generals Graham and Brewster.[3] He haunted the White House to solicit posts for these deserving veterans, on March 5th writing the President a little snappishly, "I have waited since ten A.M. & presume some duties make it impossible for you to see me today . . ."[4]

By mid-March he was back in Charleston, taking with him his daughter Laura, now a pretty but headstrong child of thirteen. One might have thought the death of Teresa would have wiped away the stain of scandal, but it was not so. The general sought to place Laura in a fashionable academy operated by one Madame Tivane. She was rejected with specious excuses, and the irate father finally gave the girl's tutelage over to a more forbearing schoolmistress.[5] By now, coping with Mrs. Grundy had become fairly routine for Sickles, but in the sensitive child her years of living in an atmosphere of shame and mistrust had left their mark. Laura was a creature of moods, high-strung and at times defiant.

Now in the Carolinas, the influential whites were fighting a battle for the preservation of some fragment of their civilization against a Congress that seemed determined to stamp it out by sponsoring negro rule. Confronted by resentment and opposition, Sickles' hot temper occasionally exploded. When the Charleston fire companies planned a parade in April, the general flatly ordered that the United States flag be carried.[6]

A storm of protest arose, for traditionally the fire companies had carried only their own colors. Sickles was inflexible. On the day of the parade the firemen swallowed their pride and carried flags on their equipment as ordered. However, one fireman had slyly removed a star from one of the flags as a hint that South Carolina wanted no part of such a union. This "insult" was noted and the offending fireman spent a month in jail without trial, then was publicly reprimanded.[7]

But if the general was hasty and ill-advised in his public relations, he still regarded himself as an exponent of mercy toward the South and proved it in the larger issues. In the bankrupt Carolinas some 60,000 lawsuits were pending for debts from twenty dollars upward.[8] Destitute widows of soldiers were being evicted from their homes. Even returned soldiers were cast into prison for debt. Governor Orr, aghast at this, had sponsored a law suspending executions for indebtedness, but the law had been declared unconstitutional by state courts. Orr, his hands tied, went to Sickles for help to protect the people against their own laws.[9]

Sickles helped. He issued his General Order Number 10,

which superseded the ruling of the court, abolished imprisonment for debt, and stopped foreclosures for twelve months.[10] It
was a move painfully needed and designed to ward off utter
chaos. It was supported by many local newspapers and prominent citizens, but denounced by some commercial interests, and
Sickles was accused of high-handedness and usurpation. Possibly
the general had a way of issuing even wise orders in a manner
that rubbed raw sensibilities, but at any rate his General Order
Number 10 raised a storm whose eddies blew into the White
House and caused consternation in the Cabinet.[11]

The President was now an object of hatred and contempt to
the radicals. He had been tipped off by his canny Secretary of
the Navy, Gideon Welles, that his own Secretary of War, Edwin
Stanton, was playing him false.[12] Stanton saw perfectly how the
political winds were shifting and had been conniving with the
radicals on the sly. Johnson likewise knew that Sickles was a
Stanton man through thick and thin.

When Johnson made a trip to his birthplace at Raleigh in
May to dedicate a monument to his father, he was no longer in
a mood to butter up General Sickles. He turned with sarcasm
on Sickles, who was there to give an official reception to the
President and his entourage.

"General," he said, "I am requested by several farmers, who
met me at one of the railway stations, to intercede with the commanding general for the purpose of obtaining such permission
as will allow them to shoot crows in their cornfields."

Sickles took the rebuke in stride. "Your Excellency," he replied, "no formal permission is necessary. Shooting crows in
cornfields has not been prohibited."

He then explained gravely that his order against firearms was
directed at people in streets and public places as a measure to
curb violence and did not extend to cornfields. The two men
parted with superficial politeness that only emphasized the coolness between them.[13]

The lines were now drawn for a death struggle between

Johnson and a Congress whose acts he had vetoed with monotonous regularity and which had passed them as regularly over
his veto. The time for choosing sides—Johnson or the radicals
—had all but passed. Where did Sickles stand?

The general, to do him credit, seemed sincere in occupying
a middle ground, a No Man's Land where he could not stay for
long. True, he had aroused the ire of the Carolinians by a few
intemperate acts of minor consequence. But in the larger issues
he was moved by a real desire to revive the foundering econ-
omy of the two states. In a letter to Stanton he had argued
against the "extreme tendencies" of the radicals, but being a
political realist he felt the President should make some concessions to the inevitable.[14] To Senator Browning he had complained about the carpetbaggers ostensibly sent to help the
emancipated slaves but who were more concerned about gathering them into the Republican fold. They were, he said, "tyrants,
knaves and robbers" who were doing great harm.[15] In a letter to
Senator Lyman Trumbull—still on black-bordered stationery
—he stoutly opposed the radical demand that men who took
part in the rebellion be barred from public office, saying, "Now,
more than ever, men of ability and experience in public business are needed for the State government in the South." [16]

In these opinions Sickles was far closer to Johnson than to
the radicals. For all his identification with Stanton, he still had
his own moderate views and the courage to stand by them. Impatient as he was at times with the Carolinians, he sought to
help them. That old secessionist, Governor Orr himself, wrote
Sickles, "But for your General Order Number 10, I believe an
increase of troops would have been necessary to guard the public records and insure the safety of sheriffs and other officials
against popular violence." [17]

In fact, Sickles got along very well with Orr and with Governor Worth of North Carolina, with both of whom he had to confer frequently. In one of these conferences, Orr came up with a
deathless observation:

"The Governor of South Carolina feels constrained to say to the Governor of North Carolina that in these military cabinet councils, there is a long time between drinks." [18]

Perhaps it was not so much matters of policy that soured the relations between Sickles and the President as it was the general's rather cavalier assumption that he knew better than anyone else—including Johnson—what should be done in the Carolinas. Harried on all sides in Washington, and with an edgy temper ever growing edgier, the President was not of a mind to take orders from his commander in Charleston.[19]

Sickles was no radical—not yet—but he was still Sickles. He made angry threats against the editor of the Columbia *South Carolinian* for commending ceremonies in honor of war dead at which a Confederate flag was displayed.[20] Flags meant much to him. He was high-and-mighty enough so that unreconstructed citizens spread stories about him, not all of them true. One of them which drifted northward and was picked up by the Washington *National Intelligencer* told how the general entered a horse car in Charleston while smoking a cigar and was informed by the conductor that smoking in the conveyance was contrary to the rules.

" 'Ah, indeed,' replied the great man, taking out his watch with the utmost nonchalance. 'Indeed! Then you shall consider the rules suspended for the next half hour.' " [21]

It made a good story even though untrue, as the *Intelligencer* itself later admitted.[22] General Sickles never condescended to ride in street cars. When he went abroad he was driven in a fine carriage drawn by the four black steeds the admirers of the Third Corps had given him. Apocryphal though it was, the story perhaps gave an idea of the impression he made on sensitive Carolinians. Sickles was a man who could strut sitting down even under happy circumstances, and his patience was sorely tried by Southerners who refused to see the blessings of Northern domination. His issuance of General Order Number 10 had already caused mutterings in Washington because he enforced it over the protests of state courts which pronounced it illegal. But it was in rage over the murder of three of his soldiers that he went overboard with a splash.

He defied a federal court.

This came about when four Carolinians were convicted by a military commission of the murders. A writ of habeas corpus was issued in favor of the accused men. Sickles refused to appear in answer to the writ. Federal Judge Bryan thereupon declared him in contempt of court and ordered his arrest. The ticklish question then arose: who was to arrest the general in command of all the real power that existed in the two states? The question was purely academic, for the general showed his power by flatly refusing to allow himself to be arrested.[23]

This he did with technical propriety, for he was ordered by his good friend and superior, Secretary of War Stanton, "not to give up the prisoners nor submit to arrest but to take into custody any and all persons attempting either." [24] In giving this order, so contrary to Presidential policy, Stanton was in open revolt and in fact it was one of his last acts as a government official. Johnson demanded his resignation, got a curt refusal, and dismissed him on August 12th. He moved Grant, whom he believed loyal, up to the Secretaryship.[25]

To Sickles in Charleston, the ousting of his ally was a clear signal that the time for choosing sides between Johnson and the radicals was all but past. If there was any doubt as to which way the general would jump, it was resolved when the President proceeded to go to work on him. Johnson got an opinion from Attorney General Stanbery that Sickles was acting illegally in superseding the courts. Sickles came back with a tart telegram asking to be relieved from command and declaring, ". . . the declaration of the Attorney General . . . disarms me of means to protect life, property or the rights of citizens and menaces all interests in these States with ruin." [26]

Johnson's patience was rubbed raw. "A conceited cuckold," he snapped, "is an abomination in the sight of God." [27] Secretary of the Navy Welles, solidly behind the President in his fight with the radicals, was angry too.

"Sickles should . . . have been cleared out some time since," he wrote in his diary. "The President showed me after the Cabinet adjourned an impertinent and presuming letter from King Sickles, who insists on obstructing the Federal Courts . . . I advised the President to make short work with King Sickles." [28]

As for General Grant, the military man, he seemed out of his depth in this question of legal technicalities, but he was inclined to side with Sickles. However, on Johnson's order Grant dispatched a telegram to Sickles on August 13th, saying in part, "Authority conferred on Dist. Commanders does not extend in any respect over the acts of Courts of the United States." [29] The general-in-chief slept on it, and when he awoke next day he thought differently. On his own, he sent another telegram to Sickles nullifying the order of the day before and permitting Sickles to continue in his course pending the preparation of a report as to his reasons.[30]

When Welles learned of that, he was of the opinion that Grant's action was motivated by something more than woolly-headedness. The Navy Secretary suspected that Grant had already deserted the administration and had secretly gone over to the radicals even while paying lip service to the President.[31] Washington was now a hotbed of double-dealing and suspicion in which the harassed President could not even be sure of the loyalty of some of his Cabinet and key officials.

On August 27th, Johnson finally heeded Welles' advice and finished off King Sickles. He relieved the general from his command for what the Attorney General called "high misdemeanors," replacing him with General Canby.[32] Sickles returned in bitter dudgeon to New York, with Governor Orr and many others regretful at his dismissal but with some feeling quite contrariwise.

"We affirm," observed the Charleston *Mercury*, "that here in this city there was an universal feeling of relief at his departure." [33]

As always when he met rebuff, Sickles felt himself a victim of injustice. True, his almost two-year rule had been well-intentioned and in many respects wise. But it had to be admitted that the general was temperamentally unsuited for a post requiring the maximum in patience and tact. He had needlessly given offense in matters themselves of minor import. Then too, there was a little matter of superior authority. No one—not even General Sickles—should have defied the President and the courts of the land.

But in New York he was feted as a hero by the arch-radical Union League Club, and there was no longer any doubt as to where Sickles stood. He was with the radicals. He was out to do all he could to have President Johnson's head.

CHAPTER XXVIII

The General Calls on a Lady

The headhunting was already well under way. It was merely a question of how the President's head should be lopped, and on what pretext, as punishment for his dogged refusal to junk the Constitution and leave the South to the wolves. Impeachment talk had been bandied about for months. Earlier in the year Congress had passed over Johnson's veto (*everything* was passed over his veto) the insultingly mischievous Tenure-of-Office Act, which forbade the President to remove certain officials including members of his own Cabinet, without the Senate's consent. This had the satisfying effect of humiliating the executive and curbing his powers, but with a push from Edwin Stanton it was to accomplish a good deal more than that.

Lincoln's ferocious war secretary was universally honored for his loyalty and tireless service to the cause during the conflict, but now he had become the intriguer again. Johnson had long seen the evidence mount that Stanton was secretly working against him with the radicals. Johnson dismissed him in the belief that the Tenure-of-Office Act was unconstitutional, and felt this a good opportunity to test the act in the highest court.

Well, muttered the radicals, we will see about that.

When Sickles reached Washington in mid-September, vengeance was brewing. His good friend Stanton was also one of the "outs," and thereafter Stanton came into the open with his enmity for the President. General Grant, too, even though he was now Secretary of War ad interim, was giving way to radical pressure and moving into the camp of the opposition. He saw fit to give a reception for Generals Sickles and Sheridan—both of them removed by the President from commands in the South—and thereby gave public notice of the direction of his sympathies.[1]

Sickles had already addressed a letter to Johnson denying "each and all of the allegations" against him and demanding a court of inquiry to investigate his actions.[2] In other words, as Welles scoffed, he "wanted to try the President and Attorney-General for disapproving his conduct." [3] Grant advised Johnson to accede to this request because "Genl. Sickles' professional reputation is suffering." [4] But the President decided that if Sickles was suffering it was his own precious fault, and refused—an act that heated the New Yorker's choler still further.

Now began a serio-comic game of musical chairs revolving around Edwin Stanton and the War Department. The Senate lost no time in voting that Johnson's removal of Stanton was illegal and that Stanton was therefore still war secretary. Thereupon Grant became absent-minded and forgot Johnson's request that he hold the office despite any Senate action and force a test of the constitutionality of the Tenure-of-Office Act. Grant tamely handed the keys to Stanton, who once more took over. This time Stanton barricaded himself in the office with all the grim determination of a man prepared to stand off a siege.

The President, wondering whom he could trust, all but plucked a name out of a hat and appointed General Lorenzo Thomas, adjutant general of the army, as temporary secretary. Thomas marched with military stride to the War Department building. Reaching the office, he found the door barred by soldiers. When he insisted that he was the rightful secretary, Stanton even placed him under temporary arrest.[5] Stanton, a year earlier talking of resigning his post, could not now be removed from it by anything short of dynamite. His control of the army proved useful in ways not strictly military. He had a soldier named Walter Dunn stationed in the White House as a spy to keep watch on Johnson, and Dunn dutifully noted all callers and conversations.[6]

Located somewhere on the periphery of this bitter intrigue, but actually the focus of its intent, was General Ulysses S. Grant, the man of Appomattox, the popular hero whose name was a household word. There was no doubt at all that Grant could be elected President in 1868, and now he was safely in the radical camp, the center of a ruthless struggle for power. We will elect Grant in 1868, the radicals said, but first there is another matter to attend to—finishing off Andy Johnson for good and all.

Congress appointed a committee to prepare articles of impeachment.

As for Sickles, he was never far from the eye of this gathering hurricane. Unworried about the propriety of a major general plunging headlong into politics, he addressed a big Grant-for-President rally in New York in December.[7] He went on to Connecticut, New Hampshire, and New Jersey, sounding the trumpet for Grant and dashing off enthusiastic letters to Grant's old political sponsor and fellow citizen of Galena, Illinois, Representative Elihu Washburne. Washburne, once a participant in the Congressional scuffle that had toppled Representative Barksdale's wig, was now a radical promoting the interests of his townsman Grant. To Washburne Sickles urged drastic action against Johnson, whose "inglorious Career is nearly ended," and went on:

> Here let me express the hope that Congress will take no Counsel from fear— The people will never follow timid leaders,—in truth the present Crisis demands Courageous leadership . . . & that is why the Masses all intuitively look to Grant who Combines good sense, tact and firmness.[8]

The one-legged general was a dynamo of activity, rushing from one city to another to wave the Grant banner and rally the Republicans in local elections. From Boston he wrote Washburne:

The battle for New Hampshire "goes bravely on"—My meetings are always as large as the largest Halls admit of, and hundreds go away unable to get in. It is the same in Connecticut— On Wednesday night last I addressed the largest meeting ever held in New Haven—the stronghold of the opposition. We shall carry New Hampshire and recover Connecticut. *Chase is not reliable—This I know—He is for Johnson.* Our friends must secure him if possible—A failure now in the Senate will be fatal to us and a decisive victory for Johnson . . .

My address is Concord N. H. until the victory is won.[9]

There were many other letters to Washburne and others, advising on strategy and urging unity and energy in the assault on the President. Undoubtedly Sickles would have been happier if he could have managed the impeachment proceedings himself, but this duty had devolved upon others and anyway the general could not be quite everywhere at once.

But when the impeachment trial began in March, 1868, with Chief Justice Chase presiding and the Senate sitting in judgment on the President, Sickles was back in Washington to take part in a show calculated to demolish the man who had dismissed him from his post in the Carolinas. It was his second wrecking job in the capital. The first, against Meade, had misfired, but the New Yorker was looking for more destructive results this time. Strangely, the bitterly radical Senator Ben Wade was once more a leading member of the wrecking crew. Senator Wade, as president pro tempore of the Senate, would succeed Johnson in the Presidency on his impeachment, a fact which would have caused a man of delicate perceptions to disqualify himself from voting. Wade did not disqualify himself. He would vote against Andy Johnson if it was the last thing he did, and he was so certain of the result that he was already selecting his Cabinet.[10]

By now the feeling against Johnson had mounted to such virulence that all reason and fairness fled. Stanton, cheered by the radicals, was still fortified in his office, eating and sleeping there lest some minion of Johnson attempt to storm it in his absence. Yet the President still had friends in the Senate, and there were others teetering on the fence who were revolted by the lynch-law tactics of the impeachers. There had even been an abortive attempt to prove that Johnson had master-minded the plot to kill Lincoln. As the trial wore on, the political pressure exerted against Senators whose minds were not yet made up as to how they would vote, was enormous. The doubtful ones were threatened and cajoled. Spies kept watch on them, and it was said that bribes were offered.[11] But with the approach of the day of Johnson's judgment, Stanton and others of the whipcrackers were still unsure enough to feel it necessary to send out emissaries to canvass and dragoon Senators who had not yet made known their stand.

One of the doubtful ones was forty-year-old Senator Edmund G. Ross of Kansas. A Republican, Ross was at first believed "safe" until he dropped a few remarks leading to the awful suspicion that he might not be quite sure he would vote against Johnson on all of the articles of impeachment.[12] In a fight so close that one vote either way might mean the difference between victory or defeat for the impeachers, Ross immediately became a person of gigantic importance. The radicals busily looked into his background, hoping to find scandal with which he might be intimidated.[13] Stanton was so worried that Sickles went to Ross in the Senate and put the question to him point-blank. According to Sickles, Ross flatly denied that he was wavering, and the impeachers breathed more easily.

"I cared nothing about the politics involved in the controversy," Sickles later said with a perfectly straight face, "but I was the friend of Grant and Stanton, and Johnson had treated them badly. In common with all friends of Grant and Stanton, I was doing my best to rid the country of Johnson." [14]

Came Sunday night, May 15th, the eve of the vote which would decide Johnson's fate and would also decide something else—namely, whether the Senate of the United States could be cowed and subverted by thug tactics. The tension on both sides was painful. Hasty canvasses had confirmed that the vote

would be close. No one slept much that night. One of the impeachers, Senator Cassel of New Jersey, was still worried about
Ross. It was almost eleven when Cassel drove to the apartment
Sickles was sharing with the man who had fought with him at
Chancellorsville, General Pleasonton. Knowing Sickles' powers
of persuasion, the Senator asked him to talk with Ross and make
sure the Kansan was "right."

Senator Ross was lodging at the home of Mrs. Matilda Ream,
mother of Lavinia "Vinnie" Ream, a talented young sculptress
who had been commissioned to execute a statue of Lincoln and
was presently working on it in a studio in the crypt of the Capitol. Cassel said that Miss Ream was a Johnson supporter, and
worse yet, she had a good deal of influence over Ross. She might
even win the wavering Senator over in the eleventh hour. In
selecting Sickles for this mission, Cassel could hardly have been
forgetful of the general's ingratiating ways with women.

So Sickles got a carriage and rode to the Ream establishment
near Capitol Hill. The driver got lost en route, and it was past
midnight when they arrived, but the general could see a light in
the sitting room and also one in the upper room occupied by
Senator Ross. He glided to the door on his crutches, which he
used more often than his artificial leg, and knocked. He later
gave an account of the interview, certainly one of the most fantastic on record.

Vinnie Ream, who was something of a prodigy, being only in
her early twenties, answered. She recognized Sickles but did
not invite him in. When she told him the Senator was not in, he
replied that he would come in and wait. Still she did not ask him
in. The general was in no mood for gallantry. "I pushed my way
in," was the way he described it.

"You know what I came here for," he said. "I came to save
Ross. You can help me."

The word "save" was in keeping with the spirit of the hour.
In the minds of the impeachers, the only way to salvation was
to vote Andrew Johnson into the political trash heap. But the
attractive Miss Ream was obviously not disposed to help. Sick-

les knew she was a precocious young woman who had proved
her adeptness at influencing Congressmen when she won the
commission to execute the Lincoln statue.[15] It was said that Senator Ross had a high regard for her judgment. Sickles felt that if
he could only win her over, Ross would be "saved." He used
all his gifts of persuasion in outlining the President's crimes,
not forgetting to warn that Ross would be cast into political
oblivion if he voted to acquit.

The young lady was not impressed. In fact, she scarcely made
any reply at all to the eloquent general. Her coolness made it
plain that she would be happy if he left. Miss Ream had already
been importuned by other radicals eager to bring her over to
the side of holiness, and she was growing impatient at the endless pressure. Furthermore, it was late and she wanted to go to
bed. Sickles determined that if this was to be an endurance contest, he would not be outlasted. He heard footsteps upstairs as
if two men were there, and he was convinced that Ross was one
of them.

Seated in a comfortable chair, he tried to draw the sculptress
into conversation, but failed. Now and then she went to the
door and held whispered discussions with someone the general
could not see. Time dragged on. At length, for want of anything
better to do, he asked her to sing, knowing she was musical. Miss
Ream complied. But the tension was telling on her too, and
soon she burst into tears and fled from the piano. Sickles grimly
continued his vigil, sitting there until four A.M. Then he stirred
in his chair.

"You are going?" she asked eagerly.

"Not until I see Ross," he snapped. "He is in the house. Bring
him to me."

By now she was almost hysterical. "No, no," she sobbed. "It
would do no good."

"Then he has bound himself to vote for acquittal?"

Miss Ream nodded. "He will support the President."

The general gathered his crutches and rose. "He is in your
power," he said angrily, "and you choose to destroy him."

He clumped out into the darkness, and as he went he saw the light still burning in Ross's room.

Washington quivered with excitement when morning came. Senator Ross was still pursued by pleading, threatening radicals right down to the very hour of the vote, but even without him the impeachers felt reasonably hopeful. Senator Grimes, known to be in favor of the President, was gravely ill and surely would be unable to come. These hopes were blasted when the pallid Grimes was carried bodily into the chamber.[16] In the end the vote was thirty-five to nineteen in favor of impeachment, one short of the two-thirds necessary.

President Johnson remained in office by virtue of the hardihood of Senator Ross, who did indeed find his political career destroyed because of it. Or possibly it was the hardihood of Vinnie Ream. At any rate, the radicals were furious enough to eject Miss Ream from her Capitol studio, restoring it later on when they had cooled somewhat.

Sickles did not cool. He never forgave Ross. Twenty-eight years later, when the name of Ross came up and it was mentioned that he was working as a typesetter, Sickles bristled.

"He'll die in the street," he growled. "That will be his end." [17]

CHAPTER XXIX

A Deep Sense of Propriety

Any politician understands the value and necessity of alliances. With Daniel Edgar Sickles, mere alliances were not enough. From the days when he was cutting his teeth on Tammany methods of running New York, he sought intimate friendship with politicians whose views he shared and particularly with those who held promise of gaining power or already had it. This inclination was not entirely selfish. He really cherished his friends, sometimes even suffered for them, and did favors for some who were outside the pale of political preferment. Still, it can hardly be said that he was oblivious to the main chance.

Thus, in the early days he had identified himself successively with Brady, with Fernando Wood, with Pierce, with Slidell. Moving onward and upward, he had scored a minor miracle by lashing his colors to the Buchanan mast. Then came Stanton, Lincoln, and Hooker, followed by a brief wooing of the despised Johnson.

Now, in 1868, the man for Sickles was General Ulysses S. Grant. Stanton was still a valued friend and would remain so, but the fact had to be faced that the bearded monster was ailing and his great days were behind him. But Grant—here was a soldier, a man with a future, so covered with laurels that his somewhat dissembling participation in the impeachment fiasco scarcely showed. Here was a man whose political possibilities seemed limitless.

While Sickles may not have been the very first to climb aboard the Grant bandwagon, he was not far behind and when he got on he swarmed all over it. In so doing he bolted the Democratic Party he had sworn by for thirty years and became a Republican. For him it was a dramatic switch, but not without portents, for in '64 he had backed the Republican Lincoln against the Democrat McClellan. He was far from alone in switching. The raging issue of how the South should be reconstructed had snapped old ties and caused a fairly heavy shift of political bedfellows.

Now he had established cordial relations with Representative Washburne, whom he had known since his days in Congress. This friendship with Washburne had at least two heart-warming aspects. For one, Washburne, like Sickles, had once been a printer and the two could josh about old days with the stick. For another, it was Washburne who had rescued Grant from miserable failure as a shopkeeper in Galena by helping him get his army commission early in the war. Grant never forgot his kindly sponsor, and the teetotalling Washburne was now pushing the Grant boom with all his might. It could almost be said that if one stood well with Washburne, he stood well with Grant.

In May, however, Sickles got a rude shock. He went to Albany, where he was chosen chairman of the New York delegation to the Republican national convention to take place in Chicago. After accepting the post, he was taken aside by a former comrade of the Army of the Potomac, General Sharpe.[1] Sharpe said that Grant had requested him to tell Sickles that he preferred that Sickles should not go to the convention. Was Grant beginning to wonder whether the fading cloud of disrepute that still clung to Sickles might do the campaign no good?

Sickles hastened to write Washburne about this dilemma "which *Embarrasses* me . . . I regret I had not been sooner advised of the General's wishes, for I could have declined in good season; but now, having accepted the position & also the Chairmanship, it is not easy to retire without risk of Misapprehensions. Still, if Gen'l Grant desires it I will retire at once, & so that no time may be lost in filling my place . . . I would

have written to General Grant direct, but presume he prefers
not to write on these matters . . ." [2]

Sickles was more than embarrassed. He was reflecting on how
difficult it could be for a man to live down past indiscretions,
even after losing a leg at Gettysburg. Happily, the objection
was withdrawn and Sickles went on to Chicago at the head of
his delegation, where he made a speech denouncing the seven
Republican Senators who had voted to acquit Johnson, and led
cheers for Grant.[3]

After the election of Grant that fall, Sickles had the comfort-
ing assurance that he would be offered some substantial reward
for his labors in the vineyard when the new President took office
in 1869. While he waited, he was busy at the law and with a few
excursions into stock investment. Investment fever was in the
air. Railroads were booming, capitalists were emerging as a
force to be reckoned with, and a pair of cunning intriguers
named Jay Gould and James Fisk had made millions simply by
deft and larcenous manipulation of stock they held in a road
they controlled, the Erie. Among the stockholders who took
financial lickings as a result were Sickles' friend August Belmont
and a promoter named James McHenry.

McHenry, once a grocery clerk, had shown enterprise in
launching an exporting business specializing in shipping American products to England, and had grown rich at it. Foreseeing
the inevitable expansion of American railroads, he had invested
heavily in Erie as well as gaining control of a smaller tributary
road, the Atlantic & Great Western. In his many trips to England he had talked enthusiastically of the profits to be made in
American railroads, and as a result some $20,000,000 had been
invested in Erie by wealthy Britons.[4]

McHenry and his British friends were outraged when they
took losses instead of profits because of Jay Gould's conscience-
less maneuvers. His cup of woe ran over when Gould, through
devious stock-jobbing, threw McHenry's Atlantic & Great Western into receivership and made himself the principal receiver.
McHenry was wild for revenge. He went to London to organize

Erie stockholders there in a solid bloc against Gould. When he returned, he looked up General Sickles and proposed that Sickles mount a legal offensive designed to crush Gould and place the two railroads in honest hands.[5]

The fact that the canny McHenry selected Sickles for this formidable chore is a fair gauge of the general's standing in the less polite realm of legal infighting. Any assault on the redoubtable Gould would involve a judicious massing of strength and a gift for intrigue.

Sickles agreed to take the case, but he counselled delay. Gould, the archetype of the rising group of ruthless robber barons, had made such effective use of bribes and influence that his position at the moment was unassailable. He had bought and paid for three New York judges who would issue any writ he desired. He also had the Tammany city government as well as the governor and state legislature eating out of his hand. Sickles urged a quiet, underground organization of forces against Gould which would gather strength and strike when the time was ripe.[6] McHenry, much as he yearned to fly at Gould's throat, saw the wisdom of this. The bargain was struck and Sickles had a secret assignment that was to occupy a cranny of his busy brain for more than three years.

Characteristically, however, the largest cranny was reserved for politics. Early in March, Sickles entrained for Washington to see Grant inaugurated as President and to rejoice with the ailing Edwin Stanton over a happy political situation which they had taken a large part in engineering. True, they had failed in their cherished objective of impeaching Andrew Johnson, but look at Johnson now! A broken has-been down in the hills of Tennessee. On the night of March 5th the general was crutching his way among a throng of triumphant Republicans at the inaugural ball held in the Treasury building.[7] He could not dance with Mrs. Grant—the absence of a leg was a sore trial at times like this—but he could still fascinate a group of listeners with his irresistible charm. And he was the only person there for whom General Grant was the fifth consecutive occupant of the White House whom he could address on terms of intimate familiarity.

Grant, the nation's honored general who was soon to prove that military mastery was no guarantee of executive wisdom, did not forget his friends. For Secretary of State he picked his old ally Elihu Washburne. While Washburne was a seasoned legislator, he was totally unfit for the critical State Department task and he knew it. Possibly the appointment was meant only as a temporary one, made as a gesture to increase Washburne's prestige for his next job, for Washburne stayed in office hardly long enough to warm the swivel chair. He was then appointed minister to France while Hamilton Fish, former governor of New York and United States Senator, became Secretary of State.

With the change in administration, there were hundreds of plums loading the patronage boughs, and thousands of deserving party stalwarts waiting in hope under the tree. Among them was Sickles, who expected something handsome for his all-out espousal of the cause. He was keenly disappointed when Fish wrote to offer him the legation at Mexico City.

Mexico! To the general it seemed close to a rebuff. He wrote Fish to decline this offer and to suggest that he would be more inclined to accept one of the major European legations more commensurate with his rank.[8]

So the matter was taken up with Grant and other members of his new Cabinet. Stanton, retired but still a powerful force behind the new regime, loyally urged Sickles for an important post. Secretary of War John Rawlins, Grant's faithful sidekick who had served as his stern duenna during the early years of the war, warning him away from bottled temptation, suggested naming Sickles as minister to Spain.[9] Rawlins was eager to acquire Cuba, then in revolt against Spain, and he was well aware that Sickles had been hot for incorporating Cuba into the republic ever since the days of the lamented Ostend Manifesto. Grant fell in with this suggestion even though Fish was inclined to throw up his hands in horror at it.[10]

Fish, a proper man and devout Episcopalian, had a low opinion of Sickles that dated back far earlier than the Key killing. Back in 1840, when both Fish and Sickles were young gentlemen in New York, Sickles had given Fish a note for five dollars drawn on the Silver Lake Bank—a bank which he discovered did not exist. Fish found it necessary to address several letters to Sickles asking him to replace the "five dollar Bill which proves to be a fraudulent note." [11] Five dollars was hardly enough to get excited about. Still, there was a principle involved and in Fish, a man of probity, this little exchange had aroused doubts about Sickles which had been strengthened by certain things that had happened since. Furthermore, he regarded the hero of Gettysburg as too unstable in temper and lacking the patience and tact required for the delicate Spanish mission.

But Grant wanted Sickles. Fish bowed to political expediency. The offer was made, and early in May Sickles accepted.

Now at last, Sickles may have thought, my old sins and errors may be forgotten and hidden behind the looming record of my services to the Union. If he thought this, he was wrong. The New York *World*, a bitterly Democratic organ, let out a prolonged shriek that was to last for weeks. Bennett's *Herald,* Henry Raymond's *Times,* and Horace Greeley's *Tribune* approved, but the old enemy, the *Evening Post,* was aghast, and even the Republican *Harper's Weekly* shook its editorial head.

"Of the ability of General Sickles there is no question," said *Harper's,* "nor of his faithful service during the war and as a commander of a department . . . But, with all that may be said in favor of the General's appointment to Spain, there is, it seems to us, a certain deep sense of propriety that forbade it . . ." [12]

Harper's itself showed a deep sense of propriety in failing to mention the specific shortcomings of the general that this "deep sense of propriety" should be exercised about. Others were not so charitable. Their utterances hurt even though the general's hide had been toughened by years of obloquy. He was discovering that it was a good deal harder to brighten a tarnished reputation than to make good a bad check on the Silver Lake Bank.

However, there were compensations. Quite apart from civil office, Grant had given notice of his gratitude to Sickles by making him a full major general on the retired list of the regular army—one of the highest honors paid any soldier after the war, West Point or not. This was a gesture that delighted Sickles. Though he had held a dozen offices, the military was his dearest love, his missing leg a badge of sacrifice and glory, and anyone who addressed him otherwise than as "General" had better watch out. Now the mighty Grant had done more for him than he had asked of Johnson two years earlier.

The difficulty was that the accursed Johnson administration had passed an act in 1868 providing that army officers who took non-military foreign missions thereby automatically forfeited their commissions, so that other officers could be promoted into their places. Much as he wanted to go to Spain, Sickles would sooner lose his remaining leg than give up his two-star rank (retired) in the *regular* army. He hurried to Washington to consult Grant in the matter. Grant assured him that since he was a retired officer and would serve in Spain without army pay, he would not lose his commission.[13]

Relieved, Sickles joined his ally John Forney in a call on Stanton, lying ill at his home on K Street. It was evident to both of them that Stanton was failing rapidly. Yet he was still keeping a close watch on the political scene.

"I wanted to see you both," he said warmly; "you, General, as the new minister to Spain, and you, Forney, as my steady newspaper friend."

Spain, he declared, would eventually be a republic, and then Cuba would become a part of the United States. Stanton, whose influence had been at least partially responsible for Sickles' appointment, knew the general like a brother and was well aware that his extraordinary abilities were too often submerged by impatience and hot impulse. He gave the younger man a friendly lecture on the touchy nature of the Spanish mission and the necessity for tact and forbearance.[14] For Stanton to preach tact and forbearance to Sickles was much like two Bengal tigers sitting down to discuss the advantages of a herbivorous diet.

But Sickles solemnly agreed on the herbivorous line and returned to New York, where an event was brewing that gave him much pleasure. General Graham, Chauncey Depew, Henry Raymond, and other New York friends had arranged a grand reception in honor of his appoinment as minister to Spain. The affair had been planned as a gesture of affection for the general and also as a rebuke for such newspapers as the *World* which had been hurling dead cats at him.

This was an event for which the *World* had been lying in wait with a licking of chops. The burning issues of the day had corroded the two major parties with a virulence that inspired some of the most frantic newspaper abuse ever seen. Edited by the able, acid Manton Marble, the *World* despised all Republicans but reserved a special spleen for "traitorous" Democrats who had moved over to the opposing camp during the ambush on Andrew Johnson. In its list of political lepers, Daniel Sickles held a position at the very top.

The reception for Sickles was scheduled for the evening of June 30th at the Everett House on Union Square—the same hostelry where he had staged the mammoth greeting for Buchanan when he returned from England thirteen years earlier. With a malicious sense of timing, the *World* that very morning came out with one of the most withering, vindictive (and unfortunately largely true) personal assaults ever set in bold-face type in a metropolis whose newspapers were never known for moderation. Its seven-bank headline set the pace:

DANIEL E. SICKLES
Public Reception of our new
Minister to Spain
SOME ACCOUNT OF HIM
His Career as Rowdy, Mail Robber, Spy,
Murderer, Confidence-Man, "General,"
Satrap, Politician, Etc.

"We propose," the *World* purred by way of introduction, "to take up Sickles' career . . . in order that all who go to the Everett House this evening may know precisely the man whose hand will be extended to greet them."

The *World* thereupon filled all of its front page and a large part of page 2 with an unflattering "biography" of the general. Its researchers had dug deep in the morgue for material. The story described Sickles correctly as "one of the most remarkable men of our time," and went on to assert that he was remarkable chiefly for villainy. Starting with Sickles' boyhood, it dredged up all that was discreditable in his career. It recounted his youthful follies and jousts with the law. It depicted him sleeping in a drunken stupor in a brothel with Fannie White. It recalled the rumor that he had taken some of the proceeds from Fannie's bawdy house to further his political ambitions. It asserted that he had had the unparalleled audacity to take Fannie to London with him when he became Buchanan's secretary of legation, and present her—a prostitute—to Queen Victoria. It did not forget his attacks on George Peabody in London ("scurrilous"), his election to Congress ("fraudulent"), his killing of Key ("deliberate"), and his reconciliation with his wife (to prevent disclosure of forgery and other crimes). It moved on to his service as a general (incompetent and conniving) and his term as "satrap" in the Carolinas ("arbitrary and tyrannical"). All these items and many more were covered in the most searching and libellous detail. The *World* had fruitful ground to till and it made the most of it.

"During the last Presidential election," it finished, "while drawing pay as an officer in the Army, Sickles traversed the country making political speeches for Mr. Grant. Grant was elected, and Sickles is Minister to Spain." [15]

The *World* sold out that day. New Yorkers accustomed to political brickbats had never seen anything quite like this. Sickles was raging, but his indignation did not keep him from the Everett House that night. "Clad in full evening dress, and resting upon the arm of a chair, with a crutch by his side," he received some 200 well-wishers, among them Emanuel Hart, Horace Greeley, John Graham, Thurlow Weed, and Peter Cooper.[16] Many of those who came to do him honor had known him for years and still regarded him with admiration as a friend despite all the newspapers could say. He made a speech of appreciation which for him was remarkably brief. He avoided any mention of the *World* onslaught.

While he may have felt that the Spanish post was proffered grudgingly, and was somewhat less than he deserved, Sickles wanted it not only as a just political reward but also as an opportunity to realize his long-cherished desire to bring Cuba under the flag. His appointment was not yet secure, for he was in precisely the same situation as when Lincoln had nominated him as a brigadier general. He still had to be confirmed by the Senate. The publicity he was getting was not the sort likely to woo the Senate.

Daily the baleful *World* continued its asault. "The claim that the man atoned for his hideous offenses against decency and good morals by his services during the war are utterly unfounded," it said. "He was one of the most conspicuous failures of the war." [17]

That struck to the heart of the man who believed himself the hero of Gettysburg. It gave him small comfort to reflect that Manton Marble and his *World* had a gigantic cheek to be heaping vituperation on anyone for "services during the war." What were the services of Marble and his sheet when the Union was struggling for its existence? Marble, safe in his New York office, had been the leader of the Copperhead press, attacking the Union cause, smearing Lincoln with insult, and demanding an end to the conflict while Sickles was giving flesh and blood in the fight.[18] But if Marble had a short memory about war services, he nevertheless was out to impale Sickles on one of the most caustic pens of the day.

"It is a great abuse and prostitution of our foreign missions," the *World* declared, "to convert them into asylums for broken reputations. They are instituted for the public good, not for the private advantage of male Magdalens . . . Our government has no right to thrust into foreign society a man whom the social code of every civilized community would exclude . . . a man who has forfeited by a life of infamy every title to be admitted within the sacred precincts of a virtuous home." [19]

The *Evening Post* seemed anticlimactic by its very calmness when it agreed that the country would be "dishonored by being represented abroad by a person so infamous as Sickles." [20]

The venom of these continuing attacks was made all the more insupportable because Sickles was defenseless against them. While he had been careful to keep his overt life above moral reproach for a decade, his enemies were happy to dig up the errors of earlier years and parade them before the public—and before the Senate. Despite his good work in many issues of later years, he *had* once been scandalous and immoral, and any attempt to seek redress by lawsuits would only prove it. Like a human target at a sideshow, all he could do was dodge as best he could and hope that the support of the *Times, Tribune,* and *Herald* would save him.

For all his natural desire to escape this vituperation, Sickles had work on the Erie project which he told Fish would occupy him in New York until July 15th. But Fish was anxious to get the Cuban crisis settled before it got worse. He tartly informed Sickles that in that case he would ask Grant to appoint another minister. [21]

The general capitulated. Early in July he sailed for Spain, taking with him Laura and his elderly mother and leaving his father at home. His head was bloody but not noticeably bowed even by the *World*'s parting shot: "It is to be hoped that General Sickles, before leaving for Spain, will deliver an address at Cooper Institute on the importance of increasing the perils of homicide and improving the inducements to conjugal fidelity." [22] He was taking a chance on being confirmed by the Senate, and in fact that body was reluctant enough to delay confirmation for almost a year.

CHAPTER XXX

Tact and Forbearance

The master of Bloomingdale, the man who had dispensed hospitality at the Stockton Mansion, hobnobbed at the White House and Delmonico-ized an Army of the Potomac tent was not likely to become an ascetic as the chief representative of the United States in Spain. In Madrid Sickles took a handsome suite of rooms at the fashionable Hotel de Russia on the Carera de San Geronima,[1] on a lower floor out of consideration to his missing leg. Although he owned an artificial leg and had used it occasionally, he was impatient with its caprices and now almost invariably made his way about on crutches. There were some who said spitefully that the general made dramatic use of those crutches and was never forgetful that they were a badge of heroism and sacrifice at Gettysburg.

Perhaps Madrid was as cheerless and bare as John Hay said it was, but it had its Prado, its Escorial, its bull ring, its theaters, and an aristocracy accustomed to the better things of life. In the hierarchy of State Department importance, Madrid came at least third after London and Paris, but before long it would be first in crisis.

In Spain, Sickles was dealing with a country almost as chaotic and bankrupt as South Carolina in 1865 and fully as jealous of its traditions. But here he could not issue an edict and back it up with the might of his regiments. Here his weapon would be diplomacy. He was embarking on parleys that would require all the "tact and forbearance" Stanton had advised. It was a mission that could make or break him.

Now aged forty-nine, and looking years younger, he still burned with ambition that seemed to give spring to his compact frame and sharpness to his eye. There was yet time. For him, the Spanish mission might be a means, not an end. After his untiring services for Grant, the Republicans had not been excessively generous in their rewards, and yet—might not the ultimate reward come to the man who could at long last fulfill the glittering dream of making Cuba a part of the United States? Yes, there was time. Here in hot Madrid lay opportunity enough to make a man's pulse misbehave, and Daniel Sickles was never one to doubt his own ability to seize opportunity when it struck.

Spain in 1869 was a morass of disgruntled factions in perfect agreement that they had been subjected to decades of misrule, and in utter disagreement as to what to do about it. During the previous year, the pleasure-loving Queen Isabella II—the same lady to whom Sickles had been presented in 1854—had been driven into exile after a series of increasingly violent revolutions. The country was now under the nominal leadership of a regent, handsome General Francisco Serrano, whose own marked intimacy a few years earlier with the unconventional queen had caused eyebrows to rise.[2] But the real power in an almost powerless government was General Juan Prim, the rough-hewn patriot who had led the revolution. Prim was working doggedly at the almost hopeless task of preserving Spain's far-flung empire when he was having more than enough trouble maintaining order on his own rebellious peninsula. There was crisis almost everywhere in Spain and its possessions. One of the greatest of them was in Cuba, the Caribbean island which Americans had coveted for decades and more than once had tried to buy. Cuba was in massive rebellion, and had been for a year. The Spanish authorities there were unable to suppress it. American filibusters, with an eye to easy riches, had jumped at this opportunity to aid the revolutionists, one of them being Gen-

eral Thomas Jordan, the former Confederate officer. Illegal
boatloads of men and arms were sneaking into Cuba, American
adventurers being killed for their pains, and legitimate American
property in the island was being ravaged or appropriated as violence raged.

The result was a growing exasperation in the United States.
Influential men including Henry Ward Beecher were demanding the acquisition of Cuba. Spain had long since demonstrated
her incapacity to maintain even nominal order there, their reasoning went, and it was high time for the United States to take
over. Some seemed oblivious or careless of the fact that such a
step taken by force would almost surely mean war with Spain.
In the Cabinet, Secretary Rawlins was eager for Cuba, and
President Grant himself wanted the island.

Now, with the Spanish exchequer almost empty and the nation's resources being still further drained by the fruitless war
in the island, seemed the time of all times for Cuba to come
under the Stars and Stripes. By agreeing to its sale for a handsome price, General Prim could in one stroke replenish his exhausted treasury and rid himself of a distant and costly struggle.

When General Sickles reached Madrid, he carried instructions from Secretary Fish to push for Spanish permission for the
island to purchase its own independence, with the United States
proffering its good offices and guaranteeing the payments. It
was felt certain that under this arrangement Cuba would soon
become a United States possession. As a preliminary step, the
United States insisted on the abolition of slavery in Cuba.[3]

With the shaky Spanish government all but backed into a
corner, it must have seemed to Sickles a fairly simple task to
persuade Prim to part with Cuba. What else could the Spaniards
do but sell? Sickles was to discover that even a beggar has pride
and that the machinations in Madrid could be easily as devious
as those he had known in Washington. At any rate he was happy
in having as his secretary of legation young John Milton Hay,
whom he had last seen in the White House as Lincoln's secre-

tary and who had since served in diplomatic posts in Paris and Vienna. The general could go nowhere without meeting someone he knew.

Sickles made the usual formal tender of credentials in an audience with the regent, and was warmed when General Serrano said, "I take pleasure in assuring you that the President of the United States could have made no choice for the honorable post which he has conferred to you which could have been so agreeable to us as that of yourself." [4] It was nice to know that Serrano was not unduly influenced by the New York *World*. Sickles then secured an interview with General Prim, President of the Council and the real government leader. To Prim he gave the views of the United States in settling the Cuban problem.

He found Prim quite receptive to the United States offer of good offices in the matter. He was willing to discuss independence for Cuba in return for being bailed out of bankruptcy, but he admitted some doubt as to whether he could persuade the Spanish people to agree to the sale. Without putting it in so many words, he was admitting that his own government was so precarious that he was walking on eggs and giving close heed to public opinion. Still, the overtures were encouraging and Sickles felt that progress was being made.

But it soon turned out that Prim's doubts were all too well-founded. In September, when it leaked out that the transfer of Cuba was being discussed under American pressure, the Spanish press flew into a frenzy. Here was a Yankee insult! What business did the Americans have to meddle in Cuba, a sovereign Spanish possession? Spaniards demonstrated in the streets and demanded more troops to quell the Cuban revolt. Down with the Yankee meddlers! [5]

Much as he needed good American dollars, Prim was affrighted at the temper of the populace. He told Sickles that the whole matter would have to wait.[6] So the general, disgruntled, protested at the "atrocities" in Cuba and settled back to practice the qualities which were least prominent in his makeup—namely, tact and forbearance.

Balked in his first foray in the direction of Cuba, he turned to extend the reconnaissance of the Erie citadel he had begun in New York. In this effort he enlisted friends in America, dangling before them the prospect of juicy profits. He wrote Emanuel Hart, asking him to make cautious inquiries into the Erie-Tammany cabal and telling him of McHenry's plan to merge the Erie and the Atlantic & Great Western. "If this operation can be effected," he wrote, "a handsome fortune can be made for us in the Combination. The securities of both roads . . . will go up to a comparatively high figure—and if you desire for yourself a position in the reorganization I can give you the support of my Clients." [7]

He wooed Wikoff, suggesting that he join in the espionage against Erie and promising, "I do not doubt McHenry will see that you receive enough to enable you to go back to London and write your Memoirs 'in Clover.' " [8]

He wrote General Pleasonton congratulating him on his appointment as Commissioner of Internal Revenue and promptly turning the appointment to advantage by urging Pleasonton in his new office to make a searching probe into the fraudulent Erie bookkeeping and tax structure.[9]

He wrote Charles Graham and John Graham, soliciting their aid against Erie. He wrote Forney, picturing a rosy future when the brigand directors of Erie were unseated: "Some day I hope we shall be able to make a direct continuation line running broad gauge from New York to St. Louis. Perhaps I may be President of that Corporation wielding more than [$] 100,000,-000 of Capital . . ." [10]

If Jay Gould was not blasted sky-high, it would not be because Attorney Sickles was not busily laying demolition charges. In his effort to marshal every available weapon against the enemy, he was not overlooking the government in Washington. He made President Grant himself privy to the secret offensive against Erie and solicited his cooperation. Possibly he anticipated that Grant might not regard Erie matters as the legitimate concern of the government or the minister to Spain, but he got around this neatly. He pointed out that the Erie thievery had given American enterprise a sorry reputation in Europe and would harm honest American industry because European investors would be fearful of entrusting further funds to the Yankee pirates. Further, Erie was hand in glove with Tammany, no friend of the Republican administration. Grant agreed at least to the extent of approving the minister's leadership in the undertaking.[11]

"Good news from Washington," Sickles cabled McHenry. "Government with us." [12]

Meanwhile, the practical General Prim, concerned about his tottering government, was shopping for a king to give the volatile Spaniards a new focus of patriotism. Late in 1869 he offered the crown to a Hohenzollern prince—an offer so infuriating to the French, who suspected Spanish-Prussian intrigue, that despite the prince's refusal the fever burst into the Franco-Prussian War.[13] At length Prince Amadeo of Savoy, son of the king of Italy, agreed to become the Spanish monarch although there were plenty of Spaniards, both monarchists and republicans, anxious to shoot him on sight as a foreign interloper. As a gauge of the Spanish temper, stout-hearted General Prim was set upon by assassins on December 27th, 1870, and murdered shortly before the new King Amadeo I arrived.[14] It was Amadeo's first official duty to gaze sadly at the bullet-riddled corpse of the general who had sponsored him.

Sickles immediately presented his time-worn representations about Cuba to the new king's government under Serrano. Unhappily, the national climate was anything but beneficent for the settlement of such a matter. Spain seethed with discontent and violence. A Carlist war raged in the north and there were smaller uprisings elsewhere, while in Madrid one patchwork cabinet succeeded another with such maddening regularity that Sickles found himself dealing with an endless parade of foreign ministers, none of whom occupied the post long enough to say anything more decisive than *mañana*.

Tact and forbearance. Those were Stanton's words, but with

Sickles patience was a thing of short limits. The mission which
had started so promisingly was striking unexpected snags. War
still raged in Cuba, Americans were being slain, and other adventurous Yankees were still aiding the revolutionists with illegal arms and men, but all of the minister's politely-worded
requests for an end to this disorder came to nothing. In fact, the
Spaniards were inclined to place a large share of the blame
on the United States for failing to stop the filibustering which
they claimed was keeping the revolution alive. Much as Sickles longed for the big stick, here in Madrid he could only ask
and ask and ask, and be met by that same infuriatingly courteous Spanish temporizing. He was growing testy about the
whole business.

"It is next to impossible to do anything with these people,"
he complained. "They do not know their own purposes from
day to day. Pride is always in the way of their interest." [15]

It was not long before the well-intentioned King Amadeo,
who was hated by many of his subjects simply because he was a
foreigner, also had the animosity of the American minister to
cope with.

Before Sickles, like a vision of the Grail, loomed the exciting
prospect of tying up Cuba in silken ribbon and presenting it on
a platter to the United States. He was moved by a sincere conviction that in so doing he would be accomplishing a patriotic service of the first magnitude, one that would benefit generations of
Americans to come. Probably he was not unaware that such a
feat could hardly fail to bring immense popularity at home,
with attendant newspaper headlines and perhaps even statues in
bronze. But who could have dreamed it would take so long?

It was fortunate that the general had other matters to occupy
him. For one thing, he was still marshaling his forces for the
onslaught on Jay Gould and the Erie Ring. Now and then he
hopped aboard the Paris express to confer with European stockholders in the French capital. While there, he renewed his
friendship with his wartime colleague, the Comte de Paris,
whom he had last seen on the Peninsula of Virginia, and also

had an opportunity to discuss American politics with Washburne, now in Paris as American minister.[16]

For another, his relish for social diversion had not waned. In
Madrid he had rapidly become known as a lavish host whose
dinners and wines were unexcelled and whose conversation
could run the gamut from Goya to Gettysburg, with authorita-
tive emphasis on the latter. His weekly entertainments, one observer noted, were attended by "the elite of Madrid society . . .
Ministers, Senators, Deputies and public men of all kinds, distinguished writers, painters and artists. There, too, were not
wanting the gentle sex." This last was scarcely a necessary observation. The gentle sex still vied with politics as the grand passion of his life. His receptions eventually outgrew his facilities
at the Hotel de Russia, causing him to move to a magnificently
furnished house at No. 12 Calle Isabel la Catolica, where his gatherings continued and "music and dancing became the order of the
day." [17]

One of the guests at the Sickles salon was a dark-eyed senorita
in her early twenties, Caroline Martinez Guerrera, whose father
had died in her infancy and who had taken the name of her stepfather, Senor Jose Creagh. Bred in a convent, Caroline de
Creagh was a niece of the Marquise de Novaliches. She had
been an attendant at the court of Isabella II, and although that
monarch had been deposed, Caroline and her family were still
loyal to the Bourbons. She had taken a solicitous interest in
the younger Laura Sickles. Now it was noticed that General
Sickles was showing marked attention to Caroline de Creagh.[18]

This did not mean that the general, though progressing into
the years of discretion, had forsworn his old philandering and
was entertaining the thought of settling down. His restless eye
still roved. On one of his trips to Paris it lighted on a queen,
deposed it is true, but still a queen for all that—Isabella II, the
same regal lady whom he had met in 1854 when his designs, as
now, were centered on Cuba. Isabella was now presiding over a
court-in-exile on the Avenue Kléber in Paris, and in his visits to
the French capital Sickles became a frequent caller there.[19]

In the roll of errant royalty, this headstrong daughter of the Bourbons had won a niche peculiarly her own. Forced by political pressure into loveless marriage at sixteen with her own cousin, she had retaliated by indulging in a scandalous series of affairs which made her the talk of Europe. Warm-hearted and well-intentioned, she was yet so heedless of public opinion that she had flaunted her fondness for a succession of lovers including General Serrano, General O'Donnell, and an opera singer named Marfori.[20] Of her it was said, "It is believed that she suffered from a trouble which made normal standards of morality almost impossible for her." [21] A nymphomaniac and a thoroughgoing Bohemian, she had had five children about whose paternity there was widespread speculation.[22] She had been accused of "high treason against the cause of virtue and morality," and was not noticeably disturbed by the charge.[23] Now forty-one, she had grown excessively fat. Yet even her critics conceded that in her bulk there was no grossness, that her proud carriage invested her ample curves with heady allure, and that she had a "très grand air." [24]

General Sickles, in the summer of 1871, became a frequent passenger aboard the Madrid-Paris express on matters not strictly chargeable to legation business. Perhaps it was inevitable that with his hedonistic inclinations and his knowledge of the deposed queen's purple past, he would take more than a platonic interest in her. Along the boulevards it was whispered that *la reine* had a new *affaire de coeur*. The one-legged American war hero who handled his crutches with such élan, it was said, had won her favor. Paris buzzed with Gallic witticisms about *"Le roi américain de l'Espagne"*—the Yankee King of Spain.[25]

Certain it is that these two—alike in recklessness, pursuit of pleasure, and scorn for convention—were cast from the same eccentric mould. The New Yorker had known many women of assorted degree since his liaison with the prostitute Fanny White a quarter-century earlier, and assiduous effort had at length elevated him to the very royalty of dalliance.

But unconventionality carried certain penalties. Even in her

Parisian romancing, Isabella never forgot that she was the daughter of Ferdinand VII, that her ancestors had held the crown for
nearly a thousand years. She was actively grooming her fourteen-
year-old son Alfonso for the day of whose ultimate arrival she
had no doubt, the day when he would return in triumph to
Madrid and resume the throne. In this she had the loyal support
of a monarchist faction in Spain resentful of the foreign King
Amadeo and determined to restore the Bourbons. These supporters were now outraged by her open affair with the American
general—a scandal which they felt would imperil the growing
movement for the recall of Alfonso. They urged her to have done
with her lover.[26]

So the general had several kettles on the hob in addition to
the slowly simmering problem of Cuba. He had already drawn
a handsome £1500 retainer from McHenry for his groundwork
in the mobilization against Gould,[27] without any worries about
the propriety of accepting side commissions while receiving
$16,800 a year for representing his country in Madrid. His van-
tage point in Spain was useful in allowing him to confer personally on occasion with the European investors in Erie whom Mc-
Henry represented. It also was a distinct disadvantage in forcing
him to delegate the New York end of the enterprise to others. He
was coolly plotting to overthrow the shrewdest and most powerful titan of finance in America, a man who had a habit of demolishing his opponents. To McHenry he wrote with clear understanding of the immensity of the project: "I am maneuvering to
divide the enemy . . . To succeed with what I have undertaken,
I must break up the alliance between the Erie Managers and the
political and Judicial power . . ."[28] But in a letter to General
Graham, who had fought with him on the Peninsula and in the
Peach Orchard, he showed his inborn confidence:

> . . . I am offered the Presidency or any other position I choose
> to take in the new organization & great inducements have been
> offered to me to go to New York and take charge of the fight . . .

When we get control of one or both of the roads, I can get you all the engineer work . . .

Remember us all to Mary. My Mother & Laura are well— Laura is hard at work at German and I should not be surprised to see her soon writing a letter in German to Mary. We have charming weather here this autumn. We are keeping house—and have a handsome room for you and Mary whenever you will come to make us a long visit.[29]

Sadly, it was not entirely true that Laura was "well." She would never quite recover emotionally from her years of shame and proscription as the daughter of That Woman in the Key affair, nor from a feeling that her father was not innocent of blame. To be shunned and insulted by New York children who should have been her playmates was too bitter an experience for any child to escape unscathed. In Madrid she was no longer shunned nor insulted, but the rescue came too late. She had grown to a slender, aloof girl of sixteen, cursed with more than her share of her father's headstrong nature and instinctive hostility to restraint. When Sickles put a stop to a burgeoning affair she was having with a young Spanish officer, her defiance had touched off an unhappy scene. The relations between father and daughter were no longer warmly filial.[30]

Despite his real affection for her, the general was so engrossed in a multitude of projects that he had no time to bestow more than occasional love and attention on the daughter who needed love and attention above all things. To her he had given the same infrequent and fleeting tenderness that had mortified the late Teresa Sickles. It was not enough.

So the general kept busy. In August, 1870, he was sorry to lose the services of John Hay, who was leaving the diplomatic service to take an editorial post with Greeley's New York *Tribune*. But Sickles had a genius for turning even untoward circumstances to advantage. He was never forgetful of the power of the press. Before Hay left, he enlisted the younger man's aid in urging a stepped-up editorial campaign against Jay Gould, bolstering the idea with a personal note to Greeley.[31] Considering Sickles' friendship with Greeley, it is not unlikely that he aided Hay in landing the job with the *Tribune,* thereby gaining another newspaper friend in a spot where it would count.

Sickles knew exactly whom he wanted to replace Hay, and he got him. The new secretary of legation was a twenty-eight-year-old scholar with the grandly alliterative name of Alvey Augustus Adee, a nephew of Sickles' friend Charles Graham. Adee, whose hearing was impaired as a result of scarlet fever, liked to dash off facile verses for the newspapers and was an able and efficient young man perfectly designed for the practice of tact and forbearance. He was to have little time for verse, for his chief soon loaded him with a heavy assortment of chores, many of them having no connection with diplomacy. As though it were something new, the minister was asking the Spanish government for action on the Cuban problem and reiterating the demand for the abolition of slavery there. Sickles was getting along beautifully with Secretary of State Fish now, for Fish well realized the difficulties of the Spanish mission. The general even sent him a half-pipe of sherry from Jerez with his compliments.[32]

Fish would have been horrified had he known that his minister was so soured on the government of the new King Amadeo that he was beginning to connive secretly with revolutionists whose purpose was to depose the king and install a republic. He was enraged at the government's continued efforts to suppress the Cuban rebellion at all costs, cabling angrily to Fish:

> Sixteen hundred of the worst class of convicts are at Cadiz awaiting transportation to Cuba [to fight the revolutionists]. I have again remonstrated without result.[33]

But in the midst of remonstrances, amours, trips to Paris, Nice, Lisbon, and Seville, and schemes to upset the Spanish monarchy and the directorate of the Erie Railroad, the general did not neglect the pleasures of life. Fluent in Spanish as he was, he enjoyed the theater and opera not only because he sincerely loved music and the drama but also because he was keenly aware of the social value of these entertainments. He was never satisfied with anything but the best. He subscribed to the *Teatro Nacional de la Opera* for 1750 *reals* and selected his box with care. Possibly his contempt for the new king had given offense, for the box he chose was turned over to someone else and his tender of the payment refused—a slight that outraged him. He wrote a heated 2000-word letter of protest to the theater agent claiming damages for being refused the box even after "I sent a *Tapicero*, Mr. Landa, to the opera house with orders to place a carpet on the floor of my box and to see that the furniture was sufficient . . ." [34]

The new secretary of legation, Mr. Adee, was kept furiously busy not only with state affairs but also with arranging little luxuries for his chief. Adee wrote to Paris to order *"Vin Tonique"* for *"Le Général Sickles,"* urging *"grande vitesse."* He wrote to order Sauternes, Chablis, St. Estephe 1864, and five different kinds of champagne. He wrote to Tarragona saying the general was much pleased with the sherry known as "Dry Old Gentleman 1820" and ordering forty gallons more, as well as muscatel for Sickles' mother. He wrote to a tailor on Savile Row to settle a bill. He wrote to La Rochelle for special patés favored by the general. He wrote to London for four kinds of visiting cards for the minister, "of finest ivory Bristol board." Adee must have felt somewhat like a combination housekeeper and amanuensis as he ordered—also from London—sterling silver spoons bearing the monogram "S" with a star on each side. Major General Sickles was not going to let anyone who drank his tea forget that he was a major general. [35]

While Sickles and thrift had always been on distant terms, in Spain the coolness reached outright rupture. His fees from McHenry and his $16,800 salary were stretched taut. McHenry received occasional notice of this in messages from the general such as, "If you can conveniently give me a further Credit, I shall feel obliged." [36] Possibly rich old George Sickles in New York helped to satisfy the vintners and silversmiths, since Mrs.

Sickles was with her son. The United States government likewise found the minister going over the usual quota, and obliged by sending $1,529.16 for "extraordinary expenses." [37] "Extraordinary" was perhaps the correct word in more ways than one.

Even with an ocean between, the vengeful New York *World* still kept an eye on the minister. In February, 1871, he attended a meeting in a Madrid theater of Spanish liberals who were pushing for the abolition of slavery in the nation's colonies. Sickles, who had long been pressing his government's petition for abolition in Cuba and Puerto Rico, made a speech warmly urging the emancipation of the slaves.

The *World* of March 9th took note of this with an editorial headed "The Scoundrel Sickles Speaks," commenting that the general occupied, "as is his modest custom, the most conspicuous box in the theater" and adding that "The other speakers were gentlemen. There is no reason to suppose that any of them had been a thief, or a forger, or a dependent upon outcast women, or a murderer."

In discussing Sickles' statement that he had "given his life to the sacred cause of negro emancipation," the *World* erupted molten lava:

> Mr. Sickles has shed a certain amount of blood—especially the blood of the late Philip Barton Key—but he did so for his own selfish purposes, and not in support of any cause that could be called sacred. He joined the army because it was his last chance of gaining recognition among honest men, at a time when he was ostracized as that most infamous of men—a trader in the virtue of his wife . . .
>
> He might, with equal truth, have claimed that all the acts of his remarkable life were performed in the interest of the negro race. He should have said that it was to free the negroes that he had stolen money, robbed the post office and forged checks. That he had held the position of bully in a house of ill-fame solely in the interests of emancipation, and that he had disgraced his wife, and murdered the man whom he had permitted to be-

come her lover, with a single eye to the sacred cause of emancipation . . . the impudent mendacity of his recent speech is one of
the least disgraceful of the acts by which he has become notorious.

Greeley's New York *Tribune,* where Sickles' friend Hay was
now working as an assistant editor, did not allow the blast to go
unchallenged:

The *World* is positively hysterical over the fact that its filthy
abuse of Gen. Daniel E. Sickles produces no effect here or abroad
. . . There is one efficient answer to this unwholesome black-
guardism. At the time when these men assert that Gen. Sickles
was doing all these disreputable things, he was the trusted and
honored leader of the Democratic party in New-York City. Their
libels of today dishonor their past. For ten years Gen. Sickles has
acted with the Republican Union party—years full of glorious
history . . .[38]

While this was some balm, the *Tribune* did not so much defend Sickles against the asserted crimes as to place them in the
Democratic era. The general groaned under the *World* lash. It
was apparent to him now that the skeletons in his closet would
never be allowed decent interment. Still, this incessant public
waving and rattling of the bones was agonizing to a man who
liked to be liked. "In June 1869 the 'World' published similar
libels against me," he wrote in anguish to General Graham.
". . . My subsequent confirmation by the Senate was generally
regarded as sufficient answer to these gross calumnies—But it
seems that the malevolent purposes of the 'World' are not satisfied." He went on:

It is true I have ever believed that the best answer to abuse was
the faithful performance of all my duties as a citizen—And such
a refutation would ordinarily be sufficient.—But this journal
pursues me with fiendish purpose—It wounds my aged parents—

It tortures my child, now grown to womanhood—It offends all
who honor me with their steadfast and noble friendship [and is
calculated to] embarrass me seriously in my duties here as the
representative of my Country at a foreign Court.

So what was the general going to do about it? He admitted
that he would prefer not to prosecute the *World,* for "such a
mode of vindication would be at best tardy, partial and unsatisfactory. And, if it could be avoided, I would rather not appear
personally in the business." Sickles asked Graham to discuss the
problem with Hart, Forney, or John Graham. He suggested the
appointing of impartial referees to decide whether the *World*
libels were justified. He would deposit $5000 with the referees to
be given to a home for soldiers' orphans if the attacks were found
truthful, and would demand that the *World* forfeit the same
amount to the same charity if the newspaper was found to be in
the wrong.[39]

This proposal evidently came to nothing. A month later the
general was again writing Graham about a new grievance. He had
learned that the *World* libels had been reprinted in *El Cronista,*
a Spanish-language paper in New York, and the *World* had taken
the trouble to send copies of the *El Cronista* reprint to newspapers in Madrid with the request that they publish it. While
the Madrid papers had refused to do so, their editors had nevertheless read the unflattering appraisal of the American minister.
Sickles was simmering over this proof of the *World*'s vindictive
effort to defame him in Spain as well as America.

"I don't care what may be the consequences," he wrote stormily
to Graham, "I will not stand it any longer. I am on the War-
path." [40]

But his warlike spirit cooled, for no action was taken against
the *World.* Although that newspaper obviously was motivated
by malice and politics, there was enough truth in its attacks to
make any public airing of them via the courts an embarrassing
and possibly fruitless business.

The general, in truth, was so busy with diverse enterprises that he scarcely had time to quarrel efficiently with the *World*. He was frequently off to Paris to see Isabella and to push other affairs there. France was in the throes, having suffered humiliating defeat at the hands of the Germans, and was desperately seeking moderate peace terms. Through his friendship with the Comte de Paris, Sickles became acquainted with Adolphe Thiers, provisional head of the French government, and was not at all diffident about offering advice on how to treat with Count Bismarck. In the light of his many journeys, amours, and side interests, the wonder is that he had any time at all for sleep, or for attention to his duties at the legation.

While Sickles possessed the energy of several ordinary men, the only possible explanation of his multifarious activities is that he accomplished everything he did—including his romances—with lightning speed. Action drove him every waking hour. He had no leisure, wanted none. The fact is that he did find time to continue his appearances at the foreign office, as well as to carry on a hand-written correspondence so voluminous and beautifully phrased that it would alone comprise a heavy chore. He was also poking his nose into an enterprise far beyond his authority and not without peril.

This concerned nothing less than the monarchy of Spain. Sickles' tact and forbearance had long since frayed. He had despaired of getting any settlement of the Cuban question out of the government of the unfortunate King Amadeo, who had been shot at several times. His solution for this impasse was characteristically direct. He was taking action to get rid of Amadeo.

Madrid was a very nest of political machination, with a dozen factions seeking change or plotting revolution. Quite heedless of State Department policy forbidding American ministers to meddle in foreign politics, Sickles secretly threw his weight behind a group that sought to overthrow Amadeo and establish a republic. Not that he was forgetting Isabella and her hopes for the restoration of Alfonso—not at all. Possibly the Bourbons would be reestablished in God's good time. God's good time was too slow for the general. He had waited now for two years for the

accomplishment of his Cuban dream and was fairly groaning to
have it realized. To his logical mind it seemed inevitable that if
Spain became a republic—a well-nigh bankrupt republic, of
course—then he, as the emissary of another friendly republic,
could speedily close the deal for Cuba. His house on the Calle
Isabel la Catolica became the meeting place for a group of republican plotters, and also for agents of the Cuban revolutionists. To
both of these conspiratorial cabals Sickles gave his advice and aid,
even helping them compose their documents. It was his considered intention to become the personal, though unofficial, sponsor
of a republic in Spain.[41]

The general did not seem at all diffident about playing chess
with a throne. Perhaps he carried it a little far, for he went out
of his way to show studied disrespect for the king. When a baptism ceremony was held for Amadeo's infant son, the American
minister was conspicuously absent. He likewise failed to attend
a royal banquet at which his presence had been requested.[42]
These and other slights so offended Don Mateo Sagasta,
Amadeo's chief minister, that he began to entertain the idea of
asking for Sickles' recall.

So the general was in a position common to him—at the epi-
center of a gathering storm. He seemed unworried about it. He
sent off a letter to McHenry containing the potent sentence, "I
have my plan of campaign all made." [43] In it he discussed the
proposal that he take a post with reorganized Erie, but gracefully declined it on the ground that President Grant would be
upset if he resigned at this delicate moment. He had already
asked Grant, and been given, a three-months leave of absence
to depose another king—Jay Gould, the monarch of Erie. While
this could hardly be classified as the legitimate enterprise of a
man serving as United States minister to Spain, Grant's conception of such proprieties were not too clear and besides Sickles
stressed "the mortification every American minister [is] compelled to feel" at such corruption and thievery as Gould was per-
petrating at the expense of the road and its stockholders.[44] He

did not mention that he expected to draw the most handsome fee of his entire legal career when the battle was over.

Two empires were being privately undermined at the same time—one financial, the other monarchical—and Sickles was the busy sapper in both tunnels. One would have thought that now, surely, he had all the responsibilities he could possibly shoulder. Not so.

All his life Daniel Sickles had been a specialist in surprise, the conceiver and executor of acts both good and bad but generally surprising. This element of surprise arose not only from the nature of his decisions but also from the blinding speed with which he acted on them. He was never a muller, a ponderer. With him, decision was swift and action almost simultaneous.

In the autumn of 1871 it was announced that he would marry the Senorita Caroline de Creagh. Madrid society was atwitter when the banns were published and the general, to whom religion had never been a paramount consideration, took the necessary step of conversion to Roman Catholicism. It was at first planned that the wedding would be solemnized in the following spring, but when the bridegroom-elect found that certain confidential affairs would summon him soon to New York it was decided to hurry the nuptials so that the bride could accompany him.

"The suddenness of the notice," wrote the New York *Herald* correspondent, "compelled the wedding to be a private one. Under other circumstances the General would gladly have thrown his doors open to his large circle of friends and acquaintances."

So the service, held at the legation on November 28th, was a small affair. Even so, it was not lacking in distinction. The rites were performed by the Patriarch of the Indies, the highest dignitary of Catholicism in Madrid, assisted by three others of the clergy. One of the *Padrinos* was none other than General Francisco Serrano, the ex-regent and a grandee of Spain. He was aided by the Prussian and French ministers, a juxtaposition looked on as a happy one in view of the late war. Old Mrs. Sickles and the bride's parents, along with a few Spanish generals, gazed on fondly as Laura Sickles appeared in a dress of pearl silk to act as bridesmaid. If Laura was seething underneath the pearl silk, she did not show it. The bridegroom, meticulous in full dress, was the soul of cordiality as he greeted his guests.

"The bride," wrote the *Herald* scribe, "who looked lovely, went through her part without the emotion usual to young ladies under such 'trying circumstances.' There were no hysterics, no faintings nor sobbings, over this union of one of Spain's fairest daughters with one of America's bravest sons."

The hysterics and the sobbings would come later. Now, with the services read, the party retired to the crystal-chandeliered dining room for a quick round of refreshments, for there was a train to be caught by the bridal pair. General Serrano proposed a spirited toast in champagne to the health and happiness of the newlyweds, a toast that was responded to with enthusiasm. Within an hour, General and Mrs. Sickles were whisked away and were soon aboard a carriage of the Ferro Carril del Norte on their way to England and America.[45]

It would take more than good wishes and toasts drunk in champagne to bring happiness to the fair young senorita in her union with a man more than twice her age—a man with too much ambition, too many enterprises, a man whom wedlock would never lock.

Did the general, as it has been written, enter into the union at the urging of Isabella, solely as a marriage of convenience which would serve as a cloak so that these two could continue their liaison unmolested by the tiresomely proper Bourbon bloc? Was Caroline simply a sacrifice in the interest of decorum? [46]

It is only known that on November 28th, aboard the northbound express with his Spanish bride, the general was reviewing long-laid plans soon to explode in combat that should—with luck—bring him fame and fortune. He was en route to New York to slay a dragon.

CHAPTER XXXI

St. Daniel and the Dragon

Jay Gould was a slight, bearded, soft-spoken man of thirty-six who hid a steel-trap brain and the instincts of a buccaneer under a deceptively mild exterior. For years he had manhandled the Erie Railroad with such a marvelous disregard for rolling stock and maintenance that it was said that any man who rode on the Erie took his life in his hands. Gould had no interest in rolling stock or passenger safety. By slick manipulation of stock and wholesale corruption of governing officials, he had milked the road of something more than $60,000,000,[1] robbed stockholders blind, gobbled up smaller railroads, ruined opponents and competitors, driven at least one of them to suicide, and made himself the most feared financial freebooter in the nation. Victims were always suing Gould and being annihilated for their pains. It was because Sickles had seen the uselessness of suing Gould that he had spent two years and a half constructing a battering ram of a different kind.

Gould had secured his immunity through an alliance with that cynical Tammany colossus of the fix, "Boss" William Marcy Tweed, the uncrowned king of New York State. Tweed was a member of the Erie board of directors, sharing in the spoils. Tweed's man John T. Hoffman was governor of the state. Tweed's man A. Oakey Hall was mayor of New York. Tweed controlled the Tammany city administration, the state legislature, and the supreme court. Tweed controlled everything, and through Tweed, Gould controlled everything.[2]

333

But the man who had advanced his troops into the Peach Orchard was not afraid of Gould. For one thing, there were signs of cracks in Erie's foundation. When a Tweed hireling turned informer, New York City was treated to some astonishing news, viz.: a plasterer had been paid $138,187 for two days' work on the courthouse. Another valuable artisan received $1,149,874.50 for repairing plumbing and gas-light fixtures in the building. Thermometers had cost the city $7500 apiece. These charges seemed dear. The Boss was arrested and although he was out on bail, a reform movement was hammering away at the greatest temple of fraud New York had ever seen.[3] If Tweed could fall, why not Gould?

When General Sickles arrived in New York with his bride on December 22nd, 1871, he was questioned by reporters about a rumor that he was employed in some aspect of Erie affairs.

"There's nothing to it," he said with a wave of the hand. "I'm here on vacation with my wife, that's all." [4]

He went on to Washington to pay his respects to Secretary Fish and President Grant, then returned to New York for the business at hand. Setting up headquarters at the Westminster Hotel, he joined forces with Samuel L. M. Barlow, attorney for the Atlantic & Great Western, in a last discussion of strategy. It was apparent to them both that Gould's hold on venal politicians and judges still made him impregnable against the usual legal injunctions. Some other chink would have to be found in his armor.

The chink was found in the person of O. H. P. Archer, vice-president of the railroad. Archer was opposed to Gould's methods but unable to do anything about it. Possibly Archer's willingness to aid a foray against his dreaded boss was accelerated when Sickles showed him claims against Erie for over $23,000,000 and pointed out that these claims were valid against the personal estates of the company's directors, which included Archer himself. In any case, Archer agreed to serve as Trojan horse and operations got under way.[5]

Sickles learned that a sizeable majority of Erie's seventeen directors were antagonistic to Gould but too fearful of his power to oppose him openly. The general resolved to capitalize on this discontent. He aimed to pull the board of directors right out from under Gould. There ensued many weeks during which Sickles and Barlow were quietly working on the dissident directors in an effort to convince them that they would profit by joining the uprising, or suffer by failing to join it. All this had to be conducted in back-room secrecy, for if Gould got wind of it the scheme would be blown sky-high. It is doubtful that the general relied solely on persuasiveness in reasoning with the directors. It was later said that they were cudgeled with a judicious combination of promises, bribes, and threats. At least some of these gentlemen had taken part in sharp practices as Erie directors so that they felt vulnerable when they realized the strength of the movement Sickles represented. There was an endless amount of reasoning, cudgeling, and possibly bribing, and when it was over Sickles had eleven of the directors on his side.[6]

The general and Attorney Barlow had likewise made undercover arrangements with a group of prominent and respectable Erie stockholders who were aroused at the continued looting of the road and were willing to step in as new directors when the time was ripe. Among them was the upright General John A. Dix. Another was a wartime comrade of Sickles', General George B. McClellan, now president of McHenry's Atlantic & Great Western Railroad, which had been more cruelly treated by Gould than McClellan's Federals at Fair Oaks. The stage was now set and ready. But there was still a large question as to whether all the actors would perform their roles in the letter-perfect style essential for success. Sickles could be forgiven for a case of nerves as he contemplated the groundwork which was the fruit of more than two years of his toil, and realized it would result either in the greatest financial triumph or the most humiliating fiasco of the decade.

Came Act I in this drama of deceit. Several of Erie's directors had asked Gould to call a board meeting to take some action which might repair the "general want of confidence in the credit of the company." Gould, in his customary high-handed manner, ignored the request. Nothing could have satisfied Sickles more, for Vice-President Archer now took his cue to perfection. Archer himself called the meeting, to take place at the Erie offices on March 11th, 1872.[7]

The Erie offices, properly enough for this fantastic railroad, were located in the six-story white marble Grand Opera House at Twenty-third Street and Eighth Avenue. Gould and his late partner in larceny, James Fisk—recently shot dead by a love rival—had bought the ornate pile with Erie money but taken title to it themselves and then leased it to the road for $75,000 a year. This was merely a routine example of the kind of management which had been profitable to Gould and Fisk but ruinous to lesser stockholders. In the Opera House, Erie's moguls could indulge their taste for luxury by stepping on thick rugs in mirrored and frescoed offices and sitting in Mancotti chairs studded with gold nails.[8]

Act II saw the climax approaching. On the afternoon of March 11th General Sickles began his sortie. Along Twenty-third Street he led a caravan of carriages carrying Barlow, Dix, McClellan, Archer, and others of the purification forces. They were properly armed with injunctions and had thoughtfully brought along a brigade of police and other strong-armed fellows just on the off chance that there would be resistance. They pulled up in front of the Opera House and the fireworks began.

As it happened, Jay Gould was not caught entirely napping. He had surrounded himself with a group of policemen and plug-uglies, but he had underestimated the strength of the assault and his forces were outnumbered. The hero of Gettysburg dispatched a company of musclemen to clear the ornate entrance. Then he led his invaders into the building.

There ensued more than an hour of wild disorder, shouting, and struggling in which a few bruises were suffered. The confusion was heightened by the fact that both Gould and Sickles had detachments of police on their side, both of them claiming to be fortified with legal right. But Gould, overpowered, was forced to retreat to the president's room, where he locked himself in.[9]

"Very well," Sickles said. "We will proceed without Mr. Gould."

The military phase was over and Act III unfolded in comparative quiet. The old directors of Erie sat down in the board room and resigned their posts as they had agreed. The new board of directors was elected, with General Dix as president—a development that left L. D. Rucker, general superintendent of Erie, fairly goggle-eyed with bewilderment. Rucker pleaded that he did not know which directors to recognize. Sickles fixed him with a gimlet gaze.

"You had damned well better recognize the new ones," he snapped.[10]

After a hurried conference with other operating executives of the road, the disheveled Rucker announced that he and all the rest were at the command of the new regime.

A crowbar was now brought to bear on the door of the glittering office where Gould had barricaded himself. The lock gave way and Sickles and his minions poured in. Gould tried to flee but was cornered. An official served him with a paper notifying him that he had been removed from office and directing him to surrender all Erie property.

"This is illegal!" Gould shrieked, apparently not realizing the irony of the complaint.[11]

Sickles still had qualms about the political aid the little fox could muster. He was anxious to persuade Gould to resign voluntarily and thus avoid a protracted court battle over the legality of the ouster. With John Graham as his chief of staff, he closeted himself with Gould and a battery of attorneys and was said to have shown the financier proofs against him of a "serious criminal nature."[12] He also purred the kind of words Gould liked to hear—profit.

"If you resign," he said, "Erie will go up fifteen points. You can make a million dollars."[13]

So in the end Gould capitulated and handed in his formal resignation. All this was as incredible as if the Reverend Henry
Ward Beecher had preached a sermon warmly advocating drunkenness and debauchery. Editors went into hysteria. The impregnable bastion of Erie, ringed around by crooked judges and
bribed legislators, had been taken by storm. The newspapers
filled front pages with ecstatic copy about what they agreed was
the most amazing financial coup in history.

"The blow has fallen at last on the Erie thieves and banditti,"
crowed the *Herald*, "and not a fragment of their once great conspiracy remains." [14] The *Tribune* described with admiration the
secret moves made by the hero of Gettysburg and added, "Yesterday General Sickles appeared publicly as the master spirit who
directed the campaign against Erie, and had won it." [15] In an interview, Sickles told of his three-months leave of absence from
Spain for the Erie project.

"The work is accomplished," he said, puffing comfortably at
a cigar, "and I have twelve days left." [16]

This was one of the moments the general lived for. He received
more newspaper space than he had since Gettysburg, and this
time there was no doubt that he was on the side of righteousness.
The operations of Gould were so notorious that Sickles was presented as a plumed knight who had ridden bravely in and scattered the forces of evil—a warming experience for a man whose
newspaper publicity had not always been flattering. His absorp-
tion in the Erie intrigue had made his bride a lonely woman in
New York, but the former Caroline Creagh must have felt reflected glory to find the name of the husband she so little understood emblazoned in headlines all over the city. Sickles was also
pleased at the fee he drew from McHenry and the British stockholders, as well as by the large block of Erie stock presented him
by the new board of directors, who also made him a gift of a fine
house at 23 Fifth Avenue. It was pleasant to be a hero again, and
doubly pleasant to be in pocket.

Another man who was in pocket, though not precisely a hero,

was the vanquished Jay Gould. Sickles' estimate that Erie stock would go up fifteen points was short of the mark. It went up twenty points on the strength of an enthusiastic conviction that under honest direction the shares would pay handsomely, and Gould, with his large holdings of stock, made a fortune.[17] Sadly, the change in directorship could not work a miracle. Gould & Company had so thoroughly looted the railroad that it was crippled by debt for years and not until 1891 did it pay a dividend.[18]

Still, the general had headlines to bask in, hands to shake, applause to acknowledge. Perhaps he knew there was one newspaper that would never give him applause or even grudging approval—his old enemy, the New York *World*—but what of that?

The *World* took a little time showing him what of that. In this Presidential election year, there were signs of a liberal Republican revolt against Grant. Horace Greeley was being mentioned as a possible candidate against the President.[19] This placed Sickles in an awkward position, since the mercurial Greeley was a friend who had applauded his war services, supported him for the Spanish post and given editorial acclaim for his Erie coup. The *Tribune,* now more than ever with Hay on its staff, was a powerful ally which Sickles did not want to alienate.

But Sickles was no fence-sitter. He was for Grant, and in a New York speech he came out strongly for the President even while admitting that he honored Greeley.

The *World* leaped out snarling at that. In an editorial headed "The False Sickles" it blasted him for his Grant speech and loosed a new discourtesy. It called the general a pimp.[20]

It was undoubtedly the first time a prominent public figure and war hero had been referred to by a metropolitan newspaper as a pimp, although this milestone is not recorded in the textbooks. While it did not specify, the *World* probably used the word in recollection of the old unverified rumors that Sickles had appropriated proceeds from a brothel twenty-five years earlier at the time of his excursions with Fanny White.

A pimp! In a fury, Sickles consulted John Graham. The next day's *World* published a letter from Graham threatening suit on behalf of Sickles unless the newspaper retracted.

George Templeton Strong, who was still recording New York doings in his diary, was amused at the very idea of Sickles suing anyone for libel. "One might as well try to spoil a rotten egg," he sniffed, "as to damage Dan's character." [21]

But in commenting on Graham's threat, the *World* retreated to the extent of admitting regret over the use of the word "pimp," conceding with an air of doubt that "we do not believe he deserves the epithet." Then, with joyful malice, it hurled once more the tested thunderbolts it knew were libel-proof:

> We have repeatedly and deliberately called Sickles an acquitted murderer—a man who shot the alleged seducer of his wife, and afterwards exciting the loathing disgust of gentlemen and men of honor by creeping back to the bed which he had killed another man for defiling—cohabiting again with the dishonored wife whose shame he had published to the world and proved in a court of justice as a means of saving his neck from the gallows . . .[22]

There it was again. All this had happened thirteen years earlier, but the remorseless *World* would not let it be forgotten. Sickles, the vulnerable, swallowed his choler and did not sue. By now he knew that even though he had slain the dragon of Erie —even if he should make the United States a present of Cuba— his past would be a millstone around his neck until he died.

Overstaying his leave by a month, he went to Washington and learned that his hopes for Cuba had gone glimmering. He was not wanted in Spain. Foreign Minister Sagasta had sent word to Fish that Sickles would not be welcome as the American minister. The general had been too open in his dislike for King Amadeo and in his sympathy with the republicans. Sagasta would be pleased if another minister were appointed.[23]

Even the patient Secretary Fish, who had no knowledge of Sickles' meddling in Spanish politics, was growing testy over the endless palaver that never got anywhere. The war in Cuba was now more than three years old. American interests were still suffering, American freebooters still being killed. Fish instructed Sickles to return to Spain carrying his letter of recall with him, but also carrying a warning: If Sickles were recalled, he might not be replaced. The departure of the minister would be an ominous sign of worsening relations which might or might not prod Spain into a settlement on Cuba.[24]

Sickles sailed for Spain on April 27th along with his bride, who must have inquired into the meaning of the American word "pimp" and experienced shock and puzzlement. Though his days as minister seemed numbered, an incident of turbulent Spanish politics had the effect of saving his job. By the time he arrived in Madrid the hostile Sagasta had fallen from power and the cabinet had been reconstructed with a large republican element. The new foreign minister, Christin Martos—himself a republican—greeted Sickles with open arms and begged him to stay.[25]

Sickles stayed. Secretary Fish was exultant enough to write him, "I congratulate you on your triumph over Sagasta. You remain—where is he?" [26]

CHAPTER XXXII

The Big Stick

The general was bubbly and beaming for a time. Spain, he felt, was moving in the direction of a republic, and with the republic installed the avenue would be broad and open for him to negotiate terms on Cuba. Once again he plunged enthusiastically into intrigue with the Spanish republicans and the undercover agents of the Cuban insurrectos. Both groups met frequently at his residence, with the benefit of his counsel. He was untroubled with any concern over the paradox of the American minister accredited to the court of King Amadeo doing his secret but energetic best to wreck Amadeo and become the personal sponsor of a new government in Spain. When Sickles had what he considered a laudable end in view, he did not hesitate to demolish a monarchy that happened to be standing in his way.

But the demolishing took time. He kept pressing for action on Cuba, and instead of complying the Spaniards came back at him with protests against the activities of American filibusters in the island. Amadeo still clung to his tottering throne. Sickles was not only out of patience with the dilatory tactics of the Spaniards but was growing increasingly annoyed with his own government for what he felt was a failure to back him with a stern enough attitude toward Spain. A few months later, in vast disgust, he let Secretary Fish know it was high time to do something more than petition and plead:

If the President . . . has no purpose of initiating a policy of rigorous pressure on Spain with respect to Cuba, I wish you would instruct me to present my letter of recall in January or February. I Confess I am tired of my useless work here and of these vacillating people. If the President is satisfied with my services and you feel justified in recommending my promotion to any vacancy that may happen in one of the higher Missions (except Russia where the Climate is too severe for me) I shall be glad to continue in the Diplomatic Career—otherwise to retire, if not on "my laurels" at least I trust without loss of reputation.[1]

Perhaps Sickles hoped this neatly worded complaint might prod Fish and Grant to adopt the stiffness he felt was needed. In any case, Fish soothed his momentary pique and he stayed on. At long last, on February 12th, 1873, he had reason to believe that his long stint of forbearance, if not tact, had borne fruit. King Amadeo abdicated and fled to Portugal with his queen. The republic was proclaimed in Spain.

Sickles could be forgiven for feeling pride in the infant government, since he was at the very least its godfather. The new government felt the same about him. The *Americano* general who had nursed the republic from a mere backroom dream to a joyous reality was showered with attentions and honors. When he paid a call on President Figueras to announce American recognition of the new government, he walked between rows of crack Spanish infantry presenting arms and was serenaded by a band playing the *Star-Spangled Banner* and the *Marseillaise*.[2] His intrigue against the monarchy, like his campaign against Jay Gould and the Erie Ring, had bubbled in privacy for many months and had burst forth on an astonished world with the same conclusion—complete success and gratifying public acclaim.

Now, surely, the project on which he had set his heart for almost four years—the settlement of the Cuban question— would soon be accomplished. He felt gleeful enough to twit Washburne on the slowness of the French to install a republic.

"If you don't hurry up the Versailles people," he chaffed, "we shall have the Spanish Republic organized and ready for business before her French sister is *en toilette* . . . I believe we shall now be able to settle all our questions with this Government satisfactorily." [3]

But to his growing exasperation, Sickles discovered that the temporizing attitude of the Spanish was just as prevalent among republicans as monarchists. Not even the government he had helped to install was anxious to let loose of the rich Caribbean isle. Regardless of party, many influential Spaniards seemed of the opinion that a large part of the blame for the violence and rapine in Cuba was on the illegal American filibusters who were aiding the revolutionists there. What was more, the establishment of the republic in Spain won widespread approval in America, with public opinion inclined to give the new government time to find its bearings. This subsidence of popular indignation was reflected in Secretary Fish, who was disposed to deal softly with the republic. The pressure was off.

For Sickles, the parleying and the waiting began all over again, with no big stick in the form of a peremptory American government behind him. But in one man's view the general did not lack for diversions while he parleyed. Secretary Fish, the proper Episcopalian, must have gazed with some incredulity at a letter he received which was signed only "An American Citizen Just from Spain" and which read in part:

> Can the Department of State be aware, or rather ignorant, of the infamous character of Gen. Dan. E. Sickles?
>
> While in Madrid his conduct with women has been simply disgraceful. For months before his marriage with Caroline Creagh, who is heartily sick of her bargain, poor girl; he lived in open and notorious adultery with Madame or Senora Domeriquy, a Cuban conspirator, even at the U. S. Legation, to the shame of our countrymen abroad.
>
> An American by the name of Belknap supplied this creditable Minister with child virgins for the purposes of prostitution.

His conduct with lewd women of the town was and *even is* shocking.

Are we to have another Philip Barton Key affair in Spain?

This state of things is pleasant and gratifying for American families traveling in Spain—wives, sisters, daughters—who respect themselves or their nation . . .

P.S. Sickles could never have discharged the duties of his post with credit, *so licentious has he been,* if it were not for the great talents of Mr. Adie [sic] the Secretary, a gentleman of virtue and learning, as all know who have visited Spain.[4]

The American Citizen Just from Spain might have got more action on his complaint had he addressed it to Manton Marble of the New York *World* instead of to Fish. Alarming as all this was, Fish had too many troubles on his hands to give ear to anonymous gossip-mongers. The Secretary of State was well aware of Sickles' gamy reputation and had not wanted him as minister in the first place, but he had gradually come around to the view that the general had done well on a mission brimming with difficulties and wanted him to see it through. Perhaps he would have seen it through had it not been for a highly irregular American ship named the *Virginius*.

For three years the *Virginius* had been a notorious blockade runner, illegally sneaking arms and soldiers into Cuba to aid the insurrectionists. On October 31st, 1873, the vessel was engaged in its usual illicit enterprise when it was overtaken by Spanish men-of-war between Jamaica and Cuba, captured and brought into Santiago. Its crew and passengers were taken prisoner, and despite the protests of the American consul it appeared that they would be executed.

These men were largely a hardened lot of adventurers who had cheerfully flouted the law. Nevertheless they were entitled to a fair trial under the provisions of a treaty with Spain. Under instructions from Fish, Sickles made representations to the Spanish government not to allow any executions without proper trial.[5] The Spanish authorities so ordered their officials in Cuba, but this message was delayed in transmission. In Santiago, the local Spanish governor, General Juan Burriel, let his rage at American filibustering get the best of him. With no more than a mock trial, the *Virginius'* master, an American named Joseph Fry, and fifty-two passengers and crewmen—many of them likewise Americans—were lined up against a wall and shot. Spanish soldiers completed the ghastly business by jamming their guns into the dead men's mouths and shooting their heads off.[6]

News of the atrocity touched off a blaze of anger in the United States, where public feeling had long been smouldering over the violence in Cuba. Mass meetings were held in scores of cities. Furious citizens howled for war with Spain. Jingoistic newspapers fanned the flame. Secretary Fish—as well as General Sickles—was faced by crisis.

Though he knew the *Virginius* was an outlaw ship and had some doubt as to its right to fly the American flag, Fish denounced the executions as "butchery and murder." He instructed Sickles to demand the release of the vessel along with the surviving prisoners, a salute to the American flag, and the signal punishment of the officials responsible for the slaughter. If these demands were not granted within twelve days, he was to close the American legation and leave Madrid—an ominous step toward outright war. However, Fish warned Sickles to proceed with discretion and to avoid "all appearance of menace."[7]

This was no more effective than Stanton's old counsel of tact and forbearance. The general was breathing fire over an affront to the flag. Discretion went glimmering, for he was consumed with what Fish had warned him against—menace. He quickly became involved in an acrimonious exchange with the foreign minister, Jose de Carvajal, that greatly offended the Spaniard. Sickles' wrath mounted when a throng of excited Madrilenos, incensed at news of the American demands, mobbed the legation and had to be dispersed by the police.[8] The American minister, who a few months earlier had been given every honor in Madrid, was now being hissed and reviled. When five days passed and Carvajal had not given in on all points, he was all for quitting his post without giving the Spaniards the extra week of grace they had been offered.

"I propose, unless otherwise ordered, to close this legation forthwith, and leave Madrid," he cabled Fish, adding resentfully the next day, "Popular feeling runs high here against the United States and this legation. Press violent and abusive, advising government to order me out of Spain." [9]

In Washington, Fish was straining every fiber to prevent war, but the general in Madrid seemed almost willing to let it come. The United States Navy was already getting on a war footing. It was at this point that the Secretary of State began to grow a little mistrustful of his minister. For one thing, he was taken aback by Sickles' aim to close the legation after giving the Spaniards only five days of their promised twelve. It appeared as though the minister was trying to force his hand. For another, Fish was startled to find some of the general's confidential communications published in the New York newspapers at the same time as they were received at the State Department. While he never accused Sickles of sending this material to the press, he was aware of the minister's affinity for the newspapers and began to wonder if General Historicus was rearing his head again. Was Sickles trying to bolster his "big stick" policy by inflaming American public sentiment?

"It really appeared," Fish later wrote in confidence, "as though he [Sickles] took the violence of the *Herald,* the *Sun,* & other kindred sheets, as evidence of the popular sentiment, & that the Country was to rush to arms, & that he was preparing his sword & Epaulettes to be at the head of the Movement. A pacific solution, under such circumstances, would naturally be a disappointment . . ." [10]

Fish instructed Sickles to remain at his post. The general seemed to interpret this as a sign of weakness, and he dispatched a telegram telling the Secretary what was what:

If we hesitate, it will be asserted and believed in Spain and Cuba that we pause before the defiant attitude assumed by this government and people . . . Misapprehending our forbearance, Spain would abuse any success obtained by duplicity and delay, and show herself more than ever arrogant and regardless of our rights and dignity . . .

I have the best reasons for the opinion that my prompt withdrawal from Madrid . . . will convince Spain we are in earnest, and she will yield to our terms.[11]

History was repeating itself. Just as in the Carolinas, General Sickles was acting more like a policy-maker than as a representative carrying out policy directed from Washington. Again Fish, after conferring with President Grant, ordered the minister to stay.

In New York, the *Herald* had already declared war against Spain. Old Bennett had died the year before,[12] but the product of his peculiar genius was as irresponsible as ever. In a series of inflammatory articles on the crisis, the *Herald* acted as if it had a direct wire from Minister Sickles in Madrid, backed up his "tough" policy to the hilt, ridiculed Fish for temporizing, and beat the drum for war. A random sampling of headlines and subheads from the paper give the tone:

ON TO CUBA!!! . . . *Spanish Barbarism* . . . WAR BELIEVED TO BE INEVITABLE . . . *Our Insulted Flag* . . . *A Mad Mob Menace Our Minister* . . . *Immediate Redress or Immediate War* . . . HOSTILITIES IMMINENT . . . *Outrageous Onslaught on Minister Sickles.*[13]

The *Herald* published the result of a "canvass" which showed the overwhelming sentiment of various parts of the West and South for war, and solemnly headed one item, "Hoboken For War." [14] "Since noon today," said the same issue, "the story of the assassination of Minister Sickles has been current in Washington." Someone was a little over-eager there, for five days later the *Herald* announced, "In conversation today General Sickles said that he did not see how war could be avoided." [15]

The New York *Times*, suspicious of the source of the *Herald's* "inside" reports from Madrid, took a careful guess and said they were "doubtless inspired by Mr. Sickles . . ." [16]

By now the embattled minister in Madrid was the center of a windy editorial tempest in America, some papers depicting him as the heroic and abused exponent of national honor and others agreeing with the *World* in calling him a "bullying marplot." "It was always a public disgrace," said the *World*, "it is now a public injury, that Sickles should represent us in Madrid." [17]

While the general fulminated in his legation, the Spanish government played a deft trick on him. Through its minister in Washington, Admiral Polo, it informed Fish that it was ready to negotiate a settlement and requested that the discussions take place in Washington rather than Madrid. Without precisely saying so, the Spaniards were asking that the militant General Sickles be removed from the parley.

Fish agreed. He did so because the Spanish proposal was conciliatory enough to make him wonder whether Sickles had been misinforming him somewhat as to that government's attitude. In any case it was clear that Sickles was at swords' points with the Madrid government so that there was little chance of agreement there.

A few days later—without Sickles having even a little finger in the pie—the Spaniards came substantially to terms and the flaming *Virginius* crisis was snuffed out. It was a settlement that some hot-headed Americans, not the least of them General Sickles, regarded as groveling. The *Herald*, without reporting the reaction in Hoboken, termed it "a national disgrace." [18]

It was hardly that, and it had the great advantage of averting war with anyone but Sickles.

In Madrid, the general was in a rage. He had been sidetracked, dead-ended, pushed out of the negotiations by the wily Spaniards, and Fish had betrayed him by accepting their proposal. The Secretary of State had offered him up as a sacrifice to the Spaniards whom he would have forced to eat crow. This oblique maneuver caused him to become the butt of jokes in the Spanish capital, and if there was anything he could not stomach it was derision. He handed in his resignation. His diplomatic career ended with a splash heard in every chancellery in Europe and which caused the New York *Times* to comment, "good riddance." [19]

While Sickles' humiliation was deserving of sympathy, the blame for it was largely his own. He had lost his temper with the Spaniards. Worse yet, he had tried to force his own rough-shod policy, feeling that Fish and Grant were feeble in their stand. With this in mind he had even subtly misrepresented the Spanish attitude, cabling to Fish the less reasonable of their contentions and omitting some of their conciliatory ones.[20] He had made himself so resented by the Madrid officials that they had cheerfully euchred him out.

The general had succumbed to the same inherent weakness that overmastered him in 1859 when he raced around Lafayette Square bristling with loaded pistols, in 1864 when he determined to destroy Meade, and in 1867 when he defied the federal courts in the Carolinas. He had gone considerably beyond ordinary prudence. Ordinary prudence, unfortunately, was not in him or he might easily have realized the ambition that now had glimmered out for good—to become President.

CHAPTER XXXIII

Au Revoir *and* Goodbye

Sickles lingered morosely in Madrid for a time, preparing for the arrival of his successor, Mr. Caleb Cushing. It was not until February 27th, 1874, that he left for Paris with his wife, his mother, and Laura.

His castle in Spain had collapsed in ruin, but it was a good deal worse than that. Sickles, the man who made a career of nurturing political friendships, was on the outs with the potent Fish and the all-powerful Grant.[1] Sickles, the passionate lover of politics, was in the political scrap heap and he knew it. What ached most of all was his conviction that he was right and Fish and Grant were wrong. He had no doubt that had he been allowed to handle the *Virginius* crisis in his own way, Cuba would have been ours and his efforts would have been capped with triumph instead of something approaching disgrace. After more than four years of striving and reaching, the island had been all but in his grasp, only to be snatched away by what he considered the timorousness of Hamilton Fish.

The general was bitter almost unto desperation. Loving as he did to control events—a planner whose gaze was always far ahead—he seemed riven by violent emotional upheaval whenever control was taken from him. Thus, when young Lorenzo Da Ponte died, Sickles had acted like a man bereft of his senses, kicking and screaming at the funeral so that he had to be carried away bodily. When he learned of Teresa's affair with Key, he had wept and groaned not for minutes but for many

351

hours, shaken by a terrible inner tempest that was quite apart from his violence in killing Key. Now, with his long labors in Spain rendered futile, his high hopes crushed, he reacted in a paroxysm of rage against the man he believed responsible, Secretary Fish. Vengefulness overmastered him. Apparently he even contemplated a frontal assault via the newspapers on the secretary who had jettisoned him. Rumblings of this reached Washburne in Paris, who lost no time in relaying them to his chief:

> . . . I cannot imagine why he should get up such trumpery un-
> less he has become mad with the whole world and is striking out
> wild. It is said here that he gives out that he has a rod in pickle
> for you—that he has become possessed of compromising informa-
> tion in regard to you and that you are to be demolished on his
> return home. It is well perhaps that you should be advised of it
> in order that you may be prepared to be demolished with de-
> cency . . .[2]

For Sickles to be gored by Secretary Fish was bad enough, but to be kicked at the same time by President Grant, who had backed up Fish, was the *coup de grace*.

But disaster was a companion of many campaigns, and before long he accepted it with his old elasticity. When he met Wash-burne at Bordeaux in March, he was "very pleasant," and while he felt that the United States had lost a golden opportunity to appropriate Cuba—a belief he held to the end of his life—he cast no reflections on Fish.[3]

For the first time in more than three stormy decades, Daniel Sickles was out of politics with no visible chance of getting back in. Such a rebuff as he had suffered would have killed in any man the itch for office—any man but the general. In him the itch merely lay dormant for a while.

Soon he was on to London with his family, where he took a house and inquired into an enterprise that had lain in the back of his mind since his trip to Panama for Lincoln. He was looking into the market for a loan for the construction of a canal across the isthmus.[4] This project never materialized, but he enjoyed visits with the American minister and draw-poker expert, General Robert C. Schenck, and the consul general, Adam Badeau, both of them well-liked political cronies. His love for horseflesh had never flagged, and he made up a party to drive to the Derby in a four-in-hand drag.[5] Leaving his family in London, he made a brief trip to America that summer. When he returned he set up his family in a small estate at Chantilly, also taking rooms nearer the center of things at 8 Rue de Presbourg in Paris.

Why he chose to settle in Paris may not be an unanswerable question. For one thing, Sickles loved Paris and spoke the language with passable fluency. His wife Caroline had objections to moving across the sea to a land strange to her. Then too, the deposed Queen Isabella was still in Paris.

Isabella had purchased the Hotel Basilewski on the Avenue Kléber, renamed it the Palace de Castile, and was squandering the allowance given her by the Spanish government.[6] Still intriguing for the return of her son to the throne, she had time to bestow extravagant largesse on indigent artists and musicians, and there were occasions when she had to pawn the family portraits.[7] Nor had she forgotten the charm of the one-legged American general. It was said that the two were inseparable.[8]

Under the circumstances it is not surprising that the Sickles menage knew moments of discord. Caroline was not in agreement with her husband's definition of marriage, an elastic definition that placed no tether on his half of the bargain. There were other troubles. Sickles' mother, whose puzzlement at her son's erratic ways had never dimmed her love for him, became ill with advancing age and died in a Paris sanitarium. Then there was the crisis with Laura, now grown to young womanhood.

The relations between Laura and her father had worsened ever since they arrived in Europe, at last reaching outright hostility. She was likewise on unhappy terms with her stepmother. The high-strung girl broke irrevocably with her father and returned to New York.[9] Thereafter they went separate ways, with Laura leading a gay but disillusioned life on the allowance the general sent her.

Trouble there was, and yet Sickles seemed unbowed by it. Though technically unemployed, he kept busy. With France under a provisional government, the hopes of the royalists were high and the Yankee general took part in subtle but vain maneuvers to make his good friend the Comte de Paris king.[10] There was almost no political problem in that part of the world so knotty that he did not feel qualified to solve it. Yet he was still a watchful defender of all things American, as shown by a note he dispatched to the Duke De Caze while Washburne was away at Cannes:

> In the absence of Mr. Washburne I feel it my duty as an American Citizen to inform you that I am told on what seems to me good authority that M. Alexandre Dumas new play, 'L'Etranger' which is about to be produced at the Theatre Francaise, contains offensive reflections upon Mr. Washburne in his official character.
>
> I hope you will kindly regard this intimation as made with no other motive than a sincere desire to preserve the most friendly sentiments between France & the United States.[11]

In 1875 the general's wife bore him a daughter who was named Eda—his first official offspring since Laura was born. When in the following year Mrs. Sickles bore a son, there was nothing Latin about the names given him. The infant was christened George Stanton, honoring his hoary old grandfather in New York and the late political autocrat who had once defended Sickles' life for protecting the "sanctity of his home." The sanctity of the home was a convenient concept on occasion, but not in Paris in the Middle Seventies.

One might have thought a life of such irregularity would alienate conservative colleagues, but the Sickles charm and friendliness were as winning as ever. Staid old Washburne, who had been critical immediately after the Spanish explosion, soon warmed up and with his wife was often a dinner companion of the Sickleses. Probably Washburne, like many others, threw up his hands, came to the conclusion that Sickles was a brilliant eccentric not to be measured by ordinary bourgeois standards, and let it go at that. In any case, the general seldom stayed in one place long enough to become bothersome. He took his wife on a tour of Germany and Italy. He was constantly flitting off to London, and made several trips alone to America. Along the way the *Virginius* wounds had healed somewhat and in his convalescence his marrow-deep predilection for politics came once more to the surface. As he was about to leave for Havre to embark for New York in September of 1876, he dashed off a note to Washburne, saying, "I hear there is good news from Vermont," in the same breath mentioning having heard that Washburne's Scotch cook was now disengaged and wondering if she might work for Mrs. Sickles.[12]

He spent more than six months in America, a good deal of it in Washington, where he took pains to make peace with Grant, now nearing the end of his two unhappy terms as President. Although he claimed blandly that he had "come home to vote,"[13] it was hardly coincidence that he was in the United States in time to take part in the campaign for Rutherford B. Hayes, the Republican nominee for Grant's successor. When Hayes was judged to have beaten the Democratic entrant, Tilden, in a most highly irregular election, Sickles was exultant.

"In all political History there is no record of any such Contest," he wrote Washburne. "We have won—yet to win it was necessary that every one of a hundred contingencies should turn in our favor." He added in semi-humorous vein: "I shall soon see you in Paris—where my wife says I have been sometime 'overdue.' "[14]

Possibly he was overdue, but not long after his return to Paris he was back in London again on a fussy little errand on behalf of the French Republic. General Grant, his Presidential labors over, had started on his aimless world tour and had reached England in June. France was next on his itinerary—

a plan that troubled Sickles' friend Thiers, because Marshal MacMahon, a legitimist, was now president and an election would soon be held. For Grant to visit France now might be construed as giving his tacit approval to the legitimist faction and thus influence the election. Washburne had already written Grant suggesting that he change his itinerary, but Thiers was fearful that the point was not pressed hard enough. At his suggestion, Citizen Sickles was off to London to see Grant. The ex-President and his wife were agreeable, leaving for Germany via Belgium and giving France a wide berth until after the election.[15]

For his various services to the republic, the French government conferred on Sickles the insignia of a Commander of the Legion of Honor [16] —a decoration that may have stirred pride in his troubled wife, though she had little opportunity to congratulate him. She saw her peripatetic husband for only a fraction of his time. Early in 1878 he was en route to America again, enjoying on May 7th a reunion of the Third Army Corps Union at Newburgh, New York. There he gathered with comrades of Chancellorsville and Gettysburg, among them Joe Hooker and Chaplain Twichell, now the pastor at Hartford's big Asylum Hill Church. With Twichell and Hooker he made a pilgrimage to West Point, where Fighting Joe—now a semi-paralyzed oldster filled with a brooding sense of wrongs done him in the war—recalled pranks of his cadet days.[17] Sickles loved nothing better than the camaraderie of those who had survived the baptism of blood with him. During the course of an after-dinner speech he told the graying or balding Third Corps veterans, "I expect to be here with my family permanently in the ensuing autumn." [18] When he returned to Paris he knew it would not be for long.

Meanwhile the Spanish republic Sickles had brought to life in 1873 had died in infancy. Early in 1875 Isabella's son returned to Madrid amid wild acclaim and was crowned Alfonso XII. Despite the chilly attitude of the Spanish people toward their exiled queen, they could hardly ban the mother of the popular king. From then on Isabella spent part of her time in Madrid, still maintaining the Palace de Castile in Paris.

In 1879 Washburne finished his ten-year tour of duty in Paris and returned to America, his old campaigner's nostrils quivering at the early scent of political trends for the election year of 1880.

If Washburne's nostrils quivered, Sickles' were positively aflutter. The politician in him had been starving so long that at last the hunger was unbearable. And time, always disregarded as a tagalong of no account, had suddenly grown big enough to climb up on his shoulders and breathe down his neck. The years of youth had trickled away unnoticed in restless activity. He had been planning for 1880. His frequent visits home, augmented by a flood of letters to potent Republicans, had managed to bring some semblance of repair to his damaged fences. Now, 1880 loomed not so much as a year of opportunity as a year perilously close to his last chance to recoup fortunes that had dwindled through what he believed the errors of faint-hearted men.

When he informed Caroline that they were going to America, the lady put her foot down. She refused to go. Instead, she insisted that they return to Madrid, where her mother lay ill. Furthermore, as she later disclosed, "I learned that my husband had been untrue to me." [19]

Sickles wanted no more of Madrid, a place with bitter memories. Probably there were tears and hysterics, but his mind was set. With him, the ties of matrimony—even his real fondness for children who were bone of his bone—gave way to the relentless drive of ambition and the need to do what he wanted when he wanted to do it.

He said goodbye to Caroline, and *au revoir* to little Eda and George Stanton. Late in 1879 he was on his way back to New York to stake everything in one last throw of the dice at the political gaming table.

CHAPTER XXXIV

Return of the Native

The erect, meticulously-dressed, one-legged man who opened bachelor diggings on Fifth Avenue, was in his sixty-first year, but no one seemed to know this. The impression in New York was that the general was born in 1823 and was therefore fifty-seven.[1] Whether this was merely a chance error or a misconception Sickles allowed to persist out of vanity or a feeling that a man of sixty-one had considerably less chance for political advancement than one of fifty-seven, the fact was that he looked much younger than fifty-seven. The years had been kindlier than events. The scars of fast living and a hundred ordeals were somehow invisible in the smooth skin and alert eye of this determined man who had been climbing the slippery cliff of fame for four decades and had several times come near gaining the heights.

The city he knew so well may have lacked the beauties of Paris, but no one could say it had not gone on a spree of expansion. Brooklyn Bridge was abuilding, the elevated railroad was a roaring miracle, and there were electric lights along a part of Fifth Avenue. A few adventurous citizens had installed in their homes a remarkable new means of communication, the telephone. A blonde young lady named Lillian Russell was beginning to create a stir. Some of the old faces were gone. Hooker was dead, joining Brady, Meagher, and Hart in the beyond. But old John B. Haskin, rich as Croesus, was still in Fordham. General Butterfield, who made a fortune in railroads and in somewhat clandestine deals with Jay Gould, inhabited a mansion on upper Fifth Avenue. General Sherman, up on Madison Square, was a living monument to the Union. General Grant came back from his world tour, out of employment and speaking with the coyness of a man who would accept a third Presidential term if it was thrust upon him—an attitude Sickles encouraged with some strenuous thrusting. He had settled on Grant as the great hope of 1880, the man who could surely win and who in victory would not forget his supporters.

Over in Brooklyn, a pathetic Laura Sickles was living with her grandmother, the widowed Mrs. Bagioli. Laura had contracted an unhappy and short-lived marriage as a climax to a childhood of insecurity, and was finding in drink and dissipation the only refuge from her despond. The general sent her an allowance and that was all. He had turned his back on her.[2]

In his quarters at the corner of Ninth Street Sickles established a veritable museum of trophies. The walls were hung with the skins of tigers, leopards, and other deceased animals he had brought from Spain. There were scrolls, medals, crossed swords, battle flags, photographs in uniform and *en civil*. Maybe the future looked uncertain, but the general was not forgetting that he had a romantic and glorious past, nor did he allow anyone else to forget it. His vanity was of an open and ingenuous kind that, far from antagonizing, seemed to endear him to friends who may have chuckled a bit about it in privacy.

Now his sensitive political antennae were vibrating in the direction of the upcoming Republican convention. Was there yet time? Sickles thought there was. He hurled all his spring-steel energy into the third-term boom for Grant. Late in May of 1880 he was off to the national convention in Chicago to see what could be done about climbing that cliff again.

In Chicago he joined an old Confederate antagonist, General James Longstreet, and other veterans in campaigning for Grant.[3] The man of Appomattox seemed a cinch for the nomination despite the strong challenge of James G. Blaine. The prospects for Sickles were taking on a rosy hue again. With Grant in the

White House there seemed no doubt that he would recover the ground lost in the Madrid debacle and more.

But at this hectic convention the experts were given a repeat reading of the ancient text that in politics nothing is certain but uncertainty. One man who took a hand in twisting destiny was none other than Grant's long-time standard bearer and Sickles' good friend, Elihu Washburne. Washburne had come to the realization that he would not mind being President himself. When his name was placed in nomination, he did not withdraw it in Grant's favor—an omission Grant never forgave and which likewise chilled the Sickles esteem.[4] Washburne showed no real strength and yet the votes he got came at the expense of Grant, who could not quite muster the total necessary for victory. After a feverish succession of ballots, the impasse was solved by the nomination of the darkest of dark horses, James A. Garfield.

Grant was mortified at what he felt was a humiliation. Sickles was a good deal more than mortified. He was stunned and bitter at a freakish whimsy of fate that seemed directed at him personally. He had put all his eggs in the Grant basket and the basket had gone smash. As a last-ditch Grant man he could expect nothing from Garfield when the Ohioan went on to election, and it was plain as a pikestaff that he had shot his political bolt. Indeed, even if Garfield had been inclined to toss some plum to the late minister at Madrid, he was a hard man to suit. Minor posts were not for him. He was in the awkward position of having been intimate with five Presidents, having held many posts of high authority, and thus having established a level of official dignity below which he could not descend without loss of face.

In New York, General Grant forswore politics and became a Wall Street broker, an innocent soon to be shorn of every penny he had. In New York, General Sickles, who was a good deal less innocent than Grant and would never forswear politics as long as breath remained in him, looked about for something to fill the vacuum in his life. Daniel Sickles, private citizen, was a man in chains.

"Under his cool, placid, polished demeanor," one observer commented, "he hides a restless and unsatisfied ambition, and has become so used to the pride and power of office that he can never be truly contented . . . unless he is serving the people in some public capacity." [5]

His father was likewise a man of boundless vitality feeling a certain lack in his life. Despite his millions, crusty George Sickles was living simply out in New Rochelle, commuting to his Nassau Street office every day, and entertaining his friends by flapping his arms and crowing at the conclusion of his meals to demonstrate his vigor.[6] In 1881, at the age of eighty-one, he showed his vigor in another way. He took a bride—forty-eight-year-old Mrs. Mary Sheridan Sawyer, a widow with three daughters. Although the general had never allowed convention to hamper him, possibly he did not approve of this May-December union. He did not attend the wedding.

More than ever, Sickles' pet horror was idleness. To him, idleness meant having less than a dozen full-blown projects at once on which he could pull simultaneous strings like a master of marionettes. He was back at the law, he was taking fliers in Wall Street, he was serving on various public committees, he was president of the Society of the Army of the Potomac and the leading figure in the Third Corps Union, he was a fixture at the opera, where the Vanderbilts reserved a chair for him in their box, he seldom missed a first night at Wallack's Theater, and in the midst of a busy social life he was performing the melancholy duty of helping to bury old comrades.[7] He was carrying on a heavy correspondence, he was smitten by one pretty face after another, and he was watching the political arenas both in the state and the nation with the keen eye of an insider who was yet on the outside. Judged by ordinary standards the general was furiously busy, yet he was gnawed by discontent. He had ridden in the main stream of history for decades. Now he had been shunted by some vile eddy into a stagnant backwash where all he could do was watch events flow past him.

A change came over him. He began to look critically at the
Republican Party which had shelved him and to feel that he
had always been a Democrat in principle.[8]

In New York the general was regarded with respect as one of
the city's most colorful characters—a war-horse who could not
forget the fray, but withal a man of rapier wit, roving interests,
and an astonishing disregard for money. His hair and mustache
were only lightly touched with gray. No longer the dandy, he
dressed now with mature discernment and was always as spruce
as a whip. He was known for his "sweet, pleasant smile, and
the fascinating manner and address of a courtly and accomplished man of the world."[9] Yet a faint odor of scandal still
clung to him. Why had he left his Spanish wife and two small
children in Europe to live in bachelor splendor in New York?
The general never spoke of that, but people wondered. Nor had
they forgotten the Key affair, now a quarter-century past. One
night when Sickles was sitting in a private box at the Standard
Theater—he never sat in anything but a private box—he looked
down and saw the son of Philip Barton Key in the stalls. Observant eyes did not miss this dramatic encounter, and it was
said, "They recognized each other undoubtedly; but neither gave
any sign of recognition."[10]

In his unwelcome estate as private citizen, the general was
seized anew with the memory of the glory and the tragedy of
the days of '61–'65 when the Union would have met extinction
but for the men who fought and bled for it. He began to cajole
and lobby for better treatment of the veterans of the Blue and
for more fitting memorials to the nation's struggle. In this work
he was never without the feeling that he personally had contributed in no small measure to the victory, and was outraged
at any notion to the contrary.

While no one suggested that he had not fought gallantly,
there were those who dared to criticize his judgment. In the
Seventies and early Eighties some of the more thoughtful and
scholarly of the Civil War histories were published. Not a few
of them took critical exception to Sickles' advance into the

Peach Orchard at Gettysburg, declaring that it had cost the Army of the Potomac needless casualties. Even Sickles' close friend, the Comte de Paris, who had labored for years over a monumental history of the war, could not refrain from writing, "Sickles does not seem to have appreciated the importance of the Round Tops." [11]

To the general, all this was close to blasphemy. He had been shorn of office but one thing he was determined no one would take away from him was his mantle as the hero of Gettysburg. Bristling, he set out to fight Gettysburg all over again. In an address given at a reunion at the battlefield on July 2nd, 1886, he repeated the old story that General Meade had been of a mind to retire from Gettysburg and to form again at Pipe Creek, and declared that it was the advance of Sickles' Third Corps that forced the battle, made withdrawal impossible, and saved the field for the Union. General Meade, fourteen years in his grave, could not defend himself from this interpretation, but a former colleague, Colonel G. G. Benedict, was still vigorously alive. The resentful Benedict made public a confidential letter he had received from Meade in 1870 defending his generalship and criticizing Sickles' forward move.[12] The New Yorker would have shown magnanimity and wisdom had he conceded that errors had been no man's monopoly that day and that possibly even he had been not without fault in decisions drawn in the stress of crisis. But he was hanged if he would admit that his missing leg was a needless sacrifice. He wrote a detailed public reply to Colonel Benedict, again emphasizing Meade's disinclination to fight and justifying his own moves. It was written with such persuasive clarity as to be almost convincing to a casual reader, but it failed to explain his strange neglect of the all-important Little Round Top.[13]

"I was in the right place to defend Round Top when I put myself in front of it," was a devious sentence that could have been demolished by anyone so inclined.

The general harmed his own case by being so positive of his own superlative correctness. Truth to tell, he was a little testy and unreasonable on this point which was so sacred to him, but in other ways he was as genial as ever. In his frequent trips to Gettysburg—a place he came to regard with a somewhat possessive attitude—he was chagrined to see that the battlefield had taken on a dingy aspect, with its few monuments placed without a master plan and showing the mutilations of vandals. The hallowed field was under the joint and unsatisfactory control of the several Northern states whose dead lay there. It became clear to him that Gettysburg should be a national memorial maintained by the federal government to do honor not only to the Union but to the Confederate forces who had fought there. So zealous was his devotion to the rehabilitation of the field that in 1886 he was appointed chairman of the New York State Monuments Commission, in charge of the design and erection of Empire State memorials at the site. It was perhaps a minor post for the former counsellor of Presidents, but this was a cause near to his heart and he threw himself into the work with unflagging energy. Indeed, his pride was a little chastened now, and just to keep his hand in he allowed Governor David B. Hill to thrust a couple of other minor offices on him—Chairman of the State Civil Service Commission (1887) and sheriff of New York County (1890) to complete the term of the resigned incumbent.

In 1887, old George Sickles was hurrying the construction of a great marble tomb at Beechwood Cemetery in New Rochelle. He got it finished none too soon, for he died in March only a fortnight after its completion.[14] The general, who had failed to attend his father's wedding, was present at the funeral and provided dinner at the Huguenot Hotel for 150 funeral guests.[15] Since his father left an estate of something more than $5,000,000, the financial specters that had haunted him for most of his life were exorcised, it seemed, for good. It was pleasant to have money, admittedly, but money was only incidental to the man who thirsted for action above all things.

George Sickles did not forget his granddaughter, Laura,

leaving her some property in his will.[16] Sadly, Laura was beyond the point where a legacy would help her. She had abandoned herself to a life of recklessness that was already proving ruinous to her health. "If Gen. Sickles ever sought to reclaim his daughter," one observer noted, "the public never knew of it." When she died in 1891 in a rented room in Brooklyn, friendless and alone, the unforgiving father did not attend her funeral.[17]

Now it was Gettysburg that absorbed a large part of his attention. He became as familiar in the little Pennsylvania town as he was on Fifth Avenue, swinging along on crutches as he examined sites for projected monuments and aided in the dedication of those erected. He could be sharp when circumstances beyond his control allowed errors that offended his sense of justice. On September 24th, 1891, he made an oration at Gettysburg to dedicate a memorial to the 42nd Regiment, New York State Volunteers, known as the Tammany Regiment—a massive column surmounted by an Indian brave standing with his musket before a tepee. In tones bristling with anger he finished:

> . . . I have the honor to place this memorial in the custody and care of your Association. I cannot fitly perform this duty without giving expression to the suprise and indignation felt by the veterans of this famous battalion when they see their monument standing in a rear line, from which they advanced and repulsed the approaching enemy, whilst troops that refused to advance [probably a reference to General Barnes' command] in obedience to the repeated orders of their brigade commander, are permitted to place their monument on a line much further to the front than they ventured to march, until after the victory was won. I know that the trustees of the Battle-field are in no sense responsible for this outrage upon history.[18]

Clearly, he had a bone to pick with the supervisors of the field. He knew he was fighting a losing struggle against its mismanagement and decay unless it could be taken from the divided control of many states and handed over to the sole re-

sponsibility of the federal government as a national shrine.
What did he propose to do about that? Daniel Sickles, a man
who got things done, knew precisely what to do. As a member
of a committee of seven old soldiers considering the problem,
he pushed for federal ownership.[19] And with the project under
way, he ran in 1892 for Congress on the Democratic ticket to
dragoon it to completion in Washington.

The general was roundly cheered when he appeared at Miner's
Eighth Avenue Theater to make a campaign speech, hobbling
to a chair in the center of the stage. As colorful a spellbinder
as ever, he attacked the claim that the Republicans had won
the war.

"Gettysburg was the decisive battle of the war, as admitted
on all sides, and who fought it?" he trumpeted. "On the right
wing was General Slocum commanding an army corps, a Democrat; on the left was General Reynolds, till he was killed, a
Democrat . . . in the Devil's Den was a man named Sickles,
a Democrat." [20]

That, as the newspapers admitted, brought down the house.
Sickles was elected. In 1893, in his seventy-fourth year, he was
off to Washington again to mingle with a new breed of legislators, some of them born since he served his first term in
Congress. In a House inhabited by the shades of Keitt and
Clingman and the echoing calls for secession, he spent much of
his time pressing for federal purchase of the battlefield, which
to his infinite disgust was marred by such monstrosities as a new
electric railway occupying important lines of battle.[21]

The general mounted an irresistible offensive. He introduced
his bill. He got it passed. The Gettysburg we know today is
in great part a testimony to the efforts of the Third Corps
leader who lost a leg there.[22]

Meanwhile, although he had turned the page on his wife he
was maintaining an affectionate correspondence with his son
Stanton and daughter Eda in Madrid. Eda, who had only a
vague childhood memory of her father, was now eighteen and
charmed by his letters. "My love for you is deeper each day as

my age advances," she wrote him in Spanish. "I do not want to grow old without seeing you." [23]

Possibly the general sometimes wondered if he had erred in leaving his family. But not for long. In Washington he formed one of the most cherished friendships of his life. It happened to be with an old enemy—the man, in fact, who was indirectly responsible for shooting away Sickles' leg—General James Longstreet of the late Confederate army. He had again met the gigantic Old Pete, now growing somewhat deaf, at a gathering of Union and Confederate generals at Gettysburg in 1893,[24] and from then on the two were warm friends. Founded on sincere affection, their friendship if anything was cemented by the fact that both had been criticized for their generalship on that terrible July 2nd when Longstreet's First Corps assaulted Sickles' smaller command. In the view of touchy Southerners, Longstreet had committed not one but three unpardonable sins. He had become a Republican after the war, had accepted office under his old West Point classmate Grant, and had ventured to find fault with the revered Lee's strategy at Gettysburg. There were many down in Dixie who looked on Old Pete as an outcast and were laying the loss of Gettysburg squarely on his shoulders, saying that if he had not waited so unconscionably long to attack, the Union forces would not have been up and the day would have been a victory for the Gray.[25] Longstreet, like Sickles, had to fight the battle over again a hundred times. His unpopularity was painful to him, and he was glad to find a sympathetic ally in Sickles. Each of the two generals agreed that the other had moved with blameless skill that day.

The halls of Congress, with their behind-the-scenes maneuvering and attendant social whirl, held their traditional attraction for Sickles. True, Cleveland, whom he had fought, was President and the White House was no longer a place he could burst into at will. The old days of power, of membership in councils that set national policy and made Presidents, were a memory. Yet Congress gave him the interplay of motive, the thrill of persuasion in debate, and the sense of conflict and

accomplishment that was meat and drink to him. He knew all
the tricks like the back of his hand. He wanted more. In 1894
he ran for reelection and was defeated.[26]

It was a disappointment fit to make an oldster of three-
quarters of a century go into rapid and final decline. But Sickles
was not ready to die. He was not even resigned to rocking chair
and slippers. Still chairman of the Monuments Commission,
he threw his energies into coaxing appropriations from Albany,
consulting with engineers and sculptors, executing a map showing the positions of the various military units at Gettysburg,
and demanding hairline historical correctness in the placing
of New York State memorials. He was still practicing law, still
plunging in Wall Street, still dispensing largesse to war veterans
in need, still attentive to women. He liked to dash off to the
Adirondacks in summer to escape the heat, and during one
sojourn there he wrote not entirely waggishly to his good friend
Horatio C. King, "If I had a girl or two with me I wouldn't
return at all." [27]

With King, a fellow New Yorker, Gettysburg survivor, and
colleague on the Monuments Commission, he was on terms of
intimate affection.[28] His frequent letters to King, scribbled in
his inevitable hurry, gleamed with rare good humor and good
sense, mirroring a never-ending round of travel, visits, and
enterprises that would have exhausted an athlete. A few fragments tell a tale of awesome septuagenarian gusto:

"Yours of 21 inst., after journeying from Lake Placid to
Buffalo & thence here again, reached me this morning . . ."
"All right—will take seats for Thursday or Saturday night for
Sothern's Hamlet, if you like it. Shall we go together—or do
you care to take your best girl?" "Here I am tramping through
the Northern forests & hills—Enjoying big log-wood fires night
and morning." "As I see the President is busy with Congress
on sundry important questions it seems to me best to wait a
while, lest I might embarrass him in the steps he is taking."
"I am afraid you won't know common folks this summer, now
that you are President five or six times over, and smothered

with so many dignities." "Rode a Camel at Buffalo, with Grace Adams! Don't scold!" [29]

In 1897 Sickles enjoyed a reunion with a young lady he had not seen for some seventeen years—his daughter Eda. Startlingly beautiful at twenty-two, Eda was now the wife of Dayrell Crack-anthorpe, a British diplomatic attaché temporarily assigned in Washington. The general was delighted with her. He escorted her down to Old Point Comfort, Virginia, where the Third Corps Union held its annual meeting, and showed her off proudly to his comrades.[30] He went to Washington for a time to be with her, writing King with amiable enthusiasm:

> I am enjoying these days with my daughter and her family —although I have only seen her in the brief intervals of Washington gayety. Poor girl, she seldom goes to bed on the same day she gets up; I am waiting for her now,—10:30—to return from a dinner & go with me to Lady Pauncefote's Reception, at the Embassy—and after that I believe there is a Ball! . . .[31]

Washington was a place that drew him like a magnet quite apart from family ties. Though he no longer held national office, he went there occasionally on Gettysburg business. He was friendly with many Senators and Representatives. He could no more avoid the center of national politics than he could take a detached attitude toward women.

When William Jennings Bryan became the Democratic candidate for President in 1896, Sickles did not hide his scorn for the silver-tongued orator of the Platte. The Democrat-Republican-Democrat proclaimed his independence once again and came out for the Republican candidate, a handsome young Ohio politician named McKinley. It did not take any argument on the part of Mark Hanna to persuade Sickles to join his Gettysburg comrade, General Oliver O. Howard, and other aging officers in a rail-car speechmaking tour for McKinley that covered twelve states and roamed as far west as Kansas. With the snowy-bearded Howard minus an arm and Sickles lacking a leg, the troupe was known as "the wrecks of the Civil War" [32]—a misnomer as far as Sickles was concerned. He gave rousing speeches from the rear platform at scores of tank-town stops, showed his colleagues how to mix a favorite cocktail, and gaily whistled airs from *Rigoletto* as the caravan rattled across the prairies.[33] The wrecks did good work, and McKinley after his election showed his fondness for them.

True, it was felt that General Sickles was too handicapped to lead United States forces against the enemy in Cuba during the Spanish-American War—an offensive he would cheerfully have commanded against a nation he had never ceased to dislike. But there were compensating bits of patronage. He secured for Longstreet, now ailing and impoverished, a post as commissioner of railroads. He won for his son Stanton, whom he had not seen since he was a small boy, an appointment as attaché in the legation at Madrid. (Madrid again!) When he could do a favor for a friend, or make a loan from his seemingly inexhaustible resources, he did it with a graciousness that sprang from sincere generosity. Only one thing he insisted on—that no one misunderstand the perspicacity of his move with the Third Corps into the Peach Orchard.

Horatio King, an incurable poetaster, bore this in mind when the hoary Third Corps Union held its annual banquet in New York in 1903, forty years after the battle. King got up before the aging diners and read a poem of seven stanzas that left no doubt as to who the guest of honor was:

> Turn out the guard! The General comes,
> A grand old hero he.
> Our Bismarck, rugged, bold and strong,
> And young at eighty-three.

For a wonder, King had the age right. The general *was* eighty-three although he didn't look it. He must have been pleased at these opening lines, but undoubtedly it was the fifth stanza that really caught his fancy:

> I see him on that famous field,
> The bravest of the brave,
> Where Longstreet's legions strove to drive
> The Third Corps to its grave.
> The fight was bloody, fierce and long,
> And Sickles' name shall stay
> Forever in the Hall of Fame
> As he who saved the day.

Ah—that struck the right note! One can picture how the general glowed at this affirmation of the high merit of the maneuver which shallow critics had carped at. King's verses may have come short of soaring, but they were sincere, and he was sincere when he declaimed:

> Hail to the Chief, our loving friend,
> May many years be thine!
> We toast thee in our heart of hearts,
> And not alone in wine.[34]

However the poesy limped, Sickles' sentimental heart was touched because he knew that every man in the room felt that way about him. He had become a landmark—a charming, pigheaded, lovable old rip whom nobody would want any different. The old odor of scandal had subsided to a mere whiff faint enough to be interesting rather than objectionable. In his agile octogenarian years he had come near to achieving what for him was something remarkably close to respectability.

But if anyone thought that at long last his life would gutter out in sedate quiet, he was mistaken. The general still had a few headlines left in him.

CHAPTER XXXV

A Grand Old Hero He

I have just come home, and have your dear note, many many thanks for it has made me very happy to know you still think of me. It is now six o'clock and to [*sic*] late to meet you. It is best for I might sin . . . My husband is sitting looking strait at me. Love me still dear Edgar it is so sweet to be loved by one so dear to my sad heart. I am afraid I shall always be so, God forgive me! and bless you my so dearly loved one.[1]

This unsigned note Sickles did not consign to the fireplace as he must have done with countless others. He preserved it in his papers and marked it "Private" out of a sentiment he cherished despite a parade of other amours that absorbed his attention. Even in his eighties, with the Twentieth Century staring him in the face, his fascination with the feminine was something that lingered like a taste for rare wine.

Time seemed to have all but erased the bitterness in his heart at the knowledge that in his dearest ambitions he had been a failure. Since youth he had sought high political place with a fierce passion. Several times over the years he had come within a hair's breadth of the prize only to miss it. Somehow, in those precious moments when opportunity had struck, something had always happened to thwart him. *If* he had not been so free-and-easy with women and with debts . . . *If* he had not shot Key . . . *If* he had not arranged that ambush for Meade . . . *If* he had not been so violent in Madrid . . .

The guess is that the general did not ascribe his failure to any personal shortcomings but rather to ill luck and circumstances beyond his control. His mind, so quick and brilliant in appraising others, had a blind spot when it came to self-analysis. He never seemed to reach awareness that these big "ifs" in his career, those moments when opportunity had beckoned and then coldly turned her back, were not isolated instances of mischance but repeated betrayals by his own inner weaknesses. More than once he had been the Coming Man. Always, in the supreme moment, he and no one else had made the error that brought doubt, anger, and ruin. In him the "tragic flaw" of classic drama came into painful life. He had in wild abundance every quality needed for success—everything but a deep sense of responsibility. But if he was a failure, he gave to failure an indomitable distinction it had seldom known. He invested it with a grandeur, a roll of drums, and a sounding of trumpets that never accompanied men who achieved humdrum success. He was the most spectacularly successful failure of the century.

Now in the early Nineteen Hundreds, the general had enough affairs to keep only two or three ordinary men busy, so he found time to sit occasionally for his portrait. He was hale and hearty but for his eyes, which he sometimes favored with an eyeshade. A melancholy fact he had to face was that he already had outlived all but a few of his contemporaries. Grant had long since passed on. Sherman, Butterfield, Slocum, Wikoff, and the two Grahams were no more. Sickles mourned them and many others, and yet his genius for companionship surrounded him with as wide a circle of friends as ever. He was somewhat annoyed to see the formerly sacred precincts of lower Fifth Avenue subtly changed by a scattered infiltration of commerce, including the establishments of the Messrs. Knabe and Chickering, piano merchants. He lived simply among the relics of his career, attended by an aging negro valet named Frazier Moseley and a spinster housekeeper, Miss Eleanora Earle Wilmerding.

Miss Wilmerding was an attractive woman in her middle

years, clearly devoted to the general. Her exact status in the household was a subject of some speculation. She had a tendency to address the master affectionately as "dear," and there were those who felt that her attitude was considerably more familiar and attentive than one would expect of a servant. Otherwise she was unassuming and quiet—so quiet that one would never have expected her to stir up a waspish controversy that was to furnish gossip for every scandalmonger in Manhattan.

The general was "a fine, fiery old gentleman," Frederick Van Wyck recalled, "a picturesque figure filled with positive notions which he was not at all afraid to express on all occasions." [2]

He was a prodigal old gentleman too. Always reckless with money even when he had little of it, now that he was rich he indulged in peculiar orgies of extravagance. He was playing the market with the same zeal he had once devoted to betting on the horses. He donated heavily to aid needy war veterans, was generous to friends down on their luck, and despite Miss Wilmerding's anxious clucking he lavished gifts on a succession of women who caught his attentive eye. If he approved of an actress' portrayal of her role, or admired a dancer's thighs, she might become aware of his approval by receiving a costly diamond or emerald. Possibly there were some who capitalized on this weakness.

"Do help me dear General," wrote one unemployed lady of the stage. "I would not ask you if I was not really hard up. I am studying very hard and waste no time on flirtation or guile . . ." [3]

The stock market seemed to hold a special fascination for the gambler whose whole life had been a gamble. He took losses. He went back to take more losses.

Was it an oppressive sense that youth was gone that fired him to furious battle against age? Despite his handicap, he flitted about like a moth. Returning from a vacation in Cuba in 1901, he was just in time to hurry up to Hartford, where his beloved

Third Corps Union was holding its annual meeting. In Cuba he had bought a fifteen-foot boa constrictor which he intended to present to the Central Park Zoo. First he decided it would be a splendid thing to show his army comrades. At his Hartford home, the Reverend Mr. Joseph Twichell was bewildered when the Adams Express wagon arrived with a crate containing a live snake of frightening proportions. Excited neighbors gathered to view the exhibit. The mystery was explained when Sickles reached Twichell's place, resplendent in his major general's uniform.

As he did annually, Sickles took possessive charge of the reunion with such effervescent good will that no one could resent him. "Gen. Sickles, though in his 77th year [he was actually in his eighty-first], was in excellent health and spirits," Twichell recorded in his journal, "and, as usual, was the hero-in-chief of the occasion." [4] The clergyman who enjoyed intimate acquaintance with many of the great could look on the general's little vanities with good humor.

If the Sickles good will was infectious, his scorn was sharp. He could still intimidate the mighty with splendidly articulate disapproval. The fact that Cuba was not a part of the United States even after a war had been won there filled him with disgust which he did not hesitate to voice in a speech delivered at Fredericksburg with his friend President McKinley listening beside him.

"Cuba would have been ours today," he growled, "as it should be ours, if we had not chosen to renounce that island by a self-denying ordinance in which wisdom was sacrificed to sentiment." [5]

The general's crusty dignity was enough to influence a friend of longer standing, John Hay, now Secretary of State.[6] In Madrid, Sickles' son Stanton had become secretary of legation and apparently had been involved in some difference with the minister, Bellamy Storer. Storer wanted to have young Sickles transferred, but Hay explained why this was impossible:

I know you have felt aggrieved that we have not been able
to make a change in the Secretaryship of the Legation . . .
President McKinley was influenced by precisely the same feeling which influences President Roosevelt; that is, the desire to
avoid an open and painful quarrel with General Sickles. To remove Mr. Sickles somewhere else would offend the General
scarcely less than to dismiss him from the service . . . were
you in my place you would probably do as I do—that is, avoid
as much as possible open feuds and wrangles in the party.[7]

Although it would seem that he had established by sheer
weight of argument and repetition the sagacity of his movements
at Gettysburg, the general was yet plagued by a festering suspicion that there were still a few doubters, a few heretics. In
1902 he addressed a letter to Longstreet in Washington, inviting him to attend the unveiling at Gettysburg of the impressive equestrian monument to General Slocum which Sickles
in his capacity as head of the Monuments Commission had
seen to completion. Old Pete replied regretfully that a painful
lameness forbade his attendance. Then he added a few lines
that filled General Sickles' heart with a benediction of joy:

On that field you made your mark that will place you promi-
nently before the world as one of the leading figures of the
most important battle of the Civil War. As a Northern veteran
once remarked to me, "General Sickles can well afford to leave
a leg on that field."
I believe that it is now conceded [here Longstreet stretched
a point pretty far] that the advanced position at the Peach
Orchard, taken by your corps and under your orders saved that
battlefield to the Union cause. It was the sorest and saddest
reflection of my life for many years; but, to-day, I can say, with
sincerest emotion, that it was and is the best that could have
come to us all, North and South; and I hope that the nation, reunited, may always enjoy the honor and glory brought to it
by that grand work.[8]

Here was the last, the clinching vindication! Who could
doubt it now, coming from the very general who had opposed

him there? If Sickles had formerly felt affection for Longstreet, he now regarded him with nothing short of love. He saw to it that the letter was read at the Slocum statue dedication. He sent a copy of it to Hay. He had more copies printed and sent them broadcast to other friends. A few months later, on a trip to Boston, he was recognized by C. W. Bardeen, the Bostonian who had fought under Sickles at Gettysburg. Bardeen introduced himself, and there is hardly need to mention what the conversation got around to.

"I have maintained all these years," Bardeen said, "that the battle of Gettysburg was won by the advanced position taken by your corps under your own orders."

Sickles beamed. "That is absolutely true and demonstrated," he replied. "Only last fall I had a letter from General Longstreet affirming what he had already published in his history of the war. I will send you a copy." [9]

He sent Bardeen a copy. He sent copies to all the surviving Third Corps veterans whose addresses he had. He was still sending out copies nine years later. The letter of General Longstreet attained a circulation comparable to some of the books of Mr. Howells. The old lion of the Confederacy died in 1904, and when his young widow, Helen D. Longstreet, published a loyal defense of her husband titled "Lee and Longstreet at High Tide," the letter was reprinted therein. Sickles wrote a preface that was alternately breezy and poignant. He did not fail to uphold his late antagonist's every move at Gettysburg.[10]

Possibly the Gettysburg monomania could be wearisome, and yet the general had friends of many years' standing who bore it and swore by him. Up in Hartford, the Reverend Joseph Twichell, a member of the Yale Corporation and one of New England's outstanding clergymen, seemed to have derived an indelible impression of wonder and admiration out of his long acquaintance with Sickles. Twichell's closest friend was Mark Twain. In the course of long walks they took together around Hartford, and on one excursion to Europe, the humorist heard many a tale Twichell had to tell about General Sickles. Mark

Twain later moved to New York, just across Ninth Street from the general, and got to know him personally. One rainy night in 1906, he and Twichell dropped in on Sickles for a visit that moved him to a sharp bit of character analysis. He found Sickles to be "a genial old fellow; a handsome and stately military figure," seated in a room cluttered up with trophies, medals, flags, and animal skins. The atmosphere struck him as odd:

> You couldn't walk across that floor anywhere without stumbling over the hard heads of lions and things . . . it was as if a menagerie had undressed in the place. Then there was a most decided and unpleasant odor, which proceeded from disinfectants and preservatives and things such as you have to sprinkle on skins in order to discourage the moths . . . It was a kind of museum, and yet it was not the sort of museum which seemed dignified enough to be the museum of a great soldier—and so famous a soldier. It was the sort of museum which should delight and entertain little boys and girls. I suppose that that museum reveals a part of the general's character and make. He is sweetly and winningly childlike.

Mark Twain admitted that to listen to Sickles talk was an experience extraordinary enough to require a fairly searching inquiry:

> [The general] talks smoothly, in well-constructed English— I may say perfectly constructed English. His talk is full of interest and bristling with points, but as there are no emphases scattered through it anywhere, and as there is no animation in it, it soon becomes oppressive by its monotony and it makes the listener drowsy. Twichell had to step on my foot once or twice. The late Bill Nye once said, "I have been told that Wagner's music is better than it sounds." That felicitous description of something which so many people have tried to describe, and couldn't, does seem to fit the general's manner of speech exactly. His talk is much better than it is. No, that is not the idea—there seems to be a lack there somewhere . . . Maybe Nye would say that "it is better than it sounds." I think that is

it. His talk does *not* sound entertaining, but it *is* distinctly enter-taining.

The humorist recalled Twichell's story of how the general, when he was wounded at Gettysburg and felt himself to be a dying man, was interviewed by a newspaper correspondent. In what he believed to be his last interview, Sickles "put aside everything connected with a future world in order to go out of this one in becoming style."

Now when we sat there in the general's presence, listening to his monotonous talk—it was about himself, and is always about himself, and always seems modest and unexasperating, inoffensive—it seemed to me that he was just the kind of man who would risk his salvation in order to do some "last words" in an attractive way . . . And also I will say this: that he never made an ungenerous remark about anybody. He spoke severely of this and that and the other person—officers in the war—but he spoke with dignity and courtesy. There was no malignity in what he said. He merely pronounced what he evidently regarded as just criticisms upon them.

I noticed then, what I had noticed once before, four or five months ago, that the general valued his lost leg away above the one that is left. I am perfectly sure that if he had to part with either of them, he would part with the one that he has got.[11]

General Sickles did not know, as he chatted there among his relics, that he was being observed and analyzed by an expert. Or if he knew, he did not care. What he did know was that no one in the world—not even Mark Twain—had lived such a life as he had.

CHAPTER XXXVI

I See Him on
That Famous Field

On August 27th, 1908, a vessel tied up at a New York pier carrying on its passenger list two persons who, though they bore olive branches, were fated to turn the last years of General Sickles' life into a bizarre peepshow. They were Stanton Sickles and his mother Caroline, who had not seen her husband in almost three decades. The Spanish lady's aged stepfather had recently died in Madrid, leaving her free to travel. She had taken a surprising notion. She had decided that surely time would have melted the differences that held her and the general apart. Warmly seconded by Stanton, she wanted to resume the marriage that had ended with such finality in that bitter quarrel in Paris in 1879.

She put up at a hotel while her son, now a matured secretary of legation, made cautious diplomatic overtures toward his father aimed at arranging a meeting and reconciliation between his parents. Stanton, who kept a brief journal, noted in it in French two visits he made with his father, apparently by way of preparation. Then, the protocol agreed upon, he escorted his mother to the flag-bedecked museum at 23 Fifth Avenue. It was a meeting so charged with drama that Stanton's dry journal sprang into momentary capital-letter enthusiasm showing how keenly anxious he had been to bring it about:

"*Samedi, 29: PREMIERE ENTREVUE DE MES CHERS*

PARENTS APRES VINGT SEPT ANS! *A midi—½ heure chez lui."* [1]

So Caroline and Daniel Sickles gazed at each other across a chasm of time and trouble and dissonance. They were both old now, even though the lady could have been the general's daughter. They talked, both of them undoubtedly recalling the glitter of Madrid and Paris in days long gone by, their memories stirred with a thousand recollections of pleasure and pain, of two children now grown and having children themselves, of the lust for power that somehow withered the contentments of domesticity. They talked, and their first meetings were pleasant enough. Then they came up against an immovable barrier— the general's iron will.

Perhaps Caroline should have known that even after twenty-seven years, Daniel Sickles would not make an agreement with a woman except on his own terms. In truth, it was expecting a good deal of a man hard upon ninety to demand that he alter the unruly tenor of his life for the sake of propriety.

The rock on which the negotiations broke was the housekeeper, Eleanora Wilmerding. Mrs. Sickles sensed that the devoted and possessive Miss Wildmerding had won a place in the general's affections that would be embarrassing. The lady's firm stipulation was that Miss Wilmerding should be dismissed before a permanent reunion could be effected.

General Sickles bristled. Had his wife, after a twenty-seven-year separation, come across the Atlantic to dictate terms on how he must live? All right then, he rumbled, there will be no reunion. Miss Wilmerding will not be dismissed.

Hurt but still determined, Mrs. Sickles and Stanton retreated to the Albert Hotel, a few blocks away on Eleventh Street. There were discussions on strategy between son and mother. There were further parleys with the general. The old warrior was adamant. He would not dismiss Miss Wilmerding. New York was puzzled at the spectacle of General Sickles and his Spanish wife living a short distance apart, apparently in a state of uneasy truce.[2]

Possibly there was some suspicion that Mrs. Sickles was more
interested in inheritance than in reconciliation. Though the
general was known to have suffered heavy losses in investments,
he was still regarded as an immensely wealthy man. He acted
the part. If anything, his seizures of extravagance had grown
more ungovernable, especially toward women who caught his
fancy. He was a valued customer of several fashionable jewelers.
In his bedroom he reserved a dresser drawer for baubles—
brooches, lavallieres, earrings, bracelets—so that he would never
be caught without a pretty bijou to signalize his admiration for
some fetching creature who walked into his ken.[3] It was also his
pleasure to appear in front of his house every Sunday and dis-
tribute largesse to war veterans, some of whom may in truth
have been veterans and needy.

The cornucopia seemed bottomless. And General Sickles,
angered at continued remonstrances on the part of his wife and
Stanton, testily cut them out of so much as a penny. He made
over his will, leaving everything to the lady they wished him
to cast out of his home, Miss Wilmerding. The war clouds that
had hovered around his head ever since his youth became a fixture in his old age.

The cruel fact was that the general was teetering with his
crutches on the edge of ruin, although he blithely ignored the
portents. His lifelong recklessness with money had taken a long
time catching up with him, but now it was hard behind. He
had lost some $4,000,000 in Wall Street.[4] No one knew how
much he had cast away in other careless disbursements. Still he
refused to recognize any danger. When his good friend Representative William Sulzer of New York presented a bill in Congress in 1910 which would have retired Sickles as a lieutenant
general and raised his pension of $7500, the move seems to have
been designed as an honor rather than as a needed increment.

"He needs no eulogy," Sulzer told the House. "The record
is glory enough." But Representative Gardner of Michigan
pointed out that Sickles was rich in his own right and had already received more than $200,000 as a major general on the

retired list—a figure Sulzer disputed, but the measure was defeated.[5]

Money? It meant nothing to the general. While his wife settled down to permanent, helpless indignation at her lodgings a five-minute walk away, he continued to comport himself like a maharajah. He was not quite satisfied with the portraits previously painted of him and was desirous that his true likeness be preserved for posterity. He commissioned Princess Lenott Parlaghy to paint it, promptly becoming infatuated with her. When the princess admitted that she had always wanted to own a lion cub, Sickles was his old gallant self. He presented her with a litter of six.[6] After the canvas was finished and the princess planned a reception to view it, the general gave her a list of some 200 friends including Andrew Carnegie, Admiral Schley, Theodore Roosevelt, Chauncey Depew, Charles Evans Hughes, Thomas A. Edison, and William Glackens.[7]

The cornucopia was not bottomless. General Sickles was borrowing money. The first rumbling of disaster came in 1911 when his daughter, Mrs. Eda Crackanthorpe, sued to prevent his disposal of properties she felt entitled to as her share in her grandfather's estate.[8] It began to appear that she was suing for a mythical equity. Widening fissures of debt became visible in the ancient structure. In 1912 the Bowery Savings Bank initiated foreclosure proceedings against the general. August Heckscher sued him for recovery of $8000 loaned on a promissory note. The Bank of the Metropolis attached his property for failure to repay $5050. The Lincoln Trust Company joined the throng of claimants by obtaining a court order for a sheriff's attachment against his personal property for failure to meet a judgment for $8200.[9]

The general was broke. Worst of all, the attachment against his personal property meant that his most dearly prized possessions—his war relics, his swords, medals, and flags—would go under the sheriff's hammer unless some miracle intervened.

The miracle came to being. Mrs. Sickles, who had been living nearby for four years in the unhappy status of unwanted wife,

now had her chance to prove that her vigil was not a mercenary
one. She paid the $8200 judgment. She took a second mortgage
on the general's house to save him from eviction. She pawned
her jewels to pay another $5050. But when it became evident
that even this was not enough, she threw up her hands in dis-
may.

"I cannot beggar myself entirely to save him," she said.
". . . my heart was filled with sympathy for my husband in spite
of the great wrong he had done me. I pawned my jewels to save
his treasures. The general has his pension to live on, and I can
do nothing further for him . . . I will welcome him with open
arms if he wishes to make his home with me, but I will not put
up all my money to save his house to have it occupied by him
and his housekeeper to the exclusion of me." [10]

A few days later the general abandoned his reveries of distant
battles long enough to issue a snappish statement attacking his
wife's motives and insisting it was not necessary for her to pledge
her jewels.[11]

Meanwhile Sickles was still unpaid chairman of the New York
State Monuments Commission, an office he had held for twenty-
six years, though of late he had delegated many of his duties to
younger members. Late in 1912, State Controller William
Sohmer went over the books and discovered that $445,641 in
state funds had been given to the commission for expenditure
on monuments. Sickles' expense vouchers accounted for only
$417,165 of this, $28,476 less than the total given him.

What happened to that $28,476?

The general was queried about it. He did not seem to have
the slightest idea about what had happened to the $28,476.
There was embarrassment and consternation in Albany. Something had to be done. Something had to be done even though
Stanton Sickles, who had been spending much of his time trying
to mend the breach between his parents, came forward and paid
$5000 of it. That still left a shortage of $23,476. Attorney General Carmody reluctantly initiated proceedings against the entire monuments commission, a group of eight men.

General Sickles thereupon showed that his military heart was still as stout as oak. He addressed letters to Carmody and Controller Sohmer declaring that he was solely responsible for the commission's funds and thereby baring his own leathery neck for whatever axe would fall.[12]

No one wanted to use an axe on the ninety-three-year-old hero, but the law was the law. General Sickles was deposed from the monuments commission. A civil order was secured for his arrest. The unpleasant duty of executing this order fell on Sheriff Julius Harburger, a warm admirer of the general who did not forget that Sickles had once held the office of sheriff himself. Harburger, a benevolent-looking little man with drooping mustaches, was almost tearfully torn between reverence and official obligation. He received the arrest order on Saturday, January 25th, 1913, but he was in no hurry to carry it out. The least he could do, he felt, was to allow the general a quiet weekend.[13]

On Sunday, Sickles' negro valet hung three silk American flags out the window of 23 Fifth Avenue. If the citadel fell, it would go down with colors flying. Amazed New York sat back to witness the pathetic crumbling of a dynasty that had once seemed impregnable. The news had gone out over the wires, and it speedily became apparent that the old warrior's name still held magic. One unknown admirer, William Dodge of Indiana, wrote to announce that he would take Sickles' note for the entire deficit. Down in Gainesville, Georgia, where the widow of Longstreet served as postmistress, Helen Longstreet was moved to indignant fury. She wired Sickles:

MY SOUL IS SORROWED BY YOUR TROUBLES. AM WIRING THE ATTORNEY GENERAL OF NEW YORK THAT I WILL RAISE MONEY AMONG THE RAGGED, DESTITUTE, MAIMED VETERANS WHO FOLLOWED LEE TO PAY THE AMOUNT DEMANDED IF THE NEW YORK OFFICIALS WILL ALLOW SUFFICIENT TIME. WE ARE WRITING INTO OUR HISTORY THE STORY OF DEGENERATE DESCENDANTS OF HEROIC SIRES. THE REPUBLIC, WHOSE BATTLES YOU FOUGHT, WILL NOT PERMIT YOUR DEGRADATION.[14]

Reporters, hovering outside the Sickles museum that Sunday, peered in a window and noted that the general was puffing vigorously at a cigar and seemed unworried. In this emergency he was visited by Stanton and Mrs. Sickles, who agreed to help him on one condition—that Miss Wilmerding quit the place at once. Sickles wrathfully refused the ultimatum and they left in hopeless exasperation. "It was said," the *Times* commented, "that they were through with the general for good." [15]

Not so. Stanton and his mother were nothing if not determined. While the old soldier had never been the retiring sort, now he was seeing his domestic dilemma—a matter properly of some privacy—aired in the newspapers like a street brawl. Indeed, neither he nor his wife nor his son seemed concerned about keeping their differences on a confidential basis. On the contrary, each of them at times seemed to appreciate having in the public press a convenient medium for presenting his or her side of the quarrel.

"We are the best of friends," Mrs. Sickles told a reporter, "but he is very old and consequently refuses to let anyone tell him what he shall do. It is stubbornness that makes him keep that person in his house and exclude me. I have said, 'I will not return here unless Miss Wilmerding leaves,' and he immediately gets angry and says he will be master of his own house. Yet he told me he is very glad I became friends with him again, and begs me to forgive him for the past . . . It would be foolish for me to say I love my husband, as he is so old and I am many years his junior. But my heart is overflowing with sympathy for him . . ." [16]

Newsmen were also clustering around the harassed Sheriff Harburger, whose duty it was to place Sickles in the Ludlow Street Jail—the same barred ruin where Boss Tweed had died. Harburger announced that he was contributing one hundred dollars to a national subscription started by Controller Sohmer to pay off the general's debt to the state.

"Will you put him in a cell?" a reporter asked.

"My goodness, no," the sheriff replied, aghast. "I shall see to it that he has every attention and all the comforts of a good home . . . He won't even know he is in jail, so fine will be his treatment." [17]

On Monday, when Sheriff Harburger advanced reluctantly by carriage up Fifth Avenue to take his prisoner, he was followed by a retinue of reporters. The valet Moseley admitted them. They found Sickles seated in a big chair in a rear room. Miss Wilmerding was with him, her face mirroring scorn for a law that would dare interfere with her venerable charge. He was clad in a black suit and wore an eyeshade. The sheriff shook hands with him.

"I'm glad to see you, general," he said feelingly.

"And I'm glad to see *you*, sheriff," Sickles replied with a smile, apparently forgetting the object of the visit.[18]

But there was reason for his placidity. He had friends, as he always had friends, who stood by him regardless of any errors or omissions on his part. The sheriff was delighted to learn that through the last-minute efforts of these well-wishers, a surety company had agreed to pay $30,000 bond for Sickles. He would not have to arrest the general after all. The hero of Gettysburg proudly displayed the telegram he had received from Helen Longstreet. The sheriff eyed it with proper appreciation, then mentioned that $5.29 was due as a bond fee.

"Ah, yes," the general said. "Eleanor! Please get me $5.29."

"Yes, dear," Miss Wilmerding replied, and brought it.[19]

When Sheriff Harburger returned to his office, he found there a letter from Sickles. In it the general recalled that there had once been ill-advised criticism of his tactics at Gettysburg but that this unfortunate error had been laid once and for all by a statement made by Longstreet, his adversary there, which he enclosed.

"You will see from the statement of General Longstreet," he wrote, "that I won the great and decisive battle of Gettysburg." [20]

Gettysburg aside, the general had won his last grim battle but one. Although his fiscal affairs were still in chaos, he had

routed a flanking movement of the minions of the law. He settled down to peaceful pursuits again, with Mrs. Sickles resuming
her troubled stay at the hotel nearby. Despite all the rebuffs she
had been dealt, her remarkable determination was unbroken,
her hope for final reunion still strong. Stanton was at her side,
and growing testy. To a newspaperman he hinted that because
of his mother's payments on Sickles' house she would eventually become its owner.

"General Sickles will be welcome to it as a residence," he went
on, "but a certain person in his household will get this." And
he executed a violent kick with his right foot.[21]

For a mousy little housekeeper, Miss Wilmerding was causing
a deal of turmoil. She made no statements to the press but remained on in quiet triumph, undoubtedly relishing the dis-
comfiture of her enemies.

*   *   *

Early in July a sprinkling of aged veterans of the Blue and the
Gray gathered at Gettysburg to celebrate a peculiarly solemn
event—the fiftieth anniversary of the battle that had shaped the
Union. Sickles was there, of course. Nothing less than death
could have held him away. He was too old to trust himself with
crutches on uneven terrain, so his valet Moseley guided him
about on a wheelchair. The quiet Miss Wilmerding had also
accompanied him.

The fighter who had been born in Monroe's time listened to
a speech by President Woodrow Wilson. For another ceremony
he was given a seat of honor on the porch of the Rogers house [22]
—the same farmhouse where a pretty girl named Josephine
Miller had baked biscuits for some of Humphreys' men back in
'63 as they awaited an ordeal whose proportions they luckily
could not measure. From the porch he watched a nostalgic pag-
eant that brought tears to his eyes—the uncertain and shaky
charge of the remnants of Pickett's command, executed by
white-haired men in their seventies, just as they had done it a
half-century earlier. At the crest they were met by equally

white-haired survivors of the Army of the Potomac. There was
no shooting this time. The old Grays were embraced warmly by
the old Blues as an emblem of the union born out of blood and
travail that was at once foolish and glorious, even as the long
life of General Sickles had been foolish and glorious.

The general could be forgiven for feeling emotion as he surveyed the field which had been a fond part of his mind and
heart for fifty years. During those five decades he had stubbornly
built up a legend not quite in accord with historical fact but
which nevertheless had attained pure reality for him. He could
recall with senescent pride the verses of Horatio King which so
beautifully upheld the legend and yet were not too far from
fact:

> I see him on that famous field,
>   The bravest of the brave,
> Where Longstreet's legions strove to drive
>   The Third Corps to its grave.
> The fight was bloody, fierce and long,
>   And Sickles' name shall stay
> Forever in the Hall of Fame
>   As he who saved the day.

Where were they now, those soldiers who had been with him
when he made the dashing maneuver that saved the day? Hancock, De Trobriand, Pleasonton, Humphreys, Howard, even
the cautious Meade (he did his best to lose the battle, that fellow)—all of them, and a host of others, under the sod.

No, not quite all. Twichell was there, eighteen years Sickles'
junior, a splendid-looking, snowy-maned man of seventy-five.
Twichell, who knew so well the general's weaknesses without
ever forgetting his vast strength, had stopped in New York to
accompany his old commander to the field.[23] Now the warrior
and the clergyman recalled for the last time the tormented day
when the leg was lost whose loss was never really a loss. Horatio
King—bless him for those verses!—was hovering nearby. Helen
Longstreet was there too, representing a Southern newspaper—

a spirited young woman who saw in Sickles a weathered but gallant symbol of glory so long gone by that it was fading from the memory of all but a thinning few.

Strange that among all those marble representations of men afoot, men on horseback, men perpetuated in the throes of mortal combat, there was no memorial to General Sickles.

The general had an answer to that. The whole damned field was his memorial.[24]

*   *   *

He went back to New York, a man who had survived himself. He went back among his medals, his flags, the relics that for him were the only important reality. In February, 1914, the bodily obstacle to a reconciliation with his wife was removed with the death of Miss Wilmerding. The obstacle of resentment was as strong as ever. While Mrs. Sickles—joined again by Stanton— still waited on Eleventh Street, the general made a new will naming his three grandchildren as heirs and leaving bequests to Moseley and Horatio King. He seemed unaware that the wolves of debt were breathing close to him now and that he was assigning moneys that did not exist.

The reconciliation had to wait until April 24th, when Sickles suffered a cerebral hemorrhage. In tears, Moseley went to inform the wife and son. They were with the semi-conscious soldier until he died on May 3rd, 1914, in his ninety-fifth year.

So General Sickles made his last flurry of headlines in the newspapers that had heaped praise and blame on him in what seemed another age. The public press had a little trouble appraising the career of this man who had not always been right. If he belonged in the hall of fame, then the hall might require some altering. But the *Times* said something nobody could deny:

"He was a truly adventurous spirit." [25]

APPENDIX

$\mathcal{N}otes$

Chapter I. THE PEOPLE'S CHOICE

1. The Diary of George Templeton Strong, Vol. I, pp. 77–78.
2. New York Times, March 5, 1857.
3. The same.
4. Philadelphia Evening Bulletin, March 6, 1857.
5. Harper's Weekly, March 15, 1857.
6. New York Times, March 5, 1857.
7. Harper's Weekly, June 13, 1857.
8. The same, March 12, 1859. Also, Recollections of Men and Things at Washington During the Third of a Century, by L. A. Gobright, pp. 160–163.
9. Harper's Weekly, February 26, 1859.

Chapter II. POLITICKING ON THE POTOMAC

1. Harper's Weekly, April 9, 1859.
2. The Washington Tragedy: Trial of Daniel E. Sickles, reported by Felix G. Fontaine, p. 38.
3. The entire Murphy episode is related in the New York Times, May 9, 1857.
4. The same.
5. The same, May 12, 1857.
6. New York Evening Post, May 13, 1857.
7. Washington Daily National Intelligencer, March 28, 1857.
8. The same, May 7 and May 9, 1857.
9. A Belle of the Fifties: The Memoirs of Mrs. Clay of Alabama, edited by Ada Sterling, p. 45.
10. The same, p. 97.
11. Frank Leslie's Illustrated Newspaper (hereafter referred to as Frank Leslie's), March 26, 1859.
12. Harper's Weekly, March 12, 1859.
13. Marse Henry: The Autobiography of Henry Watterson, p. 63.
14. Recollections of Men and Things at Washington During the Third of a Century, p. 178. Also, Reminiscences of Sixty Years in the National Metropolis, by Ben Perley Poore, Vol. I, p. 532.
15. Trial of Daniel E. Sickles, p. 70.
16. A Belle of the Fifties, p. 97.

17. Frank Leslie's, March 19, 1859.
18. The same, March 26, 1859.
19. Trial of Daniel E. Sickles, p. 34.
20. The same, pp. 36, 37.
21. The same, p. 40.
22. The same, p. 70.

CHAPTER III. AFTER THE BALL

1. The Trial of Daniel E. Sickles, p. 70. A large number of the conversations and incidents relating to Mrs. Sickles' affair with Key in Chapters II to VI inclusive, are drawn from this published report of the trial. The writer supplies footnotes for only the more important.
2. The same.
3. The same.
4. A Metrical Description of a Fancy Dress Ball, by Major John De Havilland.
5. A Belle of the Fifties, pp. 126–137, gives an eyewitness description of the ball. Also Harper's Weekly, April 24, 1858.
6. A Belle of the Fifties, p. 132.
7. Thompson's testimony, Trial of Daniel E. Sickles, p. 72.
8. The same, p. 71.
9. Frank Leslie's, March 26, 1859, commented: "It is placed beyond all doubt that whatever may have been Mr. Sickles' failings at one period of his life, however wanting in morality, since his marriage he has been a changed man . . ." Harper's Weekly, April 9, 1859, said "the most searching inquiry" failed to show any impropriety on Sickles' part in Washington and that he had "replaced pleasure by nobler ambitions."
10. New York Herald, June 13, 1858.
11. The James Gordon Bennetts, by Don C. Seitz, pp. 130–131.
12. Dougherty's testimony, Trial of Daniel E. Sickles, p. 39.
13. New York Herald, September 1, 1858.
14. The same, September 3.
15. The same, November 3.
16. Trial of Daniel E. Sickles, p. 39.

CHAPTER IV. SIR, I DO ASSURE YOU

1. Lafayette Square of that era is described in an article by Major Gist Blair, Records of the Columbia Historical Society, Vol. 28, 1926, pp. 133–173. Also in Historic Homes of Washington, by Mary S. Lockwood, pp. 154–164.
2. Reminiscences of Peace and War, by Mrs. Roger A. Pryor, p. 47.
3. Trial of Daniel E. Sickles, p. 40.
4. Mystery of "A Public Man," by Frank Maloy Anderson, pp. 126–129.
5. Reminiscences of Sixty Years in the National Metropolis, Vol. II, pp. 25–26.
6. Letters of Lawrence O'Bryan Branch, 1856–60; North Carolina Historical Review, 1933, Vol. X. Partial quotation from two letters, p. 62 and p. 64. Harper's Weekly for January 29, 1859, observed, "Mr. and Mrs. Sickles are universal favorites. Nowhere is there a more refined or generous welcome."
7. A Belle of the Fifties, p. 86.
8. Quoted in New York Evening Post, March 1, 1859.
9. Trial of Daniel E. Sickles, p. 66.
10. The same, Mrs. Brown's testimony, p. 67.
11. Reminiscences of Sixty Years, Vol. II, p. 26.
12. New York Times, March 15, 1859.

13. Cooney's testimony, Trial of Daniel E. Sickles, p. 72.
14. Trial of Daniel E. Sickles, p. 52.
15. The same, p. 35.
16. The same, p. 76.
17. The same, p. 42.
18. A Belle of the Fifties, p. 98.
19. Trial of Daniel E. Sickles, p. 72.

Chapter V. BUT ONE COURSE LEFT

1. Trial of Daniel E. Sickles, p. 75.
2. The same, p. 73.
3. The same, p. 75.
4. The same, p. 40.
5. The same, p. 42.
6. The same, p. 46.
7. The same, pp. 42, 43.
8. Harper's Weekly, March 12, 1859.
9. The same.
10. Trial of Daniel E. Sickles, p. 74.
11. The same, pp. 17–21. While this high-flown speech sounds more like something out of melodrama than what a man would say under such stress, several witnesses were in substantial agreement that this is what Sickles actually shouted at Key.
12. The same, p. 19.
13. Bonitz recorded his witnessing of the killing in his diary, now in the hands of his son, Fred W. Bonitz of Charlotte, N. C. The father related verbally to his son Buchanan's perturbation and his remarks upon hearing the news. Mr. Bonitz still has the razor given his father by the President.
14. Trial of Daniel E. Sickles, p. 84.
15. Harper's Weekly, March 19, 1859. Also Philp's Washington Described, p. 206.
16. Frank Leslie's, March 12, 1859.

Chapter VI. THE DIGNITY OF A HOMICIDE

1. New York Times, February 28, 1859.
2. A Belle of the Fifties, p. 97.
3. Letters of Lawrence O'Bryan Branch, p. 64.
4. Diary of George Templeton Strong, Vol. II, p. 438.
5. Washington Evening Star, February 28, 1859.
6. New York Times, February 28, 1859.
7. Frank Leslie's, March 12, 1859.
8. Harper's Weekly, March 12, 1859.
9. Trial of Daniel E. Sickles, pp. 66, 68, 69.
10. New York Times, February 28, 1859.
11. Harper's Weekly, March 12, 1859.
12. Major Gist Blair, work cited in Footnote 1, chapter IV, p. 164.
13. New York Times, March 1, 1859.
14. The same, February 28, 1859.
15. Frank Leslie's, March 12, 1859.
16. Harper's Weekly, March 12, 1859.
17. Frank Leslie's, March 19, 1859.
18. New York Times, March 1, 1859.
19. Diary of George Templeton Strong, Vol. II, pp. 440–441.

20. Harper's Weekly, March 12, 1859.
21. The same, March 19, 1859.
22. Excerpts from three editorials in the New York Evening Post, issues of
    February 28, March 1, and March 8, 1859.
23. Brooklyn Times, March 1, 1859.
24. Trial of Daniel E. Sickles, p. 73.
25. Reminiscences of Sixty Years, Vol. II, p. 27.
26. Trial of Daniel E. Sickles, p. 15.
27. The same, p. 58.
28. The same, p. 95.
29. The same, p. 80.
30. Harper's Weekly, March 12, 1859.
31. Trial of Daniel E. Sickles, p. 85.
32. Reminiscences of Sixty Years, Vol. II, p. 27.
33. Harper's Weekly, May 7, 1859.
34. New York Times, April 27, 1859.
35. Baltimore Patriot, April 27, 1859.
36. Harper's Weekly, May 7, 1859.
37. A Diary from Dixie, by Mary Boykin Chesnut, p. 132.
38. Harper's Weekly, May 14, 1859.

Chapter VII. END OF A CAREER

1. Harper's Weekly, March 12, 1859.
2. Dan Sickles, Hero of Gettysburg and "Yankee King of Spain," by Edgcumb
   Pinchon, p. 134.
3. The same, p. 135.
4. July 16, 1859.
5. July 17, 1859.
6. July 16, 1859.
7. July 17, 1859.
8. New York Herald, July 19, 1859. In this issue Bennett published a "roundup"
   of New York newspaper comment on the reunion.
9. July 20, 1859.
10. New York World, June 30, 1869.
11. Diary of George Templeton Strong, Vol. II, pp. 456–457.
12. Henry Watterson was one of the few who took a sympathetic view. In his
    autobiography, written almost sixty years later, he commented (p. 63) with
    admiration on Sickles' generosity and courage in taking back his wife, add-
    ing, "He was by no means a politician after my fancy or approval, but to
    the end of his days I was his friend . . ."

Chapter VIII. FATHER TO THE MAN

1. Dan Sickles, by Edgcumb Pinchon, p. 8.
2. Harper's Weekly, April 9, 1859. This issue contains a sketch of Sickles' early
   years, which has been drawn upon freely in this chapter.
3. Lorenzo Da Ponte, Poet and Adventurer, by Joseph Louis Russo, pp. 21–40.
4. Trial of Daniel E. Sickles, testimony of Rev. Bulkeley, p. 54.
5. New York World, June 30, 1869.
6. Forty Years of American Life, by Thomas Low Nichols, M.D., p. 289.
7. Harper's Weekly, April 9, 1859.
8. The same.

9. A Political History of the State of New York, by DeAlva Stanwood Alexander, Vol. III, p. 8.
10. The History of Tammany Hall, by Gustavus Myers, p. 158.
11. New York World, June 30, 1869. Also, letter from David Graham to Sickles dated October 25, 1851, Sickles Papers, New York Library. Graham, attorney and elder brother of John and Charles Graham, defended Sickles in the mortgage suit.
12. New York World, June 30, 1869.
13. Forty Years of American Life, pp. 289–290.
14. New York World, June 30, 1869.
15. Dan Sickles, p. 23.
16. Harper's Weekly, April 9, 1859.
17. Anecdotes of Public Men, by John Forney, p. 79.
18. J. S. Carpentier to Sickles, May 19, 1852, Sickles Papers, New York Library.
19. Richard Schell to Sickles, July 23, 1853, Sickles Papers, New York Library.
20. Anecdotes of Public Men, p. 320.
21. New York World, June 30, 1869.
22. Sickles to Robert Dillon, March 16, 1853, Sickles Papers, New York Library. Sickles apparently was impressed by his own sentiment, for he preserved a copy of the letter in his papers until he died.
23. New York Herald, March 2, 1853. It may be that the civil marriage was kept secret, since the Herald announcement for both ceremonies was published at the time of the last.

CHAPTER IX. THE COLONEL AT COURT

1. Anecdotes of Public Men, p. 318.
2. The same.
3. The same.
4. New York World, June 30, 1869. Also, Ordeal of the Union, by Allan Nevins, Vol. II, pp. 65–66.
5. Ordeal of the Union, Vol. II, p. 66.
6. Letter from Sidney Webster to Sickles, July (undated), 1853, Sickles Papers, New York Library.
7. Letter dated April 11, 1853, Sickles Papers, New York Library.
8. Letter in August (no date), Sickles Papers, New York Library.
9. New York World, June 30, 1869.
10. The Works of James Buchanan, edited by John Bassett Moore, Vol. IX, p. 62.
11. The same, p. 66.
12. The same, p. 283.
13. Anecdotes of Public Men, p. 318.
14. New York World, June 30, 1869.
15. America's Ambassadors to England, 1785–1929, by Beckles Willson, p. 282.
16. The American Secretaries of State and Their Diplomacy, edited by Samuel Flagg Bemis, Vol. VI, p. 178.
17. America's Ambassadors to England, p. 284.
18. Dan Sickles, p. 40.
19. America's Ambassadors to England, p. 277; Ordeal of the Union, Vol. II, p. 65.
20. Dan Sickles, p. 53.
21. Reminiscences of Sixty Years, Vol. I, p. 444.
22. The same.
23. Harper's Weekly, April 9, 1859.
24. The Life of George Peabody, by Phebe A. Hanaford, p. 69.
25. New York Herald, November 4, 1854.
26. The same.

27. New York Herald, November 8, 1854.
28. The same, quoted from an anonymous letter signed "Vindex." The quarrel
    was fought again in the Washington Daily National Intelligencer, which
    published a long letter from Sickles giving his version in its November 6,
    1854 issue, and a reply from Peabody in its December 1, 1854 issue. Judged
    as a debate, Peabody's unruffled account seems more convincing.
29. New York Herald, July 25, 1854.
30. New York Herald, August 7, 1854.
31. Ordeal of the Union, Vol. II, pp. 355 and 357.
32. Harper's Weekly, April 9, 1859.
33. The Works of James Buchanan, Vol. IX, p. 283.
34. Hamilton Fish: the Inner History of the Grant Administration, by Allan
    Nevins, p. 189. Also, New York World, June 30, 1869.
35. The Works of James Buchanan, Vol. IX, p. 290.

CHAPTER X. TARGET, WASHINGTON

1. The Allen Trials, one of a collection of pamphlets concerning Sickles, New
   York Library Annex.
2. Argument of the Hon. Daniel E. Sickles in the Senate of the State of New York
   on the Trinity Church Bill.
3. Diary of George Templeton Strong, Vol. II, p. 440.
4. Ordeal of the Union, Vol. II, p. 456.
5. The same, Vol. II, p. 495.
6. The People, ex rel. D. E. Sickles, vs. James Gordon Bennett, New York County,
   Court of General Sessions.
7. The History of Tammany Hall, p. 189.
8. Sickles to L. E. Johnson, Sickles Papers, New York Library, letter dated
   February 5, 1857.

CHAPTER XI. MAN WITH SMALLPOX

1. Harper's Weekly, December 24, 1859.
2. A Diary From Dixie, p. 247.
3. Remarks of the Hon. D. E. Sickles of New York delivered in the House of
   Representatives Dec. 13, 1859. Pamphlet, 1860.
4. Recollections of Men and Things at Washington During the Third of a
   Century, p. 243.
5. Speech of the Hon. Daniel E. Sickles of New York delivered in the House of
   Representatives Dec. 10, 1860. Pamphlet, 1860.
6. James Buchanan and His Cabinet, by P. G. Auchampaugh, p. 160.
7. Men and Memories, by John Russell Young, pp. 25–26.
8. Sickles Pamphlets, New York Library Annex.
9. Abraham Lincoln, A History, by John G. Nicolay and John Hay, Vol. II, pp.
   149–151.
10. "The Republic is Imperishable"—speech delivered in H. of R. Jan. 16, 1861.
    Pamphlet, 1861.

CHAPTER XII. THE MAKING OF A GENERAL

1. Dan Sickles, p. 137.
2. New York World, June 30, 1869.
3. Four Years With the Army of the Potomac, by Philippe Regis de Trobriand,
   p. 426.

4. Journal of the Military Service Institute of the U.S., Vol. VI, No. 22, p. 142.
5. War Letters of Joseph Hopkins Twichell (hereafter identified as "Twichell"), letter dated May 8, 1861.
6. The same.
7. Same as Note 4 above, p. 142.
8. The same, p. 143.
9. The same, p. 151.
10. Twichell, letter dated May 15, 1861.
11. Journal of the Military Service Institute of the U.S., Vol. VI, No. 22, p. 151.
12. The same, p. 145.
13. Twichell, May 14, 1861.
14. Journal of the Military Service Institute of the U.S., Vol. VI, No. 22, p. 151.
15. The same, p. 150.
16. The same, p. 146.
17. The same, p. 148.
18. New York Tribune, July 2 and July 4, 1861.
19. The same, July 2, 1861.
20. Twichell, May 15, 1861.
21. The same, July 5, 1861.
22. New York World, June 30, 1869.
23. Journal of the Military Service Institute of the U.S., Vol. VI, No. 22, p. 149.
24. New York Tribune, July 22, 1861.
25. The same.
26. New York World, June 30, 1869.

Chapter XIII. THE UNMAKING OF A GENERAL

1. Journal of the Military Service Institute of the U.S., Vol. VI, No. 22, p. 145.
2. New York Tribune, July 22, 1861, says there were five regiments totalling 4300 men.
3. Anecdotes of Public Men, pp. 366–367.
4. Mary Lincoln: The Biography of a Marriage, by Ruth Painter Randall, p. 303.
5. The Man Who Made News: James Gordon Bennett, by Oliver Carlson, pp. 336–337.
6. Home Journal, August 31, 1861.
7. Fighting Joe Hooker, by Walter H. Hebert, p. 66.
8. Memorial to Horace Greeley, p. 53. Also, Fighting Joe Hooker, p. 67.
9. Letter from Sickles to Wikoff, August 28, 1861, Abraham Lincoln Papers, L. C. The letter discloses that Wikoff had talked with Lincoln in Sickles' behalf, that McClellan had vouched for Sickles, and adds, "When you see Mr. Bennett, thank him for his good wishes . . ."
10. Fighting Joe Hooker, p. 59.
11. The same, p. 66.
12. Sickles Papers, New York Library, October 27, 1861.
13. The same, dated November 5, 1861.
14. Fighting Joe Hooker, p. 59.
15. History of the 1st Regiment, Massachusetts Infantry, by Warren H. Cudworth, p. 101.
16. Twichell, October 1, 1861.
17. The same, October 26, 1861.
18. The same, November 30, 1861.
19. Lincoln Finds a General, by Kenneth P. Williams, p. 143.
20. History of the 1st Regiment, Massachusetts Infantry, p. 99.
21. Aeronautics in the Union and Confederate Armies, by F. Stansbury Haydon, pp. 348–350, p. 357, and p. 278. Also, New York Herald, November 24, 1861.

22. Sickles to Wikoff, January 30, 1862, Sickles Papers, L. C.
23. Reminiscences of Sixty Years, Vol. II, p. 143.
24. The same.
25. Mary Lincoln: The Biography of a Marriage, p. 255.
26. Reminiscences of Sixty Years, Vol. II, p. 143.
27. Twichell, January (date illegible), 1862.
28. The same, March 26, 1862.
29. The same.
30. Sickles Papers, L. C.
31. The same, April (date illegible), 1862.
32. Abraham Lincoln Papers, L. C., letter dated March 21, 1862.
33. Sickles Papers, L. C., dated April 6, 1862.
34. Civil War Letters of Felix Brannigan, 1861–1863, L. C., letter dated April
    20, 1862.

CHAPTER XIV. ON TO RICHMOND!

1. Sickles described his efforts in a letter to Horace Greeley, April 25, 1862,
   Greeley Papers, New York Library.
2. Letter dated April 14, 1862, Sickles Papers, New York Library.
3. New York Herald, April 8, 1862.
4. This seems borne out by events chronicled in Chapter XVIII.
5. Johnson's aid is mentioned in a letter from Sickles to Wikoff, January 30, 1862,
   Abraham Lincoln Papers, L. C.
6. Washington National Republican, April 26, 1862.
7. Sickles to Greeley, letter cited in Note 2 above.
8. Twichell, May 16, 1862.
9. History of the Third Regiment, Excelsior Brigade, 72nd New York Volunteer
   Infantry, by Henry LeFevre Brown, p. 29.
10. Letter of May 9, 1862.
11. New York Times, June 2, 1862.
12. New York Herald, May 8, 1862.
13. Fighting Joe Hooker, p. 97.
14. New York Times, June 4, 1862.
15. History of the Third Regiment, Excelsior Brigade, 72nd New York Volunteer
    Infantry, p. 40.
16. Four Years With the Army of the Potomac, p. 257.
17. The same.
18. Letter dated June 12, 1862.
19. New York Tribune, July 29, 1862.
20. These incidents are described in Twichell letters dated June 15 and June 25,
    1862.
21. Reveille in Washington, by Margaret Leech, p. 113.
22. Oration at Fredericksburg, by Daniel E. Sickles, pp. 9–11.
23. Twichell, June 19, 1862.
24. Fighting Joe Hooker, pp. 101–102.
25. New York Tribune, July 3, 1862.
26. Twichell letters, June 7 and June 25, 1862.
27. Twichell, July 5 and August 21, 1862.

CHAPTER XV. BACKWARD FROM RICHMOND

1. New York Tribune, July 3, 1862.
2. Fighting Joe Hooker, p. 115.
3. Civil War Letters of Felix Brannigan, L. C., letter dated July 16, 1862.

4. Twichell, July 19, 1862.
5. Sickles Papers, New York Library, letter dated May 21, 1862.
6. Personal Papers, Miscellaneous, L. C., letter dated May 19, 1862.
7. Twichell, July 19, 1862.
8. Memorial to Horace Greeley, p. 53.
9. New York Tribune, August 7, 1862.
10. Twichell, July 19, 1862.
11. New York Tribune, August 16, 1862.
12. Men and Memories, pp. 56–57.
13. Twichell, September 7, 1862.
14. The same, October 19, 1862.
15. History of the Third Regiment, Excelsior Brigade, 72nd New York Volunteer Infantry, p. 79.
16. The Journals of Joseph Hopkins Twichell, unidentified newsclipping found under entry for December 16, 1905.
17. The Fredericksburg debacle is vividly described in Glory Road, by Bruce Catton, Chapter I.
18. Twichell, January 1, 1863.
19. Four Years with the Army of the Potomac, p. 398.

Chapter XVI. BARROOM AND BROTHEL

1. Harper's Weekly, December 13, 1862.
2. C. F. Benjamin, a War Department official, in Battles and Leaders of the Civil War, Vol. III, p. 240.
3. Grant and his Generals, pp. 237–238.
4. The Campaign of Chancellorsville, by John Bigelow Jr., pp. 40–42.
5. The Life and Letters of General George Gordon Meade, edited by George Meade, Vol. I, p. 351.
6. Diary of Father Joseph B. O'Hagan, entry for February 2, 1863.
7. The same, entry for February 15, 1863. While Sickles was nominally a Protestant, it appears that he occasionally attended army mass.
8. Ten Years of My Life, by the Princess Felix Salm-Salm, p. 34.
9. The same, p. 41.
10. Twichell, letter dated March 1, 1863.
11. Four Years With the Army of the Potomac, p. 425.
12. Ten Years of My Life, p. 41.
13. Twichell, March 8, 1863.
14. The Irish Brigade, by Capt. D. P. Conyngham, pp. 373–374.
15. Memoirs of Gen. Thomas Francis Meagher, by Michael Cavanagh, p. 479.
16. Major General Hiram G. Berry, by Edward K. Gould, p. 243.
17. Charles Francis Adams, an Autobiography, p. 161.
18. The same.
19. Four Years with the Army of the Potomac, p. 398.
20. The same, p. 426.
21. Ten Years of My Life, p. 43.
22. General Daniel Butterfield, by Julia Butterfield, p. 160.
23. Oration at Fredericksburg, pp. 18–19; Washington in Lincoln's Time, by Noah Brooks, pp. 68–70; General Daniel Butterfield, p. 160. Strangely, the Princess Salm-Salm, who was not a diffident lady, did not mention the kissing episode in her book, Ten Years of My Life. One might dismiss it as amiable fiction were it not related as fact by at least two contemporaries (Butterfield and Brooks) in addition to Sickles himself. The humor seems genuinely Lincolnian.
24. The Journals of General M. R. Patrick, L. C., No. III, entry for April 28, 1863.

CHAPTER XVII. THE ENEMY MUST INGLORIOUSLY FLY

1. War of the Rebellion: A Compilation of the Official Records of the Union and Confederate Armies (hereafter referred to as "O. R."), Series I, Vol. XXV, Part 1, p. 171.
2. The Campaign of Chancellorsville, p. 221.
3. The Story of the 63rd Regiment, Pennsylvania Volunteers, by Gilbert Adams Hay, p. 178.
4. The Campaign of Chancellorsville, p. 279.
5. The same.
6. Berdan's U. S. Sharpshooters, by Capt. C. A. Stevens, pp. 247–248.
7. The same, p. 251. Professor Lowe, aloft in his balloon, had already reported Jackson's movement.
8. O. R., Series I, Vol. XXV, Part 2, p. 363.
9. The Campaign of Chancellorsville, p. 42.
10. Chancellorsville and Gettysburg, by Abner Doubleday, pp. 25–26. Also, the Campaign of Chancellorsville, p. 288.
11. O. R., Series I, Vol. XXV, Part 1, p. 387.
12. Chancellorsville and Gettysburg, p. 37. But there was later disagreement about this phase of the battle. So much odium was unfairly heaped on the out-numbered Eleventh Corps that one of its officers, Augustus Choate Hamlin, years later undertook an investigation. In his book, The Battle of Chancellorsville: Jackson's Attack, he charged that Sickles' excursion to Hazel Grove and beyond was "the cause of the failure of the campaign" (p. 48). He blamed Sickles because his maneuver isolated the Eleventh, leaving it to face greatly superior enemy forces alone. He accused Sickles and others of deliberately making the Eleventh the scapegoat for the defeat. He also claimed (pp. 88–90) that Sickles' and Pleasonton's reports of how their cannon and infantry stopped Jackson's charge was self-glorifying fiction. According to Hamlin, Jackson's charge stopped long before it ever reached Sickles' position because of Confederate confusion in the underbrush and the need to reorganize. All that Pleasonton's cannon stopped, Hamlin said, was a small party of rebel foragers.
13. O. R., Series I, Vol. XXV, Part 1, p. 916.
14. The same, p. 917.
15. New York Herald, May 26, 1863.
16. Chancellorsville and Gettysburg, pp. 45–46; Lincoln Finds a General, p. 593.
17. Four Years with the Army of the Potomac, p. 460.
18. Lincoln Finds a General, pp. 594–595. Fighting Joe Hooker, p. 211.
19. The Campaign of Chancellorsville, p. 355; Fighting Joe Hooker, p. 212.
20. History of the 12th Regiment, New Hampshire Volunteers, by Capt. A. W. Bartlett, p. 104.
21. Lincoln Finds a General, p. 594.
22. Three Years in the Sixth Corps, by George T. Stevens, pp. 200–205.
23. The Campaign of Chancellorsville, pp. 419–420.
24. O. R., Series I, Vol. XXV, Part 1, p. 512.
25. The Autobiography of Oliver Otis Howard, Vol. I, p. 379.
26. The same.

CHAPTER XVIII. SICKLES IS THE MAN

1. New York Herald, May 8, 1863.
2. Quoted in Harper's Weekly for May 23, 1863.
3. Journals of General M. R. Patrick, L. C., No. III, entries for May 8 and May 10, 1863.

4. Diary of George Templeton Strong, entry for May 17, 1863.
5. A Cycle of Adams Letters, edited by W. C. Ford, letter dated May 24, 1863.
6. O. R., Series I, Vol. XXV, Part 1, p. 392.
7. The Irish Brigade, p. 406. Meagher later rejoined the army, was relieved of command early in 1865 for drunkenness, then resigned his commission for keeps.
8. O. R., Series I, Vol. XXV, Part 1, p. 385.
9. The same, p. 394.
10. The same, pp. 773–774.
11. James Gordon Bennett Papers, L. C. Sickles' letter to Bennett was dated May 26, 1863.
12. Two Days of War, by Henry E. Tremain, p. 1; New York Herald, May 30. According to Doubleday (Chancellorsville and Gettysburg, p. 50), Sickles had been slightly injured at Chancellorsville by a "spent shot or piece of shell, which struck his waist-belt."
13. A Cycle of Adams Letters, letter dated June 25, 1863. On June 18, young Captain Adams had seen bloody action at Aldie's Gap, Va., losing 61 of his 94 men in killed and wounded.
14. General Patrick's diary entry for June 19 reflects his scorn for Hooker's complaints: ". . . He has declared that the enemy are over 100,000 strong— it is his only salvation to make it appear that the enemy's forces are larger than his own, which is all false & he knows it. He knows that Lee is his master & is afraid to meet him in a fair battle."
15. Even the Herald itself (June 29, 1863), evidently giving up on Sickles, praised Meade's appointment.
16. Report of the Joint Congressional Committee on the Conduct of the War (hereafter referred to as "C. C. W."), 1865, Vol. I, p. 302.

CHAPTER XIX. "THIS IS A GOOD BATTLE-FIELD"

1. C. C. W., 1865, Vol. I, p. 302.
2. General Daniel Butterfield, p. 112.
3. Lincoln Finds a General, Chapter XXI.
4. O. R., Series I, Vol. XXVII, Part 3, p. 399.
5. The same, p. 420.
6. C. C. W., 1865, Vol. I, p. 296.
7. Two Days of War, p. 14.
8. The same, p. 19.
9. Lincoln Finds a General, p. 687.
10. C. C. W., 1865, Vol. I, p. 296.
11. Two Days of War, p. 21.
12. A Little Fifer's War Diary, by C. W. Bardeen, p. 217.
13. History of the Third Regiment, Excelsior Brigade, p. 99.
14. O. R., Series I, Vol. XXVII, Part 3, p. 468.
15. Life and Letters of General George Gordon Meade, Vol. II, pp. 66 ff.
16. Two Days of War, pp. 41 ff.
17. New York Times, August 14, 1886.
18. C. C. W., 1865, Vol. I, p. 331.
19. The same, p. 297 and p. 450.
20. The Battle of Gettysburg, by the Comte de Paris, p. 152.
21. Berdan's U. S. Sharpshooters, p. 303.
22. The same, p. 304.
23. Birney's report, O. R., Series I, Vol. XXVII, Part 1, p. 482.
24. Personal Recollections of the Civil War, by John Gibbon, p. 136.
25. The Battle of Gettysburg, by Frank A. Haskell, p. 41.

26. General Gibbon of the Second Corps, concerned about this gap, sent out two regiments to the Codori house, a midway point, "so that his [Sickles'] connection with the main line might not be entirely lost . . ." (Gibbon, Personal Recollections, pp. 136–137.)

27. Williams (Lincoln Finds a General, p. 695) points out that Big Round Top, further south, was of less significance since it was too rugged to scale with artillery and was beyond effective infantry range.

28. Lincoln Finds a General, p. 699.

29. Longstreet was later blamed for his delay by many Southerners who felt that an earlier attack would have caught the Union forces not fully up and would have resulted in a Confederate victory.

30. C. C. W., 1865, Vol. I, p. 299; Two Days of War, p. 63.

31. Two Days of War, p. 64.

Chapter XX. NEVER CALL RETREAT

1. Four Years with the Army of the Potomac, p. 497.
2. The same, p. 494.
3. The same, p. 497.
4. C. C. W., 1865, Vol. I, p. 367.
5. Battles and Leaders, Vol. III, pp. 307–309.
6. New York Herald, March 12, 1864, in anonymous letter signed "Historicus."
7. Brannigan Papers, L. C., in a letter about Gettysburg whose first page is missing so that the date is lost.
8. Haskell, The Battle of Gettysburg, p. 46.
9. The same, p. 42. Colonel Haskell, who showed personal dislike of Sickles, was misleading in saying that Sickles had abandoned a "crest" for lower ground. A contour map shows parts of the area around the Peach Orchard as being 580 feet in elevation, forty feet higher than parts of Cemetery Ridge which Sickles had left. The Wheat Field, considerably lower, is at about the same elevation as the lower parts of the so-called "crest." While elevation is only one aspect of a defensive position, it is clear that Sickles did not abandon high ground for lower.
10. New York Times, July 18, 1863. According to Private Brannigan, however (letter cited above), Sickles' adjutant was "more collected than his superior."
11. History of the Third Regiment, Excelsior Brigade, p. 104. Another account (Campfire and Battlefield, by Rossiter Johnson, p. 266) says that Sickles half fell to the ground when wounded. "He was very pale, and evidently in most fearful pain as he exclaimed excitedly, 'Quick, quick! Get something and tie it up before I bleed to death.' "
12. Two Days of War, p. 88.
13. History of the Third Regiment, Excelsior Brigade, p. 105.
14. Lincoln and Episodes of the Civil War, by William E. Doster, p. 217.
15. Two Days of War, p. 90.
16. The same.
17. Glory Road, p. 319.
18. O. R., Series I, Vol. XXVII, Part 1, p. 178.
19. The Battle of Gettysburg, p. 154.

Chapter XXI. TELL IT TO LINCOLN

1. Two Days of War, p. 94.
2. New York Times, July 18, 1863.
3. The same.
4. Reminiscences of Herman Haupt, by John B. Anderson, p. 221.

5. Two Days of War, p. 99.

6. Doctors in Blue, by George W. Adams, p. 116.

7. Two Days of War, p. 99.

8. Men and Things I Saw in Civil War Days, by James F. Rusling, pp. 12–14.

9. New York Herald, July 11 and July 12, 1863.

10. Two Days of War, p. 101.

11. Abraham Lincoln, a New Portrait, by Emanuel Hertz, Vol. II, p. 901.

12. O. R., Series I, Vol. XXVII, Part 1, p. 82.

13. Two Days of War, p. 100.

14. The same, p. 107. "Poor Sickles!" Major Tremain wrote in a letter dated July 7. "He is not the man he was. Utterly prostrate, weak and feeble as a child, he still lies on his back on the same stretcher on which he was placed after the amputation of his leg."

15. The same, p. 105.

16. Sickles' right tibia and fibula are still on display in a glass case at the Armed Forces Medical Museum in Washington. The exhibit card reads in part: "The amputated leg was received at the Army Medical Museum in a rough coffin with a visiting card of General Sickles. On the card was written: 'With the compliments of Maj.-Gen. D. E. S., U. S. Vols.'
"It is said that after the war, the General would visit the museum from time to time, to see the bones preserved from his leg."

17. New York Herald, July 19, 1863.

18. The same, July 24.

19. The same.

20. The same, July 28.

21. Edwin M. Stanton Papers, L. C., letter dated August 7, 1863.

22. Stanton Papers, L. C., dated August 10, 1863.

23. New York Times, August 13, 1863.

24. The same, August 12, 1863.

25. The same, September 9, 1863.

26. The same.

27. The same.

28. The McGarrahan Claim, one of the Sickles Pamphlets, New York Library Annex.

29. Abraham Lincoln Papers, L. C., dated August 15, 1863.

30. Pamphlet cited in Note 28 above; letter dated August 22, 1863.

31. Harper's Weekly, October 24, 1863. Graham was feted by his friends at a Delmonico dinner and after recuperation was assigned to General Butler's Army of the James.

32. The Diary of George Templeton Strong, entry for August 21, 1863.

33. New York Tribune, September 29, 1863; Harper's Weekly, October 10, 1863.

34. Pamphlet cited in Note 28 above.

35. Harper's Weekly, September 19, 1863.

36. O. R., Series I, Vol. XXVII, Part 1, p. 116.

37. This rumor is mentioned in War Letters of John Chipman Gray and John Codman Ropes, 1862–1865, p. 256.

38. New York Tribune, October 19, 1863, reported: "General Sickles arrived in the front last night, prepared to take the field if a fight ensue. His friends there, however, think his valor carries him too far in his present physical condition."

39. C. C. W., 1865, Vol. I, p. 304.

40. Four Years with the Army of the Potomac, p. 530.

41. The same, p. 531.

42. Daniel E. Sickles Papers, New York Library, letter of O. W. Davis to Sickles, August 21, 1863.

43. History of the Tenth Massachusetts Battery, by John D. Billings, p. 105.

44. Four Years with the Army of the Potomac, p. 546.

45. Although the possession of Little Round Top was vital to the Army of the Potomac, Meade seemed hardly more aware of this than Sickles. If Meade had doubts of Sickles' sagacity, he would have done well to take time to look at his left. If, on the other hand, he respected Sickles' judgment, it seems that he should have paid more heed to Sickles' repeated expressions of dissatisfaction with his position and suggestions that he had a better one in mind. In his own later testimony before the Committee on the Conduct of the War, Meade said (C. C. W., 1865, Vol. I, p. 332), "I had indicated to him in general terms, that his right was to rest on General Hancock's left; and his left was to extend to the [Little] Round Top Mountain, plainly visible, if it was practicable to occupy it." If that was his order, Meade clearly had not found time to examine Little Round Top personally, did not know whether it was "practicable" to occupy it, and left that question for Sickles to decide.

Sickles certainly erred in making his change of position without informing either Meade or the corps commanders. He afterward admitted (C. C. W., 1865, Vol. I, p. 299) that in taking his advanced position he spread his corps extremely thin, but assumed that reinforcements would be given him promptly—a rather rash assumption, since not all the Army of the Potomac had arrived at the scene. Sedgwick's Sixth Corps was still marching toward Gettysburg, and the only reserve Meade had was the Fifth, part of which had just arrived and was weary after a hard march. But Sickles acted wisely when, at Emmitsburg, he heeded Howard's appeal for help and marched most of his corps to Gettysburg despite earlier orders that he hold at Emmitsburg. A finicky general might have sat down and awaited further orders from Meade.

CHAPTER XXII. CERTAIN GRAVE CHARGES

1. The Diary of Gideon Welles, Vol. I, p. 472. Welles' comment that Sickles used Howard as a "set-off" is a canny one, for Sickles had an uncommon ability at making himself the central figure in any narrative.
2. O. R., Series I, Vol. XXVII, part 1, p. 16.
3. Diary of M. R. Patrick, L. C., entry for December 16, 1863. The officer mentioned is Colonel G. H. Sharpe of New York, formerly Patrick's deputy and a friend of Sickles.
4. Lincoln's War Cabinet, by Burton J. Hendrick, pp. 280–283; Lincoln and the Radicals, by T. Harry Williams, p. 339.
5. Ben Hardin Helm, by R. Gerald McMurtry, p. 57.
6. Mary, wife of Lincoln, by Katherine Helm, p. 228.
7. Abraham Lincoln Papers, L. C., January 11, 1864.
8. The same, letter dated January 27, 1864.
9. The Complete Works of Abraham Lincoln, edited by John G. Nicolay and John Hay, Vol. IX, p. 299.
10. Abraham Lincoln Papers, L. C., February 2, 1864.
11. Manuscript at Brown University Library, dated February 20, 1864.
12. The Life and Letters of General George Gordon Meade, Vol. II, p. 164, letter dated December 28, 1863.
13. The same, Vol. II, p. 169.

CHAPTER XXIII. THE CAMPAIGN OF GENERAL HISTORICUS

1. Lincoln's War Cabinet, p. 281.
2. The Life and Letters of General George Gordon Meade, Vol. II, p. 169.

3. Meade reached Washington on March 5. The Journal of the committee for March 4 reads in part (C. C. W., 1865, Vol. I, p. XIX):

"The chairman [Wade] directed the stenographer to enter upon the journal that, having become impressed with the exceeding importance of the testimony taken by the committee in relation to the army of the Potomac, more especially in relation to the incompetency of the general in command of that army, he and Mr. Chandler had believed it their duty to call upon the President and the Secretary of War, and lay before them the substance of the testimony taken by them, and, in behalf of the army and of the country, demand the removal of General Meade, and the appointment of some one more competent to command. They accordingly did so yesterday afternoon; and being asked what general they could recommend for the command of the army of the Potomac, they said that for themselves they would be content with General Hooker, believing him to be competent; but not being advocates of any particular general, they would say that if there was any general whom the President considered more competent for the command, then let him be appointed . . ."

4. C. C. W., 1865, Vol. I, p. 4.
5. The same, p. 14.
6. The same, p. 298.
7. The same.
8. The same, p. 299.
9. One member of the committee, Representative Moses F. Odell, of New York, was clearly annoyed at the steam-roller tactics of his colleagues. He asked some questions designed to bring out points favorable to Meade. But the voice of Odell, who was not running the show, was all but unheard.
10. C. C. W., 1865, Vol. I, p. 357. This report, relayed by General Howard to General Hancock, was an injustice to Doubleday. Howard arrived at the scene in time to see a couple of First Corps regiments retreating into the town, and jumped at conclusions. Actually, the remainder of the First under Doubleday fought well and turned back the enemy until Confederate reinforcements forced a withdrawal. But Meade, unaware of this, must have taken the report at face value.
11. C. C. W., 1865, Vol. I, p. 311. In his book Chancellorsville and Gettysburg (p. 32), Doubleday later pointed out a fundamental fallacy of hearings such as this one—that a subordinate officer would not be inclined to testify against a superior still in command, and "any officer that did so would have soon found his military career brought to a close." Ironically, after the hearings Doubleday fought no more but remained assigned to duty in Washington.
12. Zachariah Chandler Papers, L. C., February 30, 1864.
13. C. C. W., volume cited, p. 419.
14. The same, p. 424.
15. However, Butterfield does not seem to have been entirely candid, for during the battle he apparently had no doubt that the order was for emergency use only. According to General Gibbon (Personal Reminiscences, p. 139), Butterfield mentioned the order to him at Gettysburg. Gibbon exclaimed that surely Meade did not intend to retreat. Butterfield "rather carelessly answered to the effect that the order was merely preparatory . . ." Since the order was not used, it was destroyed and did not become part of the official record.
16. Not even against Sickles. In his testimony before the committee (volume cited, pp. 331–333), Meade merely said, "I found that General Sickles had taken up a position very much in advance of what it had been my intention that he should take." He went on, "It is not my intention in these remarks to cast any censure on General Sickles. I am of the opinion that General Sickles did what he thought was for the best; but I differed with him in judgment."
17. O. R., Series I, Vol. XXVII, Part 1, p. 128, letter dated March 15, 1864.

18. O. R., volume cited, p. 137, letter dated March 20.
19. The same, p. 139, dated March 29.
20. C. C. W., volume cited, p. 436.
21. New York Herald, March 18, 1864.
22. The same, April 4, 1864.
23. Life and Letters of General George Gordon Meade, Vol. II, p. 182.
24. The Round Table, March 12, 1864.

Chapter XXIV. A BETTER GENERAL

1. Grant in Peace, by Adam Badeau, p. 382.
2. While Meade remained in command of the Army of the Potomac until the war's end, Grant stayed with that army almost constantly and kept a sharp eye on its operations.
3. A. K. McClure, in Lincoln and Men of War Times (p. 107) said that Sickles was sent to Tennessee to report on Johnson's administration there so that Lincoln could appraise Johnson as a possible Vice Presidential nominee in 1864. Nicolay and Hay flatly denied this, said Lincoln had nothing to do with Johnson's selection. The present account follows Sickles' own story (New York Times, July 10, 1891), in which he made no mention of eyeing Johnson as possible timber for candidacy.
4. Andrew Johnson Papers, L. C., Sickles to Johnson, undated.
5. General Daniel Butterfield, p. 147.
6. Abraham Lincoln Papers, L. C., telegram dated May 17, 1864.
7. The same, letter dated May 31, 1864.
8. Two Days of War, p. 205.
9. Abraham Lincoln Papers, L. C., August 10, 1864.
10. Sickles Papers, New York Library, September 19, 1864.
11. Tremain wrote in Two Days of War (p. 42), "He [Sickles] habitually welcomed suggestions, when coupled with useful information, from his staff officers, whether those suggestions were acted on or not . . . For such things a martinet of a general might give the staff officer a 'frost.' I never was 'frosted'—by General Sickles." The two remained firm friends after the war and fellow spirits of the Third Corps Union.
12. Daniel E. Sickles Papers, L. C., dated November 8, 1864.
13. Abraham Lincoln Papers, L. C.
14. New York Herald, November 2, 1864.
15. "Dr. Moreland is highly pleased with your complimentary notice of his nervous tonic," George Sickles wrote his son a few months later (Daniel E. Sickles Papers, New York Library, letter dated March 24, 1865).
16. Abraham Lincoln Papers, L. C.

Chapter XXV. O, CAPTAIN, MY CAPTAIN!

1. Colombia and the United States, 1765-1934, by E. Taylor Parks, pp. 246-247 and 276-277. With no transcontinental railroad, the "quick" way to get from one American coast to another was to make two ocean voyages separated by a journey across the narrow isthmus.
2. Daniel E. Sickles Papers, New York Library, letter dated January 22, 1865.
3. The same, letter dated March 24, 1865.
4. Journal of the U. S. Military Service Institute, Vol. VI, 1885, p. 261.
5. Parks, volume cited above, pp. 246-247.
6. Edwin M. Stanton Papers, L. C., letter dated May 2, 1865.
7. Source cited in Note 4 above, p. 261.
8. The same.
9. The same, p. 262.

Chapter XXVI. PEOPLE ARE TOO PRAGMATICAL

1. Grant and his Generals, p. 238.
2. The Sequel of Appomattox, by Walter Lynwood Fleming, p. 73.
3. Among Sickles' former Southern friends who did not survive were Lawrence O'Bryan Branch, killed at Antietam, and Lawrence Keitt, killed at Cold Harbor.
4. Journal of the Military Service Institute of the United States, Vol. VI, No. 23, p. 264.
5. South Carolina During Reconstruction, by F. B. Simkins and R. H. Woody, p. 66.
6. One of Sickles' favorite quotations, which he repeated frequently in public addresses, was a speech by Colonel Damas to Claude Melnotte in Bulwer-Lytton's "Lady of Lyons": "It is astonishing how much I like a man after I have fought with him."
7. Grant in Peace: From Appomattox to Mt. McGregor, by Adam Badeau, p. 384.
8. Edwin M. Stanton Papers, L. C., letter dated July 19, 1866.
9. Annual Report of the Secretary of War, 1866, p. 64.
10. The same, p. 66.
11. The same, pp. 59 ff.
12. South Carolina During Reconstruction, p. 70.
13. The Tragic Era: The Revolution After Lincoln, by Claude G. Bowers, pp. 143 ff.
14. Grant in Peace, p. 385.
15. Edwin M. Stanton Papers, L. C., July 19, 1866.
16. Personal Papers, Miscellaneous, L. C., Sickles to Liebeman, March 4, 1866.
17. Daniel E. Sickles Papers, New York Library, dated October 2, 1866.
18. The same, letter dated March 21, 1867.
19. Edwin M. Stanton Papers, L. C., dated July 19, 1866.
20. Annual Report of the Secretary of War, 1866, p. 60.

Chapter XXVII. LETTERS EDGED IN BLACK

1. The quotations are from the New York Herald for February 10, 1867. The Charleston Mercury for February 8, possibly reflecting some animosity toward the general, covered Teresa's death in one curt line: "General Daniel Sickles' wife is dead."
2. Andrew Johnson Papers, L. C., dated February 26, 1867.
3. The same, Sickles to Johnson, March 5, 1867. Sickles recommended Graham and Brewster for positions in the Internal Revenue Service.
4. The same, also dated March 5 but a different letter.
5. Dan Sickles, p. 225.
6. Charleston Mercury, April 29, 1867. There were seven hand engines and seven steamers parading on the Citadel green. Sickles issued detailed orders concerning the address to the flag, writing his subordinate in charge of the Charleston post in part: "I desire that you will at once send for the Chief of the Fire Department and inform him that the national standard must be borne in front of the column; that an escort of honor to consist of two members of each company present will be detailed by himself to march with the colors; that the colors be placed opposite the reviewing personages on the ground designated for the review, and that every person in the column shall salute the colors by lifting his hat or cap on arriving at the point three paces distant from the colors and carrying the cap uplifted marching past the colors to the point three paces distant from the same . . ."
7. South Carolina During Reconstruction, p. 68.
8. Journal of the Military Service Institute of the U. S., Vol. VI, No. 23, p. 266.

9. South Carolina During Reconstruction, pp. 46–47.
10. Charleston Mercury, April 15, 1867.
11. In reply to a critical editorial in the New York Times, Sickles wrote an able and measured defense of his order to Henry J. Raymond, editor of the Times (Andrew Johnson Papers, L. C., Sickles to Raymond, June 10, 1867), saying in part: "Believe me when I tell you that General Orders No. 10 were promulgated for no other purpose than to relieve a population, four-fifths of whom were impoverished debtors, from the utter ruin to which they were driven by remorseless Creditors, who had compromised on their own terms their own large indebtedness to Northern Creditors."
12. Diary of Gideon Welles, Vol. III, p. 65.
13. Journal of the Military Service Institute of the U. S., Vol. VI, No. 23, p. 267.
14. Edwin M. Stanton Papers, L. C., Sickles to Stanton, July 19, 1866.
15. The Age of Hate, by George Fort Milton, p. 385.
16. Andrew Johnson Papers, L. C., Sickles to Trumbull, July 1, 1867.
17. Charleston News, September 27, 1867.
18. Journal of the Military Service Institute of the U. S., Vol. VI, No. 23, p. 268.
19. The usually courteous Sickles was growing snappish even toward the President, beginning one letter to him (via the adjutant general): "I have the honor to state that in the present condition of these states it is not practicable to afford adequate security to persons and property unless the Commanding General of the District is authorized to remove Civil Officers who fail to perform their duties . . ." (Andrew Johnson Papers, L. C., Sickles to adjutant general, June 14, 1867).
20. South Carolina During Reconstruction, p. 57.
21. Washington Daily National Intelligencer, August 12, 1867. The same newspaper charged that Sickles was trying to "curry favor" among Carolinians because he intended to run for Senator from South Carolina—anything but an indication that General Order No. 10 was oppressive. In fact, the order ran directly contrary to feeling among the more rabid Northern radicals, who had no wish to help the South but were even desirous of outright confiscation of "rebel" property. It is hard to agree with historians who have characterized Sickles' regime in the Carolinas as harsh. Had the general kept his temper in minor matters—and kept on friendly terms with President Johnson—it would seem that his administration would have been eminently fair and successful.
22. The same newspaper, August 24, 1867.
23. South Carolina During Reconstruction, p. 57.
24. Andrew Johnson Papers, L. C., Sickles to adjutant general, August 17, 1867.
25. The Tragic Era, pp. 166–167.
26. Andrew Johnson Papers, L. C., Sickles to adjutant general, June 19, 1867.
27. The Age of Hate, p. 441.
28. Diary of Gideon Welles, Vol. III, p. 176, entry dated August 22, 1867.
29. Andrew Johnson Papers, L. C., August 13, 1867.
30. The same, dated August 14, 1867.
31. Diary of Gideon Welles, Vol. III, p. 185.
32. Charleston Mercury, August 30 and September 2, 1867.
33. Quoted in New York World, June 30, 1869.

CHAPTER XXVIII. THE GENERAL CALLS ON A LADY

1. Grant in Peace, p. 386.
2. Andrew Johnson Papers, L. C., Sickles to adjutant general, September 11, 1867.
3. Diary of Gideon Welles, Vol. III, p. 207.
4. Grant so indorsed Sickles' request in passing it along to the President.

5. The Tragic Era, pp. 175 and 177.
6. Edwin McMasters Stanton, by Frank Abial Flower, p. 331.
7. U. S. Grant, Politician, by William B. Hesseltine, p. 102.
8. Elihu Washburne Papers, L. C., dated January 12, 1868.
9. The same, March 1, 1868.
10. The Tragic Era, p. 179.
11. The same, pp. 192–193.
12. The Impeachment and Trial of Andrew Johnson, by David Miller DeWitt, p. 537.
13. The same, p. 538.
14. New York Sun, October 25, 1896.
15. The Impeachment and Trial of Andrew Johnson, p. 540.
16. The Tragic Era, p. 196.
17. Sickles' strange interview with Miss Ream is taken from his own account, published twenty-eight years later in the New York Sun for October 25, 1896. He was then on a campaigning tour for McKinley with General Howard and others, and in Topeka, Kan., was interviewed by reporters. The name of Ross, a former Kansan, came up and touched off Sickles' recollections.

Chapter XXIX. A DEEP SENSE OF PROPRIETY

1. This was the same George H. Sharpe, then a colonel, who had been in charge of intelligence under General Patrick in the Army of the Potomac and had brought the news to Patrick of Sickles' fight against Halleck. A New Yorker, Sharpe, like Sickles, was now an active member of the Society of the Army of the Potomac, an organization interested in politics as well as veterans' welfare.
2. Elihu Washburne Papers, L. C., May 6, 1868.
3. U. S. Grant, Politician, p. 119.
4. The New York Herald ran a brief sketch of McHenry in its May 2, 1883 issue, shortly after McHenry went bankrupt.
5. The Dreadful Decade, by Don S. Seitz, pp. 89–92.
6. New York Tribune, March 16, 1872.
7. New York Times, March 7, 1869.
8. Hamilton Fish: The Inner History of the Grant Administration, by Allan Nevins, p. 120.
9. Grant in Peace, p. 387.
10. Hamilton Fish, p. 189.
11. Hamilton Fish Papers, L. C., Fish letters to Sickles dated December 14 and December 31, 1840.
12. Quoted in the New York World, June 1, 1869.
13. New York World, June 25, 1869.
14. Anecdotes of Public Men, p. 322.
15. While the writer has used this long and detailed account in the World as a source, in fairness to Sickles he has borne in mind that the World was a political enemy and might exaggerate or even resort to outright fabrication. Other authorities have been sought to substantiate the World's statements. In commenting on the World blast, the upright diarist Strong (entry for July 12, 1869) said the paper made "certain charges that are true, some that may be true, and one (at least) that is utterly false . . ." The latter was the charge that Sickles received $10,000 for using his influence against the Trinity Church Bill, a claim the World did not state quite as a fact but prefaced with "It is said." Investigation shows that the account is true in most details. The writer has not mentioned several charges for which other sources could not be found. All of the World's statements used in this book

have the benefit of corroboration elsewhere with the exception of the claim that Sickles took Fanny White to London and introduced her to the queen as "Miss Bennett."

16. New York World, July 1, 1869. Henry Raymond, one of the sponsors of the Sickles reception, died suddenly a few days before the event.
17. Issue of July 2, 1869.
18. The Evening Post, by Allan Nevins, p. 312.
19. Issue of July 3, 1869.
20. New York Evening Post, July 2, 1869.
21. Hamilton Fish, p. 192.
22. New York World, June 25, 1869.

Chapter XXX. TACT AND FORBEARANCE

1. New York Herald, December 19, 1871.
2. The Romance of Royalty, by Fitzgerald Molloy, p. 182.
3. Hamilton Fish: The Inner History of the Grant Administration, p. 192.
4. Daniel E. Sickles Papers, L. C., Sickles' dispatch to the State Department dated August 9, 1869.
5. Modern Spain, 1788–1898, by Martin A. S. Hume, p. 494.
6. Hamilton Fish: The Inner History of the Grant Administration, p. 301.
7. Daniel E. Sickles Letterbooks, New York Library, November 15, 1870.
8. The same, Sickles to Wikoff, January 3, 1871.
9. The same, Sickles to Pleasonton, January 21, 1871.
10. The same, Sickles to Forney, January 16, 1871.
11. New York Tribune, March 16, 1872.
12. Daniel E. Sickles Letterbooks, New York Library, dated December 27, 1870.
13. The Sacrifice of a Throne, by H. Remsen Whitehouse, pp. 57 ff.
14. Modern Spain, 1788–1898, p. 496.
15. Sickles Letterbooks, New York Library, letter from Sickles to Pleasonton, January 21, 1871.
16. Elihu Washburne, three years Sickles' senior, was in many ways his direct opposite. A conservative, kindly-looking man, he neither drank, smoked, nor played cards. From a large Maine family, he had two brothers, Israel and Cadwallader, who likewise served in Congress. Sickles had dealt with Cadwallader, then a Union general, while in Memphis on his tour for Lincoln. Unlike his brothers, Elihu spelled his surname with an "e" at the end. He had been a good friend of Lincoln, was now probably Grant's closest political ally, and was a power in the Republican party.
17. New York Herald, December 19, 1871.
18. The same.
19. Dan Sickles, Hero of Gettysburg and "Yankee King of Spain," pp. 240–242.
20. The Romance of Royalty, p. 182; The Tragedy of Isabella II, by Francis Gribble, p. 180 and pp. 236 ff.
21. The Spanish Crown, 1808–1931, by Robert Sencourt, p. 227.
22. The Romance of Royalty, p. 190.
23. The Spanish Crown, 1808–1931, p. 220, quoting the London Times.
24. The same, p. 227.
25. Dan Sickles, p. 242.
26. The same.
27. Sickles Letterbooks, New York Library, Sickles to McHenry, October 25, 1870.
28. The same.
29. The same, dated October 27, 1870.
30. Dan Sickles, p. 234.

31. Mentioned in a Sickles letter to McHenry, May 26, 1871, in Sickles Letter-books, New York Library.
32. Hamilton Fish Papers, L. C., Sickles to Fish, August 13, 1870. Fish later wrote Sickles (Fish Papers, March 10, 1871) to "express my warm satisfaction & that of the President of your management of the delicate & difficult questions which you have had to treat with the Spanish Govt . . ."
33. Daniel E. Sickles Papers, L. C., January 8, 1871.
34. Sickles Letterbooks, New York Library, January 22, 1871.
35. All of these orders and many more are in various letters in the Letterbooks.
36. The same, Sickles to McHenry, June 7, 1871.
37. Acknowledged in a note to the State Department, April 10, 1871, Daniel E. Sickles Papers, L. C.
38. New York Tribune, March 13, 1871.
39. Sickles Letterbooks, New York Library, April 17, 1871.
40. The same, May 21, 1871.
41. Hamilton Fish: The Inner History of the Grant Administration, p. 621.
42. The same, p. 634.
43. Sickles Letterbooks, New York Library, November 19, 1871.
44. New York Tribune, March 16, 1872.
45. The account of the wedding follows the narrative in the New York Herald, December 19, 1871.
46. Pinchon's biography, Dan Sickles (pp. 242–245), says the union was a marriage of convenience arranged to enable Sickles and Isabella to continue their affair, with Caroline apparently in ignorance of this. Pinchon also says (p. 246) that Sickles expected a handsome dowry in his marriage to Caroline and was disappointed when the dowry turned out to be a modest one.

Chapter XXXI. ST. DANIEL AND THE DRAGON

1. Jay Gould, by R. I. Warshow, p. 135.
2. "Boss" Tweed, by Denis Tilden Lynch, pp. 372–373.
3. The same, pp. 363–365.
4. New York Evening Post, March 12, 1872. However, the secret was kept none too well. The New York Tribune for December 16, 1871, front-paged a story headed "A Death Blow At Erie" which said in part: "Gen. Daniel E. Sickles, our Minister to Spain, returns from that country as the authorized agent of the English shareholders, and will at once take charge of their affairs in the important litigations now going on." While Gould was tipped off, he probably expected only "litigation" and not the frontal assault Sickles engineered.
5. Jay Gould, p. 130; New York Tribune, March 12, 1872.
6. New York Tribune, same issue.
7. New York Times, March 12, 1872.
8. Jubilee Jim: The Life of Colonel James Fisk Jr., pp. 270–272.
9. New York Herald, March 12, 1872.
10. New York Times, March 12, 1872.
11. New York Herald, March 12, 1872.
12. New York Tribune, March 13, 1872.
13. The Dreadful Decade, by Don S. Seitz, p. 92.
14. Issue of March 12, 1872.
15. New York Tribune, same date.
16. New York Tribune, March 16, 1872.
17. The Dreadful Decade, p. 93.
18. Jay Gould, p. 135.
19. Horace Greeley, Voice of the People, by William Harlan Hale, pp. 330–331.

20. April 19, 1872, issue. The World editorial said that Sickles in his speech tried to belittle Greeley in Grant's interest, and that when he mentioned Greeley, a "great outburst of cheering denounces the effort and forces the pimp making the effort to beat a hasty retreat from the dangerous comparison." Waiting until the cheers subsided, Sickles shouted, "I welcome the cheers, for I honor the man."
21. Diary of George Templeton Strong, from entry of April 20, 1872.
22. New York World, April 20, 1872.
23. Hamilton Fish: The Inner History of the Grant Administration, p. 620.
24. The same.
25. The same, p. 621.
26. Daniel E. Sickles Papers, L. C., dated July 17, 1872.

CHAPTER XXXII. THE BIG STICK

1. Hamilton Fish Papers, L. C., dated October 21, 1872.
2. Hamilton Fish: The Inner History of the Grant Administration, p. 634.
3. Elihu Washburne Papers, L. C., dated March 10, 1873.
4. Hamilton Fish Papers, L. C., dated May 18, 1873.
5. The American Secretaries of State and Their Diplomacy, edited by Samuel Flagg Bemis, Vol. VII, p. 182.
6. Hamilton Fish: The Inner History of the Grant Administration, p. 669.
7. Foreign Relations of the United States, 1874, p. 938.
8. Hamilton Fish: The Inner History of the Grant Administration, p. 678.
9. Foreign Relations of the United States, 1874, p. 951 and p. 954.
10. Hamilton Fish Papers, L. C., Fish to Washburne, February 12, 1874.
11. Foreign Relations of the United States, 1874, p. 955.
12. Although he had mellowed a trifle, Bennett was still one of New York's most hated men in his last years, at which time a poem of anonymous authorship was circulated, whose first stanza read:

> Should History condescend to pen it,
>   What would its verdict be on Bennett?
> 'Twould say, if truth were in its page,
>   He was the scandal of his age;
> A coward, liar, pimp and sneak;
>   A heartless robber of the weak;
> In vice to profit by, a ferret;
>   Extorter of blackmail from merit;
> With face like Pan's—if Pan had squinted—
>   And heart more foul than face e'er hinted.

13. These headlines appeared in Herald issues between November 15 and December 5, 1873.
14. Issue of November 22, 1873.
15. Issue of November 27.
16. New York Times, December 23, 1873.
17. New York World for December 5 and December 7, 1873.
18. Issue of December 1, 1873.
19. Issue of December 23, 1873.
20. Hamilton Fish: The Inner History of the Grant Administration, p. 692.

CHAPTER XXXIII. AU REVOIR AND GOODBYE

1. Grant, in St. Louis when Sickles tendered his resignation, telegraphed a reply to Fish's query: "My judgment is that Sickles resignation should be accepted

but not seeing the tone of his dispatch I leave it to your judgment.—U. S. Grant." (Hamilton Fish Papers, L. C., dated December 19, 1873.)

2. The same, Washburne to Fish, January 30, 1874.
3. The same, Washburne to Fish, March 4, 1874.
4. The same letter.
5. Washburne Papers, L. C., Sickles to Washburne, June 1, 1874.
6. The Tragedy of Isabella II, p. 268.
7. The same, pp. 300–301.
8. Dan Sickles, p. 257.
9. The same, pp. 250–251.
10. The same, pp. 258–259.
11. Elihu Washburne Papers, L. C., dated February 6, 1876.
12. The same, Sickles to Washburne, 1876 (no date).
13. The same, Sickles to Washburne, March 27, 1877.
14. The same letter.
15. The same, Sickles to Washburne, July 5, 1877.
16. Journal of the Military Service Institute of the U. S., Vol. VI, No. 23, p. 272.
17. The Story of the Third Army Corps Union, by Major William P. Shreve, p. 49.
18. The Journals of Joseph Hopkins Twichell; unidentified newsclipping attached to entry for May 6–11, 1878.
19. New York World, May 4, 1914.

Chapter XXXIV. RETURN OF THE NATIVE

1. Forney gives Sickles' age as having been born in 1823. So do Fiske, Twichell, Mark Twain, and several others. The newspapers invariably subtracted anywhere from four to six years from his real age. Horatio King got the age right in a poem mentioned later in this chapter—the only instance found of such correctness during the general's lifetime. Pinchon says (Dan Sickles, p. 3) that in his last days Sickles gave 1825 as the year of his birth. It seems fairly clear that he was not averse to having his age underestimated.
2. New York World, May 4, 1914.
3. New York Times, May 31, 1880.
4. Meet General Grant, by W. E. Woodward, p. 475. Although Sickles and Washburne had been friends for twenty years, one has the feeling that this move of the Illinoisan ended the friendship. In his two-volume Recollections of a Minister to France, Washburne studiously avoided any mention of Sickles, who had been at his elbow much of the time. Nor did Grant, in his Personal Memoirs, make any mention of Sickles.
5. Off-Hand Portraits of Prominent New Yorkers, by Stephen Fiske, p. 288.
6. New York Times, December 22, 1881.
7. Among those he helped bury was Grant, at whose funeral in New York in 1885 Sickles rode at the head of 18,000 war veterans (Fifth Avenue Events, p. 57).
8. Off-Hand Portraits of Prominent New Yorkers, p. 288.
9. The same, p. 285.
10. The same, p. 287.
11. The Civil War in America, by the Comte de Paris, Vol. III, p. 605.
12. The Life and Letters of General George Gordon Meade, Vol. II, pp. 351 ff. In a speech at the 1886 Gettysburg reunion, Sickles said Lincoln told him his forward move was right and had said, "God bless you for it."
13. New York Times, August 14, 1886.
14. New York Times, March 21, 1887.
15. Anthony J. Griffin Papers, New York Library; Griffin's diary, entry for March 21, 1887. Griffin, who had worked for many years as clerk and assistant to George Sickles, noted that he was rough in manners and speech and "extremely fond of money," but kindly under his gruff exterior.

16. Last will of George Sickles, a copy of which is included in the Griffin Papers.
17. New York World, May 4, 1914; New York Herald, same date.
18. Tammany Hall, Souvenir of the Inauguration of Cleveland and Stevenson, unpaged.
19. Gettysburg and Lincoln, by Henry Sweetser Burrage, p. 159.
20. New York Times, November 7, 1892.
21. Gettysburg and Lincoln, p. 166.
22. Slocum and His Men, p. 321.
23. Sickles Papers, New York Library, dated February 20, 1893.
24. Men and Memories, p. 328.
25. According to Douglas Southall Freeman (R. E. Lee, Vol. III, Chapter VII) Longstreet was opposed to Lee's plan of attack at Gettysburg, vainly proposed other measures, and was dilatory in mounting the attack.
26. But the race was fairly close, with the Democrats again divided. Sickles got 12,079 votes, the "State Democrat" entry 2200, and the Republican victor 14,662 (New York Herald, November 7, 1894).
27. Daniel E. Sickles Collection, L. C., undated.
28. One of Sickles' closest friends in these later years, Maine-born Horatio Collins King (1837–1918) had many interests in common with him. He was the son of another Horatio King who was Postmaster General in Buchanan's cabinet. The younger King had studied law under Edwin Stanton. He served with distinction throughout the Civil War and later was active in politics as well as in the Society of the Army of the Potomac and the Third Corps Union.
29. Daniel E. Sickles Collection, L. C.; these excerpts are from Sickles-to-King letters, mostly undated but of this period.
30. Story of the Third Army Corps Union, p. 71.
31. Daniel E. Sickles Collection, L. C., undated.
32. The Autobiography of Oliver Otis Howard, Vol. II, p. 569.
33. Hanna, by Thomas Beer, pp. 161–162.
34. Daniel E. Sickles Papers, L. C. This was not the first poetical effort Sickles had inspired. At the 1894 meeting of the Third Corps Union in Washington, a poem read by David Graham Adee began:

> 'Twas the third day of the fight
> And the guns upon our right
> Were booming shot and shell
> And we heard the rebel yell,
> When in front of his command,
> With his brave sword in his hand
> Amid flaming fires of hell,
> That our gallant leader fell
> At Gettysburg.

(It was explained that although Sickles fell on the second day of the battle, "third day" fit the meter.)

Chapter XXXV. A GRAND OLD HERO HE

1. Sickles Papers, New York Library, undated but apparently subsequent to his return from Europe.
2. Recollections of an Old New Yorker, by Frederick Van Wyck, p. 156.
3. Sickles Papers, New York Library, Annie Conover to Sickles, undated.
4. The Journals of Joseph Hopkins Twichell, entry for May 6–7, 1901. Sickles' other ex-chaplain friend, Father Joseph O'Hagan, had died in 1878 after five years as president of the College of the Holy Cross.
5. Sickles' Oration at Fredericksburg, p. 3. This event of May 25, 1900, was to

dedicate a monument to the Fifth Corps erected at the battlefield with funds provided by General Daniel Butterfield. Butterfield, too ill to make the address himself, died the following year. In his speech, Sickles did not mention Butterfield.

6. Alvey Augustus Adee, who had been Sickles' legation secretary in Madrid, was now an assistant secretary of state.
7. John Hay Papers, L. C., Hay to Storer, December 26, 1901.
8. Sickles Papers, L. C., dated September 19, 1902.
9. A Little Fifer's War Diary, by C. W. Bardeen, p. 223.
10. Lee and Longstreet at High Tide, by Helen D. Longstreet, p. 21 in Sickles' introduction.
11. Excerpts from pp. 337–342, Mark Twain's Autobiography (Vol. XXXVI of The Writings of Mark Twain, Stormfield Edition).

Chapter XXXVI. I SEE HIM ON THAT FAMOUS FIELD

1. Sickles Papers, L. C. Although the Sickles couple had separated in 1879, 29 years earlier, Sickles had made a trip to Europe in 1881 and evidently had seen his wife then.
2. New York Times, May 4, 1914.
3. Dan Sickles, p. 269.
4. According to Stanton Sickles' statement, New York Times, May 22, 1914.
5. A Bill to Retire Major General Daniel E. Sickles as a Lieutenant General; Sickles Pamphlets, New York Library Annex.
6. Dan Sickles, p. 269.
7. Sickles Papers, New York Library, 1910 (no date).
8. New York Times, May 4, 1914.
9. New York Times, January 26, 1913.
10. The same.
11. New York Times, May 4, 1914.
12. The same newspaper, January 26, 1913.
13. The same.
14. The same, January 28, 1913.
15. The same.
16. New York World, January 25, 1913. The exact role played by Miss Wilmerding remains a fascinating enigma. One has the impression that Mrs. Sickles was jealous of the housekeeper and felt that she had preempted a position as mistress of the household. In a newspaper interview after the general's death (New York World, May 4, 1914), Mrs. Sickles offered a few obscure clues. In telling of her estrangement from Sickles in 1879, she said:
   "I learned that my husband had been untrue to me, that he had loved another woman before our marriage and still loved her.
   "I was heartbroken but powerless. There was nothing for me to do but to wait and to suffer. Even the boon of divorce was barred to me by the laws of my Church.
   "When at last I came to this country . . . I found the home and heart of my husband closed to me.
   "When I pleaded with him to cease his attentions to the woman who had parted us and to discharge his housekeeper, who was that woman's cousin, he refused . . ."
   While any analysis of the general's complicated love life is a risky affair, it seems possible that Miss Wilmerding, rather than being "that woman's cousin," was "that woman" herself. This theory finds support in other circumstances, among them the newspaper statement that Sickles made a will leaving "everything" to Miss Wilmerding. Could it be that Mrs. Sickles, in

order to belittle the housekeeper's role—and showing the reluctance of a proud Spanish lady to admit that she was displaced by a mere domestic—purposely beclouded the issue?

17. New York Times, January 27, 1913.
18. The same paper, January 28, 1913.
19. New York Herald, January 28, 1913.
20. New York Times, January 28, 1913.
21. New York Herald, January 27, 1913.
22. New York Herald, July 1, 1913.
23. The Journals of Joseph Hopkins Twichell, entry for June 27–July 9, 1913.
24. While the general still does not appear in bronze or stone, he is given at least minor recognition in the establishment of Sickles Avenue at Gettysburg and Sickles Road at Chancellorsville.
25. New York Times editorial, May 5, 1914. The Times also said truly that Sickles "never quite lived down the effects of his mad act of 1859," meaning the killing of Key. According to the same newspaper (May 22, 1914) the Bowery Savings Bank held a mortgage of $118,000 on Sickles' property, and his widow a second mortgage of $40,000. With these and other encumbrances, it was felt that his debts exceeded his assets. His daughter Eda Crackanthorpe's suit to compel him to restore $47,359.79 which she claimed was due from her share in her grandfather's estate, was still unsettled at Sickles' death. Daniel P. Hays, who had acted as Sickles' attorney for some years, was appointed executor of the estate, but hurriedly withdrew from this thankless task. "I have honored the general sufficiently during his lifetime," he said (New York Herald, May 9, 1914). Stanton Sickles, who had dropped almost all other matters for six years in his effort to effect a reconciliation, said (New York Times, May 22, 1914), "Monetary matters are insignificant in view of the fact we were reconciled and that he died in the Church."

The funeral services were held at St. Patrick's Cathedral on May 8, with the late general being borne up Fifth Avenue in a mahogany coffin on which lay his sword, epaulettes and blue and gold war cap. He was buried among Third Corps comrades at Arlington Cemetery. His Gettysburg leg, badly shattered, is still an exhibit at the Armed Forces Medical Museum in Washington.

Bibliography

Biographers have neglected Daniel Sickles shamefully. The only previous book about him makes no pretense at any real search of the records and is marred by an overly adulatory approach. The reason for the neglect of the general must lie in the difficulty of getting the facts about him. Sickles left few papers, many of them being lost by theft and a fire in his home. Furthermore, he outlived all of his contemporaries. Some of those who knew him best and mentioned him in print were probably inclined to be discreet because he was still vigorously alive and exceedingly resentful of criticism. The result is that any effort to reconstruct the events of his long life involves the exploration of innumerable books, papers, and news items to find stray bits here and there which can be sorted out and fitted together like the pieces of a puzzle. Fortunately, he wrote an endless flood of letters and made good copy for the newspapers, and it is in these sources that a large part of the Sickles story was found.

MANUSCRIPT SOURCES

From the Library of Congress:
Daniel E. Sickles Papers.
D. E. Sickles Collection.
Abraham Lincoln Papers.
Andrew Johnson Papers.
Edwin Stanton Papers.
U. S. Grant Papers.
Elihu Washburne Papers.
James Gordon Bennett Papers.
Hamilton Fish Papers.
The Journals of General M. R. Patrick.
Zachariah Chandler Papers.
John Hay Papers.
Personal Papers, Miscellaneous.
Civil War Letters of Felix Brannigan, 1861–1863.

From the New York Public Library:
Daniel E. Sickles Papers and Letterbooks.
A collection of pamphlets about Sickles (New York Library Annex).
Horace Greeley Papers.
Anthony J. Griffin Papers.

From the Yale Library:
War Letters of Joseph Hopkins Twichell.
The Journals of Joseph Hopkins Twichell.

From the Dinand Library, College of the Holy Cross:
The Diary of Father Joseph B. O'Hagan, S. J.

From the Brown University Library:
Some Sickles letters in the library's special collection.

From Mr. Fred W. Bonitz:
The Diary of J. H. W. Bonitz.

NEWSPAPERS

New York Evening Post.
New York Herald.
New York Times.
New York Tribune.
New York Sun.
New York World.
Charleston Mercury.
Charleston News.
Washington Daily National Intelligencer.
Washington Evening Star.
Washington National Republican.
Selected issues of a few other newspapers.

MAGAZINES

Harper's Weekly.
Frank Leslie's Illustrated Newspaper.
The Home Journal.
Journal of the Military Service Institute of the United States.
North Carolina Historical Review.

BOOKS

(Only those quoted or cited)

Adams, Charles Francis—Charles Francis Adams, an Autobiography. Boston, 1916.
Adams, George W.—Doctors in Blue: the Medical History of the Union Army in
   the Civil War. New York, 1952.
Alexander, DeAlva Stanwood—A Political History of the State of New York,
   3 vols. New York, 1909.
Anderson, Frank Maloy—Mystery of "A Public Man." Minneapolis, 1948.
Anderson, John B.—Reminiscences of Herman Haupt. New York, 1901.
Annual Report of the Secretary of War, 1866. Washington, Government Printing
   Office, 1867.
Auchampaugh, P. G.—James Buchanan and his Cabinet. Duluth, 1926.
Badeau, Adam—Grant in Peace: From Appomattox to Mt. McGregor. Hartford,
   1887.

Bardeen, C. W.—A Little Fifer's War Diary. Syracuse, 1910.
Bartlett, Capt. A. W.—History of the 12th Regiment, New Hampshire Volunteers. Concord, 1897.
Beer, Thomas—Hanna. New York, 1929.
Bemis, Samuel Flagg (ed.)—The American Secretaries of State and Their Diplomacy, 12 vols. New York, 1928.
Bigelow, John Jr.—The Campaign of Chancellorsville. New Haven, 1910.
Billings, John D.—The History of the Tenth Massachusetts Battery. Boston, 1881.
Blair, Major Gist—Lafayette Square. Records of the Columbia Historical Society, Vol. 28, 1926.
Bowers, Claude G.—The Tragic Era: The Revolution After Lincoln. Cambridge, 1929.
Branch, Lawrence O'Bryan—Letters, 1856-60. North Carolina Historical Review, 1933, Vol. X.
Brooks, Noah—Washington in Lincoln's Time. New York, 1896.
Brown, Henry LeFevre—The History of the Third Regiment, Excelsior Brigade, 72nd New York Volunteer Infantry. Jamestown, N. Y., 1902.
Buel, Clarence C., and Johnson, Robert U. (eds.)—Battles and Leaders of the Civil War, 4 vols. New York, 1884-87.
Burrage, Henry Sweetser—Gettysburg and Lincoln. New York, 1906.
Butterfield, Julia (ed.)—General Daniel Butterfield. New York, 1904.
Carlson, Oliver—The Man Who Made News: James Gordon Bennett. New York, 1942.
Catton, Bruce—Glory Road. New York, 1952.
Cavanagh, Michael—Memoirs of Gen. Thomas Francis Meagher. Worcester, 1892.
Chesnut, Mary Boykin—A Diary From Dixie, edited by Ben Ames Williams. Boston, 1949.
Clemens, Samuel Langhorne—Mark Twain's Autobiography (Stormfield Edition, Vol. XXXVI of The Writings of Mark Twain). New York, 1924.
Conyngham, Capt. D. P.—The Irish Brigade. New York, 1867.
Cudworth, Warren H.—History of the 1st Regiment, Massachusetts Infantry. Boston, 1886.
De Havilland, Major John—A Metrical Description of a Fancy Dress Ball. Washington, 1858.
De Trobriand, Philippe Regis—Four Years with the Army of the Potomac. Boston, 1889.
Dewitt, David Miller—The Impeachment and Trial of Andrew Johnson. New York, 1903.
Dictionary of American Biography. New York, 1943.
Doster, William E.—Lincoln and Episodes of the Civil War. New York, 1915.
Doubleday, Abner—Chancellorsville and Gettysburg. New York, 1882.
Fifth Avenue Events—(No author named). New York, 1916.
Fiske, Stephen—Off-Hand Portraits of Prominent New Yorkers. New York, 1884.
Fleming, Walter Lynwood—The Sequel of Appomattox. New Haven, 1921.
Flower, Frank Abial—Edwin McMasters Stanton. Akron, 1905.
Fontaine, Felix G. (reporter)—The Washington Tragedy: Trial of Daniel E. Sickles. New York, 1859.
Ford, Worthington C. (ed.)—A Cycle of Adams Letters, 1861-65. Boston, 1920.
Foreign Relations of the United States, 1874. Washington, 1874.
Forney, John W.—Anecdotes of Public Men. New York, 1873.
Freeman, Douglas Southall—R. E. Lee, 4 vols. New York, 1934.
Fuller, Robert H.—Jubilee Jim: The Life of Colonel James Fisk Jr. New York, 1928.
Gibbon, Brig. Gen. John—Personal Recollections of the Civil War. New York, 1928.
Gobright, L. A.—Recollections of Men and Things at Washington During the Third of a Century. Philadelphia, 1869.

Gould, Edward K.—Major General Hiram G. Berry. Rockland, Me., 1899.

Grant and His Generals—(No author named). New York, 1865.

Grant, Ulysses S.—Personal Memoirs, 2 vols. New York, 1885.

Greeley, Horace (subject)—Memorial to Horace Greeley. Albany, 1915.

Gribble, Francis—The Tragedy of Isabella II. London, 1913.

Hale, William Harlan—Horace Greeley, Voice of the People. New York, 1950.

Hamlin, Augustus Choate—The Battle of Chancellorsville. Bangor, Me., 1896.

Hanaford, Phebe A.—The Life of George Peabody. Boston, 1870.

Haskell, Frank A.—The Battle of Gettysburg. Madison, 1910.

Hay, Gilbert Adams—The Story of the 63rd Regiment, Pennsylvania Volunteers. Pittsburgh, 1908.

Haydon, F. Stansbury—Aeronautics in the Union and Confederate Armies. Baltimore, 1941.

Hebert, Walter H.—Fighting Joe Hooker. Indianapolis, 1944.

Helm, Katherine—Mary, Wife of Lincoln. New York, 1928.

Hendrick, Burton J.—Lincoln's War Cabinet. Boston, 1946.

Hertz, Emanuel—Abraham Lincoln, a New Portrait, 2 vols. New York, 1931.

Hesseltine, William B.—U. S. Grant, Politician. New York, 1935.

Howard, O. O.—The Autobiography of Oliver Otis Howard, 2 vols. New York, 1907.

Hume, Martin A. S.—Modern Spain, 1788–1898. New York, 1900.

Johnson, Rossiter—Campfire and Battlefield. New York, 1894.

Leech, Margaret—Reveille in Washington. New York, 1941.

Longstreet, Helen D.—Lee and Longstreet at High Tide. Gainesville, Ga., 1904.

Lynch, Denis Tilden—Boss Tweed. New York, 1927.

McClure, Alexander K.—Lincoln and Men of War Times. Philadelphia, 1892.

McMurtry, R. Gerald—Ben Hardin Helm. Chicago, 1943.

Meade, George—The Life and Letters of General George Gordon Meade, 2 vols. New York, 1913.

Milton, George Fort—The Age of Hate. New York, 1930.

Molloy, Fitzgerald—The Romance of Royalty. London, 1904.

Moore, John Bassett (ed.)—The Works of James Buchanan, 12 vols. Philadelphia, 1909.

Myers, Gustavus—The History of Tammany Hall. New York, 1917.

Nevins, Allan—Hamilton Fish: The Inner History of the Grant Administration. New York, 1937.

Nevins, Allan—Ordeal of the Union, 2 vols. New York, 1947.

Nevins, Allan—The Evening Post. New York, 1922.

New York County, Court of General Sessions—The People, ex rel. D. E. Sickles, vs. James Gordon Bennett. (Pamphlet, 1858).

Nichols, Thomas Low, M. D.—Forty Years of American Life. New York, 1937.

Nicolay, John G., and Hay, John—Abraham Lincoln, a History, 10 vols. New York, 1904.

Nicolay and Hay—Complete Works of Abraham Lincoln, 12 vols. New York, 1894.

Paris, Louis Philippe Albert D'Orleans, Comte de—The Battle of Gettysburg. Philadelphia, 1907.

Paris, Louis Philippe Albert D'Orleans, Comte de—The Civil War in America, 4 vols. Philadelphia, 1883.

Parks, E. Taylor—Colombia and the United States, 1765–1934. Durham, N. C., 1935.

Philp's Washington Described (no author named). New York, 1861.

Pinchon, Edgcumb—Dan Sickles, Hero of Gettysburg and "Yankee King of Spain." Garden City, 1945.

Poore, Ben Perley—Reminiscences of Sixty Years in the National Metropolis, 2 vols. New York, 1886.

Pryor, Mrs. Roger A.—Reminiscences of Peace and War. New York, 1904.

Randall, Ruth Painter—Mary Lincoln: The Biography of a Marriage. Boston, 1953.

Report of the Joint Committee on the Conduct of the War at the Second Session of the 38th Congress. Vol. I, 1865. Washington, 1865.

Ropes, John Codman, and Gray, John Chipman—War Letters, 1862–65. Boston and New York, 1927.

Rusling, James F.—Men and Things I Saw in Civil War Days. New York, 1899.

Russo, Joseph Louis—Lorenzo Da Ponte, Poet and Adventurer. New York, 1927.

Salm-Salm, Princess Felix—Ten Years of My Life. New York, 1877.

Seitz, Don C.—The Dreadful Decade. Indianapolis, 1926.

Seitz, Don C.—The James Gordon Bennetts. Indianapolis, 1928.

Sencourt, Robert—The Spanish Crown, 1808–1931. New York, 1932.

Shreve, Major William P.—The Story of the Third Army Corps Union. Boston, 1910.

Sickles, Daniel—Argument of the Hon. Daniel E. Sickles in the Senate of the State of New York on the Trinity Church Bill. Albany, 1857.

Sickles, Maj. Gen. Daniel E.—Leaves From My Diary (Journal of the Military Service Institute of the United States, Vol. VI, Nos. 22 and 23).

Sickles, Daniel E.—Oration at Fredericksburg. Washington, 1901.

Simkins, F. B., and Woody, R. H.—South Carolina During Reconstruction. Chapel Hill, 1932.

Slocum and His Men (No author given). Albany, 1904.

Sterling, Ada (ed.)—A Belle of the Fifties: The Memoirs of Mrs. Clay of Alabama. New York, 1904.

Stevens, Capt. C. A.—Berdan's U. S. Sharpshooters. St. Paul. 1892.

Stevens, George T.—Three Years in the Sixth Corps. New York, 1870.

Tammany Hall, Souvenir of the Inauguration of Cleveland and Stevenson. New York, 1893.

Thomas, Milton Halsey, and Nevins, Allan (eds.)—The Diary of George Templeton Strong, 4 vols. New York, 1950.

Tremain, Henry E.—Two Days of War. New York, 1905.

Van Wyck, Frederick—Recollections of An Old New Yorker. New York, 1932.

War of the Rebellion: Official Records of the Union and Confederate Armies, 128 vols. Washington, 1882–1901.

Warshow, R. I.—Jay Gould. New York, 1928.

Watterson, Henry—Marse Henry: The Autobiography of Henry Watterson. New York, 1919.

Welles, Gideon—The Diary of Gideon Welles, 3 vols. Boston and New York, 1911.

Whitehouse, H. Remsen—The Sacrifice of a Throne. New York, 1897.

Williams, Kenneth P.—Lincoln Finds a General (2 vols. paged as one). New York, 1949.

Williams, T. Harry—Lincoln and the Radicals. Madison, 1941.

Willson, Beckles—America's Ambassadors to England, 1785–1929. New York, 1929.

Woodward, W. E.—Meet General Grant. New York, 1928.

Young, John Russell—Men and Memories. New York, 1901.

Acknowledgments

The writer is greatly indebted to the pleasant and helpful staff of the Yale University Library, where much of the source material was found. One of the most vivid of all Civil War eyewitness accounts, the War Letters of Joseph Hopkins Twichell, was generously made available by his son, the Rev. Joseph H. Twichell of Hartford, who also permitted the writer access to his father's Journals. The intelligent research work of Miss Maud Kay Sites of Washington, D. C., has been invaluable. Dr. C. Percy Powell of the Division of Manuscripts, Library of Congress, found significant Sickles material in unexpected places in that vast treasury.

Warm gratitude is also felt for help given in a variety of ways by Mr. Robert W. Hill and Miss Jean McNiece of the Manuscript Division, New York Public Library; Mr. Robert A. Hug of the Newspaper Division of that library; the Rev. William L. Lucey, S. J., Librarian, the Dinand Library, College of the Holy Cross; Mr. Herman Jervis of Newtown, Conn.; Miss Dorothy C. Barck, Librarian, the New-York Historical Society; Miss Marion E. Brown of the Brown University Library; Mr. Fred W. Bonitz of Charlotte, N. C.; Mr. Frank White Jr. of Washington, D. C.; the Rev. Walter J. Meagher, S. J., of Boston; Mr. Henry M. Fuller, Reference Librarian, Yale University Library; Mr. E. Taylor Parks of the Historical Division, U. S. Department of State; and Lt. Col. John R. Elting, Assistant Professor, History of Military Art, U. S. Military Academy.

INDEX

Index

Suggested reading list:

Army Life: A Private's Reminiscences of the Civil War (20th Maine Volunteer Infantry) by Reverend Theodore Gerrish

Through Blood and Fire at Gettysburg: My Experiences with the 20th Maine Regiment on Little Round Top by General Joshua Lawrence Chamberlain

"Bayonet! Forward": My Civil War Reminiscences by General Joshua Lawrence Chamberlain

Soul of the Lion: A Biography of General Joshua Lawrence Chamberlain by Willard Wallace

The Passing of the Armies: The Last Campaign of the Armies by General Joshua Lawrence Chamberlain

The Attack and Defense of Little Round Top, Gettysburg, July 2, 1863 by Oliver W. Norton

Sickles the Incredible: A Biography of General Daniel Edgar Sickles by W. A. Swanberg

The Life and Letters of General George Gordon Meade by George Meade

A Diary of Battle: The Personal Journals of Colonel Charles S. Wainwright 1861-1865 edited by Allan Nevins

"Over a Wide, Hot ... Crimson Plain", The Struggle For The Bliss Farm by Elwood Christ

High Tide at Gettysburg: The Campaign in Pennsylvania by Glenn Tucker

Crisis at the Crossroads: The First Day at Gettysburg by Warren Hassler

Cutler's Brigade at Gettysburg by James L. McLean, Jr.

The Killer Angels: A Novel About the Four Days of Gettysburg by Michael Shaara

The Great Invasion of 1863 or General Lee in Pennsylvania by Jacob Hoke

At Gettysburg or What a Girl Saw and Heard of the Battle: A True Narrative by Tillie (Pierce) Alleman

A Caspian Sea of Ink: The Meade-Sickles Controversy by Richard A. Sauers

From Gettysburg to the Rapidan: the Army of the Potomac by Andrew A. Humphreys

Gettysburg Sources: 3 Volumes, compiled by James L. McLean, Jr. and Judy W. McLean

A History of the 93rd Regiment Pennsylvania Veteran Volunteers by Penrose G. Mark

Narrative of the Service of the Seventh Indiana Infantry in the War for the Union by Orville Thomson

The Personal Memoirs of Jonathan Thomas Scharf of the First Maryland Artillery by Tom Kelley

Sabers and Spurs: The First Regiment Rhode Island Cavalry in the Civil War by Reverend Frederic Denison

The History of the Fighting Fourteenth: 14th Brooklyn State Militia compiled by C. Tevis and D. R. Marquis

A History of the 148th Pennsylvania Volunteers by Joseph W. Muffley

Major-General John Frederick Hartranft: Citizen, Soldier and Pennsylvania Statesman by A. M. Gambone

The Civil War Letters of Dr. Harvey Black: A Surgeon with Stonewall Jackson edited by Glenn L. McMullen

Historical Record of the First Maryland Infantry by Charles Camper and J. W. Kirkley

The Baltimore and Ohio (Railroad) in the Civil War by Festus Summers

The History of the Tenth Massachusetts Battery of Light Artillery in the War of the Rebellion by John Billings

History of the Nineteenth Regiment Massachusetts Volunteers compiled by Ernest Waitt

The Twentieth Regiment of Massachusetts Volunteers by George A. Bruce

History of the One Hundred and Fiftieth Regiment Pennsylvania Volunteers, Second Regiment, Bucktail Brigade by Lieutenant-Colonel Thomas Chamberlin

Whatever You Resolve To Be: Essays on Stonewall Jackson by A. Wilson Greene

Lee: A Biography by Clifford Dowdey

Pickett and His Men by LaSalle Corbell Pickett

A Texan in Search of a Fight: Being the Diary and Letters of a Private Soldier in Hood's Texas Brigade by John C. West

A Lieutenant of Cavalry in Lee's Army by George Beale

Letters of a Confederate Officer to His Family During the Last Year of the War of Secession by Richard Corbin

Death of a Nation: The Story of Lee and His Men at Gettysburg by Clifford Dowdey

Four Years in the Saddle by Colonel Harry Gilmor

Return to Bull Run: The Campaign and Battle of Second Manassas by John Hennessy

Confederate Monuments at Gettysburg: The Gettysburg Battle Monuments by David Martin

To the Gates of Richmond: The Peninsula Campaign by Stephen Sears

Mine Eyes Have Seen The Glory: The Civil War in Art by Harold Holzer and Mark E. Neely Jr.

All of the above titles are available from the Publisher:
Stan Clark Military Books
915 Fairview Avenue
Gettysburg, Pennsylvania 17325
(717) 337-1728